Beyond Agile

Achieving Success with Situational Knowledge & Skills

By Mike Griffiths, PMI-ACP, PMP

RMC PUBLICATIONS™

What People Are Saying About *Beyond Agile*

In the digital age with agile teams, project management needs to evolve. Mike Griffiths, and the BAM model described here, promote that evolution, adding tools, perspective, and thinking to equip project leaders for the new world. Drawing on his own experience, Mike sets out a compendium of tools every project leader will find useful.

—Allan Kelly, Author of *Succeeding with OKRs in Agile*

Mike combines his breadth of experience with modern thinking about leadership and emotional intelligence. The book combines the best of current wisdom with a new approach to delivering projects using the best of both plan driven and Agile practices.

—Cyndi Dionisio,
Chair, *PMBOK® Guide* 6th and 7th Edition;
Author, Consultant

Mike's Beyond Agile Model builds on the twenty-year legacy of agile methods, and extends it well into the future. With clear guidance on emotional as well as organizational development and leadership, this book is a must read for all knowledge workers working towards individual and organizational success in our complex, turbulent, and interdependent world.

—Sanjiv Augustine, CEO LitheSpeed;
Author of *Managing Agile Projects* and
From PMO to VMO: Managing for Value Delivery

This book is truly a rich, and essential, resource for agilists who desire to broaden their scope and impact from delivery teams to the entire organization. Mike innovatively weaves in both agile practices and leadership EQ, and grounds himself in the agile mindset. The book is full of great insights and experiences that come from Mike's years of experience in the trenches. I strongly recommend this book as an important read for every aspiring agile coach.

—Ahmed Sidky, PhD
President of the International Consortium for Agile (ICAgile)
and Co-founder of the Business Agility Institute

I first met Mike Griffiths through our work on the Agile Practice Guide, *which was a collaboration between Agile Alliance and the Project Management Institute (PMI). As we continued to collaborate on many additional initiatives, we came to have a deep understanding that the way to approach any outcome or endeavor is to take a pragmatic approach using a combination of methods, frameworks, and skills to meet the complexity of what organizations and project leaders face on a daily basis.*

Beyond Agile *captures exactly what is needed to successfully lead and navigate projects, products, or initiatives. To think you can take a single framework off the shelf and blindly apply it as a "one size fits all" regardless of the context, situation, or complexity of the project or organization is a recipe for disaster. The Beyond Agile Model takes all the factors necessary to be successful into consideration: the agile mindset, values, and principles as the foundation, leveraging leadership and emotional intelligence to support the interpersonal dynamics, an understanding of plan-driven approaches, industry-specific knowledge, and understanding the unique variables and nuances of the organization and the project itself. When any leader, coach, scrum master, etc., is able to apply their knowledge, various "tools" and skills, focusing on what is fit for purpose the outcomes of being able to successfully navigate and deliver in the most complex scenarios are much higher.*

—Betsy Kauffman, TED Speaker;
Leadership and Organizational Agility Coach,
Cross Impact Coaching

Beyond Agile: Achieving Success with Situational Knowledge & Skills
Printed in the United States of America
First Printing
ISBN: 978-1-943704-23-1

Library of Congress Control Number: 2021935668

Illustrations by Fabián Fucci
Cover design by Jason Craft

PMI and PMBOK, and SeminarsWorld are registered marks of the Project Management Institute, Inc.

This publication uses the following terms trademarked by the Project Management Institute, Inc.: Project Management Institute (PMI)®, PMI Agile Certified Practitioner (PMI-ACP)®, Project Management Professional (PMP)®, and *A Guide to the Project Management Body of Knowledge (PMBOK® Guide)*.
PRINCE2 is a registered trademark of AXELOS Limited.

RMC PUBLICATIONS™

Phone: 952.846.4484
Fax: 952.846.4844
Email: info@rmcls.com
www.rmcls.com

To Jake and Samantha.

Table of Contents

About the Author

Mike Griffiths is an award-winning trainer, consultant, author, and thought leader in agile and project management.

He helped create the Dynamic Systems Development Method (DSDM) agile method and has been using agile methods, including Scrum and Extreme Programming (XP) for over twenty-five years. He has served on the board of directors for the Agile Alliance and the Agile Project Leadership Network (APLN).

Mike cofounded the Project Management Institute (PMI) Agile Community of Practice and helped to create the PMI-ACP® certification and exam. He led the writing team for PMI's *Agile Practice Guide* and cowrote the Software Extension to *A Guide to the Project Management Body of Knowlege (PMBOK® Guide)*. He has contributed to several editions of the *PMBOK® Guide* and was colead on the *PMBOK® Guide, Seventh Edition*.

About RMC Learning Solutions

RMC Learning Solutions (formerly RMC Project Management) develops and trains project managers, business analysts, and agile practitioners by providing the hard skills, soft skills, and business knowledge necessary for them to succeed in their careers. Since 1991, RMC has helped more than 750,000 individuals—as well as executives across the Fortune 500 and in government agencies—accomplish the following:

» Develop practical knowledge immediately applicable to their careers.

» Deliver organizational results using proven techniques and best practices.

» Attract, develop, and retain top talent to work on key initiatives.

» Consistently bring projects in on time and under budget.

» Increase the adoption of training through coaching and mentoring.

Today, RMC delivers a wide range of project management, business analysis, and agile training in multiple learning formats including traditional classroom training, live online training, self-directed eLearning, books, and software. The company also continues to reinforce its training via ongoing coaching, mentoring, and organizational transformation services.

What Makes RMC Unique

In addition to the above, RMC Learning Solutions separates itself from what has become a very crowded training marketplace by offering the following value-added advantages:

» **Proven techniques.** RMC provides individuals and teams with the opportunity to learn and use highly effective project management, business analysis, and agile practices that can be applied immediately on their current projects. We listen to students and clients, and integrate their ideas and perspectives to enrich each and every learning experience.

» **Outcome-based learning.** All RMC instruction and content focuses on a continuous cycle of learning. We plan your learning, set goals, and teach—then measure progress toward goals and adjust accordingly. RMC incorporates real-time feedback into all of its programs wherever possible, and is always monitoring for additional learning opportunities.

» **Professional instructors.** RMC actively recruits high-performing instructors who are champions of—and experts in—their respective disciplines. All RMC instructors have a deep conceptual understanding of their practice area, and use a variety of strategies designed to help students understand AND apply what they are learning in the real world.

» **An international reach.** Through our extensive international distributor and training provider network, RMC is able to offer its training in 18 languages and more than 60 regions across the globe. This ensures all RMC students receive the same quality of training and delivery, and the same training experience—no matter where they may be located.

» **Multiple ways to learn.** In addition to traditional instructor-led training, RMC offers a variety of learning modes to meet both individual and corporate training needs. From live online classes and self-directed eLearning courses to books, software, and templates, RMC offers students the opportunity to learn in multiple formats and at multiple price points.

Why This Book?

The world of work is changing. We see it in pockets right now, but a wave of change is coming. Projects are getting more complex, jobs are becoming less permanent, and people are more mobile. COVID-19 accelerated the transition, and now this trifecta of changes is spreading faster than ever into all industries. People who see the trend and can navigate the oncoming tsunami of change will be in high demand and will lead the bulk of the organizational transformations to come.

This book describes the mindset and tool kit needed to rise and thrive in the new world of work. It will show you the knowledge domains that have to be understood and how to work with others to succeed. The future will be collaborative, built upon skilled individuals. This book is a road map and workshop manual for building a smarter you, better positioned for the new realities of the future.

Agile: Integral but Insufficient

While agile approaches are the best tools we have for managing today's complex projects, they will not ensure that your project or product is successful. I have seen many agile projects fail despite using the correct agile approaches and being staffed with smart, motivated teams.

This was especially disconcerting for me since I have been deeply involved in the development and promotion of agile approaches for much of my career. I have been fortunate to work on many successful projects and with award-winning teams, and I have come to realize they all use agile alongside other strategies and approaches, sometimes at the forefront, but often in the background.

This is obvious once you see it, but it is rarely discussed or supported by business models or literature. Successful teams use a savvy combination of agile, leadership, and domain-specific tools—and traditional approaches, where they make sense. To move forward, we need to explain and provide tools to help navigate this mix of approaches and choose the best combination for the endeavor at hand. Knowledge is weightless, whereas processes and ceremonies come with a burden of execution, so we need to choose wisely which approaches we adopt and continue learning from a diverse spectrum of knowledge.

This book describes how we can determine the optimal mix of agile and other approaches to use. It describes a model we can use to rank project characteristics (such as size, organizational impact, uncertainty, internal support, and criticality) to identify a recommended mix of knowledge, skills, tools, and techniques. It also describes the ongoing need to focus on value delivery and prune back ceremonies when they no longer justify their time commitment. It is a dynamic process rather than a static framework, similar to dealing with the people on your project and in your organization.

Who Should Read This Book?

This book is for team leaders, project managers, ScrumMasters, development leads, and project practitioners who want to take their delivery skills to the next level. It provides a learning framework and integration points for using more than just agile approaches to be successful in a broader range of scenarios.

If you work on a team or your work involves coordinating the effort of others, then this book has been written for you. It explains a model of how to tackle complex projects and work effectively with people. Just as projects differ in size, type, and complexity, so too does the model, driven by your project characteristics.

How This Book Can Help You

Organizations are often complex and contradictory in their application of standards, processes, and norms. This book takes what you already know from agile and extends it to be more robust, applicable, and adaptive to real-world environments. It explains how to scale agile techniques while minimizing process load. It describes how to integrate agile approaches into traditional, non-agile environments and use soft skills such as influence, empathy, and leadership to gain more acceptance and support when processes and techniques fall short.

Finally, it shows why and how an integrated approach to mastering industry domain knowledge, traditional project management, leadership, and agile approaches delivers more than the sum of its parts. It describes a view one level up in terms of abstraction (and usefulness). It is not as much of a how-to-do-it book as a how-to-think-about-it book, which will then show you how to do it. It provides evidence-based guidance from a broad range of professional disciplines, including lean, project management, economics, psychology, sociology, process management, and change management.

This book contains a wide variety of ideas and concepts. It is designed to be read from cover to cover since the topics and themes build on from one other. However, it can also be dipped into. So, if you are looking for conflict resolution tips or guidance on showing risk reduction metrics, feel free to look it up in the index and dive straight in. My goal with this book and ever-evolving supporting website is to create a valuable set of resources for anyone navigating the new world of project complexity.

Chapter 1
The Problem and the Model

The Problem

Agile, by itself, is not enough to be successful in many project environments. We also need to add in more leadership and emotional intelligence (EI) to understand how to perform and get the best out of teams. Also, there will be times when elements of traditional, plan-driven approaches can be useful, and we need industry-specific knowledge to be viewed as credible project advisors by sponsors and other stakeholders. These facts may seem obvious and just common sense, but, unfortunately, this common sense is not commonly applied or taught. This book solves this problem.

Visual Thinkers

This book will appeal to visual thinkers who like to conceptualize the big picture before getting into the details. These people, who are sometimes called *right-brained* after the portion of the brain responsible for processing images, would rather be shown how something works than told in detail how it works. If you spend a long time getting the flow of your PowerPoint slides right before you can focus on adding content and detail then you are, like I am, likely right-brained.

Research by David Hyerle into visual thinking reports that 90 percent of the information entering the brain is visual. Forty percent of all nerve fibers connected to the brain are connected to the retina and a full 20 percent of the entire cerebral cortex is dedicated to vision, so let us use it.[1]

This book shows the stages of skills progression, it illustrates how one step builds on the previous step and provides one-page views of how things relate and fit together. Like having a good map, understanding context and structures spatially allows us more confidence to explore new territory and retreat to familiar ground when needed.

FIGURE 1.1 *Leadership and EI*

Figure 1.1 shows how *leadership* is built upon *emotional intelligence*, which itself comprises outlook, *working with others,* and *managing self.* Images like this are used to create a visual, spatial framework for thinking about projects. Just as Kanban encourages us to visualize project work so we can all collaborate on it more effectively, visualizing the elements of project high performance help us discuss and understand them.

This Book Is Experience-Based

This book draws on a blend of commercial experience and scientific theory. Some concepts are the synthesis of several academic research papers. However, where possible, preference is given toward approaches I have seen work in several organizations. Examining the origins of research claims often uncovers dated, self-referencing clusters of studies, often written by the same author, or studies that employed university students as participants that are motivated and behave quite differently than commercial sector team members.

It is not that I do not trust academic recommendations based on tests conducted in universities; I just prefer recent commercial project experiences. Likely, I am biased to some degree by my own observations. Still, I think as work environments continue to evolve at ever-increasing rates, we owe it to ourselves to seek the closest guidance to our current work teams.

Continuous Digital and #NoProjects

So far, we have talked about delivering successful "projects," but the notion of projects with a defined start, middle, and end is being challenged with recent Continuous Digital and #NoProjects concepts. As software becomes more critical to competitive advantage, projects are not ending. Instead, the software-driven products continue to live on and evolve. This is a good sign that the business values the products and services and wants to keep investing in them and developing them.

Project management in many industries is evolving into ongoing product development and delivery. Organizations are arranging themselves around value streams that deliver business benefits. The principles described in this book about improving our ability toward effective delivery of value apply equally in Continuous Digital delivery environments and the #NoProjects world.

The organizational delivery construct may no longer be "projects," and we will likely switch to more product teams and value streams. However, the tools and techniques we use to engage and motivate people and to develop these new products will still apply. As you read this book, when you see the word *project*, think also of *products*, *initiatives*, and *value streams*. They are the future but still rely on the cooperation of people toward a vision.

Why Agile Is a Great Starting Point

Agile methods provide a great platform upon which to base our project approach. These include:

- ## Prioritized on Business Value and Risk Reduction

  By focusing on the highest business priority items first, organizations stand a much better chance of obtaining the bulk of the benefits from their endeavors. Projects inevitably encounter unforeseen issues and take longer than initially hoped. By prioritizing based on business value, the major benefits should be delivered even if not all the project scope can be delivered by the deadline or before the project funding runs out.

  Also, risks and complexity thwart many initiatives, especially new, novel endeavors. By actively seeking out and driving down the risks as early as possible, teams stand a better chance of overcoming them or finding an alternative approach in time to complete the project. This combination of focusing on the highest business value first and actively attacking risks early dramatically improves the likelihood of success and is a crucial strength of agile approaches.

- ## Iterative and Incremental Development

Most of today's projects are in the knowledge-worker domain, not the industrial-worker domain. By that, we mean they are not producing something similar to a past project; instead, it is new and likely has not been done before in your organization. Knowledge-worker projects bring subject-matter experts (SMEs) together to collaborate, share information, and build something or solve some novel problem. Whenever we are making something new like this, people will have different ideas about what the end goal should look like; since we have not done this before, issues will be encountered along the way.

An effective way to operate in this environment is through iterative and incremental development. Building small increments of the solution and then getting feedback on them allows us to confirm we are on the right track with the customer and redo work with the least penalty if we have diverged from their goals. It also allows us to get feedback on elements of technical feasibility and performance (whether the interface works or the speed is acceptable, etc.) to confirm we are indeed driving down the risks.

In addition to getting feedback and confirming we are building the right thing (product) and building it right (performance), we can get feedback on how the team is performing (process). Iterative and incremental development with frequent reviews of how the process is working allows issues to be resolved quicker than approaches with fewer reviews.

- ## Adaptation and Improvement

Iterative and incremental development provide the opportunities and inputs for improving, but it is the conscious efforts of adaptation and improvement that actually move us forward. The feedback we collect at product demonstrations and suggestions collected at retrospectives are not so much lessons learned as lessons *to be* learned, since until we act on them, they are just suggestions and ideas.

Acting on feedback, changing a design, and experimenting with a new process for an iteration or two is the starting point for adaptation and improvement. We try something different and get feedback on the change, capitalizing on what goes well and learning from what does not help. In addition to the evolving product getting reviewed, our experiments and adaptations are also inspected. It is this double loop of development and improvement that allows teams to better build superior products.

- ## Increase Drive through Empowered Teams

Agile approaches that give more autonomy to workers and move local planning down to team members improve motivation and productivity. Motivation expert Daniel Pink observed that when people are given more control over how they organize their work environment, their time, and team structures, their satisfaction increases along with their commitment to organizational goals, and their productivity.

Agile approaches use lean concepts around respect for workers to build effective, empowered teams. When teams are given the authority to improve their own processes they feel more ownership of them and a stronger drive to deliver. People are great at managing complexity: they juggle home lives, work tasks, email, phone calls, and text messages. Many traditional attempts at project management ignored this capability and instead relied on sequential task lists of work to complete. Agile approaches leverage people's ability to manage complexity. They do this by presenting a high-level list of work to be completed within an iteration, but letting the workers figure out the best way to organize and deliver it. Generally, the people closest to the work will have the best insights into the dependencies and practicalities of undertaking it and will produce better plans.

- ## Safety

Linked to empowered teams and respect for workers is the concept of personal safety for contribution. It is sometimes missed by companies looking to adopt agile approaches without fully understanding the agile mindset, so I think it is worth separating out as its own topic of success for agile methods.

People only commit and try their hardest when they feel assured that trying and failing will not be punished. People only freely ask questions when they know exposing their lack of knowledge on a topic will not be held against them. A key component of building healthy teams is creating a safe environment where it is okay (and expected) that people will fail trying things and there are no dumb questions since we are all just trying to improve and learn as quickly as possible.

When we have this mindset in place, teams stretch their goals and achieve far more than when operating in an environment with fear. As my old project manager used to say, "You only have two hands to work with; if you are using one to cover your rear, you now only have one hand to work with." In short, agile approaches create safe environments for teams, thereby ensuring everyone is working with both hands at full speed.

Why We Need to Move Beyond Agile

While agile approaches offer our best starting point, they are not enough to ensure success or even deliver enough success enough of the time. Too many agile projects fail and then organizations go back to using more traditional, plan-driven approaches with lackluster performance. This is because agile by itself is not sufficient for challenging environments. Agile approaches work well for small projects in receptive, supportive environments, but we often work in large, messy, somewhat toxic environments.

Agile-scaling frameworks provide potential solutions for many of the common problems associated with larger teams and programs but carry risks associated with process weight and diversion of team focus. When presented with a buffet of processes, tools, and deliverables, teams tend to take too much because everything looks valuable (and is valuable in the right context), but when taken together too much attention and effort from delivery is diverted.

At the same time, agile tools and agile alternatives to traditional planning, estimating, tracking, and reporting approaches are appropriate if the organization is transitioning wholescale to agile, but most organizations use agile delivery within more traditional governance frameworks. Suggesting only agile solutions will be misaligned and rejected. We need to understand the reality of slow transitions and be able to integrate with traditional structures, metrics, and processes to be successful.

This is not a failure of transitioning an organization to being fully agile; it is acknowledging the truth that organizations change slowly, and many organizations may never fully adopt agile processes throughout their hierarchy. The sooner we realize that the industry and culture of the organization dictate their readiness and tolerance for transitioning to agile approaches, the sooner we will be better aligned to choose our battles wisely and be more effective. Our tool kit and skill set should contain traditional project expertise (along with leadership and domain-specific knowledge) to be successful.

Industrial Workers, Knowledge Workers, and Learning Workers

Since we are discussing organizations and work, now is a good time to define some terms and models about work.

Work has progressed through several distinct stages. Initially, humans wandered the earth as hunter-gatherers, then they started planting crops and herding animals. It changed society and work; this was the Agricultural Revolution. As a result, people wandered less, and they lived and worked where their food was and close to trading opportunities.

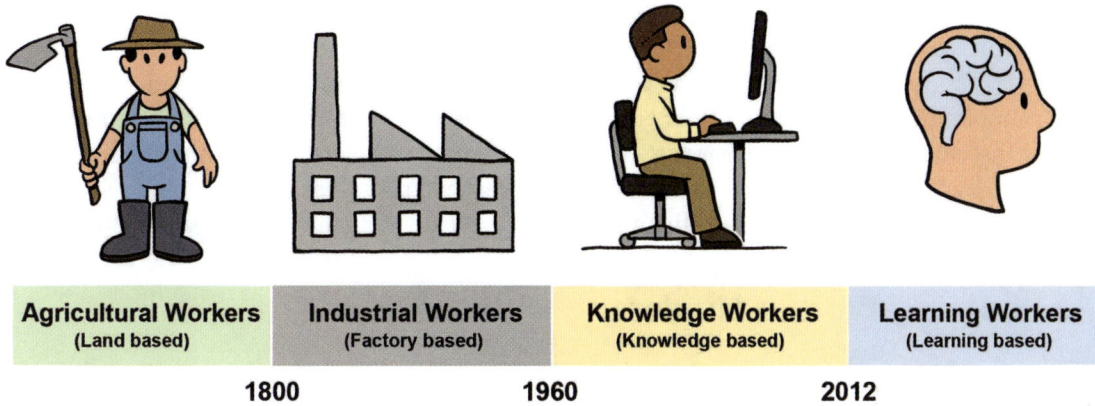

Agricultural Workers (Land based) **Industrial Workers** (Factory based) **Knowledge Workers** (Knowledge based) **Learning Workers** (Learning based)

1800   1960   2012

FIGURE 1.2 *Work Revolutions*

The next big transformation came with the development of machines and factories, when people left their farms and villages to move into cities. This was the Industrial Revolution, which eventually led to the development of many classic project management tools and concepts, including Gantt charts, functional decomposition of work tasks, and localized labor. In turn, these developments created more advanced project management tools, such as the work breakdown structure (WBS) and network diagrams.

The next stage was known as the Information Revolution. This revolution focused on information and collaboration, rather than on manufacturing. It placed value on the ownership of knowledge and the ability to use that knowledge to create or improve goods and services. Peter Drucker popularized the term *knowledge worker* and explained how they are subject matter experts who collaborate and solve problems that their organizations typically have not faced before. As work became more novel, instead of producing many copies of the

Unique Characteristics of Knowledge Workers and Learning Workers

When knowledge-work and learning-work projects became more common, people found that the research, learning, communication, and collaboration involved in these projects made tasks more uncertain and less definable than industrial work. As people tried to apply industrial-work techniques to knowledge-work projects, frustration—and project failures—increased. Agile methods were developed in response to this problem. Agile pioneers collected the most effective techniques for knowledge and learning work, adapting them for use on projects and experimenting to see what worked best. This new initiative began in the software development field, but is now used in all kinds of knowledge-work and learning-work projects.

same widget, knowledge workers built new products and services that their organizations typically had not offered before.

The final stage of work evolution (for now) is dubbed the Learning Age by Jacob Morgan, author of *The Future of Work*. New technologies are evolving rapidly and company training departments cannot provide all the things their employees need to carry out their job duties in an effective manner. Instead, with the rise of internet-based information and learning, learning workers have the skills to learn as they go. They can also adapt quickly and apply their learning to new situations and issues. Capacity to learn and a willingness to self-study are the hallmarks of learning workers.

The Learning-Worker Mindset

> *Learning and innovation go hand in hand. The arrogance of success is to think that what you did yesterday will be sufficient for tomorrow.*
>
> —William Pollard

The fact that you are reading this book likely means you are a learning worker and appreciate the need for and value in continuously updating your perspective and skill set—or you have been forced to read this book as some kind of cruel punishment!

As the rate of change continues to accelerate, our ability to learn and adapt to change will dictate our success and our usefulness to organizations.

The Institute for the Future published the report *Future Work Skills 2020*, sponsored by the University of Phoenix Research Institute. It listed the characteristics they felt most valuable for workers in 2020. It focused on ten key work skills driven by six agents of change:

1. Sensemaking: Ability to determine the deeper meaning or significance of what is being expressed

2. Social intelligence: Ability to connect to others in a deep and direct way, to sense and stimulate reactions and desired interactions

3. Novel and adaptive thinking: Proficiency at thinking and coming up with solutions and responses beyond that which is rote or rule based

4. Cross-cultural competency: Ability to operate in different cultural settings

5. Computational thinking: Ability to translate vast amounts of data into abstract concepts and to understand data-based reasoning

6. New-media literacy: Ability to critically assess and develop content that uses new media forms, and to leverage these media for persuasive communication

7. Transdisciplinary: Literacy in and ability to understand concepts across multiple disciplines

8. Design mindset: Ability to represent and develop tasks and work processes for desired outcomes

9. Cognitive load management: Ability to discriminate and filter information for importance, and to understand how to maximize cognitive functioning using a variety of tools and techniques

10. Virtual collaboration: Ability to work productively, drive engagement, and demonstrate presence as a member of a virtual team

So, in line with the need for this learning mindset, we now explore the domains further.

But Hybrid Agile Is a Diluted Abomination, Is It Not?

As soon as people suggest using agile along with other techniques, the stigma of hybrid approaches arises. When combining agile with something else, the result is something that is no longer purely agile; it is somehow diluted or tainted. When you mix beer with lemonade, the resultant shandy drink is neither as strong nor tasty as beer, nor as pure or refreshing as lemonade.

However, using two things together does not have to mean having to mix or dilute them. It is possible to use agile for development and then other techniques for approval. Instead of choosing between listening to music featuring only guitars or only pianos, we can enjoy guitars and pianos used in sympathetic combinations. Having more than one tool in your toolbox is beneficial.

> *The test of a first-rate intelligence is the ability to hold two opposed ideas in the mind at the same time, and still retain the ability to function.*
>
> —F. Scott Fitzgerald

People gravitate toward simple solutions. Having a single approach to follow is reassuring and creates a sense of clarity and security. Unfortunately, life and projects present many context-sensitive decision points and so no single strategy will be correct all the time.

Instead, we need to grow more comfortable with maintaining two (or more) opposed ideas in mind at the same time while retaining the ability to function. We must have knowledge of several different ways to tackle a situation and then apply the one that best fits the scenario and stakeholders. This creates complexity and uncertainty that many people are not comfortable with and would rather avoid.

Simple answers may be reassuring but they are typically wrong. Life is complicated and so are useful answers. Rather than providing a short pamphlet of how to operate and reach our goal, we need a map so we can make many midcourse adjustments at the junctions on the way to our goal.

The Tyranny of the OR versus the Genius of the AND

Jim Collins, author of *Good to Great and Built to Last*, describes the concept of the "Tyranny of the OR versus the Genius of the AND." The "Tyranny of the OR" is being forced into A or B choices, such as whether we should undertake this project using an agile or plan-driven approach. The "Genius of the AND" is finding ways to use the best of both approaches to create a better third alternative, option C.

In this way, agile hybrid approaches leverage the benefits of agile while also using additional approaches to increase the likelihood of success. They harness the proven benefits of prioritization, iterative and incremental development, adaptation, and empowered teams while also using successful integration, influence, and domain knowledge to deliver. Whether you call it beyond agile, hybrid agile, or agile+ does not really matter. It is this "Genius of the AND" mindset, coupled with the willingness to continue learning and apply smart practices, that increases your ability to deliver.

I have consulted for Lockheed Martin's drone software development group. They operate in the difficult space of undertaking projects using the latest experimental hardware and software systems, yet also being bound by rigorous safety and compliance requirements.

Formal specifications and extensive testing traceability evidence are basic entry criteria to working in their domain. If you do not create and use them effectively, you do not qualify for the work. At the same time, they need lots of short iterations to quickly prove approaches and test prototypes.

Lockheed Martin uses a combination of agile research and development techniques sandwiched between more predictive, formal approaches to deliver effectively while still meeting their regulatory requirements. They are using the "Genius of the AND," preserving the integrity and benefits of agile, while ensuring rigor and quality through more formal approaches.

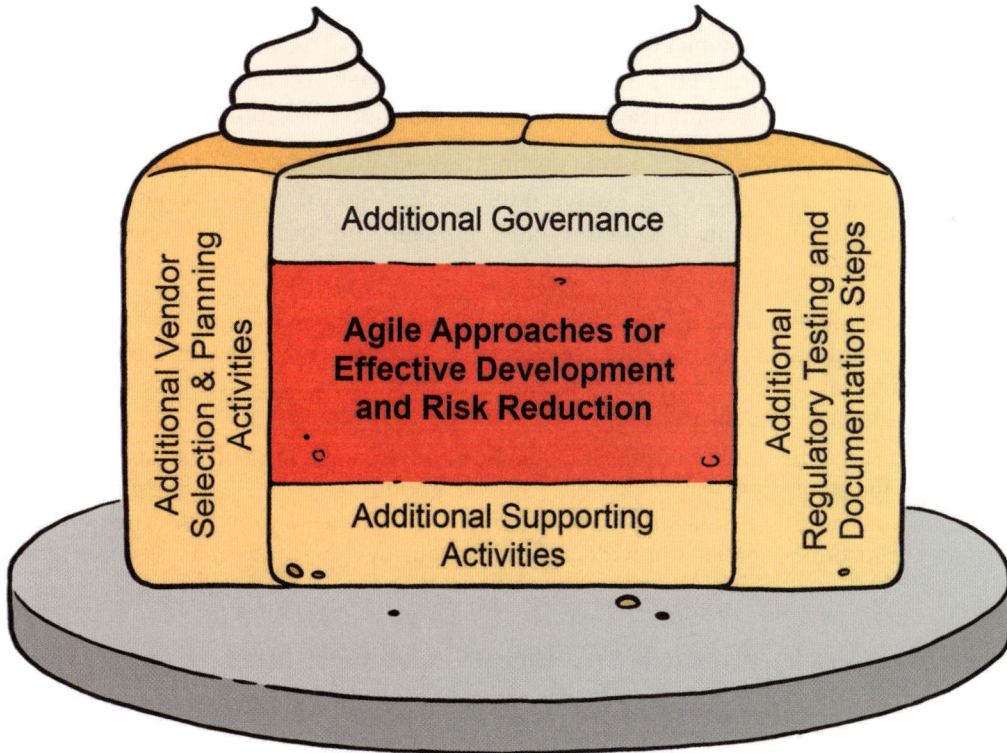

FIGURE 1.4 *Genius of the AND*

Proficiency at Tailoring

Combining and tailoring approaches is an advanced topic; it requires that we are first comfortable and competent at using approaches in the plain-vanilla, out-of-the-box form first. Before attempting to use the BAM, I recommend people be familiar and have had success with agile approaches. Only when you know how things are supposed to work and feel can you be confident that a new approach has sufficient components and balance to be successful. We will explain how this is achieved in the "Putting the Model to Use" chapter.

Another concept that is aligned with expanding approaches beyond just the core agile framework is the Shu-Ha-Ri model. Shu-Ha-Ri is a skills-progression framework, popularized in the agile community by Alistair Cockburn. According to this model, when learning a new skill or process we move through three stages, as follows:

1. **Shu:** Obeying the rules. *Shu* means "to keep, protect, or maintain." As beginners, we start by following the rules we have absorbed from our teachers, mentors, or learning experiences.

2. **Ha:** Consciously moving away from the rules. *Ha* means "to detach or break free." Once we have mastered the rules through practice, they become second nature to us—at this point, we can break free of our training and work intuitively.

3. **Ri:** Going beyond the rules to find our individual path. *Ri* means "to go beyond or transcend." In this final stage, we reach full mastery—at this point, we have integrated the rules so thoroughly that we can transcend them and strike out onto new paths for others to follow.

This is well-aligned with the BAM, using the mindset and values of agile in a larger setting, complemented by additional skills, to be more effective. Beyond agile provides a framework for finding our individual path. It does not dictate what to do; it makes recommendations and suggestions that can be evaluated and adopted or ignored as applicable.

Your projects are different than mine. It would be ill-advised and kind of arrogant to suggest a tool can provide the single best way to proceed. Instead, good frameworks provide guidance from which stakeholders can make their best-informed decisions. Gather as much information as you can, consider the recommendations provided, then use your own best judgment to decide how to proceed.

Process Has Weight, but Knowledge Is Weightless

Ceremonies and processes have weight and take time to undertake. This is okay and worth it if the process adds sufficient value to warrant the expenditure. However, often they do not add enough value, or the processes continue to be used day after day, beyond the point where they are still valuable, and instead become a net drain on a team's efficiency.

Knowledge, on the other hand, is weightless. There is no penalty for collecting knowledge. Understanding a wide variety of topics and techniques allows us to use only those that are the most efficient and appropriate for our current circumstances.

We can visualize process as the baggage and tools we carry on our project journey. Like going on a hike, some small undertakings may require no additional support. We can just turn up and do them. As projects get longer and more complicated, just like a longer hike, we might be glad of a raincoat and some food and water for the trip.

Complex and hazardous endeavors may require sophisticated tools (and knowing how to use them). The goal is to take just what we need, understanding that the more we elect to bring, the better prepared we are, but the slower we will go. The more energy you use carrying a heavy backpack of tools, the less energy you have available to move toward the project goals. So, we need to balance responsible process with goal focus and progress.

FIGURE 1.5 *Knowledge Is Weightless*

What about SAFe, DA, LeSS, Nexus, Etc.?

Currently, the agile community is abuzz with discussions of and promotions for scaling frameworks that claim to help organizations apply agile approaches to large, complex scenarios. These frameworks include SAFe, LeSS, DA, and Nexus. These and others provide models for managing large teams, multiple teams, programs, and portfolios. Many of the models also tackle the pre-project demand management funnel and post-deployment sustainment portions of the life cycle.

These frameworks offer reasonable solutions for common scaling problems. They are generally well researched and supported by a wealth of training courses, credentials, and certified consultants. However, they come with some fundamental problems as well.

Agile Myopia - Agile scaling frameworks dictate that agile approaches are the only solution. When you have only a hammer in your toolbox, all problems look like nails. However, sometimes the best way to deal with that traditional stakeholder who wants a WBS is to give them a WBS. Likewise, maybe some aspect of your project is defined and repeatable, so why not use a traditional plan-driven approach for it? It is both arrogant and ignorant to believe agile is always the best solution.

Software Focused – The agile approaches, scaling frameworks, and usage tool kits grew out of the software development space. Unfortunately, they have not shed their software-focused roots and still contain concepts based on software architecture. That might be okay for consultants who can filter out these elements and convert the ideas to other industries, but it is an impediment to sharing ideas and getting a broad spectrum of stakeholders on board.

Buffet Syndrome - As when faced with a buffet of tasty-looking food, there is a tendency to take more than you need. With so much information available in these tool kits, most organizations and teams try to adopt too much process, rigor, and artifacts, leaving too little energy for the true project goals. As we discussed earlier, it is fine to understand the theory (knowledge is weightless) but when you start using these rich frameworks the process weight overwhelms most organizations.

Instead, the speed of delivery and ability to quickly react to changes that are key agile benefits are lost by organizations now using overly heavy frameworks. As focus shifts to training, learning new terminology, and roles like Release Train Engineer, less effort is directed to project goals, with predictable results.

The BAM described in this book avoids the buffet syndrome by providing context-sensitive recommendations based on your current project characteristics. Small, simple projects get fewer recommended approaches than large, complex ones. The risk of taking on too much process and reducing effort toward the end goal is largely removed.

Strategy and Cultural Mismatches - Agile scaling frameworks support agile transformation efforts. This is the conversion of the whole organization from a traditional command-and-control structure to a more flat, lean-pull model of operation. This is a noble, worthy goal; organizations that design their structures this way gain many benefits.

However, most organizations are not ready for a wholescale agile transformation. They are content with their profit centers and annual budget cycles even though they have associated problems. Agile scaling frameworks that have strategies to perform agile transformations eventually run into deep-rooted cultural obstacles to such fundamental change and then stall. As the saying goes, "Culture eats strategy for breakfast," which stresses the importance of people's commitment and passion for a cause.

While their goals are admirable, and it would be great if we really could convert organizations to new structures and thinking models, we need to be realistic about the likelihood of really achieving it. We should continue to try but not bet the farm on it happening anytime soon.

So, for the project practitioner trying to add value and deliver successful projects for their stakeholders, agile scaling frameworks are problematic. Agile approaches are not always the best tools for the job. Like any good tool, agile tools are great for their intended purpose but are no panacea or silver bullet. Also, the size and depth of scaling frameworks create distractions of focus and dilute team effort from project goals. These approaches often try to undertake too large of an organizational change that carries an increased risk of failure.

Finally, treating an organization's agile transformation as a project itself is a valid approach, but adopting a scaling and transformation framework to help deliver a large business project adds unnecessary scope and risk. Instead, treat these frameworks as knowledge resources from which to cherry-pick. Maybe there is a model for coordination between teams that is useful, or a prioritization scheme for evaluating release candidates or features that could be handy. However, be wary of adopting one wholescale to assist with project delivery. Avoid framework consultants, training, and certification programs; we cannot afford distractions from the real goal of completing a project.

Why Now?

Agile has "crossed the chasm" in terms of market penetration, understanding, and awareness. People know about it and many organizations are using it in common practice. Most organizations are not fully agile; they are using agile approaches in pockets, but the techniques have reached a tipping point of common awareness and understanding.

Unfortunately, most companies are struggling with it. It does not integrate well into their existing processes for funding, planning, estimating, tracking, or reporting. It is also at odds with their staffing, procurement, and contracting models.

So, on the one hand, agile approaches are poised to deliver value and productivity gains. Enough people at last understand them and want the benefits. On the other hand, their potential is being held back through integration issues and overzealous adherence to agile ceremonies and terminology.

These frustrations and failed benefits delivery are unfortunately a reason why many organizations are abandoning agile and losing the great start that they were off to. Alone, it is not enough in many organizations, but now is the perfect time to start reaping the rewards of lean and agile approaches with the smart application of integrating them into existing knowledge and skills.

Another factor influencing the *why now?* question is our current time period. Since the end of 2016, there are more millennial (Gen Y) workers in the workforce than any other category. A quick primer of the different workforce generations is given in the sidebar on the next page.

The year 2016 marked an important milestone, with more millennials in the workforce than any other group. This shift, along with Gen Z starting to work, means the future of work is set to change rapidly. For instance, Gen Z has no recall of a time before the internet and mobile devices.

Instead, they grew up playing with these devices and as they enter the workforce they will define how every other generation ultimately uses technology.

Generations Primer

The Center for Generational Kinetics defines a generation as "a group of people born around the same time. People in these groups exhibit similar characteristics, preferences, and values over their lifetimes. Generation traits are not fixed or exhibited by everyone in that age group, but they likely show similar characteristics, such as communication and motivation preferences. This is because they experienced similar trends at approximately the same life stage and through similar channels (e.g., online, TV, mobile, etc.)."

It is important to remember that at an individual level everyone is different. But looking at people through a generational lens offers useful predictability for those trying to reach, inform, or persuade a large cross section of a population.

The primary generations are:

- Gen Z, iGen, or centennials, born in or after 1996
- Millennials or Gen Y, born from 1977 to 1995
- Generation X, born from 1965 to 1976
- Baby boomers, born from 1946 to 1964
- Traditionalists or silent generation, born in or before 1945

Much as millennials encouraged other generations to use social media, text messaging, and digital downloading, Gen Z could do the same for wearable devices, artificial intelligence (AI), and dependence on the cloud for storage and computing. How we engage and motivate teams is set to change too. Agile approaches, with their emphasis on inclusion (teams plan and estimate) and empowerment (teams make local decisions), are well aligned for the next generation of workers. These concepts will no longer be niche development techniques, but rather the minimum entry criteria for engaging the majority of the workforce.

The Accelerating Rate of Change

We now live in a time of accelerated change. Never before have ideas and innovation spread so quickly. In just one generation, humanity has gone from ideas being spread by books and word of mouth to the hyperconnected world we live in today. Figure 1.6 contrasts the time to adoption by fifty million people for some common technologies.

Given this trend of faster innovation and faster adoption by an increasingly connected society, our ability to adapt and innovate is critical.

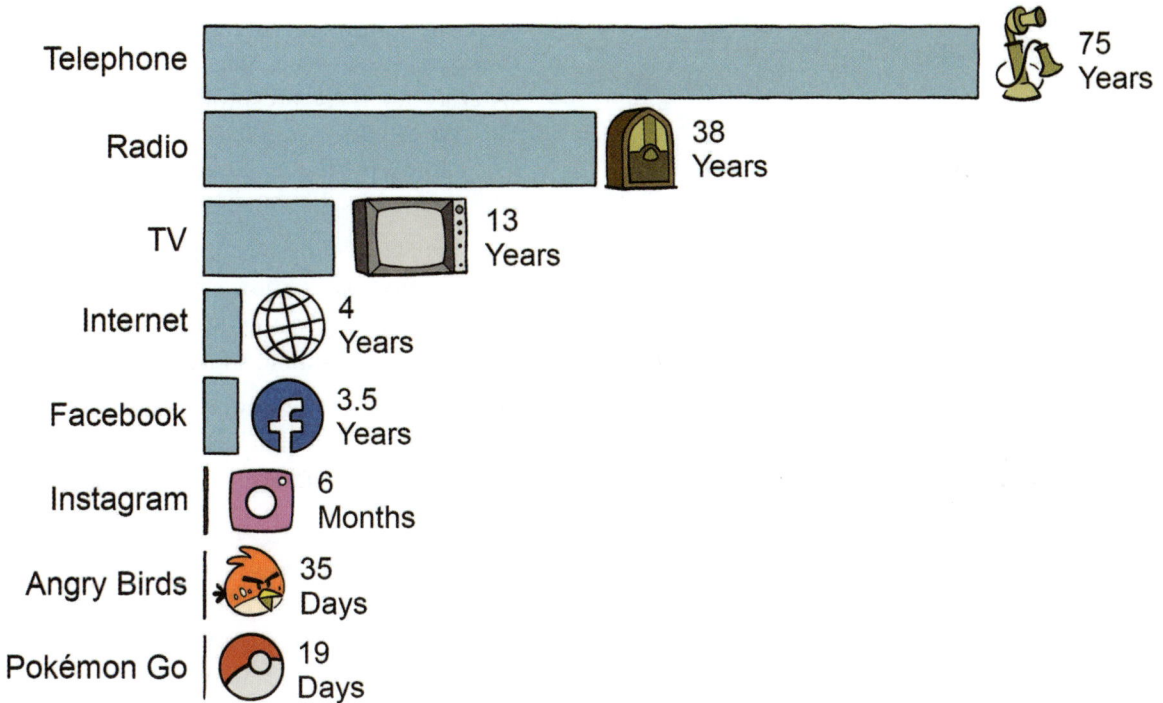

FIGURE 1.6 *Speed of Change*

Understanding the End Goal

The end goal is not to be agile, but to be successful in our endeavors. That does not mean winning at any cost. I am not suggesting we ever take advantage of people, act in a disrespectful way, or exhibit anything beyond true integrity and transparency.

Instead, the end goal is to make all our stakeholders successful. This includes the sponsors and businesspeople commissioning the work, the team members undertaking the work, and all the supporting and tertiary roles that touch or get touched by the work along the way. It matters much less what we call our approach.

There are no points for style in the approaches we follow in industry. We may well have to

> *Intelligence is the ability to adapt to change.*
> —Stephen Hawking
>
> *Anyone who stops learning is old, whether at twenty or eighty. Anyone who keeps learning stays young.*
> —Henry Ford

conform with organizational process standards and meet audit and review criteria, but these are project deliverables also. We can do so, and more besides. I have never seen a process standard that precludes additional steps that increase success rates.

We are starting with agile as the basis for effective delivery since it represents today's best way to approach knowledge-worker and learning-worker projects. If something better comes along tomorrow, we should use that instead. Heck, if wearing purple hats produced better results than using agile, we should all wear purple hats.

Our goal is improvement and growth in the journey to be more relevant and valuable. The Beyond Agile Model described in this book takes an approach-agnostic path to superior performance. The end goal is success for our stakeholders and we can use a savvy mix of techniques and superior understanding of people, process, and tools to get there.

This mindset represents the application of outcomes over outputs. Outputs are the things we create, such as prioritized backlogs and definitions of "done." Outcomes are the less tangible feelings of success, frustration, or failure that occur because of how we engage with people and work together. We should be valuing these outcomes far more than the outputs that were just temporary stepping stones. It is time to learn how to focus on outcomes and drop our affection for outputs.

Your Starting Point

The good news is that if you are already applying an agile mindset, values, and principles to your work, you are on the right track. The techniques described in this book are net additions to agile, like bonuses or power-up features in a game, if that metaphor works for you. They make you more effective, increase your likelihood of success, and make you more useful to your organization.

The bad news is they require a mindset shift and change in how we work. There is no single right way anymore; we do not just do things the agile way knowing that it is a well-researched and balanced system. Instead, we evaluate several different potential solutions and choose the most appropriate for our given project circumstances and stakeholders.

I deliberately list stakeholders separately from project circumstances despite them being part of the circumstances because it is worth stressing that culture beats strategy every time. Trying to apply a superior approach, not mindful of the people issues involved, will lead to failure. Many agile introductions fail because they were trying to do the right thing but with deliberately awkward stakeholders. We need to choose our battles carefully and understand that the smartest thing to do next may be to use an inferior but better-accepted approach this time around.

The saying "Do you want to be right, or do you want to be successful?" reminds us to choose our battles carefully. Often, being right and pointing out errors in other people's logic is a shortsighted and hollow victory because it cuts off further opportunities to make progress. Like pointing out technical flaws in arguments with your spouse, it is not really that smart in the long-term scheme of things. Another word for taking this long-term goal mindset is *Satyagraha*.

Satyagraha Mindset

The term *Satyagraha* means a "firm (but smart) pursuit of truth" and was coined and developed by Mahatma Gandhi and used in his pursuit of civil rights and freedom. It comes from compounding two words: *satya*, meaning "being," and *agraha,* meaning "holding firm to." The interesting part is the timeframe and strategy. It may take a while to get where you really want to go and there may be obstacles and compromises to make along the way.

Some of the principles include:

» Nonviolence

» Truth and honesty

» Harbor no anger at the opponent

» Suffer the anger of the opponent

» Do not be the source of quarrels

These principles were applied to civil rights movements where real physical harm was a possibility. They went on to inspire the American civil rights movement and were used by Martin Luther King Jr.

Anyone attempting to bring about change can apply these ideas. It will likely be a long journey; to be successful you have to be ready for minor setbacks. Sometimes, you must bend and flex to stay in the game and continue. However, persistent, respectful engagement wins out eventually. Hard stands, shouting, and trying to force people to do things is a recipe for failure and rejection.

We should learn from successful change agents and employ their strategies most likely to be successful. *Satyagrahi* is the persistent, respectful, engaged, and helpful way to effect any change.

Transformation (Moving to a Learning-Worker Mindset) Requires Change, and We Do Not Like Change

It's bad enough that adopting agile requires organizations to change. Adopting a Beyond Agile approach to projects requires further change; what is more, you will likely be the one to lead that change.

This moves us from a large group of people wanting the benefits of change but not willing to change themselves, to a smaller group of people willing to change themselves, then finally to the smallest (often empty) group of people willing and able to lead that change in an organization. However, if it were easy then it would likely already have happened. We can succeed where others have failed, and we will explore the process to achieve success.

As we know, changing people's minds about how to work is difficult and time-consuming. People grow comfortable working in familiar ways and nature has conditioned us to be cautious and suspicious of change. Leading people through change is an especially challenging, but also rewarding, process. We may not be successful in converting everyone and we must learn that that is okay and inevitable. A bigger issue would be not trying just because it is too difficult.

Before we can effectively change other people's minds about new ideas, we need to be convinced of the changes ourselves. Only then will we have the conviction to follow through with credibility and passion. New ideas and changes generally go through the following stages:

1. Conceptualize: First, we have to understand the idea.

2. Internalize: Then, we need to internally agree to the idea and decide to embody it.

3.   Practice: Next, we practice it in our own work, then in our behaviors and interactions with others.

4.   Radiate. Finally, we can encourage others to work this way and radiate the mindset and practices to others.

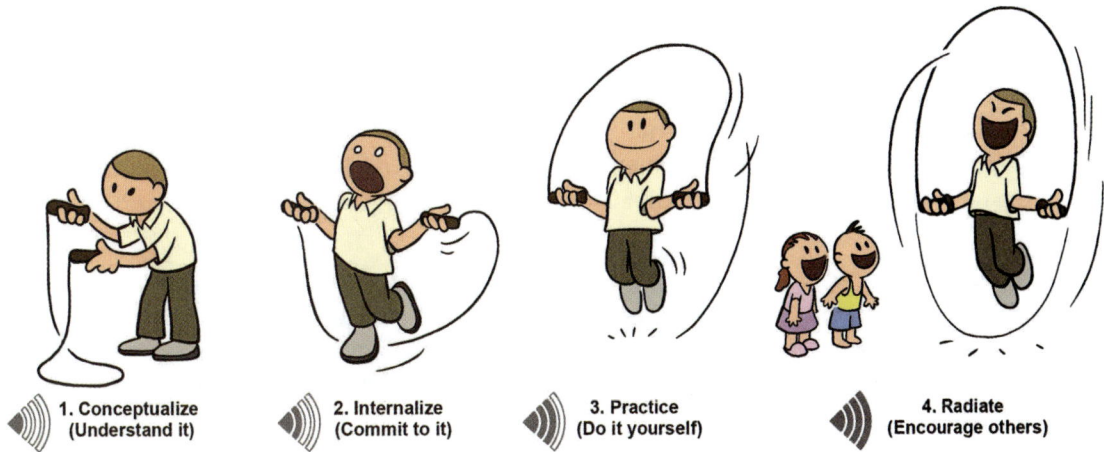

1. Conceptualize (Understand it)   2. Internalize (Commit to it)   3. Practice (Do it yourself)   4. Radiate (Encourage others)

FIGURE 1.8 *Stages of Change*

Using this approach, we first acknowledge something is a good idea and an approach we want to try. Then we learn about it and try it in our own work. When we have had good personal success, we practice it more openly and encourage others to try it for themselves. Then comes the task of sharing it with others and encouraging others to adopt it too.

Jumping to the last step and trying to roll out a change without going through the first three steps of understanding it and using it yourself will result in a lack of conviction and inability to answer the inevitable questions that people will have. First, we have to experience and be the change we want to see in the world before we can convince others.

I constantly see people rise in life who are not the smartest, sometimes not even the most diligent, but they are learning machines. They go to bed every night a little wiser than they were when they got up and boy does that help, particularly when you have a long run ahead of you.

—Charlie Munger

To get started, we need a model to understand our skills and potential gaps in our knowledge and techniques for being successful on complex projects.

What Is the Beyond Agile Model (BAM)?

The BAM is a visual thinking framework for discussing and combining concepts from lean/agile, plan-driven, leadership, and emotional intelligence. It is an approach-agnostic and combines recommendations from many approaches. It is designed for team leaders, project practitioners, project management offices (PMOs), and business representatives who want relevant high-value project guidance. BAM provides context-specific project-approach recommendations from a full spectrum of project disciplines, including lean/agile, leadership/EI, plan-driven, and industry-specific approaches.

Unlike scaling models or tool kits such as Scaled Agile Framework® (SAFe®), Large Scale Scrum (LeSS), Disciplined Agile (DA), and Nexus, it avoids agile myopia (believing everything can be solved best by agile approaches) and buffet syndrome (the tendency, when presented with ideas, to take on too much process) by being simultaneously broader and more selective in its recommendations.

BAM recognizes that processes carry implementation weight, yet knowledge is weightless. So, it recommends learning much and implementing little—just the most relevant to retain maximum team effort toward the project goal. This dynamic model changes based on project and organizational characteristics, recommending the highest-value-added approaches, knowledge, and deliverables for the situation at hand.

Some key concepts:

» There is no single, simple model for complex projects.

» Process carries weight, but knowledge is weightless.

» Guidance needs to be dynamic based on project and organizational characteristics.

Chapters 2 and 3 explore the model in more detail.

Chapter 1 Summary

Now more than ever, we need to prove our worth and be valuable to organizations that are innovating faster than ever. Agile approaches provide a decent starting point, but they are neither silver bullets nor complete solutions. Instead, we need to broaden our view and embrace the scary ambiguity offered by the *Yes, and...* approach. It is scary because the choice depends on context; there is no single Scrum process to follow, no universal WBS-to-Gantt-chart method. It depends; you have to be smart and make choices. It is how grown-ups run projects.

Key topics covered in this chapter:

» Agile is integral but insufficient: The best teams use a savvy mix of approaches, do not focus much on process, and do what is required that day to be successful.

» Thinking framework: This book provides a thinking framework for combining ideas and working in complex environments.

» We are visual thinkers: Visualization helps us separate ideas spatially and chronologically; it helps us solve complex problems.

» The BAM is a visual-thinking framework for discussing and combining concepts from lean/agile, plan-driven, leadership and EI, and industry-specific domains.

» Much of our work today has evolved from industrial work to knowledge work to learning work.

» A hybrid needs not be a dilution; it can be a powerful new formulation.

» The "Tyranny of the OR versus the Genius of the AND" describes the evolutionary step of selective combination—more difficult because there is no formula, but more powerful because it can be context unique.

» Process has weight, but knowledge is weightless. Learn all you can, then be selective about how much process you use. Continually ask *What process is no longer worth the cost?*

» Agile myopia: The idea that all problems can be solved by agile processes.

» Buffet syndrome: Frameworks tempt us to take on too much process, which takes away from delivering value.

» Rates of change are accelerating and will continue to do so.

Chapter 2

Using the Beyond Agile Model

The Beyond Agile Model (BAM) is not complex, but comprises several overlapping layers and a dynamic component. To help explain the various elements, the walkthrough below will build the model incrementally, component by component.

The Model Starts with Agile

The first element in the model is agile itself. As discussed earlier, agile is the best starting point for successful project execution in complex environments. Its focus on people, value delivery, and risk avoidance, coupled with iterative and incremental development, provides a robust framework that is tolerant of change and new discovery.

Its frequent reviews and adaptation allow the elements of product, performance, and process to be improved throughout the life cycle. Finally, its empowered teams and emphasis on team safety create productive, motivated teams who are more likely to be invested in the project's success due to the influence they have had in its design and execution.

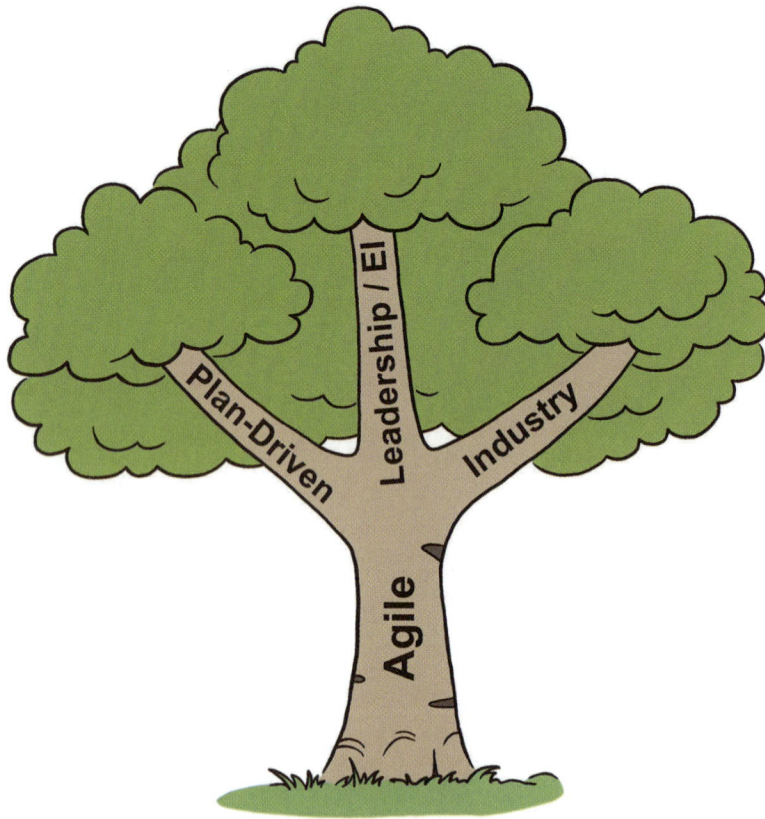

FIGURE 2.1 *Tree Model*

There are many ways to picture how agile is integral to a larger model of project delivery. Figure 2.1 above shows agile as the trunk of the tree, supporting boughs that represent the domains of plan-driven, leadership and EI, and industry-specific knowledge. Each of these domains is described next.

The circle in figure 2.2 represents the mindset, values, and principles of agile approaches. It also encompasses commonly applied agile practices used by most agile teams. In other words, the set of all things generally known as agile. While agile is integral to project success, it is not all that is required. So, additional domains of knowledge and skills are also layered into the model.

FIGURE 2.2 *Agile-domain Model*

Leadership and Emotional Intelligence (EI)

The next layer in the model is leadership and EI. While agile approaches promote servant leadership and encourage shared leadership by team members, they do not explain why or how best to achieve this. That is understandable; leadership is a huge topic, much larger and older than project management. However, there are some core concepts necessary for effective project delivery.

In addition to leadership, emotional intelligence is also a critical field of knowledge and skills. EI is the ability to recognize our own and other people's emotions and use emotional information to guide thinking and behavior. It also allows us to manage and/or adjust emotions to adapt to situations and achieve goals.

Projects are commissioned by people for people and then undertaken with people. Assuming we can be successful at executing them by becoming experts at only the analytical steps of task estimation, scheduling, execution, and tracking, is missing the most important part of the picture.

It may initially seem overwhelming to think we need to learn the large topics of leadership and EI to be successful on projects. The good news is that they overlap with the agile mindset and values anyway. The ideas of respect for workers and building empowered teams leverage leadership and EI. So, you are likely already using many leadership and EI concepts in your everyday application of agile values and principles. Learning more about leadership and EI will just provide additional diagnostic tools and more strategies to apply when faced with challenging situations.

So, while there is likely more to learn, leadership and EI are all useful net additions to what you already know. As when finding a secret door to an extra room in your house, you now have a whole new area to explore and make use of.

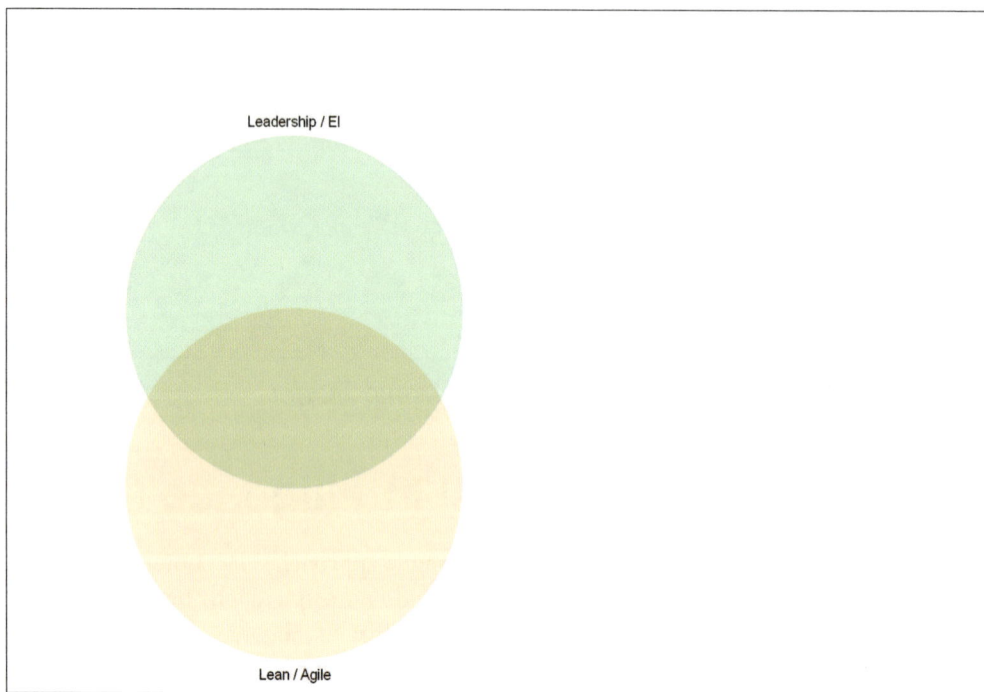

FIGURE 2.3 *Agile and Leadership/EI Domains*

Plan-Driven Knowledge, Skills, and Tools

This topic may not seem as exciting as leadership and EI, but it is still essential. The industrial worker-based, plan-driven mindset and principles are ingrained in most organizations' procedures and organizational structures. They are not going away anytime soon. Some start-ups are created with structures that deliberately avoid them; a small number of existing organizations can successfully migrate away from them. However, the vast majority of companies in existence today employ plan-driven inspired policies and practices.

It is not necessary to like or endorse plan-driven approaches, but it is necessary to fully understand them, to be able to talk the talk using all the correct terms, and to undertake them correctly. In fact, to be credible at suggesting alternative approaches, we need to be experts at these traditional plan-driven methods. Only when we clearly know more about a subject, its background, and its application can we make compelling arguments to augment it with something else and eventually move away from it.

Plan-driven approaches and alignment with PMI practices and frameworks are discussed in chapter 12.

Plan-driven approaches are not broken or invalidated in today's world of mostly knowledge-worker and learning-worker projects. They still work but are likely not the most appropriate methods or controls to use

Case Study: Out-Reporting IBM

My first taste of true agile approaches was in the early 1990s with a defense contractor, based in the United Kingdom, called Data Sciences. We used a combination of approaches including rapid-application development (RAD), popularized by James Martin, and participatory design, developed by Enid Mumford. This fusion, which involved short cycles, rapid feedback, and user-guided development, was successful. In 1994, when the DSDM Consortium was formed, Data Sciences was one of the original contributors and DSDM grew from these ideas along with additional ideas brought by other consortium members.

I was only at Data Sciences a couple of years before IBM acquired them. While IBM were themselves DSDM Consortium members, the group responsible for bringing Data Sciences staff into the IBM fold was not directly involved with it. I remember being asked to create project reports using IBM's plan-driven reporting templates and explain progress to one client using earned value (EV) reporting.

EV reporting is not incompatible with iterative and incremental approaches. However, it is based on comparison of actual progress relative to a baselined plan, which creates challenges when that initial baselined plan is flawed. Our first plans on knowledge-work and learning-work projects were created when we knew least about the project (at the beginning). These plans were "today's best guess" at the time they were created, but a week or a month later were usually woefully inaccurate. Measuring progress against a flawed map is of limited value.

However, back in the mid-1990s, this acknowledgment about initial plans being flawed was not universal. Stating that your plans were inaccurate was just admitting to needing to do more planning. As a junior project manager (PM), questioning the validity of using EV on agile projects was not an option I was qualified to raise with the new IBM project management office (PMO).

Instead, I had to learn all I could about EV, by first reading how-to books, then the original textbooks, and finally the relevant research papers. Interestingly, the more I learned, the more I discovered that the pioneers and proponents of EV were aware of the applicability limitations in high-change environments. However, if you just read how-to textbooks (there were no blogs and few online articles back then), you got the impression EV reporting was a cut-and-dried mathematical process to be duplicated the same way on every project. Yet the originators and research papers offered me cautions and shades of gray.

In the end, through collaboration with an EV white-paper author who happened to work in a different part of IBM, I was able to have a good discussion about using EV on agile projects. Back then, they were not called *agile*, but high-change, exploratory projects were understood by IBM because it undertakes a lot of research. Only after becoming well versed in EV and its limitations did I become a credible source to discuss its applicability concerns and suggest alternatives.

As things turned out, many years later after moving to Canada, I worked with a colleague to coauthor our own white paper on agile alternatives to EV; it was presented at the Agile 2006 Conference and is frequently cited. Awareness and application of plan-driven approaches can be a valuable strength that is helpful not only for undertaking approaches, but also for deciding when to replace them.

when faced with high rates of change, complexity, and the need to foster collaboration between diverse groups of subject matter experts.

However, few projects are purely knowledge-work or learner-work from start to finish in all activities. Often, early project-feasibility and funding-request stages are largely procedural and analytical. Final rollout and training work of a project to, for example, the tenth group of customers may be largely routine and readily duplicated with little scope for complexity or need for adaptation.

As such, plan-driven approaches are still relevant in many situations. It is probably not wise to base a modern, complex project around plan-driven approaches, but they are valid and valuable. This book will explain what you need to know, not only down to a step-by-step, how-to level; it will also show you how to integrate plan-driven tools and techniques with agile approaches in ways that do not invalidate agile values or principles.

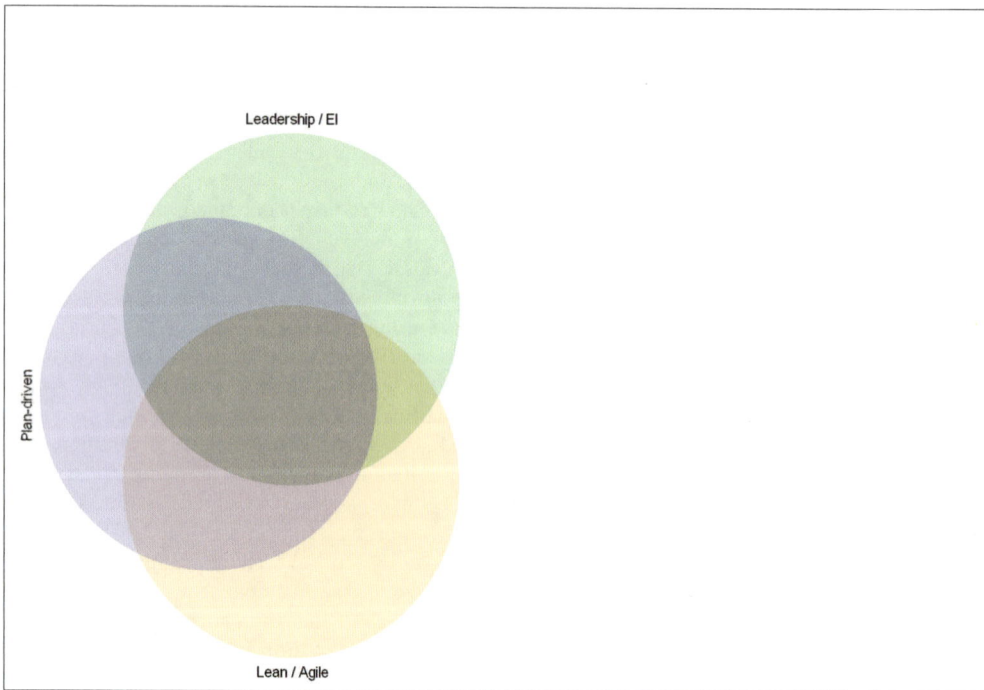

FIGURE 2.4 *Agile, L/EI, and Plan-driven Domains*

Industry-Specific Knowledge and Skills

The final component of the underlying model is industry-specific knowledge. This means understanding both the business domain of your customer and the technological domain of your project. So, if you are building a pipeline scheduling system for an oil and gas company you will need to understand the oil and gas pipeline industry and principles of scheduling.

Likewise, there will be industry-specific guidelines and requirements that must be followed just to do business. Financial projects are often bound by Sarbanes-Oxley (SOX) requirements. Pharmaceutical projects require compliance to Food and Drug Administration (FDA) guidelines. Military and safety-critical projects often need to demonstrate compliance with rigorous testing and requirements traceability needs.

These are not optional; they are the price of admission to participate in your specific domain. We cannot ignore these requirements. Instead, we need to understand them and incorporate them into our project life cycles at the appropriate points. This work is encompassed in the industry-specific domain—knowing what is required in your field and incorporating it appropriately in your projects.

Understanding the customer business and the product domain is critical, but often underestimated. To be credible and listened to by the sponsors and executives, we need to understand their day-to-day world. During the execution of large, complex projects, we will inevitably need to deliver bad news about progress or issues encountered. This might be accompanied by suggestions for simplification or requests for compromises. When the person reporting issues and suggesting alternatives does not understand the industry or core business models, it is easy for sponsors and executives to dismiss the concerns.

Project leaders should learn as much about the business and project technologies as possible so they are seen (rightly) as trusted advisors and business advocates. When project leaders build a strong understanding of the business, project goals, and issues, they can simultaneously act in the best interests of the business and the project.

For most people executing projects, this means they will always be learning. There will always be new business groups to represent, new technologies to understand, and new applications to learn. This is the realization that we are simultaneously knowledge workers and learning workers.

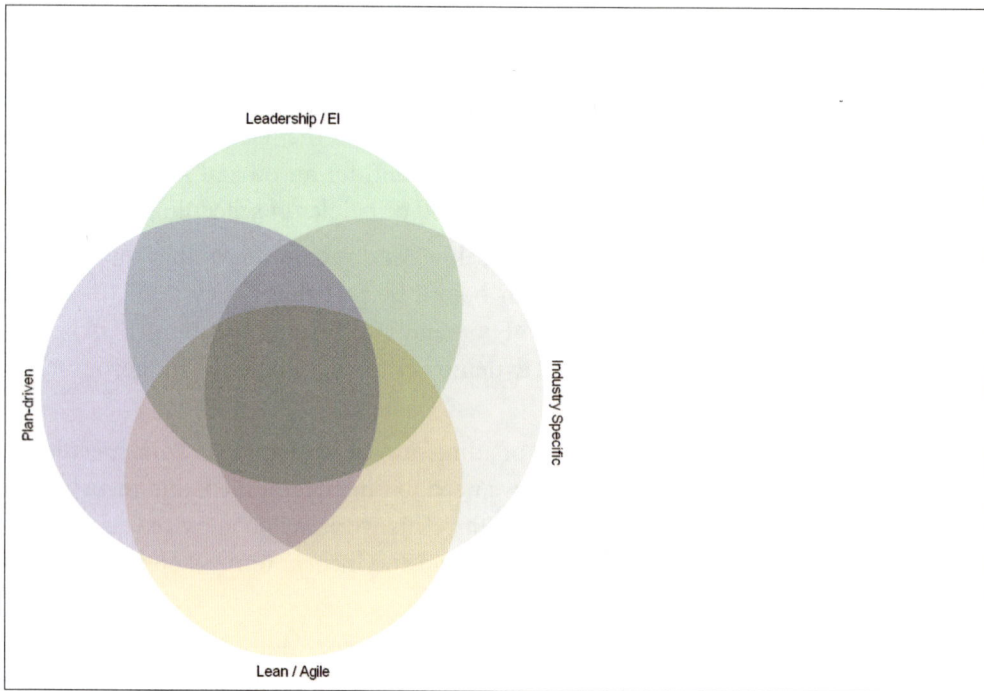

FIGURE 2.5 Agile, All Four Domains

Now that we have all four components of our project model described, we can label the resultant set as our organizational environment. This is where we conduct our projects and describe the attributes at play. Next, we can select which elements are necessary for a specific project. Remembering every process or ceremony we select has a management and delivery effort that diverts energy from building the final product or service. If the approach is necessary and delivers return on investment (ROI), we want it, but the goal is to take just enough — not as much as we can. Think about packing for a hike instead of filling up at a buffet; less is better, as long as you have minimally what you need. As with many project decisions, the real answer is complex but right, as opposed to simple but wrong.

Applying a Project-Specific Lens

All projects are different. They vary in scope and size, complexity, and the degree to which the technologies are understood or new to us. Characteristics like the criticality to the business and the experience levels of the team members will impact the rigor employed and processes we use. It is simplistic and foolhardy to assume a one-size-fits-all approach will ever be successful.

Instead, we need to tailor our approach for each project within organizational and industry norms. Large, critical projects will use more rigor than small, discretionary projects. Defined, repeatable projects with few uncertainties about requirements or technology will need less consensus gathering and fewer scope-exploration steps than new product development.

Our approaches, training, and artifacts should vary based on our project characteristics. An interactive tool to help you apply this project-specific lens can be found at www.BeyondAgileModel.com. This concept is illustrated in figure 2.6, which shows some project characteristics sliders and the resultant recommended set of approaches for such a project.

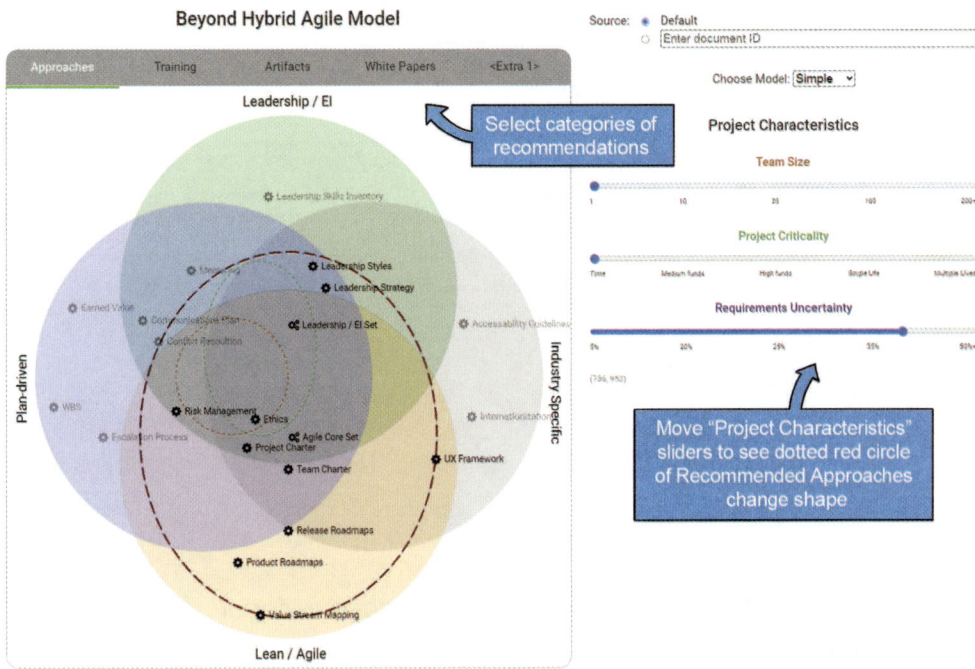

FIGURE 2.6 *Small-website Model*

In figure 2.6, we see the overlapping domain circles of agile, leadership/EI, plan-driven, and industry-specific knowledge. To the right of these circles is a *View* tab with the *Approaches* view selected; this switches which recommendations are displayed on the main canvas. In this case, recommended approaches are shown but we could switch to a different view and see recommended training or recommended artifacts.

Below the *View* tab are the *Project Characteristics* sliders. Moving these slider controls varies the size and shape of the dotted red recommendations lens. In the example in figure 2.6, we have selected some project characteristics for a small website development project. For comparison, in figure 2.7, we are viewing training recommendations for a logistics application project. The project characteristics sliders are in different positions, so the recommendations lens is a different size and shape.

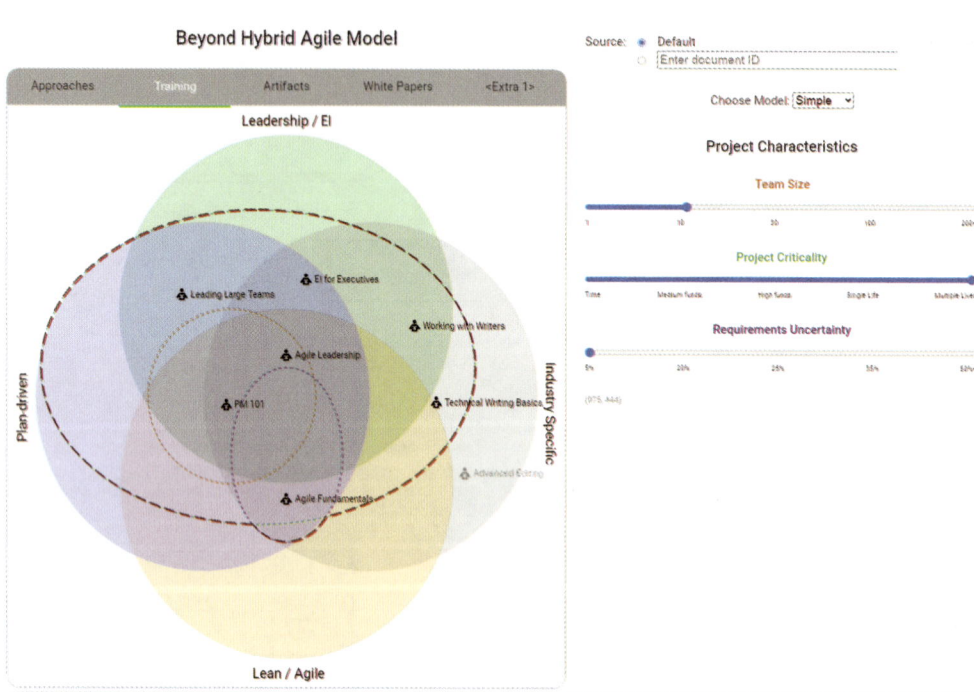

FIGURE 2.7 *Logistics-application Model*

Understanding How the Model Works

For anyone wanting to understand more about how the lens works, and why it often has an irregular, lumpy appearance, here are some more details. Each of the project characteristics sliders controls a set of recommendations. For instance, when agile adoption is low, the reliance on and need for plan-driven approaches will be higher.

Each of the variously sized sets of recommendations has a different origin (center) and set of growth characteristics based on its influence. The final recommendation lens is the union (outside line combination) of all the overlapping project characteristics recommendations sets.

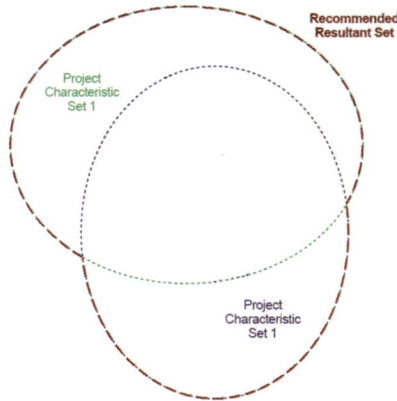

FIGURE 2.8 *Recommendations-lens Model*

In figure 2.8, there are just two intersecting sets and a single resultant set. When using the model, there will be as many sets as project characteristics configured for your environment. This additive model shows us the final resultant set of recommendations (be they approaches, training, or artifacts) based on our organizational environment (the background canvas) and our unique project characteristics.

We will discuss this model further in the next chapter.

Limitations of the Model

All models are wrong, but some are useful.

George E. P. Box, British statistician

As the quote above reminds us, models are a simplified view of reality. They help us understand concepts, and crucially, give us something to point at while discussing ideas and issues with colleagues. These characteristics make them useful. However, all models are limited and wrong in certain applications because they cannot predict every variable, interaction, or situation we will face.

So, use the model for general guidance. Moving a slider will make items become bold (to indicate it is recommended) or grey them out. Look to the trends not specific point values. Understand the theme such as increased rigor or collaboration tools, and think less about the absolute values. Remember "A fool with a tool, is still a fool." Any model, whether BAM, SAFe, or DA, have limitations and are no substitute for critical thinking and due diligence. If this stuff was easy and a model could predict it all someone would have automated it and we would be out of a job. Use the tool to inform your thinking but do not rely on it, or any other model.

Chapter 2 Summary

Our projects operate in unique ecosystems made up of industry factors, organizational factors, and project factors. Our industry often dictates safety, compliance, and materials constraints, norms, and standards. Our organization will have its own strategy, processes, and workforce strengths. Each project may be unique in its scope, goals, approach, and combination of skills and science. Managing this set of variables is complex. Assuming that two people will assess the same situation and create the same mental model of how best to operate in this situation is foolish. The model provides a way to take a visual snapshot of the situation so that we can talk about the environment and the recommended approach. It is a visual-thinking tool to promote better dialog and project design.

Key topics covered in this chapter:

» The model starts with agile.

» It extends agile with a broader view of leadership and a deeper understanding of EI.

» Plan-driven knowledge, skills, and tools still have a place.

» We will not be successful without industry-specific knowledge and skills.

» Our project operates in a unique ecosystem defined by its project characteristics, which vary within ranges.

» By manipulating the project characteristics sliders, the model shows us an ecosystem that models our project environment and makes recommendations for attributes to consider.

» Be aware of the limitations of the tool and use it for trends and suggestions, rather than single-point instructions.

Chapter 3
Putting the Model to Use

You can experiment with the model at www.BeyondAgileModel.com. Moving the project characteristics sliders and selecting different views will give you a feel for how the recommendations change based on various project features.

Remember, these are recommendations, not rules. While based on sound principles, it is okay to use approaches not recommended (just be aware of the extra process weight) and not use some techniques that are recommended (just make sure you address these points some other way or accept the risk of not using them).

The same goes for training and artifacts: They are recommendations, reasonable starting points, but not mandatory rules. If you use something extra or omit something recommended, you might want to make note of why and how any gaps will be filled. If everyone at MegaCorp agrees release plans are unnecessary, then fair enough, but you would likely still benefit from them—at least you have discussed the risks of not using them.

There needs to be flexibility like this. Good, robust systems have some flex built into them to give people options and allow independent thinking. As Dee Hock, founder and former chief executive officer (CEO) of the Visa credit card association, noted, "Simple, clear purpose and principles give rise to complex and intelligent behavior. Complex rules and regulations give rise to simple and stupid behavior."

This quote nicely describes our human ability to find ways to circumvent complex rules and inflexible processes. When governed with no flexibility or freedom to act independently, people feel over-controlled and not valued for their common sense or problem-solving skills. Instead, it is better to provide some guidelines to start from, then trust people to use their own smarts to do what is best.

It is similar to how we set up empowered teams; instead of giving them task lists and step-by-step instructions, we explain the goal and let them self-organize to best achieve it. The same is true of the BAM: it provides a well-reasoned starting point but allows freedom of choice and the application of local knowledge to override it at any time.

No Best Practices

Linked to the idea of simple, clear purpose and principles giving rise to complex and intelligent behavior, it is fair to say that in the knowledge-worker and learning-worker domain, we have no best practices. We have good practices, which are things that others in similar circumstances have found to be useful, yet they are not always the best thing to do. Today's projects are complex, dynamic, and often unique; if there were a single best way of doing (anything) it would likely have been codified and automated by now.

The fact that our work changes and relies upon people prevents us from defining single best practices. Instead, as we experiment, we uncover approaches that work (or fail) in certain circumstances. We can learn from these experiences and reuse successful ones in similar situations. These are our good practices but let us not assume they are the single best solutions.

In addition, when we attach the label *best practice*, it has a stifling effect on this approach's future development. It is now static and unquestioned, duplicated but not improved. Using someone else's best practice also reduces the user to a replicator, not a problem-solver. If we blindly apply a method or process with the assumption it is the best we can do here because it is a best practice, we have stopped innovating, adapting, and improving. So, let us use good practices and keep the brain engaged with future learning.

Note: The dangerous flip side of always encouraging people to innovate is when engineers would rather build their own wheel, gearbox, or software widget than reuse a readily available and tested version. This "not-invented-here syndrome" is an expensive anti-pattern (danger sign) that we need to be alert for. "No best practices" means in our approaches to work, not in our technical solutions. Given time-to-market and cost-of-delay penalties, often a good-enough solution is truly better.

Adding Your Own Industry-Specific Content, Branding, and Hosting

Industry-specific content is designed to be tailored for each organization. This is where you plug in all your own methods, approaches, and standards for your domain and industry. Maybe you have regulatory procedures or material standards to apply. Maybe you have labor laws or safety requirements. The domains are driven by a table of data that can be easily edited.

If you want to use the model in your own environment, there are two main options. The first is to host a version on your own corporate intranet or website. The requirements are quite simple and can be obtained from RMC Learning Solutions by contacting webmasterinfo@rmcls.com. The second option, if you do not want to host a version yourself, is to have your company-specific information uploaded to your own private instance of the BAM. Then you and others in your organization can access a version that is set up for your company with the content you need.

These sites (locally hosted or private instance) can be retitled and branded to meet organizational needs. So, if you want to call it MegaCorp Project Configurator and embed it in your PMO website, you can. Likewise, if you want to add to or change any of the content in the other domains (agile, leadership/EI, plan-driven), this can be done via configuration of the underlying tables.

It is not necessary to create your own instance of the Beyond Agile Model. The model is really just a thinking tool, a way to understand and communicate the need to vary process based on circumstance and always be reducing process costs. You can play with the project sliders and see how it operates, then just apply this thinking to the remainder of the ideas in the book, if that serves you better.

The (Un)Common Sense of Shifting Focus and Energy

Drawing from the four domains of agile, leadership/EI, plan-driven, and industry-specific knowledge as and when required may seem like common sense to you. If so, great—you already have a big leg up when it comes to how people perceive knowledge and skills. However, many people (including myself early in my career) associate project work with the completion of tasks and adherence to project process and protocol.

Many people (understandably) believe that project execution means following the steps of project execution from their traditional or agile approach. It's part of their job, and to be successful, they have a duty to do this to their best ability. Realizing or learning that it is okay, and often desirable, to deliberately de-emphasize project execution to draw more consciously from, say, EI or industry knowledge may feel alien or rebellious at first, but is ultimately more responsible than following the project execution script.

This idea of taking what is most appropriate for our current circumstance from a variety of sources is intuitive in many situations outside work. For example, when interacting with children, parents seamlessly switch between educating, entertaining, and encouraging them to do the right things, drawing from their knowledge and life experiences. We do not refrain from guiding little Billy away from hitting his sister because we were in the middle of explaining how to tie shoelaces. Instead, we switch domains, bring focus and energy to the appropriate idea, use some of that for a while, then return to the initial task.

When I started consulting, I was surprised by the reluctance people had in switching roles, focus, and energy. When coaching Mark, a junior PM at a utility company, it soon became clear that one of his biggest obstacles was getting work completed by an awkward team member. When I suggested we examine some conflict-resolution and motivation ideas, he was hesitant. He was tasked with completing the project and he would rather focus on those execution steps, even though that was at risk of not happening.

Some of this reluctance comes from the stigma and uncertainty of tackling people issues. The notion is common that all this soft-skills stuff is tricky, potentially a legal minefield if you say or do the wrong thing, and probably best left to human resources (HR). Yet, as we saw before, projects are defined by people, undertaken with people, delivered to people, and finally deemed successes or failures by yet more people. Avoiding the tricky people stuff is like trying to learn to swim without getting wet. Reading about it and trying the actions only take you a short way toward your goal.

Being comfortable in switching focus from agile execution to leadership/EI techniques, or plan-driven approaches, or industry-specific knowledge, is essential to high performance. Knowing it is both okay and desirable comes as a relief to some people who feel constrained by project-execution guidance. To others, it feels uncomfortable and scary, like having to introduce yourself to a room full of strangers and strike up conversations when you would really just prefer to go home.

As I consulted more, I saw the pattern repeat. For a variety of reasons, people did not know it was okay to de-emphasize focus and energy on one pursuit to bring it to bear in a different area. Our end goal does not change. Our project does not transform from building a trading system to sorting out the communications issues in the accounting department; but maybe that is your sole focus today.

There is a wealth of project guidance available, both plan-driven and agile, but there is little written or taught about this more important, higher-level skill of shifting focus between domains to draw on what we need today to best move our project and team toward their goals. I have over fifty books on my bookshelf that describe how to create iteration plans and release road maps, yet not one talks about this higher level of abstraction and understanding that maybe your iteration plan does not matter today.

This is why I call this concept the "(un)common sense of shifting focus and energy." It should be common sense; we only have so much focus and energy available at any given time. So, on projects, as in life, we should be drawing on our knowledge and experiences to direct ourselves and the team to where our focus is most needed.

I am not suggesting we flip-flop team activities from project delivery to team building and then EV reporting. It is more subtle and less binary than that. Instead, we seamlessly blend approaches from all four domains and shift our focus as circumstances dictate. Think of a master craftsperson with a well-stocked toolbox: When working conditions are cramped, they might switch from their favorite long-handled screwdriver to a short, stubby one that better fits the confined space. Next, they may use a plane and then some sandpaper to smooth rough edges.

Expanding our toolbox from just agile (or traditional) project delivery provides more options. Adding to these skills with leadership/EI and industry-specific knowledge creates a more accomplished project leader. They are better equipped to deal with complex projects and tricky stakeholders. They are less flustered, more effective, and better liked. Expanding your toolbox and learning to get comfortable drawing from multiple domains sounds like common sense but will set you apart as a high performer.

Stay Focused on the Goal

Expanding our awareness of different approaches is a noble end goal but it comes with its own particular risk: Taking on too much peripheral overhead or process effort and not focusing enough on getting to the project destination.

For most modern projects, the destination is a moving target and it is usually moving away from us. The longer we take to deliver a project, the more likely it is that the end point will move further away to keep up with new competitor products, industry expectations, sponsor requests, etc. I call this phenomenon *done drift* because what constitutes *done* is likely to evolve during the course of a project or product life cycle. So, we want to get to the destination as fast as we can without diverting energy on nonessential work.

When discussing the topics of project chartering and team alignment, it is common to contrast the net output of a nonaligned team to that of a well-aligned team. In figure 3.1 we can see that the team members have their own agendas and ideas of where they should be going. As when many people paddle a raft in different directions, some will cancel each other out and the net vector of movement for all that effort could be quite small and only partially aligned to the project goal.

Activities like product visioning and team chartering are designed to align everyone's ideas of what the end goal looks like and what path to take to get there. Once everyone is in alignment with these *what* and *how* questions, they can make progress toward this common goal. When everyone is paddling in the same direction, the net vector of progress toward the end goal is much larger. A 40-watt light bulb will barely light a room while a 40-watt laser can cut through aluminum, leather, and wood. It is the same light energy, just focused instead of diffused. This alignment is shown in figure 3.1 by the longer arrow toward the project goal target.

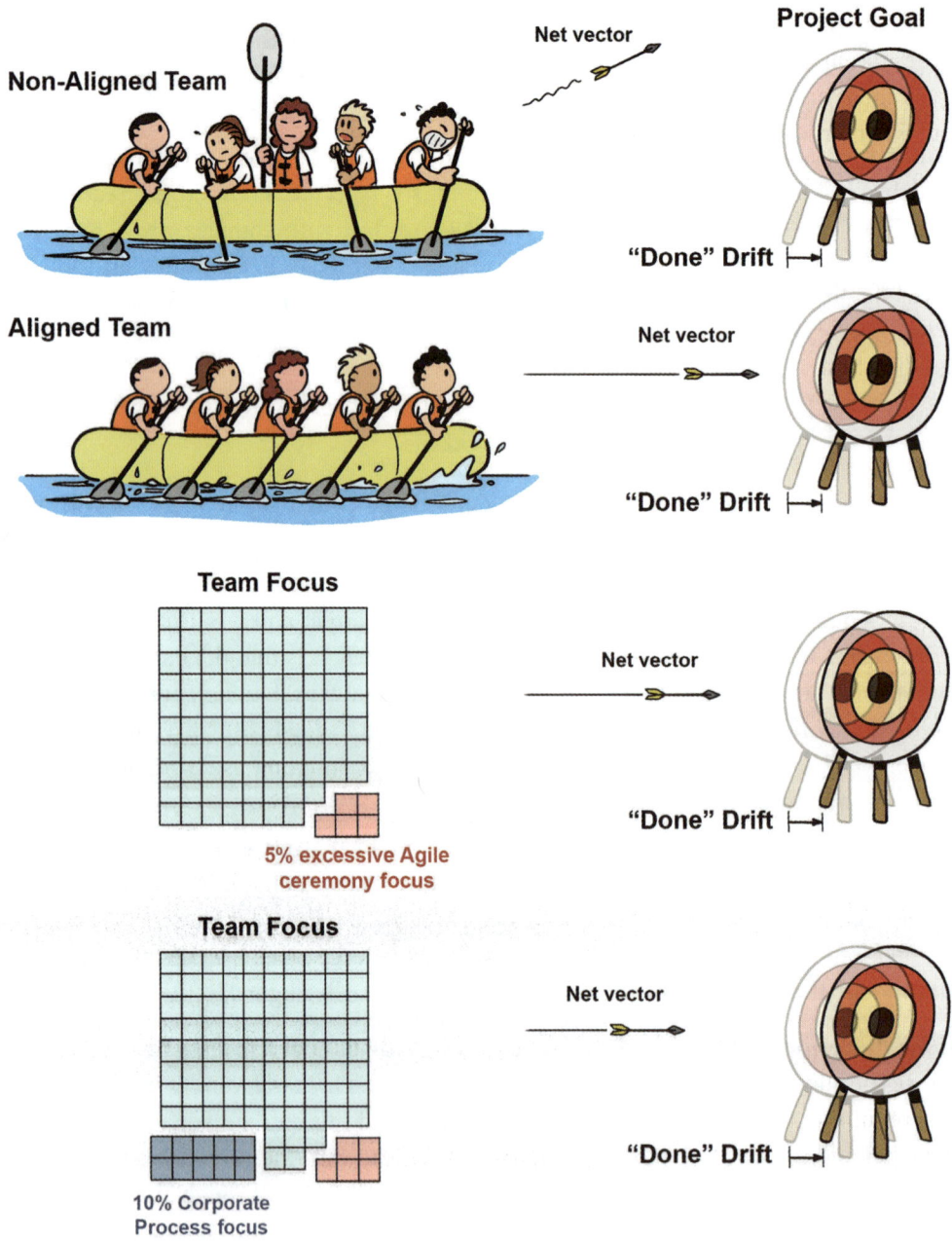

FIGURE 3.1 *Aligned and Nonaligned Teams and Team Focus*

Then we need to consider all the work, activities, and processes that do not contribute directly toward the project goal. In figure 3.1, we have removed the images of team members to show 100 squares representing 100 percent of the team's effort toward the team goal. If 5 percent of their time and energy is spent on non-value-adding process, such as excessive agile ceremony focus, they can only direct 95 percent toward the project goal, creating a gap of lost-potential in delivery value.

The more process we add, whether it is necessary corporate process or cool new team activities, the more delivery capacity we remove from the net vector of project progress toward the end goal (that is always moving away from us). In the final image in figure 3.1, in addition to the 5 percent excessive agile-ceremony focus, we also have 10 percent of corporate process focus and the net vector of progress is reduced further.

Hopefully, these images illustrate the double whammy dilemma. First, the end goal is always moving away from us—the longer we take to get there, the more we will have to do to declare success. Second, every call on the team's time takes away from their ability to make progress toward the goal.

The numbers in these examples are conservative. Think about how long you spend on your projects in value-adding activities versus non-value-adding company process, meetings, or producing three sets of time reporting, etc. All the time and focus not directed toward the end goal is a distraction. Plus, when you give people enough distractions, they lose energy and start making mistakes because of all the interruptions of constantly switching tasks.

So, while it is great to be aware of many different approaches, and blend elements of leadership, plan-driven, and other domains, etc., we must always be alert to the costs. Every interruption and call on your team's time that is not directed at the project's end goal is reducing their capacity. If the diversion results in a net increase of their capacity, then it is likely worth it. Once the dip in productivity caused by training is over, they should continue faster than before.

However, every diversion is lost capacity, so choose your extra process carefully and fiercely defend the team's goal focus. Imagine the aperture of the recommended-approaches scope as an elastic band: it should always be trying to shrink, returning to a state where less is included. Project and organizational factors will stretch it larger but also create tension. As soon as the approaches no longer justify their expenditure they should be eliminated or pared back. This might be after a few iterations once the concept is learned and now applied implicitly, or not until the end of the project if it is a truly required technique. The point is that the model is dynamic, elastic, and under tension; we do things that add value but remove them to dedicate more effort to the project goal when they are no longer required.

This dilemma of balancing production (P; getting work done) and production capability (PC; building more capability for work) is called the *P versus PC balance.* Stephen Covey talks about it in his book *The 7 Habits of Highly Effective People* while discussing optimizing results over the long term.[1] Should we just work and work (build production) or pause to train so we can work better (build production capability)? We need a smart combination to optimize the whole, balancing production with building production capability.

The same idea scales up to the team level (and company level). As a project team leader, it is your responsibility to monitor the P/PC balance for the team to maximize progress toward the project goal. We can try a couple of analogies to help illustrate and understand the competing ideas of expanding our toolbox with more tools from the domains of leadership/EI, plan-driven, and industry-specific knowledge while maintaining focus on the end goal:

- Doctors are trained in a wide field of ailments and treatments, but they are selective about which methods they use to treat a problem. Many treatments and drugs have side effects, so you would not want to use more than you need or anything unnecessary. The same goes for approaches and tools: it is useful to have a broad, detailed understanding of them, how they work, and how to use them, but we only want to use the most effective ones for this situation and only the minimum necessary to fix our problem while retaining focus on the goal.

- When driving toward a destination and trying to conserve fuel, running supplemental systems such as air-conditioning will divert energy from reaching your goal. On projects, when we add processes such as extra reporting or *Can you pilot this project tracking tool for the PMO?* it is like turning on the air-conditioning and radio and hitching a trailer to the back of your vehicle. They all consume energy that could have been directed toward the project goal.

So, while it is extremely valuable to look beyond agile for guidance, we need to maintain a strict filter on what and how much we use from any approach. Remember, knowledge is weightless, but process is heavy. So, expand your toolbox, hone your skills, become domain and tool agnostic, and then direct maximum effort toward the project goal. This process is illustrated in figure 3.2.

Expand your Toolbox   Hone your Skills   Become Agnostic   Focus on Goal

FIGURE 3.2 *Focus on the Goal*

The challenge (and skill of being a good leader) comes in using the minimum amount of the most appropriate tools and process for the situation to get the job done. We need to cast our knowledge net wide to expand our knowledge of approaches, then learn and practice these skills in our role as a lifelong learner. We need to become agnostic to approaches and choose them objectively, based on the merit of fit and value, before finally selecting the minimum needed to get the job done while directing the bulk of the team's focus on delivering the project.

This expands the familiar DevOps model:

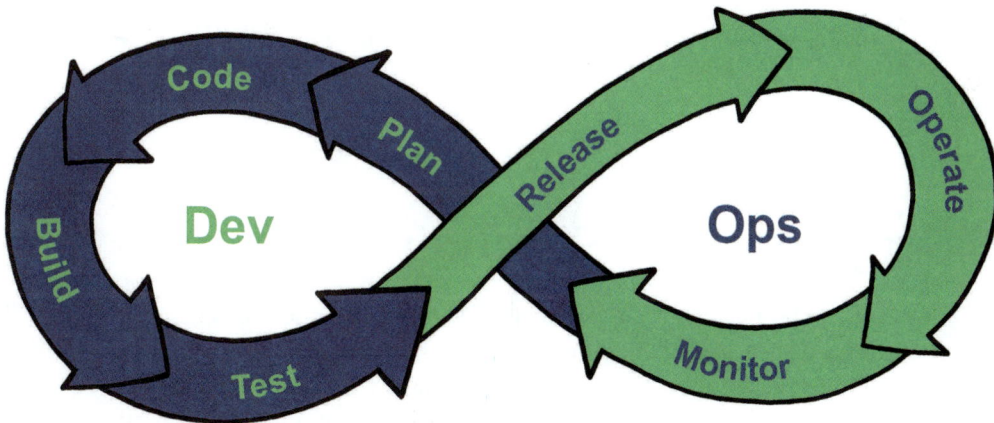

FIGURE 3.3 *DevOps Model*

With a further dimension or loop as shown in figure 3.4.

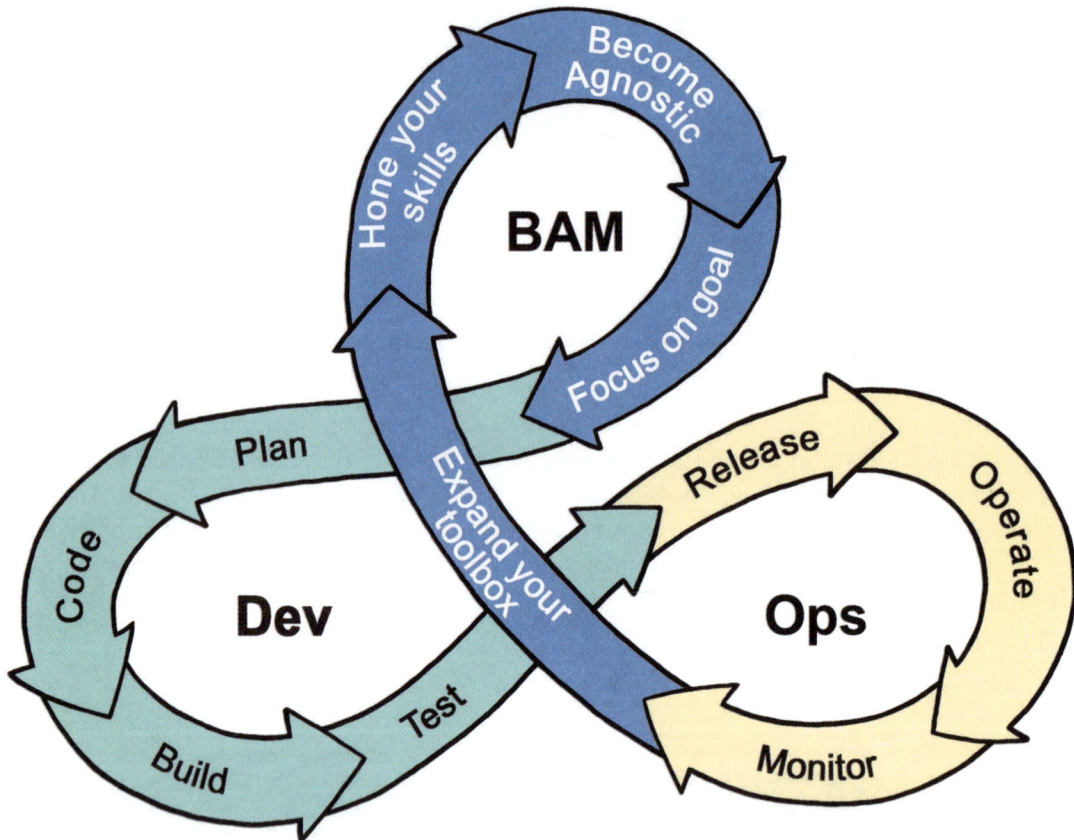

FIGURE 3.4 *BAM Model + DevOps*

The Stage and the Spotlight

The BAM discussed so far has two main ideas, the first being that the project characteristics sliders define the size and scope of the recommended approaches, training, and artifacts to consider for that project type. This is akin to setting or defining the stage we are working on. The second idea is to be careful and deliberate about what to focus our attention and our team's attention on since we can easily lose focus on the project end goals. To extend our stage metaphor, this is the spotlight that suggests what we should focus on.

These two ideas are used together in the model to define the recommendations scope—the dotted red line representing the stage encompassing everything in scope for us to call upon. Then the goal focus would be a spotlight shining on that stage, illuminating what we are to focus upon. These ideas are illustrated in figure 3.5.

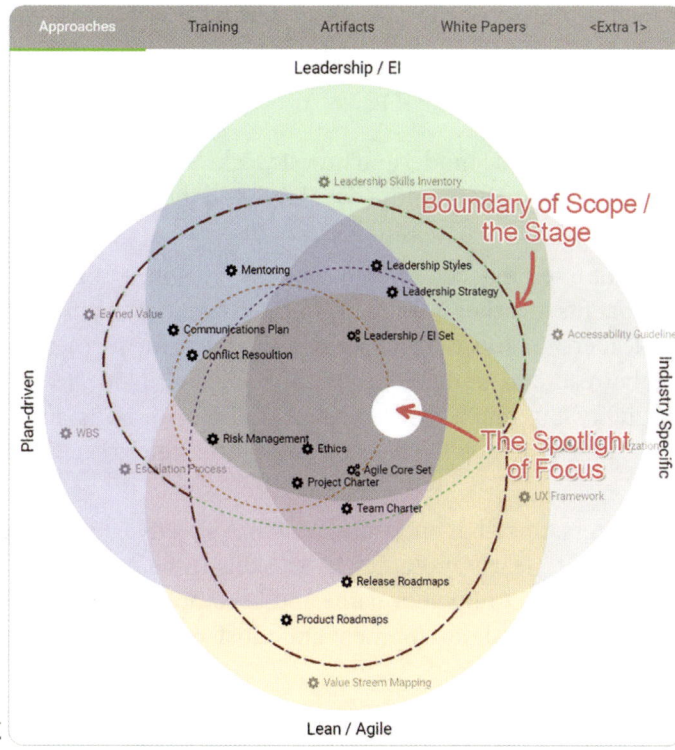

FIGURE 3.5 *Spotlight of Focus*

The spotlight is controlled by our economic view of decision-making. This means we ask *Where is the next best dollar spent for the project? Should we be building features, responding to issues, or answering a stakeholder request?*

Often, the answer to these questions is yes, simultaneously, but the idea of the spotlight is to recognize and act on the most pressing issues. As the leader of a project team, we have the ability to influence where people focus, what they move on to next, and what they select as primary and secondary objectives.

So, with a team of ten people, maybe we ask someone to look into a change request a sponsor is asking about and ask a couple of other people to make more progress on the highest priority defect fixes ahead of the demo. Perhaps the remainder of the team is developing new features.

As project lead, we continually evaluate priorities and readjust focus and work capabilities to optimize value delivery and stakeholder satisfaction. It is no use ignoring stakeholders to focus on building features, or diverting the whole team to explore every new question or request. Instead, we dynamically readjust the team focus of effort to where it brings the most valuable outcomes.

Going Deeper into the Domains

Now that we have explained the basic model and how it works, it is time to look further into each of the domains and examine the practices in more detail. We will then explore how they are combined and used as a cohesive whole to lead successful projects.

Rather than just point to established reference books on agile or EI, we describe the relevant concepts here in a way that fits together holistically in the context of the project lead role. There are lots of great books on leadership and EI (and we will list them for further reading), but they are usually generalized to be read and understood by those in multiple roles in the organization to maximize their applicability. So, much of the leadership/EI material is aimed at CEOs and HR managers, hence the need for us to apply a filter or translation step to see what applies in a project environment.

In the following chapters, this filter and translation has already been applied, leaving the steps necessary for project leaders to learn and apply these skills to be more productive and valuable. They can be considered life hacks to up your game and become more effective in your team, your organization, and your own personal development and satisfaction.

Chapter 3 Summary

You are encouraged to play with the model and see how it works, populating it with your own industry- and company-specific content. Add your organization's branding if you like. Help is available if you need it. Or just internalize the ideas and think about expanding your skills to learn as much as you can, then apply the appropriate technique for today's most critical item.

We need to understand the benefits and costs of processes. Too little process and we can go astray; too much and we waste time and effort—time and effort we might need to chase after the moving target of today's projects. Since knowledge is weightless, but process carries a weight penalty, we need to know how to expand our toolbox, hone our skills, become agnostic, and focus on the goal as much as possible. The project characteristics sliders and recommendations lens show us the stage, then we need to aim the spotlight of our focus.

Key topics covered in this chapter:

» No best practices: Complex problems do not have a single, best solution approach

» Using the model: How to use it as is, extend the data and tailor for your own needs

» Process diverts effort from the goal: "Done Drift" and the evolving nature of today's projects

» The Beyond Agile Model: Expand your toolbox, hone your skills, become agnostic, focus on the goal

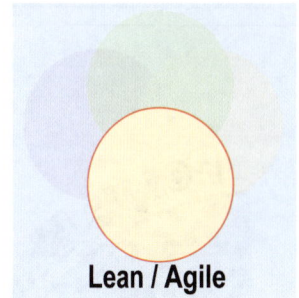

Chapter 4
Agile and Lean

This section is not intended to provide a comprehensive overview of agile and lean approaches. It is assumed, because you picked up a book whose premise is literally agile-centric, that you understand the why and how of agile and lean methods. Instead, the goal of this section is to offer some supporting views, useful diagnostic tools, and linking strategies for better integration of agile and lean approaches while avoiding common pitfalls.

The Agile Mindset—
Balancing People and Process

Agile approaches combine a mixture and equal balance of people and process approaches to project delivery. One way to picture these interwoven elements is like the twin strands of deoxyribonucleic acid (DNA). In figure 4.1, we see a blue thread of people elements such as empowerment, collaboration, and team decision-making, mixed with gold process elements such as backlogs, prioritization, and short iterations.

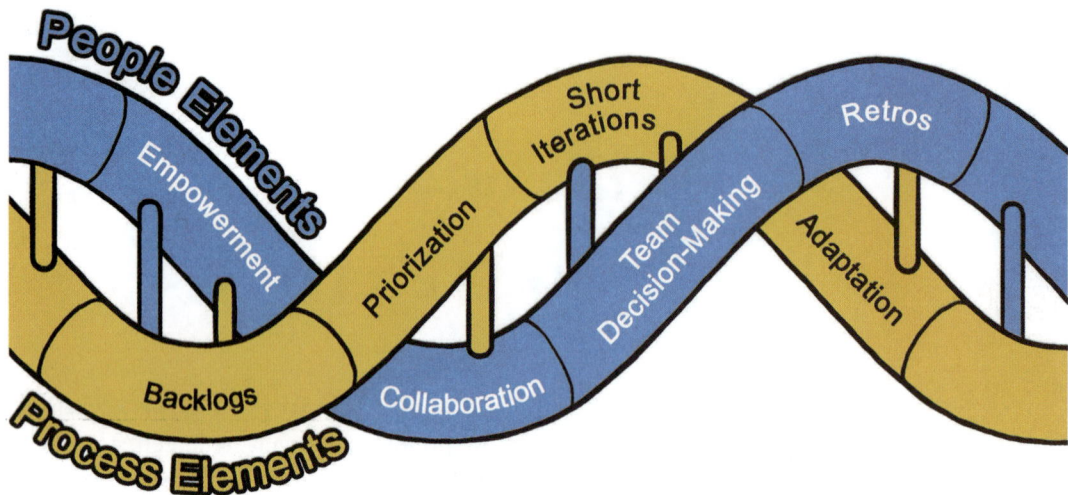

FIGURE 4.1 *Balancing People and Process*

In case you have not noticed it before, agile approaches weave people elements and process elements together through the agile mindset, values, and principles. For simplicity of understanding, we pull these elements apart to talk about them individually, but in reality, they are inextricably linked and self-supporting, like the blue and gold elements shown in figure 4.2.

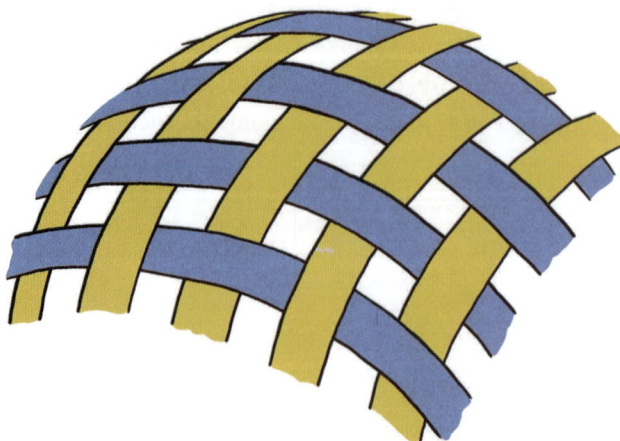

FIGURE 4.2 *Blue and Gold Linking*

The people and process elements are present in all views of agile, no matter how you slice it. Also, they are in an equal balance. This is not a matter of coincidence or hidden code, but rather the sign of a balanced system. Let us look further.

The Agile Manifesto has two values focused on people and two focused on process:

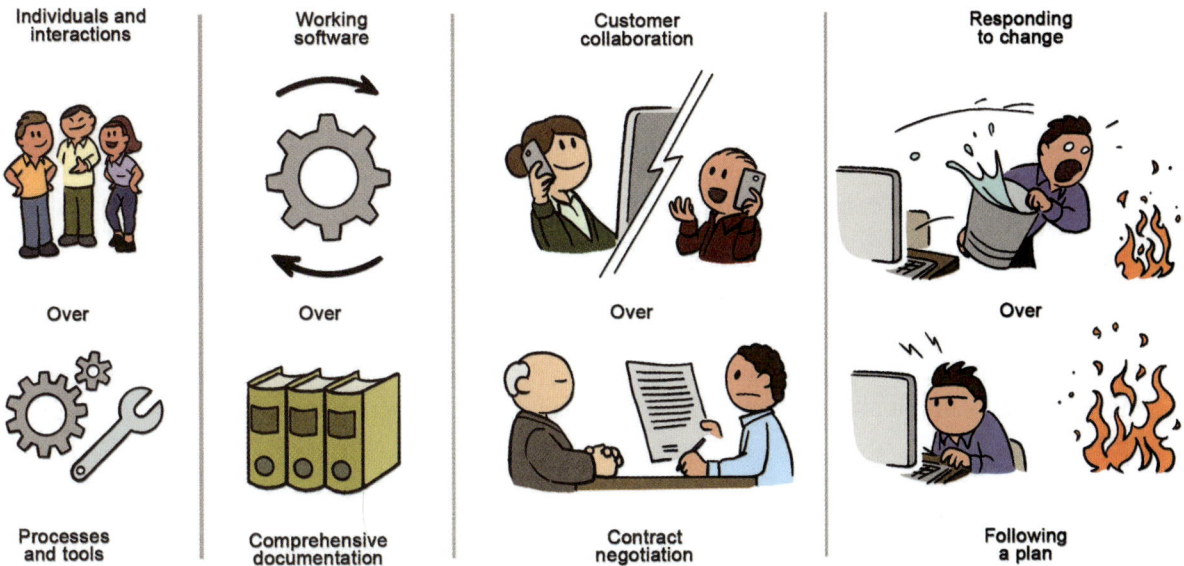

Individuals and interactions	Working software	Customer collaboration	Responding to change
Over	Over	Over	Over
Processes and tools	Comprehensive documentation	Contract negotiation	Following a plan

FIGURE 4.3 *Agile Manifesto Values*

When we examine the 12 Agile Manifesto principles again we see six focused on people (shown in blue) and a counterbalancing six based on process (shown in gold).

1. Our highest priority is to satisfy the customer through early and continuous delivery of valuable software.

2. Welcome changing requirements, even late in development. Agile processes harness change for the customer's competitive advantage.

3. Deliver working software frequently, from a couple of weeks to a couple of months, with a preference to the shorter timescale.

4. Business people and developers must work together daily throughout the project.

5. Build projects around motivated individuals. Give them the environment and support they need, and trust them to get the job done.

6. The most efficient and effective method of conveying information to and within a development team is face-to-face conversation.

7. Working software is the primary measure of progress.

8. Agile processes promote sustainable development. Sponsors, developers, and users should be able to a maintain constant pace indefinitely.

9. Continuous attention to technical excellence and good design enhances agility.

10. Simplicity — the art of maximizing the amount of work not done — is essential.

11. The best architectures, requirements, and designs emerge from self-organizing teams.

12. At regular intervals, the team reflects on how to become more effective, then tunes and adjusts its behaviour accordingly.

Let's examine the frameworks of Alistair Cockburn's Heart of Agile and Joshua Kerievsky's Modern Agile, first looking at the original models and then superimposing views of people and process.

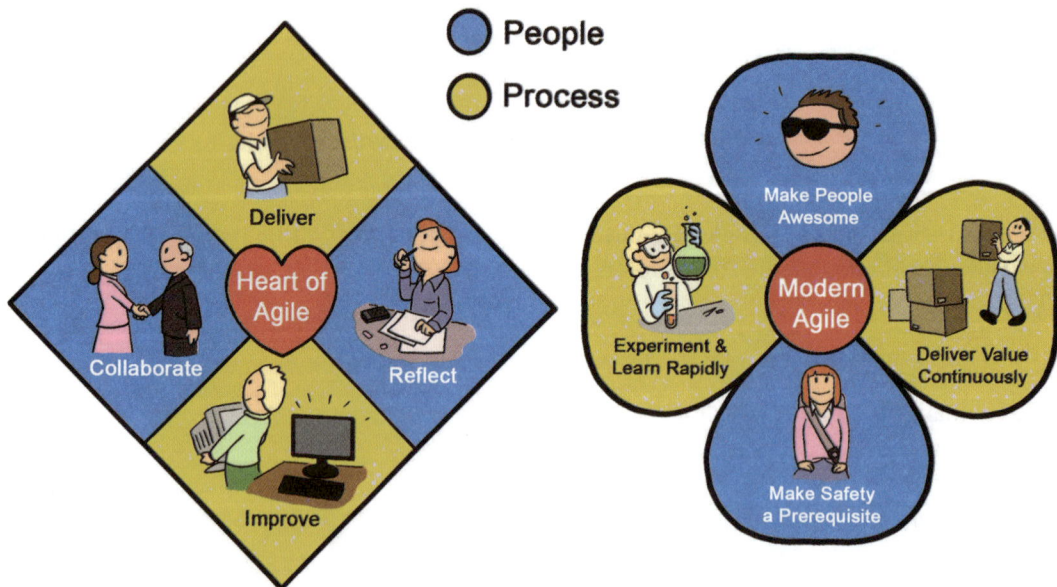

FIGURE 4.4 Heart of Agile vs. Modern Agile

In Alistair's Heart of Agile model, the *deliver* and *improve* process concepts are complemented by the *collaborate* and *reflect* people-focused concepts. Likewise, Joshua's people-focused *make people awesome* and *make safety a prerequisite* are balanced and complemented by the ideas of *deliver value continually* and *experiment and learn rapidly*.

Both models are evenly balanced between people and process advice; this fact, along with their clarity and simplicity, is what makes them both powerful and compelling.

We should always be aware of these two elements in the tools and approaches we use. Additionally, looking for a healthy balance of attention within teams is a useful diagnostic. People sometimes have a personal bias or natural aptitude for the people side of things, or for the process side of things. So why not ask the team if they think the system is in balance and, if not, what they suggest to restore to balance any imbalances?

Lean Thinking and the Kanban Method

The Kanban Method can teach agile practitioners many useful ideas about incremental change, successful organizational change, and improved team performance. So, rather than considering it as an alternative to agile approaches, I like to think of it as a complement; another source for ideas, tools, and solutions.

We have a tendency to get attached to our personal favorite agile approach, whether that is Scrum, XP, or something else, and regard alternative approaches as somehow inferior or derivative. However, the Kanban Method has some useful additions, so let us see what it has to offer.

First, many people are confused between kanban and the Kanban Method, so it is worth some clarification. The Japanese word *kanban* (usually with a lowercase *k*) means "signal," "sign," or "large visual board." Agile teams often use kanban boards to visualize their work. These kanban boards typically show queues and work in progress (WIP). They may also show WIP limits for activities and expedite paths for urgent work.

The Kanban Method (usually capitalized) is a complete process for defining, managing, and improving the execution of knowledge work. It was developed by David Anderson in 2007 and, like agile, has its own set of values, principles, and practices. More than just using kanban boards to track and manage your work, it is a full lifecycle approach for running and improving knowledge-work projects.

The term **lean thinking** was coined by James Womack and Daniel Jones to describe what they found at the heart of the Toyota Production System. Lean thinking is a business approach that provides an alternative way of organizing activities to increase the value delivered to society and individuals while reducing waste. It involves studying the flow of work, the generation of value, and the reduction of activities that do not add value (waste). Agile values and principles are related to or stem from lean thinking values and principles.

Kanban Principles

- Change management
  - » Start with what you do now.
  - » Agree to pursue improvement through evolutionary change.
  - » Encourage acts of leadership at every level.

- Service delivery
  - » Understand and focus on your customers' needs and expectations.
  - » Manage the work; let people self-organize around it.
  - » Evolve policies to improve customer and business outcomes.

Based on these principles, three parallel and ongoing agendas (themes of work) are employed:

Kanban Agenda

- Service orientation: Look outward and focus on performance and customer satisfaction. Ask *How can we meet and exceed customer goals?*
- Sustainability: Look inward to find a sustainable pace and improve focus. Make intangible work visible and then balance demand with capability.
- Survivability: Look forward to remain competitive and adaptive to more change. Scan for the emergence of disruptors and value diversity to better handle change.

Throughout all the approaches, a core set of values based on respect and collaboration is embraced. These are:

Kanban Values

- Transparency: Sharing information through straightforward terms improves the flow of work.
- Balance: The understanding that competing elements must be balanced for effectiveness.
- Collaboration: People must work together to be effective.
- Customer focus. We must know the goal for the system.
- Flow: The realization that work is a flow of value.
- Leadership: The ability to inspire others through example, description, and reflection.
- Understanding: Kanban is an improvement model that starts with self-knowledge.
- Agreement: The dynamic co-commitment to move together toward goals, respecting, and where possible, accommodating differences of opinion.
- Respect: Valuing, understanding, and showing consideration for people. A foundational value underpinning everything else.

David and I worked together in the early 2000s on the board of the Agile Project Leadership Network (APLN). He appreciated the concepts of agile and also combined them with concepts from Theory of Constraints and lean design to develop a method focused on the flow of work that could be applied to any knowledge-work scenario. Unlike agile approaches that suggest a complete switch to agile work execution, Kanban starts with the process you have right now and provides tools to improve its service.

This makes the Kanban Method much easier to adopt, as there is no big upheaval, retooling, or enterprise-wide training required. Instead, the Kanban Method principles are applied to the way things are currently done.

We can use the Kanban Method to help introduce positive change into a team or organization. The "start with what you do now" and "agree to pursue improvement through evolutionary change" concepts are nonthreatening and difficult to argue against. So, if faced with an organization or department that is reluctant to change their ways, the Kanban Method is an excellent approach.

It also brings some great insights often missed in agile approaches. For example, since knowledge work is invisible, managers may not know how much work someone has on their plate. Encouraging people to make their work visible helps them show and explain their workloads to others. It also enables coworkers to see what people are working on and then pitch in where they can.

Left-to-Right Agile Adoption

When adopting and implementing agile approaches, it is important to start with the mindset first, then apply the values and principles, and finally the practices. This encourages a *being* agile starting point, as opposed to a *doing* agile practices approach in which the practitioners may not know why they are doing things.

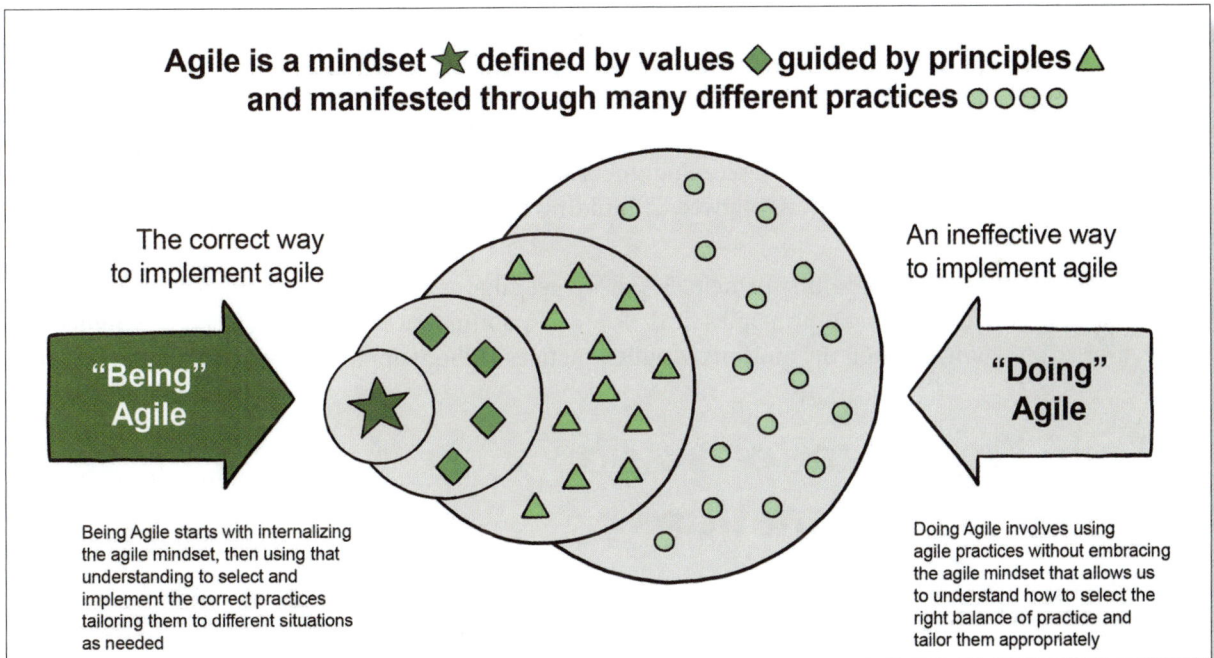

Agile is a mindset ★ defined by values ◆ guided by principles △ and manifested through many different practices ○○○○

The correct way to implement agile

An ineffective way to implement agile

"Being" Agile

"Doing" Agile

Being Agile starts with internalizing the agile mindset, then using that understanding to select and implement the correct practices tailoring them to different situations as needed

Doing Agile involves using agile practices without embracing the agile mindset that allows us to understand how to select the right balance of practice and tailor them appropriately

FIGURE 4.5 *Left-to-Right Agile Adoption*

Based on the work of Ahmed Sidky (ahmedsidky.com)

This concept of encouraging a left-to-right rather than right-to-left approach is referred to in several ways, including *being* versus *doing* agile; having an *agile mindset;* and avoiding a *cargo cult* adoption of agile, where ideas are copied in the hope of desirable results, but without understanding the underlying theory.

Regardless of the name we use, it is important that agile approaches introduced to organizations and team members are first based on the thinking involved and then, secondly, implementing the techniques. Just recommending that people blindly duplicate actions will not result in an understanding of how to adapt them to new circumstances, such as geographically dispersed teams, or part-time business input.

When discussing agile approaches with organizations and when working with agile teams, I look for signs of left-to-right adoption as confirmation that they embrace the agile mindset. When people say things like *We adapted agile approaches since they mirror how our teams naturally work anyway,* this is reassuring. When I hear things like *We rolled out the agile approaches to our teams and need some help with X*, it sets off warning bells. *Rolling out agile approaches* sounds like a right-to-left implementation of practices before embracing the mindset, values, and principles.

Look for signs like this that are indicators of deeper problems. When you encounter right-to-left implementations, the fix is often a back-to-basics examination of why agile approaches are undertaken at all. We have to reexamine the challenges of building consensus and collaboration on teams. Review the alternatives to overcoming uncertainty in requirements, which include detailed up-front analysis, or short analysis followed by building a candidate portion and iterating revisions on that until it is satisfactory.

Only after going back to first principles can we get alignment for a successful agile adoption based on mindset, values, and principles. It is slow and painful, but if you rush it, people will just revert back to going through the motions of agile practices without appreciating why.

Agile Organizations and Agile Transformations

We need to distinguish between the process of introducing an agile mindset and set of values, principles, and practices and creating a truly agile organization. Many predominantly traditional, hierarchical organizations are using agile approaches in their project teams but have not transformed their organizational structure. To truly embrace and make full use of agile approaches, certain fundamental norms need to be in place.

A small number of companies are already structured and operate with agile-aligned values. They usually have their own ways of self-organizing, distributing power, and empowering teams.

Ironically, they tend to find the suggested structures and approaches of agile overly restrictive and limiting. This is because the structures of agile were designed to exist and persist in more traditional command-and-control organizations.

Many organizations try to transition or transform part or all of a more traditional organization to operate with more agile-friendly structures, decision-making approaches, and team practices, but we should not underestimate how difficult this is.

It is much easier to introduce agile approaches into a traditional company than to fully transform a traditional company. However, they will always fit a little uncomfortably, under pressure from other aspects of the organization to revert back to more traditional ways of working.

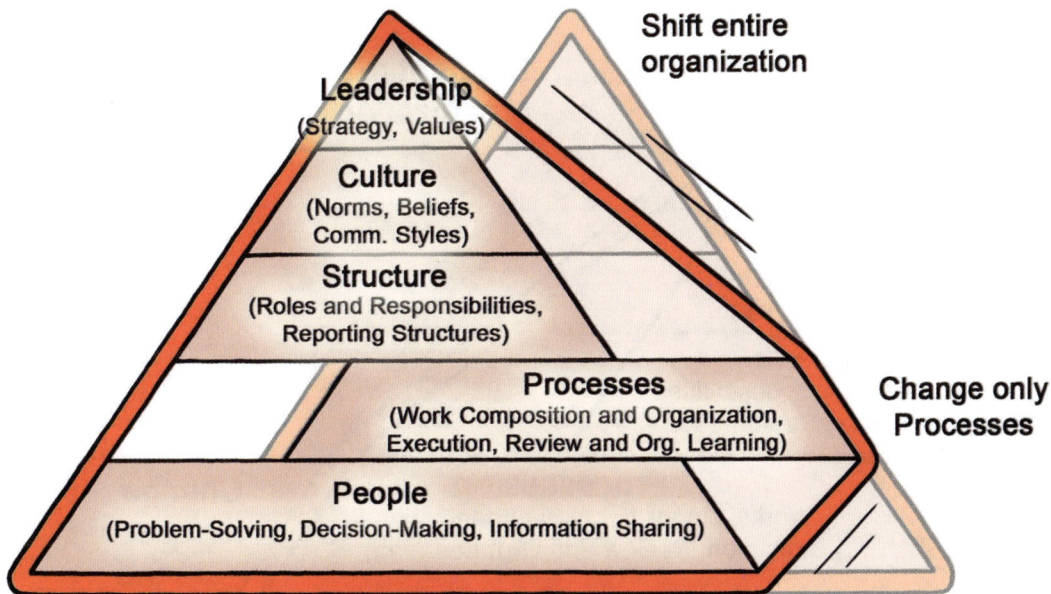

FIGURE 4.6 *Agile Transformation 1*

Based on the work of Ahmed Sidky (ahmedsidky.com)

In figure 4.6, we see that by shifting only the processes of an organization, we create tension. It is as if organizations have elastic skin: moving one element without moving the others creates this tension. It will take a concerted effort to keep them in place.

Two things can happen: First, the other elements, such as people, structure, etc., could follow suit, moving right to align with the new processes, and we would have successfully transitioned to an agile organization. More likely, however, tension from the other elements will pull the new agile processes back in. In other words, old thinking and acting prevail; agile processes are trialed, but people eventually revert to familiar ways that better align with the culture, structure, strategy, and leadership values that persist in the organization.

The different layers of the pyramid, and elastic qualities of changing just one or two elements at a time, explain some of the difficulties of establishing lasting change. To overcome the tensions created by process-focused transitions, people try a more holistic transformation approach that shifts all these elements to the right. However, we should not underestimate the difficulty of such a fundamental change and the capabilities of people required to effect it.

Many organizations or departments successfully transition their people and process to using agile approaches. In this situation, the structure, culture, and leadership of the organization remain traditional, but people successfully employ agile approaches to deliver projects.

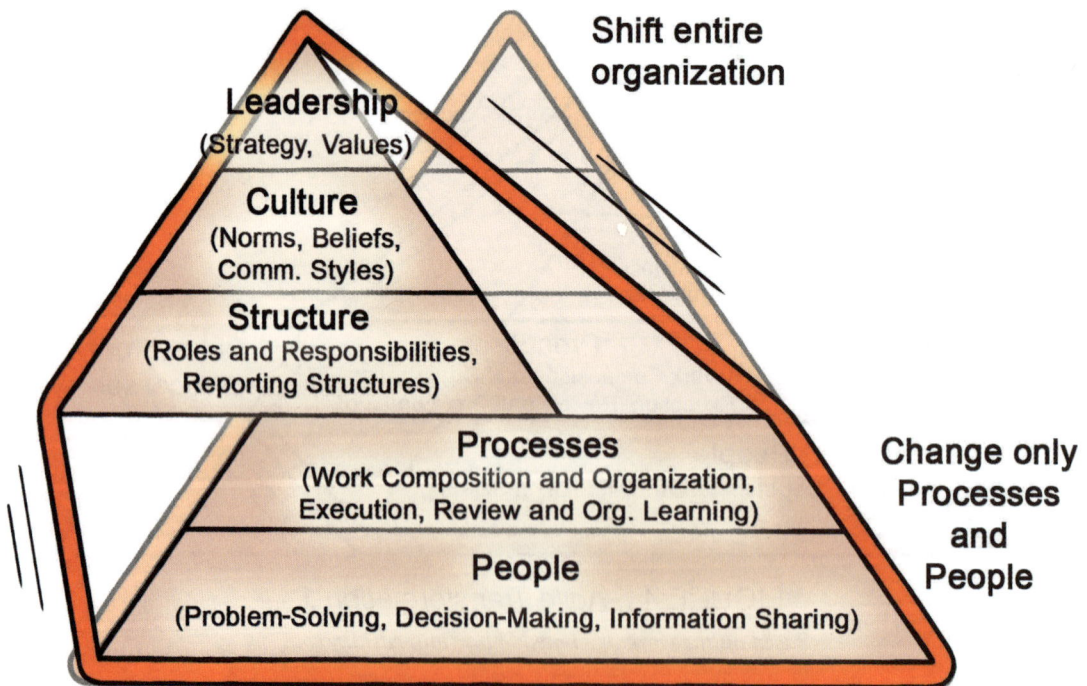

FIGURE 4.7 *Agile Transformation 2*

Based on the work of Ahmed Sidky (ahmedsidky.com)

Obviously, this is not ideal. There is still tension and a mismatch between how the teams are operating and how the company is structured and managed. However, for many groups, this is seen as an acceptable compromise. They have achieved a workable position; it is not perfect, and tensions persist, but it is sustainable.

Full Organizational Transformations

From Red to Teal

To better understand what is required for and involved with a complete organizational transformation, we need a better appreciation of corporate culture and its evolution.

It may sound surprising, but organizations are structured and operate based on the social values they reflect. In the book *Reinventing Organizations*, author Frederic Laloux describes the transition from what he categorizes as primitive red organizations to modern and futuristic teal organizations.[1]

Laloux set out to understand today's most successful organizations and how they operate. What he found was that organizations are tied to the prevailing worldview of consciousness. Every time we have changed how we think about the world, we have come up with a more powerful type of organization.

Laloux explains that humanity evolves in stages: "We are not like trees that grow continuously. We evolve by sudden transformations, like a caterpillar that becomes a butterfly, or a tadpole that becomes a frog." Likewise, the types of organizations that evolve are different and more suited to the emerging worldview than old organizations. He describes a progression of social values that categorizes organizations and assigns each category a color.

- **Red** organizations: At the most basic level of development are red organizations. These are based on fear of the leader, who exerts power over their membership or workers. These organizations operate via a command authority and division of labor. They work well in times of chaos, such as war; examples include street gangs, the Mafia, and tribal militias. In red organizations, there is no real long-term plan. Instead, they exploit opportunities as they arise and govern by fear.

- **Amber** organizations: As cause and effect are better understood, amber organizations with a longer-term view emerge. Formal roles and hierarchical structures appear with top-down command and control of the *what* and *how* steps. Planning and execution are strictly separated: planning happens at the top and execution at the bottom. Stability is valued above all and ensured through rigorous processes, and people are effectively interchangeable resources. Future success is effected by repetition of past successful approaches. The military, churches, and most government agencies exhibit these values and characteristics.

- **Orange** organizations: Modern global corporations are the embodiment of orange organizations. The goal is to beat competition and achieve profit and growth. Innovation is the key to staying ahead. Fueled by meritocracy, the idea is that, in principle, anyone can move up the ladder, and nobody is predestined to stay in their position. This drastically widens the talent pool and ability to innovate. Management by objectives is encouraged, which means command and control on the *what*, but freedom on the *how*. Organizations are viewed as machines, a hangover from the Industrial Revolution, with terminology still in use today. We talk about units and layers, inputs and outputs, improving efficiency, moving the needle, bottlenecks, and scaling solutions. Being part of a big machine can grind you down and a midlife crisis is emblematic of life in an orange organization. After twenty years of work, people realize they will either never make it to the top, or the top is not everything they hoped it would be. After chasing targets, milestones, and numbers, they yearn for something more.

- **Green** organizations: Within the classic pyramid structure, green organizations focus on culture and empowerment to achieve extraordinary employee motivation. They aim to delight their customers and build a sense of family with their employees. They do this by consulting and engaging more with their customers and employees, promoting the empowerment of workers, and building a culture of shared values. In addition to empowerment, green organizations leverage inspirational purpose. Some people scoff at the idea of such shared values, but that is because orange organizations increasingly feel obliged to follow the fad—they develop some values, post them on the wall and company website, then ignore them. Green organizations put inspirational purpose at the heart of what they do. Southwest Airlines does not consider themselves merely a transportation company; they insist they are in the business of freedom, helping customers go places they could not go were it not for Southwest's low prices. It is this strong belief and inspirational purpose that helps create a sense of "family" as a guiding metaphor.

- **Teal** organizations: Rather than having a central, hierarchical structure, teal organizations operate more like living organisms. They move operational functions out to small self-contained teams and empower delivery and local organization. They distribute decision-making powers and encourage self-management. They allow purpose to evolve organically based on people's abilities and ideas.

Characteristics and Metaphors of Organization Type

Name and Characteristics	Key Breakthroughs	Current Examples
Red organizations "Wolf pack" mentality Constant exercise of power to keep people in line. Fear is the glue of the organization. Highly reactive, short-term focus. Thrives in chaotic environments.	Command authority Division of labor	Street gangs Mafia Tribal militias
Amber organizations "Army" mentality Highly formal roles in a hierarchical pyramid. Top-down command and control (*what* and *how*). Stability valued above all through rigorous process. Future is repetition of the past.	Formal roles Stable and scalable hierarchies Processes Long-term perspectives	Churches Military Most government agencies Public school systems
Orange organizations "Machine" mentality Goal is to beat competition, achieve profit and growth. Innovation is the key to staying ahead. Management by objectives (command and control on the *what*, freedom on the *how*).	Innovation Accountability Meritocracy	Multinational companies Charter schools
Green organizations "Family" mentality Within the classic pyramid structure, focus on culture and empowerment to achieve extraordinary employee motivation.	Empowerment Values-driven culture Stakeholder model	Southwest Airlines Ben & Jerry's
Teal organizations "Organism/Community" mentality No pyramid structure. Move operational functions to provider teams. Empower delivery and local organization. Provide templates and services.	Self-management (communities of practitioners) Wholeness (distributed knowledge and decision-making)	FAVI Buurtzorg Patagonia Holacracy

Reviewing these red and amber categories, we can see the development of the classic command-and-control mindset that give rise to industrial-era project-management theory and techniques. Structure, hierarchies, and strict adherence to process underpin WBS, precedence diagrams, and change control boards.

Likewise, in the descriptions of orange and green organizations, we can recognize the agile mindset values of empowerment (freedom of *how*), focus on innovation, and fostering of care for employees. The value-driven culture, family mentality, and tapping of motivation approaches align well with agile and lean's respect for the worker and Theory Y motivation.

Teal organizations represent the next generation of organization that incorporates self-management where, instead of having centralized functions for hiring, procurement, strategy, etc., these functions are undertaken by small bands of practitioners. These small, self-managing groups are given autonomy to do what is necessary to be successful. Each group contains all the decision-making power it typically needs, supported by a lightweight group that provides templates and services.

It is quite common for one model to contain elements of previous models, nested like Russian dolls as shown in figure 4.8.

FIGURE 4.8 *Nesting Image*

So, it is possible and perfectly natural for an orange organization to still contain or use elements of amber or red thinking. Likewise, teal organizations may use elements of green or orange thinking where it makes sense. It is less of a strict sequence and more a progression of predominant social consciousness.

Agile emerged in, and aligns perfectly with, green organizations. Its theories of team and customer engagement work alongside the goals of delighting the customer and aiming to create strong cultures of shared values. Looking back at the characteristics of orange and red organizations, we see what we are up against when trying to instill agile at an organizational level. What we are trying to do is move the organization from amber or orange to green. This requires a huge change in the culture of the organization. I am not saying it cannot be done, but do not underestimate the scale of the change, or overestimate the influence you likely have.

Maybe you can be successful as an organizational transformation consultant, brought in by the top executives of the corporation to turn it around or reimagine the company for the next phase of its evolution. However, if you are a project manager or team leader who has seen success on projects using agile methods, then changing an organization from run-of-the-mill orange to empowered, shared-values green will be a difficult fight.

To make matters worse, if you, like many agile leaders, come from an information technology (IT) background, then you likely have a perception challenge to overcome too. IT projects are notoriously over budget, late, and problematic. So, an IT project leader suggesting the organization change behavior is akin to taking diet advice from a plumber: they might be right, but they are not the first source you would consult when looking for advice about making important life changes.

Neuroleadership

Another field of study worth investigating if charged with organizational transformation is neuroleadership. Neuroleadership is the application of research into the brain and psychology to better understand how to motivate people. It also helps us understand what triggers resistance to change, disengagement, and low morale.

Anyone serious about working effectively with teams and implementing change should understand the basics of how and why we think as we do. Learning how to approach change with the least resistance and the most acceptance is essential.

We must first understand that the human brain is wired for survival. Tens of thousands of years of natural selection have favored the overly cautious above the balanced risk/reward people. Evolution favors the timid and skeptical over the bold and accepting. Unfortunately, the human brain responds to social threats the same way it responds to physical threats: it tries to avoid them. This tendency for the brain to overreact to an event viewed as a threat is called the *amygdala hijack*.

This response to social threats creates "avoidance emotions" such as fear, anxiety, anger, and shame. Avoidance emotions lead to avoidance behaviors such as defensiveness, denial, attack, and withdrawal, which all get in the way of delivery.

In contrast, when we feel psychologically safe, the brain creates emotions such as excitement, trust, joy, and love. These "approach emotions" are a prerequisite for effective project delivery because they enable us to collaborate and be creative and highly productive.

One psychological tool that can help is the SCARF (status, certainty, autonomy, relatedness, and fairness) model, developed by David Rock.[2] The model is a summary of several other discoveries from neuroscience about how people interact socially at work.

The SCARF model is based on three central ideas:

1. The brain treats social and work threats and rewards with the same intensity as physical threats and rewards. For instance, when something threatens our status quo or status, it triggers our fight-or-flight response.

2. Our ability to make decisions, collaborate, and solve problems is reduced by a threat response and increased by a reward response. A downside of our threat response is focusing on aggression or escape strategies. We shut down many of our creative, collaborative, and cooperative systems, which is okay for dealing with saber-toothed tigers, but a bad reaction for dealing with workplace change.

3. The threat response is more intense and more common than the reward response. Natural selection once favored the overly cautious above the balanced risk/reward people. Now our survival does not hinge on being risk- and change-averse at work; instead, we need to consciously work on balancing threats with rewards.

The SCARF model consists of five domains:

1. Status: Our relative importance to others. A 2003 study showed that having one's status threatened or lowered affects the body in the same way as physical pain. The brain triggers a threat response and makes it much more difficult for the individual to accept and support the change.

    So, when instigating a change, we should be careful to outline how this will elevate or improve people's status. Maybe it will provide new, marketable skills or an improvement in work environment, title, salary, or visibility.

2. Certainty: Deals with our ability to predict the future. This is not the long-term future, but how we will be working weeks or months from now. People do not like uncertainty

and it impacts their ability to think about day-to-day tasks. This is why it is critical to communicate as much information as possible to reduce people's feelings of uncertainty and the debilitating brain fog this generates.

So, when involved in change, communicate, communicate, communicate. It is better to overcommunicate and bore people with the message than leave people wondering.

3. Autonomy: Our sense of control over events and work practices. We value having control over how we work. In his book *Drive: The Surprising Truth About What Motivates Us*, Daniel Pink lists autonomy as one of the key motivators in any job.[3] So, when a change comes along that might result in losing that control and autonomy, we will resist it.

    Since we are hardwired to be independent, building more autonomy into a change will make it more appealing and motivating. Let people know that the shift to agile, lean, or similar methods will also come with more autonomy to make local decisions, how they work, and maybe even the projects they engage in, etc.

4. Relatedness: This is our sense of safety with others. We make quick judgments about whether people are friends or foes. When there is no sense of relatedness with others, we are quick to be suspicious and react with fear and mistrust. This is our animalistic survival behavior kicking in. Better to be mistrusting of that strange large animal than assume it is friendly and get your head bitten off.

    When instigating change, we need to foster a sense of relatedness with the people being impacted. Otherwise, their fight-or-flight response will kick in and they will find it difficult to think cooperatively. It will be a long, slow process to gain their trust.

5. Fairness: The perception of fair exchanges between people. When we see things we think are unfair, we respond with anger. However, fairness triggers the reward center of our brain and makes us feel valued.

    We need fair, transparent policies where everyone gets heard and treated respectfully. The nature in which change is handled, communicated, and perceived is as important, if not more important, than the message or change being rolled out. Spend time analyzing the approach and optics of the rollout process to ensure it is fair and above reproach. How it is done will greatly impact how it is received and accepted.

Why Does This Matter and How Can I Use It?

Understanding how and why organizations reflect their social worldview is important for choosing our approach when dealing with stakeholders. For example, if tasked with executing a project in an amber or orange organization, I would likely strive to build a strong, cohesive team motivated around a compelling vision, and provide them with a protective shell of support and encouragement. For external stakeholders, I would map the green values of agile to the orange principles of delivering value and creating a highly efficient process.

By default, I would not take it upon myself to try to convert the organization from amber to green, unless specifically asked to. There is likely simply too much to change along with executing a project.

If, after the project completes successfully, people ask for help running their projects that way, we could discuss the mindset changes that surround agile and green thinking. However, trying to convert an organization from traditional amber to agile green, as well as executing a project, is a risky endeavor.

I used to feel conflicted about these types of decisions. Surely, as an agile consultant/coach. I was obligated to try to transition the organization as much as possible. After all, the Scrum Guide,[4] the document describing Scrum for practitioners, lists the following roles for a ScrumMaster: "Leading and coaching the organization in its Scrum adoption" and "Planning Scrum implementations within the organization."

However, I believe not every organization wants to become green or agile and that is fine, not all organizations want a lecture on becoming agile. Also, why stop at agile/green? Why not sell them on the merits of teal organizations that typically do not use agile approaches and instead organize their work more organically? Agile coaches sometimes think they need to convert the world, but not everyone is ready or wants to transform. If after observation, they seek advice, then fine, but as a default action, attempts to convert a group will likely be met with more opposition than appreciation.

Of course, if you are invited to help with an agile transformation, that is a different story. Now we can use our knowledge of the agile mindset, values, principles, and practices, coupled with the insights offered by understanding the Laloux view of green organizations, to create a road map of change.

The characteristics and work practices of green and teal organizations provide many great examples of how to structure organizations for success with agile approaches. Be available and accessible for help wherever asked, but do not confuse your own knowledge for an obligation or invitation to meddle beyond your invited scope.

Understanding Blockers and Enablers for Organizational Change

Bob Anderson's work on the Leadership Circle is a good start for additional ideas and suggestions for helping organizations and people adjust their mental models.[5] Bob describes a logical progression starting with a conversation about business performance, then linking it to the way we think and eventually to organization design.

He describes our mental models as an internal operating system through which we view and interpret the world. We cannot see this mental model or consciousness because we are looking through it. It is the lens we use to interpret everything we experience. However, it is through our consciousness, our mental model, our operating system—whatever we choose to call it—that we create our organizational designs.

Executives want to improve performance to be more effective. To do this, people need to show up differently and rise to another level of play. This involves thinking differently and explains how the business-performance conversation connects to the organization-design conversation.

Chapter 4 Summary

This chapter started with an examination of the agile mindset and the recognition of a recurring pattern of people and processes. We saw how, like DNA, it permeates every aspect of agile values and principles. We also explored how it is represented in approaches such as the Modern Agile and Heart of Agile models. All balanced systems need to consider both elements in equal proportions and find a way to balance them.

Lean thinking and the Kanban Method add the ideas of making things visible and deliberately pursuing and eliminating waste. These are the core ideas behind the sliders, circles, and spotlight metaphor in the BAM.

Then we started looking at agile adoption and organizational change. We inspected a healthy mindset and value-based change versus the dangerous cargo-cult replication of observed behaviors. We saw how trying to change only the process without changing the structure, culture, and people aspects of an organization will be difficult and likely short-lived.

Finally, we explored the red to teal levels of organizational evolution, providing a larger framework for understanding change and resistance. Neuroleadership helps explain the blockers and enablers for organizational change.

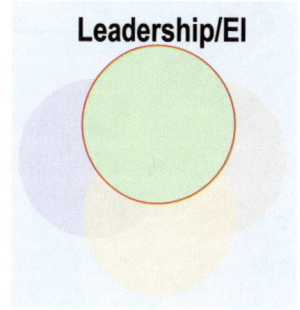

Chapter 5
Understanding EI

This section begins our discussion of the topics of leadership and emotional intelligence (EI). It is crucial that we have a firm grasp on these subjects because they underpin all aspects of successful work. If you learn only one thing from this book, I hope it will be how to improve through a better understanding of ourselves and others.

Leadership and EI work together to create cohesive, cooperative teams. The two approaches support each other and enable organizations and team leaders to build teams that overcome problems and achieve amazing results. However, to understand these topics properly, we need to decompose the system, see how the parts fit together, then tackle them in a logical sequence, which may, from the outset, seem counterintuitive.

Emotional Intelligence

Emotional intelligence (EI) involves learning how to understand ourselves, which in turn helps us work well with other people. It concerns how to communicate, support, empower, and motivate people. It's important to understand self first, because we are not going to motivate or empower anyone by being a bully, a jerk, or getting flustered.

So, while our end goal is effective leadership, which is like an electric motor that drives high-performing teams, we first need to understand that it is powered by EI—the electricity that powers the motor. For this reason, we will start with EI (which starts with ourselves) and then work up to powering the leadership engine.

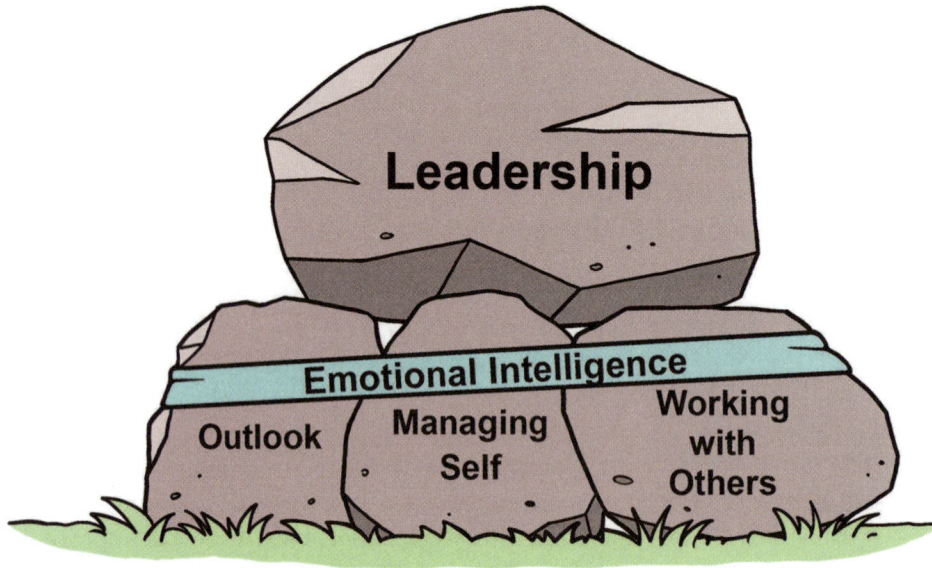

Why EI Is More Important than Intelligence Quotient (IQ)

To take advantage of our intelligence, our IQ, we first need good emotional intelligence, EI. Regardless of how intelligent or gifted we are, if we turn others off with our offensive or abrasive behavior or cave in under minimal stress, no one will stick around long enough to notice our IQ.

A quick exercise to illustrate the importance of EI over IQ is to think of a mentor who has had a significant impact on your career. List five properties that made that person such a valuable influence for you. Now examine the list and categorize the properties as EQ or IQ related. Items such as caring about you, taking an interest in your development, and demonstrating integrity and honesty are all EQ factors. Items such as master strategist, guru-level coder/architect/statistician are more IQ based.

Chances are your most influential mentor used more EQ skills than IQ—they nearly always do. That is who we are trying to emulate. It will not happen overnight, but it is better to be on the right road, heading in the right direction, than totally unaware of the destination or direction to get there.

In the June 21, 1999, issue of *Fortune*, cover story "Why CEOs Fail" reported that unsuccessful CEOs put strategy before people issues, while the most successful CEOs used integrity, people acumen, assertiveness, effective communication, and trust-building behavior. Projects are like mini organizations and the same skills apply.

Team leaders rarely struggle with core competencies in planning, change management, or reporting, yet they often struggle with communications, failing to see other people's perspective, and understanding the impacts of their actions.

Tackling the "Emotional" Elephant

The term *emotional intelligence* needs a makeover, a rebranding. The word *emotion* has too many negative connotations, unbefitting for the rocket fuel, the "secret sauce" that it really is. It should have a cool, powerful name like *results multiplier, smarts accelerator,* or *team unifier,* because that is really what it does.

However, we have inherited the term *emotional intelligence* and it seems to be sticking around for now. That is a shame, because too many people avoid it and instead stumble around researching motivation and conflict-resolution topics, hoping to get better at dealing with people, when everything they are looking for is laid out for them in the domain of EI.

So, get over any notions you may have about it being soft or too feminine to apply to your projects. If your project involves people in any way, understanding EI will improve your results. The good news is that unlike mathematical, logic, and language intelligence, which are measured in IQ tests and usually peak around age eighteen, EI develops more slowly and typically does not peak until our forties or fifties.

Better Results by Becoming More Effective

Let us start the journey with a process we are all familiar with: growing up and becoming independent adults. Stephen Covey talks about a progression of maturity and effectiveness that people go through as they get older.

Dependent   **Independent**   **Interdependent**

FIGURE 5.2 *"Levels of Effectiveness"*

Adapted from Stephen Covey

Barriers to Entry

A major barrier to understanding EI is the presence of many different models with overlapping names and ideas. Even when the same people write about emotional intelligence at different times, they create new classifications. So, even if your organization agrees to use, say, Goleman's model of emotional intelligence, which Goleman model are you using? His 1995 one, or his 1998 one? The confusion and proliferation of models is shown in the table below. Do not bother trying to distinguish between them, just appreciate the complexity and lack of standardization.

Authors	Elements in Model
Salovey and Mayer (1990)	Appraisal and expression of emotion, regulation of emotion
Goleman (1995)	Self-awareness, self-regulation, self-motivation, empathy, handling relationships
Mayer and Salovey (1997)	Perception, appraisal, and expression of emotion, emotional facilitation of thinking, understanding and analyzing emotions; employing EI, reflective regulation of emotions to promote emotional and intellectual growth
Bar-On (1997)	Intrapersonal, emotional self-awareness, assertiveness, self-regard, self-actualization, independence, interpersonal, empathy, social responsibility, adaptation, problem-solving, reality testing, flexibility, stress management, stress tolerance, impulse control, general happiness, optimism
Cooper and Sawaf (1997)	Emotional literacy, emotional depth, emotional fitness, emotional alchemy
Goleman (1998)	Emotional self-awareness, accurate self-assessment, self-confidence, self-regulation, self-control, trustworthiness, conscientiousness, adaptability, innovation, self-motivation, achievement orientation, commitment, imitative, optimism, empathy, organizational awareness, service orientation, developing others, leveraging diversity, social skills, leadership, communication, influence, change catalyst, conflict management, building bonds, collaboration and cooperation, team capabilities
Weisinger (1998)	Self-awareness, emotional management, self-motivation, effective communication skills, interpersonal expertise, emotional coaching
Higgs and Dulewicz (1999)	Motivation, intuitiveness, conscientiousness, emotional resilience, self-awareness, interpersonal sensitivity, influence, trait

One popular model is Daniel Goleman's Emotional Intelligence model, popularized in the book *Emotional Intelligence: Why It Can Matter More than IQ*. Another is Reuven Bar-On's EQ-i™ (emotional quotient inventory) model. Depending on which model you are trained in, your idea of what EQ is and how it operates will differ from that of someone trained in the other model.

This creates all kinds of problems for teams trying to apply EI but struggling to understand why other people have slightly different ideas of how things are supposed to operate. It is like trying to use Scrum and XP simultaneously on your project but calling both approaches the same name. Most of the ideas align, but there is sufficient divergence to cause confusion. Calling them both EQ just makes the problem worse.

Interestingly, both Goleman and Bar-On quote the same original research in the development of their models and that is where we will start: Understanding what EI is and how we can improve ours to better lead teams.

Another issue with EI is that it uses similar-sounding terms to describe different ideas. To the uninitiated, terms like interpersonal and intrapersonal sound alike. Also, concepts such as empathy and self-actualization might seem intangible and vague when they actually comprise simple ideas that are easy to adopt.

To help make EI more approachable and accessible, we will break it down, show how all the pieces fit together, and explain it in plain English that even the most literal engineer can follow.

We start as children, dependent on our parents for food, shelter, and support in life. How effective we are at accomplishing things grows, as we do, and eventually, we need less support. When we become teenagers and young adults, we become less dependent on adults and more independent. We eventually get jobs, move out of our parents' homes (hopefully), and are more effective at accomplishing things in life than when we were children. Our level of effectiveness, depicted in figure 5.2, gets bigger as we move from dependent to independent.

Covey says this is as far as many people progress. They learn how to be independent and contribute at an individual level. However, they are missing out on a further, more effective and productive stage called *interdependent*. This is what can be achieved when we partner and work with other people. When we learn how to collaborate and work with others, our personal limitations no longer hold us back. Other people can overcome our shortcomings.

So, if Mary is great at generating innovative ideas but lacks the patience or due diligence to see them through to fruition, she can partner with Dave, who thrives on detail and can transform ideas into completed products. When they can find ways to work together, they are both more effective than when working independently.

The bridge from the state of being dependent to being independent is called *maturity*. Parents, high schools, and the school of hard knocks move people from dependence to independence. Hopefully, there are several family members who can help with that transition.

Maturity

Emotional Intelligence

Dependent   Independent   Interdependent

The bridge from independence to interdependence is emotional intelligence. Learning how to interact, cooperate, and collaborate with others is not emphasized nearly enough. These practical life skills are hidden behind the unappealing label of *emotional intelligence*. There is much written about the process, but few people think to investigate further, at least at first. Often, family members possess it intuitively, but lack frameworks or words to effectively describe it.

We collect these EI skills as we go through life, but if you go looking for them, you can greatly accelerate and expand your knowledge of how to interact effectively with others.

Mayer and Salovey Four-Branch Model

The precursor to Goleman's EQ and Bar-On's EQ-i models was created by John Mayer and Peter Salovey, who published their research in 1990. The Mayer and Salovey model extends this maturing idea and adds layers of sophistication. It is called the Four-Branch model because it describes four branches of emotional skills, going down the table vertically in terms of sophistication and maturity, and moving from left to right horizontally from childhood to adulthood.

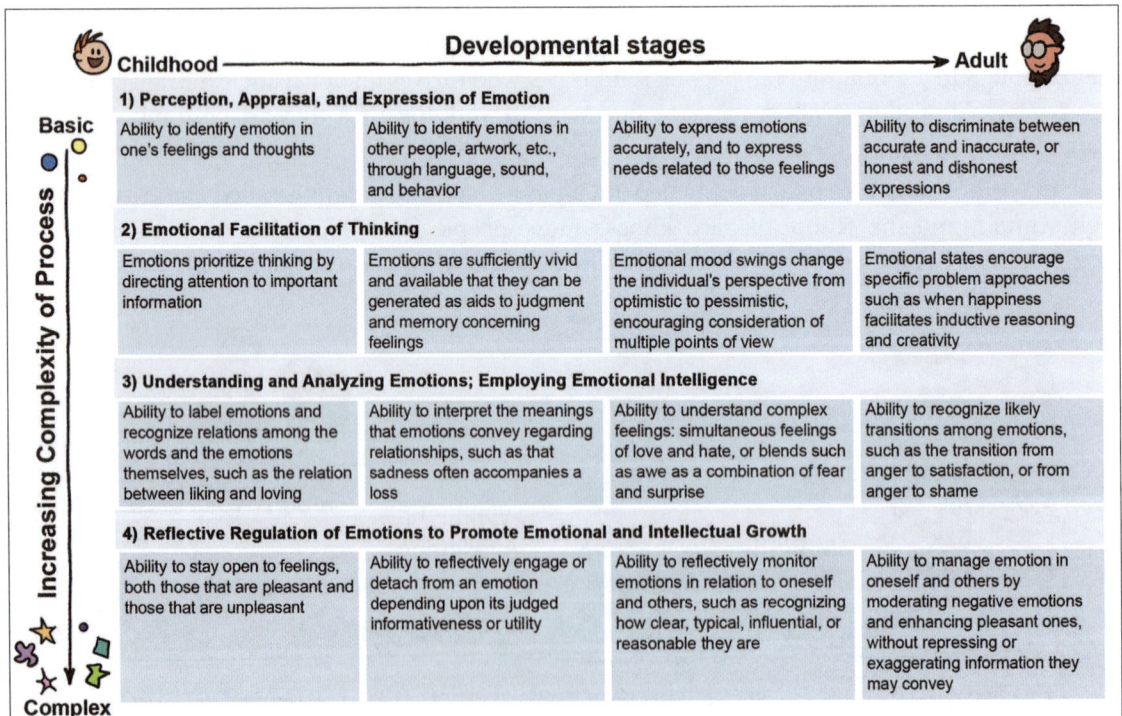

	Developmental stages		
Childhood ⟶			⟶ Adult
1) Perception, Appraisal, and Expression of Emotion			
Ability to identify emotion in one's feelings and thoughts	Ability to identify emotions in other people, artwork, etc., through language, sound, and behavior	Ability to express emotions accurately, and to express needs related to those feelings	Ability to discriminate between accurate and inaccurate, or honest and dishonest expressions
2) Emotional Facilitation of Thinking			
Emotions prioritize thinking by directing attention to important information	Emotions are sufficiently vivid and available that they can be generated as aids to judgment and memory concerning feelings	Emotional mood swings change the individual's perspective from optimistic to pessimistic, encouraging consideration of multiple points of view	Emotional states encourage specific problem approaches such as when happiness facilitates inductive reasoning and creativity
3) Understanding and Analyzing Emotions; Employing Emotional Intelligence			
Ability to label emotions and recognize relations among the words and the emotions themselves, such as the relation between liking and loving	Ability to interpret the meanings that emotions convey regarding relationships, such as that sadness often accompanies a loss	Ability to understand complex feelings: simultaneous feelings of love and hate, or blends such as awe as a combination of fear and surprise	Ability to recognize likely transitions among emotions, such as the transition from anger to satisfaction, or from anger to shame
4) Reflective Regulation of Emotions to Promote Emotional and Intellectual Growth			
Ability to stay open to feelings, both those that are pleasant and those that are unpleasant	Ability to reflectively engage or detach from an emotion depending upon its judged informativeness or utility	Ability to reflectively monitor emotions in relation to oneself and others, such as recognizing how clear, typical, influential, or reasonable they are	Ability to manage emotion in oneself and others by moderating negative emotions and enhancing pleasant ones, without repressing or exaggerating information they may convey

Basic ⟶ *Complex* (Increasing Complexity of Process)

FIGURE 5.4 *Four-branch Model*

In the Mayer and Salovey Four-Branch model shown in figure 5.4, we start, at the top left, as children with the first and most simple of the emotional skills: Perception, Appraisal, and Expression of Emotion. This first box describes being able to identify our feelings and thoughts. Are we mad, glad, or sad, for instance? Moving from left to right in the same row, we see the next step in our development is recognizing emotions in other people, artwork, etc. Moving to the right highlights skills that come with age; moving downward, we see more sophisticated and complex processes.

The second branch, Emotional Facilitation of Thinking, describes how emotions relate to thoughts and problem-solving approaches.

The third branch, Understanding and Analyzing Emotions; Employing Emotional intelligence, describes the stages of linking emotions to events, other emotions, and common patterns and chains.

The fourth and most complex process branch is Reflective Regulation of Emotions to Promote Emotional and Intellectual Growth. This branch deals with developing our skills to detach reaction from emotions and choose how we want to respond to them. It also covers the understanding of how to manage the emotions of ourselves and others without denying or exaggerating them.

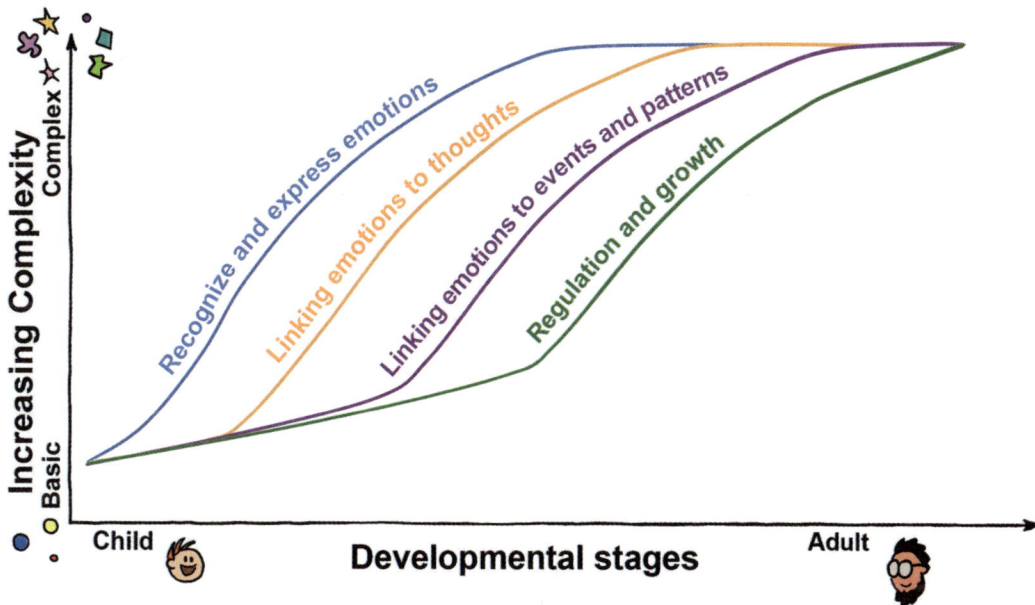

It is this fourth branch that people often need help with. It involves first realizing that there is a space between a stimulus and our response where we can choose how we want to respond. This capacity seems unique to humans; poke a bear with a stick and it will get angry every time. What makes us different is that we can choose to respond with anger or some other emotion. Learning that we have a choice in how we respond to stimuli is an important step in managing our own emotions. When people on our teams see that we do not turn into a grouchy bear whenever they deliver unwelcome news, they will be more willing to come tell us.

While receiving bad news does not immediately sound appealing, it is better than the alternative, which is having people avoid telling you bad news. To be responsible team leads, project leads, or department leads, we need to understand all the issues to have a complete picture and then start to address the issues.

Thinking about the word *responsible* can help us see the gap in which we choose our response. The word *responsible* is composed of *response* and *able*, meaning we can choose how we respond. If you are responsible for project outcomes or project teams, you should be able to choose how you respond to stimuli—both good and bad.

Viktor Frankl, a doctor and survivor of the Second World War's German concentration camps, found a way to manage the horrors of these camps that sent many people into depression and despair. He wrote about this stimulus-to-response gap in his book *Man's Search for Meaning*. He describes a difference between animals and humans in their ability to choose how they respond to a stimulus: "Between stimulus and response there is a space. In that space is our power to choose our response. In our response lies our growth and our freedom."

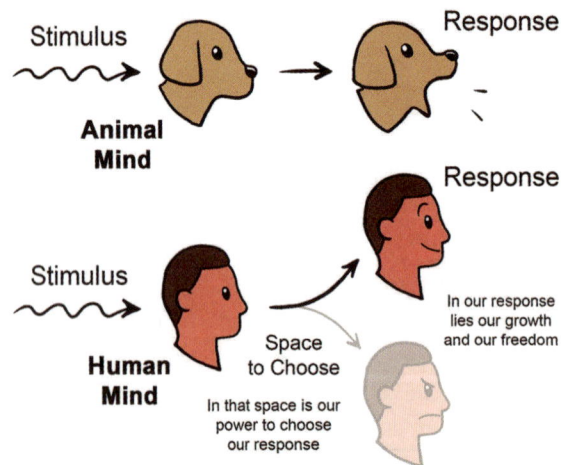

FIGURE 5.6 *Animal vs. Human Stimulus Response*

Martyn Newman, author of *Emotional Capitalists: The Ultimate Guide to Developing Emotional Intelligence for Leaders*, describes the importance of seeing and acting on the gap like: "After more than a quarter of a century studying how people make the best choices, seize opportunities, generate lasting motivation, maintain energetic mood states and develop resilience to adversity and stress… most of it depends on how much self-efficacy you possess… your ability to exercise control over your own behavior and over events that affect your life."

The bottom row of the Four-Branch model, Reflective Regulation of Emotions to Promote

Emotional and Intellectual Growth, is where we need to be to become effective leaders and coworkers. That is our end goal. Now we will explore the EQ models of Goleman and Bar-On to see how we get there.

There is a progression for organizational and project success that goes from physical, to intellectual, and finally to emotional. We need the right physical infrastructure (tools, parts, equipment), people with the right skills (intellectual), then the right culture and attitude (EQ). High performance only occurs when we have infrastructure, smarts, and culture in place.

As a project leader, you will inspire or demoralize others first by how effectively you manage your own emotions and second by how well you bring energy to the goal and renew the energy of the people you lead.

Let us start by understanding the EQ model at a high level and then drill down into the individual components and elements. Shown in figure 5.7 is a composite EQ model that takes elements from several popular EQ models.

Figure 5.7 shows three main components of EI: intrapersonal, how we perceive and manage ourselves (With Self in figure); interpersonal, how we build and maintain mutually satisfying relationships (With Others in figure); and outlook and resilience, how we approach life, deal with stress, and view the world.

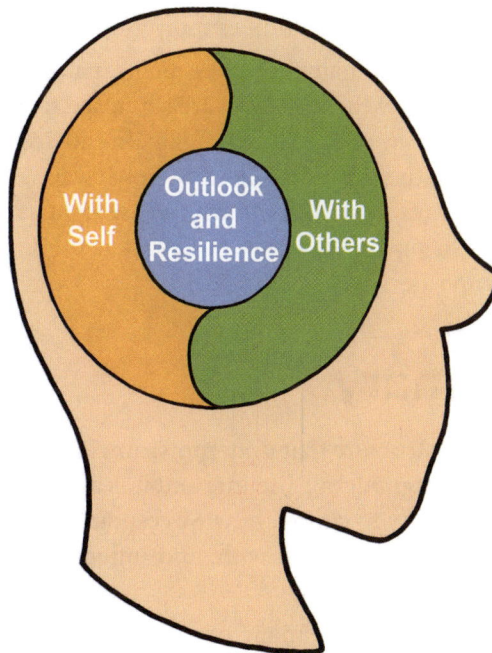

FIGURE 5.7 *EQ Model 1*

Some Warnings and Limitations About EI

I have deliberately spent a good chunk of this book talking about EI since I believe it is the single largest opportunity for people to increase their effectiveness and usefulness. All too often we see talent go to waste because smart, skilled workers are afraid to contribute their true potential, or alienate their peers, or fail to learn how to collaborate. Learning how to fix this in ourselves and then help others is a critical skill. However, it is a complex science that should come with some warnings.

EI deals with people skills that often defy scrutiny and classification. People are complex, changing entities and our behaviors rarely fit neatly into boxes and categories. The models presented here (and in any coverage of EQ) are just models, thinking tools. Do not obsess too much on whether something should be categorized as self-regard or assertiveness—just remember the general principles.

EQ is difficult to measure and while there are lots of assessments available, scores will likely vary from test to test and day to day. Think of it like your resting heart rate: it will vary from day to day and that is fine. You are looking for general trends over time, not spot measurements.

Some critics of EI argue that it is not really an intelligence and should be relabeled as a skill. I think this is probably a fair criticism and it aligns with initial ideas about the term needing a rebranding. Calling it a skill might encourage more people to study what it is and how to improve it rather than assuming we somehow are given a finite supply as with cognitive intelligence.

Finally, the self-reporting nature of many EQ assessments makes them susceptible to faking or unconscious influence. Once you know the traits you are supposed to exhibit, it is difficult to avoid gravitating toward those answers when you see them. Again, the advice is not to get hung up on the models. Read them to get the ideas, then apply them in your own way. As with assessments of agility, if we get too caught up in trying to measure the outputs, we lose sight of the mindset and values that really dictate the outcomes. Focus on the ideas; do not fall into the trap of obsessing on terms or trying to measure emotions with rulers and weigh scales.

Chapter 5 Summary

Emotional intelligence (EQ) is the structure that underpins our character and perspective. The good news is that we can develop it throughout our lifetime and it is a better determiner of success than cognitive intelligence (IQ). Our ability to choose how we respond to stress comes from our EQ. So too does our capacity to empathize with, work with, and influence others. These traits form the bedrock of leadership.

Given this significance, it is unfortunate many people are put off by the *emotional* component of the title, assuming the topic is too intangible or fickle for serious study and application. The issue is further muddied by the proliferation of EQ models, even from the same sources. Luckily, the following chapters synthesize these multiple models into a single consistent framework described in project team terms.

Key topics covered in this chapter:

» Explaining Emotional Intelligence

» Why EI is more important than IQ

» Understanding the three components of EI

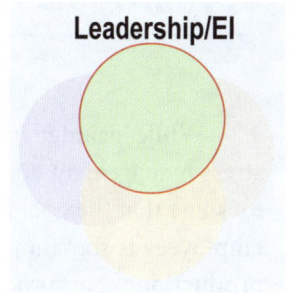

Chapter 6
EQ Outlook and Resilience

The first and most important EI category of Outlook and Resilience is concerned with establishing and developing a healthy long-term outlook toward work and life. It covers how we react and respond to stress, and how we manage our general mood.

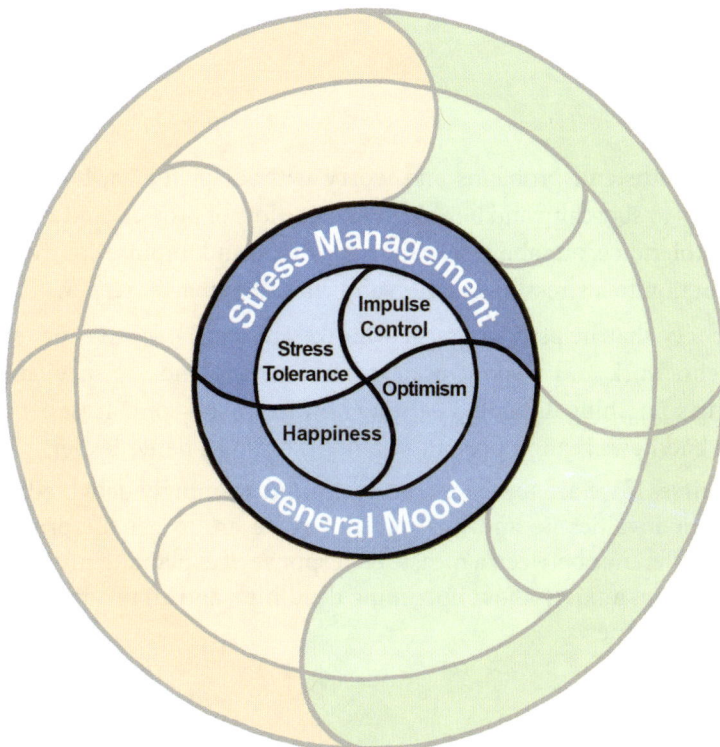

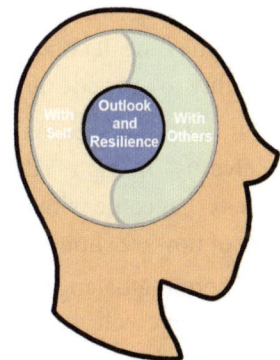

While included in both the Goleman and Bar-On models of EI, outlook and its components of stress management and general mood are often omitted from corporate EI training. This sends the message that the goal is to get people working together effectively, but the long-term happiness of employees is somehow less important. Of course, this is shortsighted; as we saw before with the production versus production capability (P/PC) balance, you have to look after the system to get the most performance in the long run.

A healthy outlook is critical to avoiding burnout. Without it, projects can appear to be a repeating cycle of unrealistic expectations, set against a backdrop of conflicting priorities, and staffed by ever more junior people. However, with a good outlook, we can see these patterns as opportunities for applying EI strategies and developing meaningful and rewarding relationships long into the future.

A good outlook is necessary to avoid going down with the ship when projects and organizations flounder. Because of the nature of the economy, and the laws of supply and demand, not every company will continue to grow and become a market leader. Not every stretch goal will be met and not every new product will be a success. We will inevitably face problems and setbacks so we better have some strategies for dealing with them

Stress Management

Stress management is the ability to withstand problems and worry without giving in, breaking down, or losing control. It is the ability to stay calm and be able to manage lots of projects and issues at the same time. It comprises stress tolerance, our ability to cope with stress, and impulse control— our ability to override our initial reaction to a stressful situation and choose a smarter response.

It is how we respond to adversity that helps distinguish who we are and how other people perceive us. Teams need leaders who work and respond well under pressure and the inevitable setbacks that come with undertaking something difficult. Learning how to react — or at least being aware of how we should react — to bad news is an important step in becoming a better leader.

There is a balance point, of course. If we are too happy-go-lucky and seemingly delighted by issues, people will wonder where our loyalties lie and how motivated we are to get the project completed. However, there is a huge difference between a measured response of explaining in a calm voice how a situation upsets us and creates anxiety about upcoming deadlines, and an uncontrolled response of yelling at the bearer of the bad news.

Stress Tolerance

Stress tolerance is our ability to withstand stress without negative impacts. It includes the ability to manage the following:

> » Choosing a course of action when problems occur
>
> » Having optimism toward our own ability to overcome a problem
>
> » Feeling that we can control or influence the stressful situation and having strategies to stay calm

Stress and anxiety (which is the undue worry about future events) trigger our primal fight-or-flight responses. Having your heart rate increase and blood withdraw from your skin, brain, and major organs might be good preparation for a fight with a lion or bear but it is poor preparation for giving a presentation, explaining a delay to sponsors, or motivating a demoralized team. In fact, the body's natural reaction to stress serves us poorly for the tasks at hand on knowledge-worker projects and can lead to long-term health risks.

While just telling people not to worry is not effective, the message is sound. To look after ourselves, we need to develop strategies for at least reducing our fear and anxiety to stay healthy and productive. Common approaches repeated throughout research and personal reports of effectiveness include:

Recognize the symptoms of stress, note them, and decide to act: Until we recognize the signs, we cannot deliberately start to counteract them. So, learn to take stock of your body and its reactions to stress. Maybe it is a dry mouth, the fluttering feeling of a racing heart rate, feeling hot under the collar, difficulty sleeping at night, repeating thoughts, or replaying conversations. These are all common feelings and experiences triggered by stress.

When you notice these feelings, alert yourself, maybe with an inner wake-up call: *Hey, I am feeling stressed. Time to do something to help reduce that.* Getting accustomed to recognizing these feelings and labeling them as stress or anxiety triggers is a critical first step to managing them. Once we can quickly and reliably identify the early signs, we can start employing techniques to help us feel better and perform better.

Talk to someone: Having someone to talk to about your issues and worries is valuable. It does not matter whether it is your spouse, a friend, a colleague at work, or a professional counselor—just find someone you can talk to. The process of explaining something out loud helps us sort through our feelings and may generate solution ideas. It also helps us put things in perspective. Once you say what is concerning you, it will likely be less impactful to you than when you had been keeping it to yourself.

Some people like to keep things bottled up because they believe talking about problems is a sign of weakness. They think of themselves as practical problem-solvers, so they need to create a strategy to solve their issues instead of sharing their worries. Well, consider talking about things as an effective stress-management strategy until you solve the underlying problem. Switching on the bilge pump of a leaking ship will not help you find the hole, but it is a smart move to prevent you from sinking while you search for and fix the hole.

Try to keep a realistic perspective: It is good to take pride in your work and try to please people, but it is not worth ruining your health by worrying too much about it. Try asking yourself if this issue will really matter in ten years, ten months, or even ten days. Sometimes we get flustered or wound up about the silliest little detail, when in reality people will not notice, care, or remember it shortly afterward. Telling yourself that this is a small issue and no one will care next month can help you put things in perspective.

Operate in your own competency sphere: Sometimes the chaos is larger than our circle of influence. Maybe a client relationship goes sour, project funding gets cut, or a competitor releases a better, cheaper product. When things are above our pay grade or not our primary concern, we obviously have a duty to help and provide input to those dealing with the issue. However, it is not on us to take on the world's problems either. When there is large-scale turmoil, stress, and change, one thing we can do is concentrate on doing our job while being available to help wherever or however we can.

Operating in your own competency sphere means focusing on your work, finding some peace and familiarity in what you know and what you are good at doing. Some things are beyond our control and while we should not bury our heads in the sand, we cannot take on the responsibility of all external issues either. So, after offering your help and between requests for input, focusing on what you do best can be a useful (and productive) strategy. When the dust settles, those that remained calm and were still able to do their work effectively are often selected for new roles (which typically come with even bigger challenges, but that is further down the line and what anxiety is for!).

Deep breathing: Breathing deeply reduces the heart rate and the immediate fight-or-flight responses caused by stress. It is important to use your diaphragm so your belly goes in and out, rather than your chest going up and down. This is the type of breathing that occurs in all mammals in a relaxed state when there is no clear and present danger. So, doing so may send *relax and reset* messages throughout the body and mind.

A slow, deep breath in through the nose or mouth on a count to ten followed by a slow exhalation through the mouth is all it takes. Think of the prompt *smell the soup, cool the soup* if it helps you. The US Department of Health and Human Services reports that a minute or two of deep breathing has been shown to lead to the relief or prevention of symptoms commonly associated with stress, which may include high blood pressure, headaches, stomach conditions, depression, anxiety, and more.

A useful aspect of deep breathing is that it is discreet and easy to do anywhere and anytime, whether just before an important presentation or during a stressful meeting.

Progressive relaxation: This approach is not so practical in a meeting but great if you cannot sleep at night because of the racing thoughts of anxiety or reoccurring dialogues you cannot stop replaying. Progressive relaxation is usually done lying down or reclined in a comfortable chair. It involves systematically tensing and then relaxing muscle groups one set at a time. It is common to start at the feet and ankles, tensing them for 10 seconds and then letting them go completely loose, then working your way up your body, tensing your calves for 10 seconds, then your knees, etc.

When you get to your shoulders, you may want to go down your arms to your hands and then up to the neck. The sequence is not as important as focusing on and activating each muscle group and then consciously letting it relax completely.

Progressive muscle relaxation is medically recommended to treat insomnia in people suffering from severe anxiety and is also effective for pain relief. It is thought that the contracting and relaxing of the muscles brings more blood to the area, which supplies more oxygen, which enhances local metabolism, resulting in reduced pain—all good benefits from an activity that can help you fall asleep quicker.

Appreciation: This is another technique that can help you combat anxiety and get to sleep more quickly. It is as simple as the adage *count your blessings* and involves consciously drawing your attention to all the things you should be thankful for. Stress and anxiety cause us to focus on problems; to some degree, this is a useful mechanism since it allows us to solve issues in the background-processing circuits of our minds. However, when we do not generate a solution quickly, it prevents us from sleeping, or performing well in the rest of lives.

Taking five minutes to appreciate all the things we have and should be grateful for helps offset recurring negative processing thoughts. Simply listing what we are grateful for is a useful exercise. These could include support of your spouse and love for your children. It could be that you get a regular paycheck, have a job, or have somewhere safe to live and access to food and water.

There are many things we likely take for granted. Taking a mental inventory helps us realize that our problems are not so bad in the grand scheme of things. Yes, they deserve our attention, but they should not define who we are or take us away from the things that we have. Mentally cataloging appreciations is a great way to counter stress and anxiety.

Physical exercise: Like progressive muscle relaxation, physical exercise pumps more blood and oxygen through our bodies and helps flush away the stress chemicals we produce when under pressure. It also releases mood-boosting endorphins that make us feel better about ourselves and our situation. Studies show that exercise is effective at reducing fatigue, improving concentration and alertness, and enhancing overall cognitive function. This is especially beneficial when stress has depleted your energy or ability to concentrate.

Personally, I enjoy running, biking, and hiking; they help me put my worries in perspective and I seem to get all my best ideas for blog articles and presentations when I am exercising. I do not consciously think about work; I am out enjoying the scenery, but ideas come to me during exercise, helping me link together elements I had not previously connected.

The type of exercise you do is less important than finding something you enjoy. If you find running boring but enjoy going to the gym or attending a fitness class, then great, go do that instead. The main thing is that it is something you enjoy and lasts for at least 20 minutes. Exercising at least three times per week, but five or six times if you can, is a fantastic way to counteract stress and simultaneously protect your own health.

Visualization: Go to your happy place. Visualizing a peaceful or pleasurable scene can help us relax, lower our heart rate, and control stress and anxiety. Identify a pleasant memory or favorite location, such as a much-loved day out or somewhere you had a great vacation. Thinking of this time and place, especially when combined with deep breathing, can dramatically de-escalate the stress/anxiety spiral.

Visualization and deep-breathing exercises are immediately available, zero resource or costs tools that nicely illustrate the "knowledge is weightless" concept. Once learned and practiced, they can be immediately applied to any situation and passed on to others who are in need of their benefits without process overhead. Take 15 minutes to practice both skills if you have never used them. It could lead to a longer, happier life.

Set priorities: Acknowledge that your time and focus is at a premium during times of stress and prioritize your attention. This means accepting that some things will not get done. During busy times, perhaps you cannot put in extra time at work, be with your family, *and* maintain a clean, tidy home. Dust bunnies and clutter for a week while you focus on work and family are a small price to pay for remaining sane and productive.

The same applies to work projects. Explaining that you will no longer meet some deliverables because of a higher-priority deadline or issue is not failure, it is mature communication and scheduling. Obviously, we have to try hard to meet all of our objectives and maybe there is some interim product we can deliver.

However, just as on major projects with prioritized backlogs, if there is just too much work, we have to sit down with our product owners and discuss priorities and sequencing. Our work product owner may be our boss or sponsors. Our home life product owners might be our spouse and kids.

When there is just not enough time to do everything, discuss with those impacted what the most important things to do are. When the realities of what can be done are laid out, most people understand the need to prioritize and would rather be involved in the process than surprised by failed promises.

Having these conversations and de-scoping some work for now is a liberating experience that reduces stress. Now freed from the impossible, we can begin to plan and execute the challenging task of getting the most done. Setting priorities provides a release valve for escalating anxiety when we see an impossible set of tasks and deadlines ahead of us.

Likely, not all these strategies will work equally well for any one person. The point is to have a repertoire of techniques to try for yourself and suggest to others you work with who are experiencing stress. The goal is to find ways to better face the problems we encounter and not surrender to feelings of hopelessness or helplessness.

Impulse Control

Impulse control is having the capability to resist or delay the urge to act. It is the opening up of that space between stimulus and response that allows us to choose how we want to respond, rather than just reacting. It creates the capacity to identify angry or mean urges, then avoid them before we make a bad situation worse. It is the opposite of being hotheaded, reactive, or flying off the handle. It also provides strategies for dealing with negative self-talk that personalizes problems (*I am such a screw up*) and catastrophizes situations (*I am going to get fired for this and become homeless*).

The thinking and behavior systems that govern how we respond to stress are described in the ABC and ABCDE models from Dr. Albert Ellis.[1] They help us understand our reactions to adversity (*activating event*) and also modify our reactions. The ABC model is as follows:

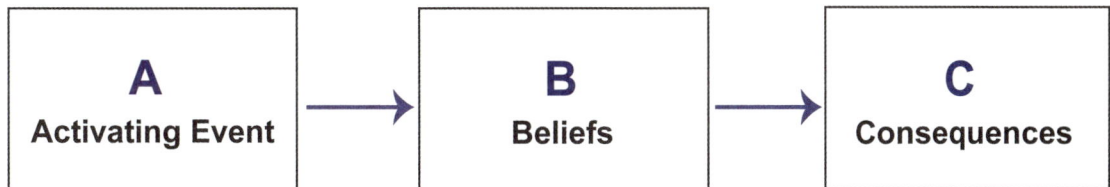

A **Activating Event**	→	**B** **Beliefs**	→	**C** **Consequences**

Let us illustrate it with a simple example that looks at two possible paths through the stimulus-response chain.

Scenario	A: Activating Event	B: Beliefs	C: Consequences
1	Ted's boss, Jim, drops by his desk and asks him to finish up his recommendations presentation as soon as possible, because he wants to look at it.	*Jim does not think I am working fast enough.* *He must think I spend too long on social media.* *Is he trying to catch me out?*	Actions: Ted says he is nearly done, when there is still much to do. Emotions: Angry, annoyed, worried
2	Ted's boss, Jim, drops by his desk and asks him to finish up his recommendations presentation as soon as possible, because he wants to look at it.	*Cool, Jim is as keen to see the results as I am!* *Wow, this must be important. I am lucky he trusted me with it.* *Great to know he knows what I am working on and cares.*	Actions: Ted explains there is more to do, but that it is his top priority. Emotions: Energized, trusted, respected

In this example, we see how the same event may be interpreted in two different ways due to the beliefs at play and the resultant outcomes and feelings. Managing the beliefs and subsequent consequences is key to impulse control and dealing with stress. When adversity strikes, we have to guard against unhealthy irrational beliefs that cause stress and nurture healthy rational ones that relieve stress.

Responses to Adversity

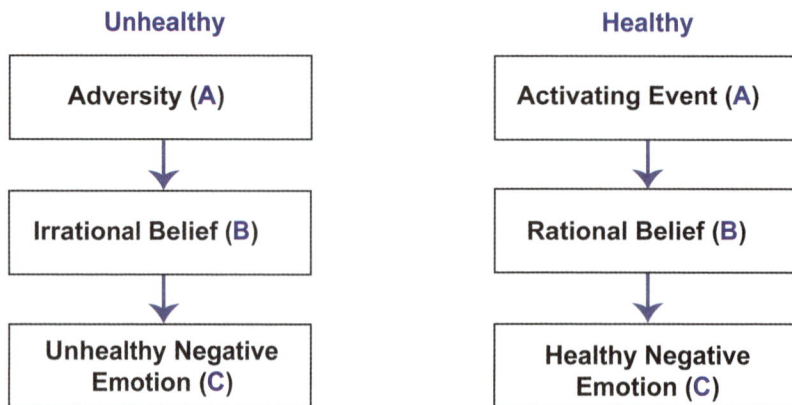

Unhealthy	Healthy
Adversity (A)	**Activating Event (A)**
↓	↓
Irrational Belief (B)	**Rational Belief (B)**
↓	↓
Unhealthy Negative Emotion (C)	**Healthy Negative Emotion (C)**

In the book *Resilience Factor*,[2] the authors map common beliefs to emotions. These B-C connections are shown here:

Common B-C Connections

Belief	**Consequences (Emotions)**
Future Threat ⟶	Anxiety, Fear
Loss of Standing with Others ⟶	Embarrassment
Violation of Our Rights ⟶	Anger
Actual Loss or Loss of Self-worth ⟶	Sadness, Depression
Violation of Another's Rights ⟶	Guilt

The chart shows that if we perceive a threat, we will feel fear and anxiety. A violation of our rights will make us feel angry. This is why, in our first example, Ted's beliefs about his boss trying to catch him out or not trusting his work ethic lead to feelings of anger and fear.

A branch of psychology called cognitive behavioral therapy (CBT) offers tools for remapping our beliefs about events to healthier ones that result in better consequences (emotions). This helps us respond to stress better and maintain a happier life, which is good for us and everyone around us.

The approach adds a *disputing* phase to harmful beliefs and an *effects noting* step that calls our attention to how we feel about various beliefs and resultant emotions. By adding these steps, we have a mechanism for regulating harmful beliefs and feelings. The *disputing* and *effects noting* steps add the D and E elements to the ABC model, creating the ABCDE model.

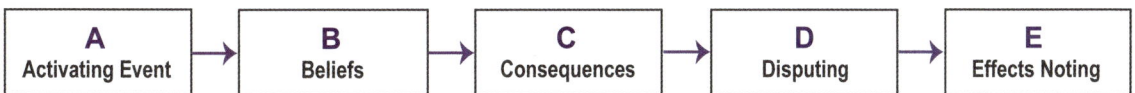

A Activating Event	→	B Beliefs	→	C Consequences	→	D Disputing	→	E Effects Noting

D: Disputing

Now when we notice negative consequences (bad feelings) about an event, we apply the *disputing* and *effects noting* steps. The *disputing* step asks six questions to dispute irrational beliefs:

1. Is my thinking here factual? Does it fit reality?

2. Does this belief best help me achieve my short-term and long-term goals?

3. Does this belief best help me protect my life and health?

4. Does this belief best help me avoid most undesirable conflicts with others?

5. Does this belief contradict parasitic thinking?

6. Does this belief best help me feel the emotions I want to feel?

These questions help us separate realistic thoughts from harmful/dysfunctional ones. Through consciously examining our beliefs in this way, we are also increasing our own self-awareness and insight into the ways we tend to think and react to situations. Let us look at another workplace example:

Scenario	A: Activating Event	B: Beliefs	C: Consequences
1	Ted's sponsor, Ellen, giggles while he is suggesting a solution in a meeting.	*She is laughing at me. She does not value my suggestions.*	Actions: Ted stops contributing ideas in meetings. Emotions: Embarrassment, anxiety

Instead of jumping to these conclusions, Ted could save some stress by applying the *disputing* and *effects noting* steps.

1. Is my thinking here factual? Does it fit reality? *No, I do not know that she is laughing at me. She could have just read a funny text or thought of something amusing.*

2. Does this belief best help me achieve my short-term and long-term goals? *No, I want to help. Feeling bad makes me want to shut down.*

3. Does this belief best help me protect my life and health? *No, it makes me self-conscious.*

4. Does this belief best help me avoid most undesirable conflicts with others? *No.*

© 2021 RMC Publications, Inc.™ • 952.846.4484 • info@rmcls.com • www.rmcls.com

5. Does this belief contradict parasitic thinking? *No, it fuels personalizing and catastrophizing.*

6. Does this belief best help me feel the emotions I want to feel? *No, it makes me feel worse.*

E: Effects Noting

Notice the effects that result from deliberately examining and disputing faulty or harmful thinking. Once we identify our emotionally charged beliefs about an event, we can begin to create an alternative line of thinking that is based upon more realistic beliefs.

The goal is to replace troublesome "irrational" self-talk with more realistic and adaptive self-talk. A statement like *I fear my presentation will be received poorly* can be acknowledged as a true concern, and then supplemented with a statement like *But I will nevertheless deliver my presentation and will probably do okay*, which leads to a calmer appraisal of the situation and a better outcome, both emotionally and objectively.

Of course, some bad events do deserve a negative response. A flooded house is bad news and there is no way around it. The appropriate response is worry and concern. However, people often beat themselves up about comments or being ignored when the more logical explanation is less sinister and we would be better served by replacing negative beliefs and emotions with positive ones.

General Mood

General mood describes our outlook on life. It includes our feelings of contentment or dissatisfaction and includes happiness and optimism.

Happiness

Happiness is your general mood regarding feeling satisfied and enjoying your life; it encompasses cheerfulness and enthusiasm. It comes from enjoying yourself and the company of others and having fun. While this all sounds nice, happiness is also an important indicator of general EI balance. People who are not happy may be suffering from worry, stress, depression, or social withdrawal. So, happiness is not just a bonus, but a central litmus test for your emotional health.

Things that make us unhappy can often be divided into two categories. The first is wishing or waiting for some event to occur, then getting upset about it when it does not happen or work out as we had hoped. The second is worrying about some event and, if it occurs, becoming sad about the outcome or, should it not occur, continuing to worry about it someday occurring.

Boiled down to these two options, we see that happiness is a mindset we apply to uncertainty and things we cannot control much. The unhealthy tactic is to base our happiness on obtaining some future goal (*I will be happy when I win the lotto*), which leaves us unhappy every time we do not, or to worry about events we cannot control (the weather for the picnic). The healthy tactic that often seems naive to natural planners and schedulers is to marvel in the grandeur of a sunrise or the simple joy of chatting with a friend. These people are "now-focused," rather than recall/regret (past-focused) or hope/worry (future-focused).

This shorter-sighted view may seem to trivialize critical issues; surely we should be worrying about the future to make it better. But if our unhappiness makes us unpopular with people or the stress affects our health, we are much less able to impact the future at those moments when we can genuinely influence things. Instead, having enthusiasm and joy for life helps us live longer and build more support and allies for action. It is actually a good strategy for effecting useful future change that is also a more pleasant way to live.

Nurturing Happiness

This *let us all just be happy* stuff may sound all well and good, but of course it is not simple. The pursuit of happiness and treatment of depression is a huge industry and the lifework of thousands of scientists. So what can we do? Well, we can learn from some generally accepted scientific principles about happiness.

When we evolved from primitive mammals, our survival depended on avoiding dangerous situations like getting eaten by predators or killed by unfriendly rivals competing for food and mates. So, quite naturally, genetics rewarded the nervous, the wary, and those willing to delay good feelings (safety, food, a mate) over more urgent feelings of fear.

The trouble is we now live in a time when these protective, intense feelings are no longer so useful. Even when we are exposed to an equal number of good events and bad events in a day, we pay more attention to the bad ones than the good ones because of our survival conditioning. To our brains, bad feelings could be useful survival lessons (the fear we felt escaping the lion, or avoiding the presentation) and could save our life in the future, so we give those feelings much more significance than the good feelings of being thanked or seeing our children play, which are unlikely to save our lives.

This tendency to forget the good feelings yet retain and replay the bad feelings can lead to unhappiness. However, understanding this mechanism is critical for increasing our happiness and resilience in the face of negative events. In the book *Hardwiring Happiness: The New Brain Science of*

Pleasure versus Happiness

Dr. Robert Lustig, author of *The Hacking of the American Mind*, makes an important distinction between pleasure and happiness. The two words are often confused and used interchangeably, especially in the marketing of consumer products, but are different.

Pleasure	Happiness
Short-lived	Long-lived
Internal and selfish	External and social
Taking based	Giving based
Can be achieved with substances	Cannot be achieved with substances
Generally experienced alone	Experienced in groups
Overexposure leads to addiction	Overexposure does not lead to addiction
Created by the release of dopamine	Created by the release of serotonin

The last difference listed in the table above relates to the neurotransmitter chemical in the brain responsible for the feeling. Dopamine is a neuron exciter; the brain protects itself from overstimulation by killing off receptor cells in a process called downregulation. To get the same pleasure response, more and more of the stimulus is required as a tolerance develops, and eventually an addiction.

The serotonin that is related to happiness is not a neuron exciter; instead, it is an inhibitor. So, its release triggers a calm, satisfied state. You do not need more and more of it to feel happy and there is no tolerance or addiction state.

You can buy pleasure, in the form of consuming things. You cannot buy happiness. Product companies knowingly and through experimentation understand the formula for creating pleasurable experiences that feed (profitable) addictions. A classic formula is for variable rewards; this was first used by one-armed bandit (slot) machines, which excite with the possibility of reward that is variable. This has morphed into cell phone addiction, where people are constantly checking their phones, hoping for a rewarding message. These systems create an itch; scratching it feels good, but feeds the itch some more, in a cycle.

Lustig asserts that the healthier happiness feelings triggered by serotonin can be created by "the 4Cs":

1. Connect: Connect with people in face-to-face settings with eye-to-eye contact that builds empathy. Connections in settings that are not face-to-face, such as social networking sites, do not build empathy, but instead rely on variable-reward-dopamine pleasure.

2. Contribute: Contribute to your communities, whether at work, with family in your neighborhood, or with interest groups through volunteerism. Serving and giving to others releases serotonin.

3. Cope: Reduce stress and allow the brain to repair dopamine damage. Sleep, mindfulness, avoiding multitasking, and taking part in exercise (a type of mindfulness) are all useful coping techniques.

4. Cook: Cooking allows us to control the amount of fructose consumed. Fructose is an addictive form of sugar that releases dopamine. Unfortunately, sugar is so cheap and habit-forming that nearly all processed foods contain it in large quantities. Cooking at home allows us to consume healthier foods in a more social and giving environment.

So, we should understand the differences between the harmful, addictive, short-term pleasures associated with dopamine and the healthier, nonaddictive, long-term happiness associated with serotonin and the 4Cs, and pursue the latter.

Contentment, Calm, and Confidence, author Rick Hanson explains how this process can be used to make us happier.[3]

He explains why bad feelings are sticky like Velcro in our minds, then outlines a process to counteract this effect by crowding our brains with good feelings. Instead of trying to stop or remove bad feelings, think of them as weeds in a garden: we can try to pull them all out, or we can choose to crowd them out by planting more "good feeling" flowers. This idea of not trying to stop bad feelings but rather focusing on the good ones takes some practice but becomes self-supporting, getting easier the more you do it.

Hanson provides the HEAL acronym to help us remember the steps:

Have a positive experience: Whenever something good happens, try to recognize it; acknowledge it to make the experience more memorable, more "sticky" in your mind, so you will be less likely to forget it. Bring it to the foreground of your thinking. Or recall a past good experience and think about why you are grateful for it.

Enrich it: Take a moment to explore the sensation through all your senses. How does it make you feel in your body and your mind? Try to find something fresh or new about it. Think about how it is personally relevant and how it can make a difference in your life. New thoughts about a familiar emotion fire more neurons in your brain, making new connections and helping the positive experience stick.

Absorb it: Let the feeling become part of you. Try to visualize that feeling, thought, and memory becoming part of your brain. You now have it; it is a part of you.

Link it: This optional fourth step involves linking this positive experience/memory to positive or negative things that occur in your life. For instance, if you recalled a positive experience about a friend and enriched the memory and absorbed the feelings, you may want to link that to situations as they occur in your day-to-day life. Now maybe an invite to a corporate event may trigger feelings of fun, not dread, as you think about the good experience you had at a similar event. If the negative thoughts drown out the good ones, just drop the link and think about the good original memory. The idea is to cultivate more positive thoughts that, over time, will become more numerous and sticky.

The process works by practicing the cultivation of positive thoughts: taking a few more moments each day to notice the little things in life that are positive, appreciating the things that go our way and what we should be more grateful for. Over time, the process of enriching and absorbing becomes more automatic and we hardwire our brains to be more positive, increasing our happiness and optimism.

If these approaches do not resonate with you, there are two others well worth investigating: mindfulness and flow. Mindfulness may sound new age, but it is centered on practical tools and exercises for silencing your inner critic, providing peace and contentment. It is about learning to focus on and love the present moment and appreciate what you have.

Mindfulness

If you are skeptical of such ideas, mindfulness can also be fairly viewed as mental training. We intuitively know that being physically fitter than most at work will mean you will usually tire later than others. Long days, long meetings to stay focused in, client site visits, and difficult travel schedules tax many people. When you are physically fit, you can withstand these demands better than most and so perform better. Mindfulness is like temperament and emotional training. It helps you develop skills for being more centered when making decisions, more comfortable with conflict, and more at peace with yourself. Developing mindfulness skills provides a mental competitive advantage. As the title of the popular book *One Second Ahead: Enhance Your Performance at Work with Mindfulness* implies, it complements happiness and EQ in general and is well worth a look.

Flow

We touched on flow briefly when discussing self-management and independence. It is that feeling of contentment with work as you get "in the zone" of being immersed in it and enjoying the process. Time passes quickly as you appreciate the creative process, wrapped up in doing what you love doing. A sense of flow can be found in a workplace setting, doing the tasks or at home. Some people love gardening, others love fishing, crafts, or music. The point is to find something you enjoy, something sufficiently mentally taxing to be interesting yet easy enough to be automatic and competent at. If it helps you feel relaxed and happy (and is not illegal), then go for it. Flow work will help you be a calmer, more productive contributor in everything else you do.

Optimism

Optimism is our ability to look at the brighter side of life situations and maintain a positive attitude, even in the face of adversity. Optimism supports resilience when facing setbacks and persistence toward goals.

Optimism and resilience in the face of problems are the best indicators of success. As noted in Angela Duckworth's book *Grit: The Passion of Power and Perseverence*, research by the University of Pennsylvania found resilience to be a better indicator of success for recruits at West Point than the standard "whole candidate score" metrics that measured many variables. From a simple survey of resilience, researchers could determine who was most likely to make it through the first difficult summer term and who was not.[4]

Woody Allen joked that 80 percent of success in life is just showing up. You certainly cannot be successful if you drop out and luck can only shine on you if you are present trying something, so being persistent certainly has its benefits.

We succeed when we commit to doing what we want to achieve, when we apply our persistence to the goal. Failure is often a withholding of that commitment and deciding to not persevere. So, persistence is key to success and an optimistic attitude is the key to persistence. They support each other like layers.

Achieving success is built upon the persistence to push on through obstacles

The will to persevere is built on the optimism that we will be successful

Optimism is the mindset that any obstacles are isolated and temporary

Cultivating Persistence

The *European Journal of Psychotraumatology* published research on strategies people use to handle stress and build resilience in the face of adversity.[5] They found that factors associated with resilience include cognitive flexibility, active coping skills, maintaining a supportive social network, attending to one's physical well-being, embracing a personal moral compass, and of course optimism.

Cognitive flexibility: Looking for the positive outcomes as well as acknowledging the negative and painful consequences of the situation.

Find and identify with a resilient role model: Find someone who has experienced adversity, disaster, or trauma whom you admire or can relate to. Imitation or modeling somebody's strength can be a powerful mode of learning by internalizing the experience of resilience.

Active coping skills: Be mindful of your thoughts about a situation. When you find yourself repeating or replaying negative circumstances or interactions, interrupt the process, then create positive statements about yourself and your situation, and look for the help and support of others.

Maintaining a social support network: Considerable emotional strength comes from close relationships with people and even organizations. Not feeling alone can help face fear and adversity. Having social support can minimize the experience of hopelessness while encouraging adaptive and active coping.

Physical activity: Attending to your physical well-being before, during, and after stressful situations can promote resilience. Exercise has positive effects on mood and self-esteem.

Face your fears instead of avoiding them: Fear is meant to tell us about danger in our environment. So, while it is important to be aware of this emotion for actually dangerous situations, it is also important to acknowledge that avoidance should not be our automatic reaction. Accepting the experience of fear and anxiety, and pushing ourself to face fears can help promote resilience when experiencing subsequent traumatic experiences. By increasing one's sense of control and mastery of stressful situations, we can learn to respond more adaptively. Practice at facing fears provides opportunities for stress inoculation, for learning to cope with fear actively, and for increasing our self-esteem.

Embracing a personal moral compass: Developing and holding a set of core beliefs that is positive about oneself and our role in the world that few things can alter. Altruistic behavior creates a purpose in life that strengthens both resilience and recovery from negative events.

In *Grit: The Power of Passion and Perseverance*,[6] author Angela Duckworth explains how talent dictates how quickly we get good at something based on the effort we apply to it using the formula:

$$Talent \times Effort = Skill$$

She then goes on to explain it is the application of further effort to this skill that generates achievement:

$$Skill \times Effort = Achievement$$

It is not sufficient to have a talent for something; you must work at it to develop a skill. You then need determination and persistence to apply that skill long enough to achieve results. Strategies for overcoming failures and setbacks are essential; for many people, pessimism interrupts the process.

Persistence is really a good-luck and success magnet. This is not a superstitious claim—it is just basic math. Luck is random: some things go well, some go poorly. To stand the best chance of success, we need to keep showing up and we need to be persistent.

In the best-selling book *Thinking, Fast and Slow*, Daniel Kahneman, that rare psychologist to have received a Nobel Prize for economics, explains the power of showing up. He says:

$$Success = Talent + Luck$$

To be successful in sports, as in any field, you need to be talented. The most successful tennis, baseball, and golf professionals need to be incredibly talented in their sport. Then you need some good luck to win. However, luck is random chance: sometimes things go well; sometimes they do not. Over a long enough period, things average out.

To illustrate this ideas, he tells the story about day-one golf game predictions and the curse of the *Sports Illustrated* cover shot.

Golf tournaments usually take place over several days. People are prone to overemphasize the results of day-one progress. If asked to predict the final outcome, people overweight the leaders at the end of day one and prematurely dismiss those who had an unlucky first day. Analysis of previous tournament results show day-one leaders go on to win only as frequently as pure luck dictates. Likewise, people who were unlucky on day one, tend to do better in subsequent days.

This is regression to the mean. Over long periods, extremes of luck average out. Since success is talent plus luck, if you stick with things long enough and have the requisite talent, you will be rewarded with good luck and success too. This is the benefit of persistence: sticking around long enough to be rewarded with some good luck.

Regression to the mean also tells us that people who have been wildly successful because of a fortunate combination of talent and luck will likely become more average in the future. This is the *Sports Illustrated* curse: seemingly everyone who makes it onto the cover of *Sports Illustrated* has a poor next season. However, we should consider how they made it onto the cover in the first place. First, they have to be extremely talented. Next, they must have experienced some good luck to produce exceptional success. Since luck regresses to the mean, it is only to be expected that exceptional results will be followed by more average results, rather than another blockbuster season.

Our takeaway should be to keep working, keep developing our skills and talent, then keep showing up and taking part so we get the ups as well as the downs of luck. If we can bank and capitalize on the random good fortunes that come our way, it should more than make up for the strange setbacks and unlucky turns that will also impact us.

Having an optimistic as opposed to a pessimistic outlook will help us cope with the randomness of life and the ups and downs of luck.

Optimistic and Pessimistic Thinking

When we apply pessimistic thinking, it short-circuits persistence. Pessimists tend to give up when confronted by adversity, even if success might be just around the corner. Much of the problem is based on how we explain or interpret problems. Pessimists have a tendency to internalize and personally own failures. They replay internal monologues, such as *It is all my fault*, *I am a failure*, and *This will never work*, that are demotivating and prevent further action. They believe problems are personal and permanent.

Optimists spin the same bad situation differently to encourage learning, adaptation, and renewed efforts at success. Optimists view failures as isolated, separate from other parts of their lives, and temporary in duration.

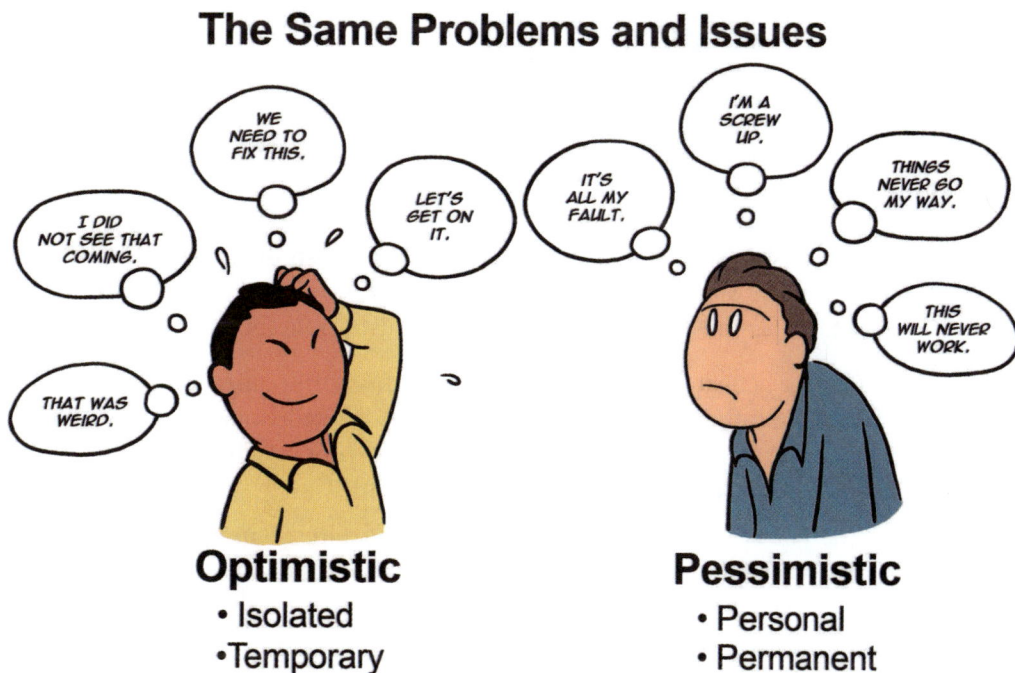

The Same Problems and Issues

Optimistic
• Isolated
• Temporary

Pessimistic
• Personal
• Permanent

A strategy for overcoming self-defeating pessimism and instead spreading some optimism within the team is to reframe problems as soon as they occur. By consciously identifying any components of the issue that are isolated (random, new, not related to previous actions), independent (not based on us), or temporary (once solved, we can quickly reuse the solution), we can prevent much of the negative thinking that leads to pessimism and a lack of persistence.

We must remember that our mood and reaction to issues often propagates through the team. If we can reframe problems and issues as temporary and isolated (i.e., consciously choose an optimistic explanatory style), we all will be more likely to be persistent and successful.

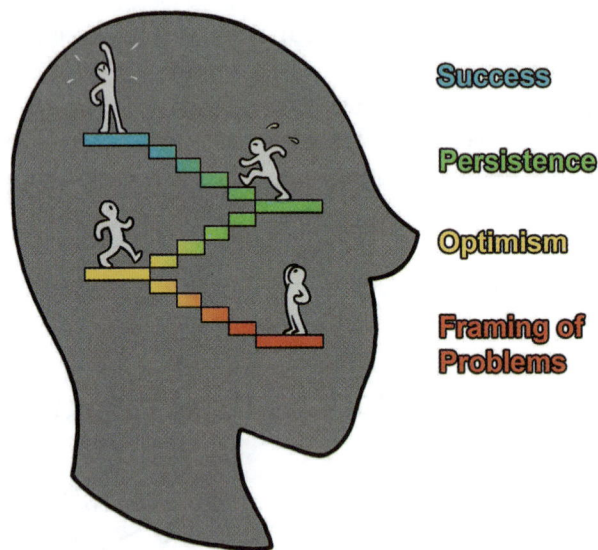

Optimism or pessimism is not a genetic character trait such as brown eyes. Optimism can be learned, or at least we can move ourselves along the spectrum from pessimism toward optimism. Additional strategies for reframing problems in a more optimistic light include:

» Looking for the benefit in every situation: Maybe this is the realization that a component failed in testing rather than in use, that the client wanted changes to a design sooner rather than later, or that at least we do not have to worry about wrapping and being careful with that vase anymore, now that it is broken!

» Finding the valuable lesson in every problem or difficulty: So now we know not to leave fragile items on the lift ramp. Double-check designs with Bill first, since he seems fussy.

» Focusing on the task to be accomplished: Determine what went wrong and why, but then get back to work quickly and focus on the goal. Do not dwell on problems; instead, move the team forward toward the destination.

Chapter 6 Summary

Outlook and resilience together form the most important, but least talked about, portion of EI. It is the basis for our general mood and our ability to handle stress and impulses. Our outlook allows us to choose our course of action when problems occur. Being optimistic about our ability to overcome an obstacle and persist when circumstances are difficult is critical for long-term success and happiness.

We examined impulse control and saw how the ABC model of activating events, which when combined with beliefs, leads to consequences. We explored how, by adding the steps of *disputing* and *effects noting*, we can reduce unhealthy reactions and start building healthier ones.

There is a difference between fleeting pleasure and more prolonged happiness. They are easy to confuse, but usually come from different sources. Finally, we looked at how persistence builds skill through talent and effort. How skill and more effort leads to achievement, and success is talent plus luck.

Success favors the persistent. Optimism, happiness and a healthy outlook help keep us going.

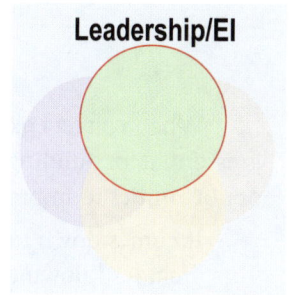

Chapter 7
Intrapersonal EQ

Intrapersonal skills are the unseen foundation of working well with others. To build this foundation, we need to understand how to work with feelings and emotions that will inevitably come up when dealing with other people; this involves self-awareness and self-management.

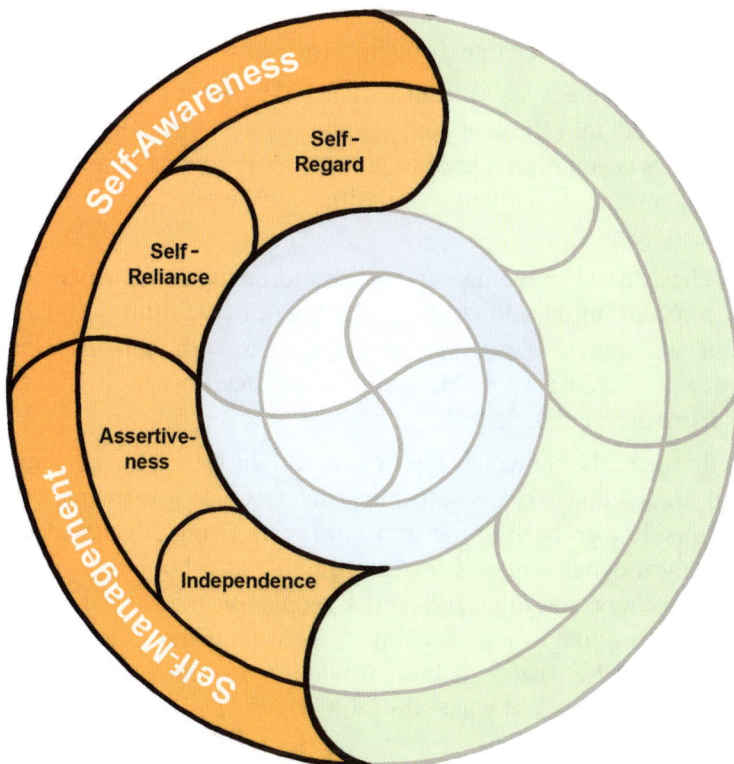

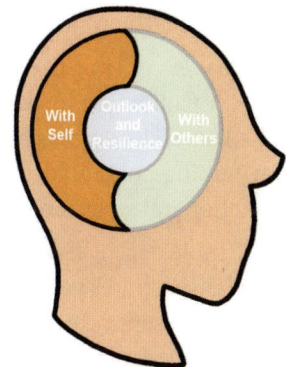

Self-Awareness
Self-Regard
Self-Reliance
Assertiveness
Independence
Self-Management

With Self
Outlook and Resilience
With Others

When you feel okay with who you are, you are more likely to admit your own mistakes, which is essential for building trust with others. If you are in denial about your shortcomings, you will miss opportunities to improve and work more effectively with others.

It comes down to liking yourself, warts and all, and knowing your strengths and weaknesses. This includes knowing your limits and capacity to ensure you do not regularly bite off more than you can chew and commit to work you cannot accomplish reasonably well.

It involves having a realistic and robust view of yourself, including not worrying too much about what others may think or say about you. Eleanor Roosevelt nicely summed up this robustness: "No one can make you feel inferior without your consent."

To be effective in motivating others, we first must be functional ourselves. Nobody will follow someone who does not have their act together. Being functional includes having confidence in our abilities and beliefs. People with low levels of EI often worry about what others will think, while people with high EI have little interest in proving themselves to others but an ongoing interest in expressing themselves.

German philosopher Hegel said, "To be independent of public opinion is the first formal condition of achieving anything great." In other words, we must get over worrying about what other people may think of us. Instead, just be yourself and be comfortable with who you are. Adlai E. Stevenson put it this way: "It's hard to lead a cavalry charge if you think you look funny on a horse."

Unfortunately, if you are in a leadership role (such as team lead or PM), people will inevitably be watching you. If, out of fear of what others may think of you, you show a lack of conviction, this will be apparent to people. The good news is you do not have to pretend to be anyone or anything you are not. Just be the committed (in a good way), authentic you, with genuine care for the project outcome and the well-being of all stakeholders.

Leaders do not need rock star charisma or outgoing personalities to be high performers. In fact, Jim Collins, in his book *Good to Great*, profiles the traits of the highest-performing leaders. These Level 5 leaders, as he calls them, are often quiet, reserved people who do much more listening than talking compared to their lower-performing peers. However, when they do talk, it is with conviction, integrity, and their own true voice, quirks and all.

People accept flaws more readily than fake showmanship or bravado. In fact, showing some flaws demonstrates you are real, open, and willing to share—attributes that resonate with people and are actively supported. To illustrate this, let's go back to the transition from being dependent on other people in childhood to becoming independent and imagine our life as a book. Our early chapters were coauthored by parents, teachers, and other influential people. Becoming an adult is about deciding to be responsible for authoring your own personal story. Becoming fully independent means overcoming an approval-seeking mindset that fuels insecurity and self-doubt, and instead accepting personal responsibility for who you are and what you want. There's a stoic saying, *Your judgment makes the insult sting, not the insult*; this is a good reminder that we have a choice in how we respond to others' criticisms and comments.

High Self-Regard, Low Self-Regard, and Imposter Syndrome

When tested in EQ assessments, entrepreneurs score high in self-reliance categories. They have independence of mind, thoughts, and values. After all, how could you run a business, whether a humble corner shop or a large manufacturing plant, if you were unsure of how to act? On the flip side of having confidence in your ability and legitimacy in a role is imposter syndrome.

Imposter syndrome is the feeling that you do not deserve to be in the role you are in and may be exposed as a fraud at any time. It is also feeling that any success you may have achieved to date is the result of good luck, not innate talent. You may also think you've deceived others into believing you are more talented than you really are. Imposter syndrome is especially common in high-achieving women.

If these feelings of being a fake, of being undeserving of praise, and of just being lucky or charming your way into roles resonate with you, do not worry. A study in the *International Journal of Behavioral Science* reported that 70 percent of people report feeling imposter syndrome at some point in their careers.

Imposter syndrome inhibits performance and erodes best efforts and contributions. While I am sure the world does not need more overconfident fools, I believe it certainly could benefit from the ideas and contributions of people who are hesitant to participate more. So, if you sometimes question whether you are deserving of your role, here are some strategies for reducing and eventually overcoming imposter syndrome:

» Name your doubts as imposter syndrome: When you notice self-doubt or dismiss your achievements, name it as imposter syndrome. Say to yourself, *Ha, there it is again: imposter syndrome!* Know that it is a common worry and try to move on.

» Seek support: Find someone with whom you can share your worries of imposter syndrome, be they a mentor or another sufferer. By explaining your feelings, the pressure is relieved and you can more easily focus on your strengths and achievements.

» Own and record your accomplishments: When you achieve something—it does not have to be huge—acknowledge that as your own achievement and write it down. Keeping a log of achievements creates a catalog of proof that can be helpful to review if you ever feel inadequate.

» Stop comparing: Do not compare your achievements or progress to others'. You are unique and the narrator of your own life's journey, not anyone else's. Be your own best you and do not worry about what others do or do not do.

» Hold firm to ambition: There will be obstacles on your path to mastery and progress. Do not take them as signs that it is not meant to be; instead, treat them as the learning opportunities they are. The Zen philosophy that "obstacles are the path" reframes problems as necessary steps toward the goal. So, stand strong and keep on going!

Self-Management

Assertiveness

Assertiveness is our ability to express feelings, beliefs, and thoughts openly without being aggressive or abusive. This may involve explaining opinions that differ from other people's, or disagreeing and taking a stand about something, even if it is emotionally difficult and even if you have something to lose by doing so. It also includes the ability to stand up for personal rights, such as not allowing others to take advantage of you.

Assertiveness can be thought of as the midpoint between being passive and being aggressive. Passive people can have difficulty expressing their emotions; they may keep emotions bottled up to avoid conflicts and can miss out on opportunities as a result.

We demonstrate assertiveness by delivering a clear message in a self-controlled manner. It involves having a calm mind and straightforward presence. It is definitely not being aggressive; when we are aggressive, we alienate people. It helps to focus your attention on the things you can control, such as your own thoughts, feelings, and actions. Also, it is useful to try to let go of things you cannot control, such as what other people think, say, or do.

Being assertive involves overcoming anxiety, confronting issues, and having difficult conversations. It also involves moving on from defaulting, the act of agreeing with others just for an easier life. I am all for choosing my battles, but when you hear a stance or plan that is counter to your project goals or values, you will often have to respectfully explain your concern.

Assertiveness is built on self-reliance and involves communicating your project vision, in your own words, toward the project goals. This involves explaining why we care for our projects and how people can contribute toward the project goals.

Team leads and PMs can do much to foster assertiveness toward a project goal by framing the project as a problem of creative discontent. The organization or market has this need, this gap, but we do not have the solution to fill it. The goal, and indeed role, of the project team is to create the product or service that fulfills the need and provides the solution.

"What lies before us and what lies behind us are small matters compared to what lies within us. And when we bring what is within out into the world, miracles happen."

—Anonymous

Independence

Independence is the ability to think for yourself and be self-controlled in your words and actions. You need to be responsible for your own planning and making important decisions. Independence also involves the ability to function autonomously without clinging to other people for emotional support or validation. Independence relies on self-confidence and inner resolve to meet expectations and obligations your way, without becoming a slave to them.

Independence builds on realizing your abilities and getting involved in those pursuits. It is about finding your passion, your calling, and dedicating your energy and time toward it. Becoming independent involves taking responsibility and letting go of an approval-seeking mindset that creates feelings of dependency and being powerless. It is about creating a distinctive vision and accomplishing something unique and meaningful for yourself.

Charisma

When discussing self-management and assertiveness, the topic of charisma often comes up. This immediately identifiable—but sometimes hard to define—quality is the combination of:

- Warmth
- Confidence
- Competence

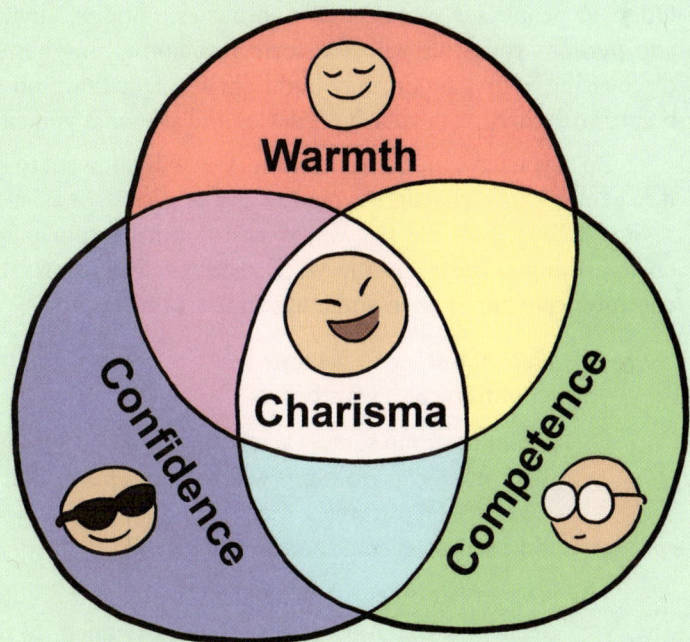

These characteristics should be in balance; otherwise, the following issues can arise:
- If someone demonstrates too much warmth, they may be taken advantage of.
- Too much confidence will be construed as being an egotistical jerk.
- Too much competence and they will be viewed as a tech nerd.

Once you discover your strengths and decide you want to dedicate your passion and drive toward them, you may realize you are not in the ideal role or organization. Maybe Greedy Corp Holdings seemed like a good career option when you were looking for a job since they offered an above-average salary. However, now that you have realized your passion is for solving novel problems, doing meaningful work, or building effective teams, it no longer seems the best place to be.

In these situations, there is nearly always a way to find an outlet or focus point for your passion within any organization. Large organizations always have volunteer initiatives, committees, and pilot groups trying to do something. They are usually happy to get help and support from anyone willing to assist them. Alternatively, within your project team, you can become the mentor to new hires or volunteer tester of new technology—whatever it is that feeds your true goals.

After you find the passion that gives you a sense of purpose and mastery, refocusing your energy within your current organization is a great way to flex your muscles in pursuit of a new role. Often, as people see some genuine enthusiasm and creativity, they will find new ways to channel it and perhaps your role will transform into something better suited to your passion. Other times discovering your passion may highlight the fact that you are in an unsuitable organization, but before you leave, push your boundaries and see what you can achieve with your enthusiasm.

Once you have found your calling, you will not want to keep it hidden and should communicate it so people know what lights your fire and can assist, or at least adjust their behavior to accommodate it. Storytelling is an effective way to communicate your passion, build support for your goals, and enlist willing cohorts for the work required. There are three types of stories that can help us communicate our passion and build support for our goals:

1. Personal story: A genuine heartfelt description of why you believe in something that communicates your beliefs.

2. Team or group story: Developing a shared sense of purpose and destiny. Explain how individual contributions will help and how other people's unique contributions will also assist. Fostering a *you need me and I need you* attitude strengthens purpose and the bonds that leverage our interdependence.

3. Destiny or dream story: Where the team is going and how it will get there, or why the team or group must change. The story needs to touch people's hearts and emotions, exciting them to action. "We are going to become the Tesla of waste disposal."

If you are not sold on the idea of storytelling, consider the advice of Harvard leadership expert Howard Gardner, who believes leaders achieve their effectiveness mainly through the stories they tell.

Believing in yourself is a crucial first step toward freedom and success. It is your self-belief, expressed in your own voice to create or improve something, that acts as the catalyst to ignite action in others. As author and politician Bruce Barton said, "Nothing splendid has ever been achieved except by those who dared believe that something inside them was superior to circumstance." Knowing (or thinking) you can make a difference is what it takes to make things happen.

The power and possibility of self-belief is nicely illustrated by what happened after Roger Bannister ran a mile in under four minutes in 1954. Until then, people thought it was impossible. In fact, there were articles in fifty medical journals explaining that it was not humanly possible to take in the oxygen required or metabolize the energy necessary to run a mile in under four minutes. Yet in the eighteen months following Bannister's first sub-four-minute mile, the feat had been repeated by forty-five people. Once they knew it was possible—once they gained the self-belief that it was achievable—they could achieve it.

The same is true with any endeavor: It is built on a foundation of self-belief. We need to take responsibility for creating something good and unique. We need to decide that we look good on that horse and get over whatever other people may think.

Self-belief is fueled by passion and mastery. Mastery is the process of getting good at something, which helps boost our emotional energy and motivation to do more of it. To keep your energy levels high, you should value your skills regularly and remind yourself of your positive efforts. Reward yourself for them; do it purposely and regularly to remain energized and motivated.

When what motivates you comes from inside, you will be less influenced or put off by negative events. Studies have shown that when people's motivations are internal and intrinsic, they are self-anchored and stronger. They exhibit more excitement, persistence, interest, and performance than people who are motivated by external demands and rewards.

Loving what you do not only helps you get better at it, but also leads to the mental state of "flow," where you get immersed in a task and time passes quickly without you realizing it. Being "in the zone" like this is an enjoyable productive state that brings satisfaction to a task.

Flow occurs when the experience of the work is intrinsically rewarding. It usually involves the interaction of three feelings:

1. Receiving immediate feedback

2. The feeling that you have the potential to succeed

3. Feeling so engrossed in the experience, that your other needs become less important

People often enjoy working with agile approaches because the opportunities for flow are present. Seeing failed tests start to pass and work in short iterations with frequent feedback provides options for immediate or shorter feedback. Breaking a complex undertaking down into more manageable features and stories, then starting with the highest priority, increases our feelings that we can achieve the end goal. Finally, minimizing interruptions and avoiding micromanagement allows people to get into the groove and do the work they enjoy with fewer meetings and status updates that interrupt flow.

The Gallup organization found that the most satisfied workers were those who answered yes to the question, *Does your job allow you every day to do what you are truly best at?* (i.e., engages their signature strengths regularly).

Team Flow

While we are still discussing the internal, Intrapersonal side of EI, it is worth digressing to learn a little about creating opportunities for flow on our teams. Mihály Csíkszentmihályi, author of the book *Flow*, describes the importance of balance between perceived challenge of the task at hand and one's own perceived skills.

Just as Goldilocks wanted her porridge not too hot and not too cold, team members also like the middle, just-right balance of engaging, but not impossible, tasks. This makes sense; people who do sudoku puzzles for fun soon get bored with puzzles that are too easy or get frustrated with those that are too hard. Wherever possible, we should try to help match team-member skills to sufficiently challenging, but still achievable, work.

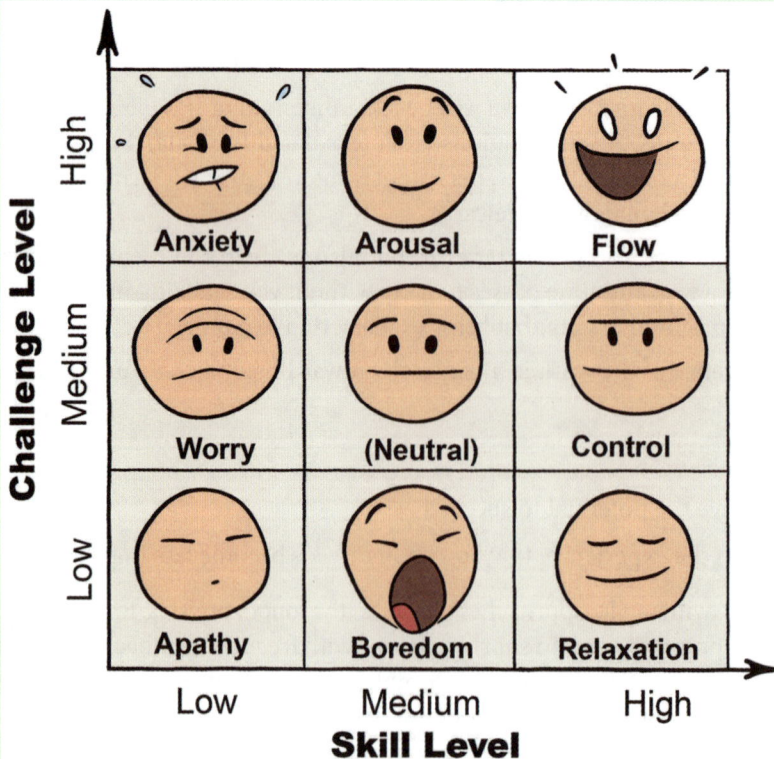

We can increase passion by focusing our attention on positive strengths. Done in moderation, this is not a selfish act but an investment in our effectiveness. When you value what you do, who you are, and what you have, you increase your feelings of well-being, happiness, and motivation. It is a pull strategy: you get pulled forward by doing the things you enjoy doing, which is always better than trying to push yourself to do the things you have to do.

It is our passion that empowers us to inspire and lead others. We should encourage people on our teams to do the same. Find out what their work-related passions are and encourage team members to pursue them. Some nice quotes that eloquently describe this include "Success isn't a result of spontaneous combustion. You must set yourself on fire" (Arnold H. Glasgow) and "Education is not the filling of a pail but the lighting of a fire" (W. B. Yeats). Once we get people excited about something, they will then do all the heavy lifting themselves.

Another benefit of being fired up with love and passion for your work, or at least for the elements of your work that you enjoy, is that it is energizing to others. People do not want to work with miserable, demotivated teammates who drain them of energy. So, be the kind of person others want to be around.

We should be careful to maintain a healthy balance of energy between our work and home life. We need time with our families, but also energy to enjoy quality activities with them. Returning from work to spend six hours with the family as an emotionally drained zombie is not the same as engaging with them in things you all enjoy. So, be sure to check your work-life balance in terms of energy as well as time.

When humans started out as hunter-gathers, the need to adapt, cope, and get along with others was a crucial skill. We stood a much higher chance of survival in groups than alone, so cooperation skills were a rewarded trait. The same is true today: the ability to get along with others allows us to stay included in the group. Our survival may no longer depend upon it, but our ability to get work done as a team does, and the skills of self-awareness and self-management are critical to continued inclusion.

Chapter 7 Summary

Interpersonal EQ is all about working with ourselves before trying to work with others. It involves self-awareness (how we recognize our feelings, such as frustration) and also deals with self-regard and self-reliance, which means coming to terms with who we are, warts and all, and knowing our strengths and weaknesses.

A low self-regard and self-doubt often manifest as imposter syndrome. We can help overcome it by acknowledging and labeling it as imposter syndrome, seeking support from others, owning and recording our accomplishments, and not comparing ourselves to others.

We saw how self-management and assertiveness allow us to express our feelings, beliefs, and thoughts without being aggressive or abusive. It is okay to disagree with people when we find the actual midpoint between passive and aggressive.

Finally, we looked at independence, the ability to think for ourselves, be self-controlled, and overcome anxiety. Finding our passion allows us to unleash the power of being authentic through storytelling and finding flow in aligned, committed work.

Key topics covered in this chapter:

» Intrapersonal skills: The foundation for working well with others

» Self-awareness: Recognizing our feelings

» Recognizing and overcoming imposter syndrome

» Self-management: Assertiveness and independence

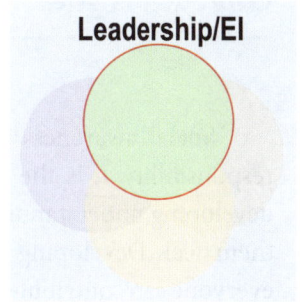

Chapter 8
Working with Others

Interpersonal (*With Others*) skills focus on building and maintaining mutually beneficial relationships with other people. There are few successful hermits because success in life involves developing and cultivating meaningful relationships with others. These relationships not only add productivity and richness to life, but also provide valuable support in times of need.

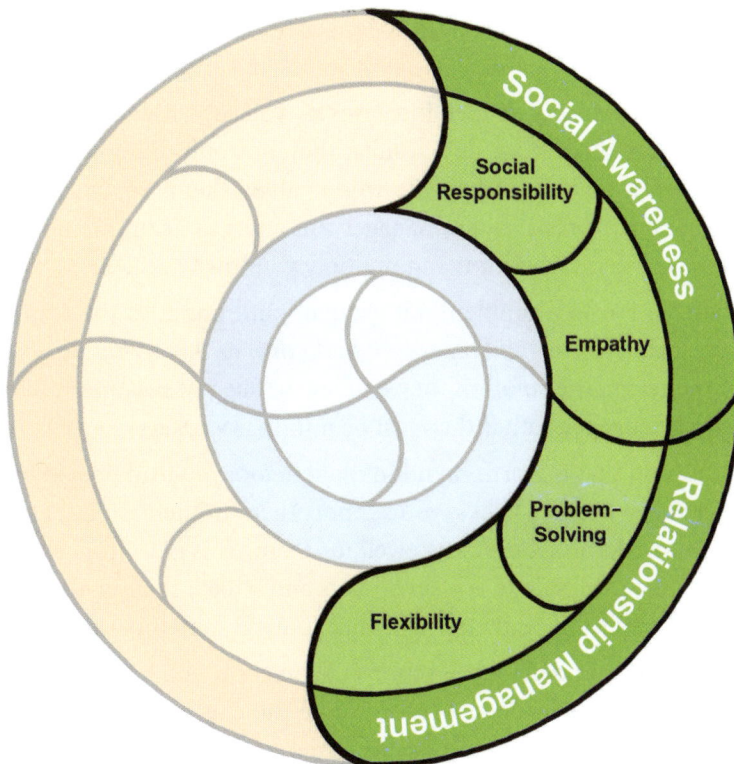

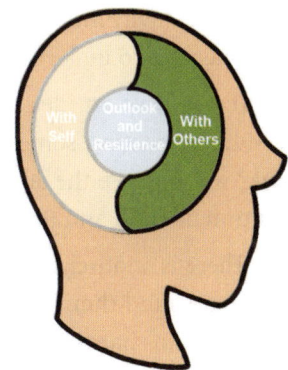

Social awareness is the category of interpersonal skills that includes empathy and social responsibility. It is the basis or necessary groundwork for effective group operation and involves developing understanding as to why people think as they do and how their thought patterns make them feel. Developing social awareness also includes a willingness to distribute power so that everyone can contribute and win. It also involves treating people as equals and creating environments where a mutual win for all partners is more likely.

It is impossible to oversell the importance of creating socially responsible teams and organizations. No single factor predicts the productivity of an employee more clearly than their relationship with a direct supervisor. Environments in which people feel cared for — through recognition or praise, regular encouragement of growth, and autonomy — are the building blocks of success. Conversely, while people can survive for short periods without these conditions, their long-term absence will cause people to physically leave—or worse, to mentally leave, no longer caring about outcomes, but remaining on the payroll.

These feelings are especially important for younger workers. Gen Y and Millennial workers believe (rightly) that the power belongs to the people. We must involve them in decision-making processes and engage with them respectfully. Carrots and sticks no longer work. It is all about values and vibes.

There is a paradox of power: your power as a leader increases as you give it away. As we encourage people to take responsibility for their work and results, they not only become more effective, but also more appreciative of and loyal to the people who enabled them. So, to create productive environments, have the fortitude to resist micromanagement and give team members the ownership to make decisions. They will thank you for it and multiply your own success.

If you have an idea or potential solution to a problem, rather than outlining it to the team, consider presenting some options. By saying, *I was thinking we could do this, or this. What do you think?* we preserve the autonomy of the team. The solution they endorse or suggest becomes their recommendation and they continue to be engaged rather than just be mindless workers.

There is another paradox or oxymoron that is worth mentioning here too: you lead people by standing behind them. This means you have people's backs, you support them in their efforts, and you step in to share the blame when things do not work out so well for them. This is an important psychological safety issue: we want people to feel safe to try new things and stretch their goals and talents toward organizational goals. A side effect of really trying is that you will sometimes fail.

Having the support of a leader to assist and defend the actions of someone who has tried but has come up short is critical for trying again. As leaders, we need to be there as a safety net and provide encouragement to get back on the horse and not be discouraged or afraid to try again.

© 2021 RMC Publications, Inc.™ • 952.846.4484 • info@rmcls.com • www.rmcls.com

Empathy

Empathy is about being aware of, understanding, and appreciating the feelings and thoughts of others. It involves tuning in to them in a nonjudgmental way and being able to put into words your understanding of the other person's perspective, even if you do not agree with it. It involves being empathetic, which can shift adversarial roles into collaborative relationships.

Empathy is not the same as pity, sympathy, or being nice. Instead, it is developing an understanding between people that creates a bond. We need to put our own emotions on hold and ask meaningful, revealing questions to unearth other people's perspectives.

Caring about someone is not manipulation; people have a deep desire to be understood. Exercising empathy and understanding people's feelings and concerns allows us to create a reservoir of goodwill and generosity that can be drawn from when we need help ourselves.

Listening well is the key to empathy, so avoid anything that gets in the way of effective listening. This includes:

Multitasking: Pay attention, switch off your phone, do not let your eyes wander from the person talking. Focus all your attention on the person speaking.

Passing premature judgment: Do not try to diagnose the problem or brainstorm solutions while someone is talking to you. Being present to hear the issues is your main task. They may or may not want your help solving problems later, but right now they want to be heard and understood above all else.

Preparing your rebuttal: Do not think about what you will say in reply when they pause or finish talking. If you do this, you are not fully focusing on what they are saying. Despite what we think, people are terrible at multitasking, so focus on listening and understanding their viewpoint.

Advising or offering premature reassurance: If someone says, *I am unsure if I can manage this role*, rather than responding with *Do not worry, you will be fine*, listen properly, make a commitment to suspend your own agenda for a few minutes, and explore their situation before offering your thoughts.

Talking too much: Active listening should be just that—mainly listening. While it is useful to ask questions and paraphrase responses to demonstrate understanding, the flow of words should come mainly from the person who is talking. "We have two ears and one mouth—use them in those proportions" is sage advice. Do not inhibit learning by talking too much.

Most research suggests 85 percent of communication is nonverbal. This means it's important to adopt an open body posture and an appropriate interpersonal space. When replying or asking clarifying questions, use an appropriate tone, volume, and rate of response that matches the person you are listening to or lead them to a more appropriate level if they are overly upset, concerned, or quiet and reserved.

What you are trying to do is place yourself emotionally in another person's situation so you can better understand how they feel. When they finish talking, pause, then paraphrase what they have said to demonstrate that you understand their feelings.

Showing empathy does not have to be limited to one-on-one settings when hearing about problems. It works with teams and vendors too. Tom Richardson, Augusto Vidaurreta, and Tom Gorman from Systems Consulting Group have created a collaborative vendor-partnership approach that emphasizes the wins for both sets of people in a commercial relationship. They introduce it like this: "Here are the wins I would like to achieve, provided that we can do business together and get a relationship going. And here are some of the wins I believe you would want to get out of the relationship. What I would like to do is learn more about your potential wins and maybe modify my own. How does that sound to you?"[1]

Framing a partnership this way acknowledges and respects the wants of both parties. It also encourages more understanding of what everyone wants to get out of a relationship and is a great model to use on teams. A manager used this approach with me quite early in my career and it had a profound effect on my motivation—so much so that I have been practicing it on all my projects since becoming a team lead or PM. However, it was not until I learned about EQ that I fully understood why it worked.

Early in the project, meet with each team member individually to outline the project goals and the way you would like to work. This involves explaining high-level problem-based objectives and letting empowered teams determine how best to solve them, as well as short feedback cycles and adaptation. Then ask the team members what motivates them and what they are hoping to get out of the project.

Sometimes, this can be quite the shock to people since nobody has asked them what they wanted out of a project before. Team members often regard themselves solely as workers on a project, delivering what the business wanted but not getting anything they wanted. So, you might have to probe further or offer some suggestions: *Perhaps there is a role, like architect, you would like to try?* or *Perhaps there is some portion of the project scope you are particularly interested in?* Usually, they soon open up and suggest some things they would like to try or that interest them.

Previously, I rushed to the next step of trying to find ways to build these activities into the project plan. Perhaps they could try being architect or shadow the architect for an iteration or two. However, this is premature. At this stage, we need to understand and reflect back our teammate's goals to make sure we really understand what it is they would like to do. Only after some confirmation that we really understand what motivates them and what they would like to get out of the project for themselves should we look for opportunities to incorporate it.

Agile projects provide great opportunities for trialing new roles, tools, and approaches. Their short iterations followed by retrospective reviews are ideal test beds for safe experimentation. In the twenty-plus years I have been asking people what they would like to learn/try/experience on projects, I have not found a request we have not been able to accommodate—and once people work with you a few times, they know this question is coming and sometimes have some lofty goals!

The real benefit of asking these questions is the shift that occurs in people. No longer is the project about them doing work in exchange for pay or other employment benefits. Now they can see how their own personal goals align with the project goals. Now they are working, in some part, for their own personal development, enrichment, and interests.

People are at their best when they have the opportunity to maximize their skills and interests. By asking what people want, truly listening, and finding ways to incorporate their requests, we can harvest everyone's full potential.

It is also important to follow up regularly. Check on how the experiments are going and ask if they have any new or follow-up goals. This reassessing and checking of goals can easily be built into an agile project's cadence of work and reviews. While iteration beginnings and ends are good opportunities for team-based coaching, mid-iteration interactions are great opportunities for one-on-one check-ins with team members to see how they are getting on and if they are maximizing their skills and interests.

> Namaste. I honor the greatness in you.
>
> In my spare time, I enjoy running and mountain biking in the Rocky Mountains where I live. They are great sports, but as I get older, I find I need to stretch more to prevent aches and pains from slowing me down. So, about fifteen years ago, I got into yoga and I find it helps, which I am grateful for. An unexpected bonus is the mindfulness and humility taught alongside the movements and breathing exercises.
>
> The practice and meaning of saying *namaste* to each other translates into "I honor the greatness in you." In other words, no matter who we are dealing with, we recognize the good elements in them. We acknowledge the struggles they face, the challenges they have to overcome, and the positives they bring forward. This is empathy at its fundamental level: understanding, accepting, and connecting at the most human level. We should honor the greatness in everyone we work with—even if some days it would be easier to swap people for a stapler!

Social Responsibility

Social responsibility is the role of being a cooperative, constructive collaborator to our team and organization. It involves acting in a responsible manner—even when you may not benefit personally—and doing things for and with others. It also covers community-oriented responsibilities and social conscience (doing what is expected of you). It involves accepting others, quirks and all, and being able to use our talents for the good of the group, not just for ourselves.

Another way to understand social responsibility is to consider what people are like when they do not have enough of it. When people are deficient in it, they are antisocial or abusive toward others or take advantage of people, which is toxic behavior. An important role of a leader is to create a socially responsible work environment that builds emotional wealth for competitive advantage.

Team leads and PMs need to model the desired behaviors of being cooperative, collaborative, and respectful in all their interactions—especially difficult ones. It is in our difficult relationships—with a group or individual blocking the progress of a project, perhaps—that we reveal our true nature. It is only when team members see you behaving responsibly in the most demanding situations that they will trust you to help them with the problems they are struggling with.

We also need to be cognizant of how we engage team members. Nobody wants to be told what to do on a regular basis. Instead, people want to solve problems toward organizational and personal goals, so we should frame work as such. As soon as leaders start telling people what to do, they have ceased to be effective.

We should also recognize, and promote, that leadership on teams is often distributed. Empowered teams are encouraged to take initiative on problems they know need fixing and enlist the help of others. So, the importance of social responsibility becomes distributed, too, and the topics of respect, fairness, organizational good, and cooperation should be covered at team chartering sessions.

Relationship Management

Once we have the social awareness component of empathy and social responsibility covered, we can start to become more productive toward project goals with people. This involves helping the team with problem-solving and being flexible in our reaction to situations and viewpoints. The role of a leader is to create an environment of healthy relationships for competitive advantage.

Problem-Solving

Problem-solving is the ability to identify and define problems, and to create and implement solutions. It is about confronting problems instead of avoiding them and doing so in a way that makes use of diverse team knowledge and problem-solving abilities.

It starts with making sure we understand the real problem and are not just viewing some side effect of a deeper underlying problem. Then we need to use a proven framework to capture and explore all the options available for use. Finally, we decide on the best solution, implement it, and determine if it is effective or if we need to repeat the process again. Let us start at the beginning by confirming the issue.

Reality Testing

Reality testing is the capacity to see things objectively, not as we wish them to be or fear that they are. It involves the ability to tune in to a given situation and determine what is actually going on, separated from any bias that we or other people bring.

Just as law professionals attempt to objectively assess a situation after hearing from victims, suspects, and witnesses, so too do project professionals when discussing issues and stakeholders. As the old adage goes, there are three sides to every story: mine, yours, and the truth. Reality testing is the ability to quickly size up the factors at play and determine what is really happening.

People with low self-regard, feelings of imposter syndrome, or general pessimism tend to fear the worst or worry too much about casual comments. For them, reality testing is a way to check for a gap between their fears and what evidence justifies. It may be as simple as asking somebody you trust. For instance: You: *Bob seemed unsatisfied with the team's progress at the demo. Did you get that impression?* Mary: *Ha, that was actually high praise! I just came from a vendor meeting with him before the demo and he went ballistic over them failing to implement a couple of low-priority enhancements. He is actually happy with how your team is performing.*

Of course, the other end of the distortion spectrum is having an overly optimistic view of the world. A strange aspect of project work is the common tendency for otherwise practical, pragmatic people to get caught up in improbable timelines: *Yes, we were late starting, but I think we can catch up*; *Yes, the proof of concept ran into lots of issues, but I think we are past those obstacles now and will go faster than initially planned*; *Yes, we had some team changes, but they are nicely gelled now and set to perform.*

I think we tell these lies to ourselves and others because we genuinely hope we will catch up. We overcame serious problems and are now all set to do better. The trouble is that smooth sailing from now on would be the exception, not the norm. Issues occur on projects and while we should not be impacted by things we have solved, we should not expect a free pass either. Take off the rose-colored glasses and own the implications of the delay. Chances are we will need more time or need to cut scope.

This emphasis on being practical and objective will help us overcome our fears and cognitive biases. It is important to see things as they really are, not how we fear they are or would like to see them. When we do encounter issues or problems on projects, we then need to figure out how to fix them. Luckily, this is not (and should not be) just our responsibility—the best problem-solving techniques involve engaging the whole team.

Problem-Solving Framework

Agile practitioners should be familiar with the problem-solving framework since it is the approach used in retrospectives. However, people are sometimes slow to adopt the approach elsewhere, or have a tendency to miss steps in the process and make suboptimal choices, when solving other problems on the project. We often have to solve problems mid-iteration or on the fly when discussing project issues with stakeholders. The process is the same, and as follows:

> » Identify: Identify that there is a problem and feel motivated to deal with it effectively.
>
> » Define: Define the problem clearly and gain consensus on an accurate synopsis.
>
> » Diverge: Generate many potential solutions.
>
> » Converge: Collectively decide to implement a single preferred solution.
>
> » Review: Assess the outcome of the implemented solution.
>
> » Repeat: Repeat the process if the problem still exists or it creates secondary problems.

There is a pattern to successful problem-solving that involves divergence of suggestions from multiple stakeholders and then convergence by the group on a potential solution. This is depicted in figure 8.2 and described next.

FIGURE 8.2 *Pattern of successful problem-solving*

Identify

First, we need to apply a filter to identify that there is a problem significant enough to warrant group participation in finding the solution. Then we must weigh the likely impact of the decision to determine the appropriate process rigor to use on this decision. There is a balance point to be struck. Group decision-making takes time and diverts attention from the project goal. When used too often, people get frustrated by the constant consultation on trivial decisions, like what type of printer paper to buy; when used too infrequently, people feel omitted and as though their opinions are not valued.

We must tailor the process to fit the impact of the decision. High-impact decisions, such as approach or technology choices, should use a more rigorous process to ensure no options or implementation steps are missed. Low-impact decisions, such as where to go for a team meal, can be tackled with less rigor (verbally, for example), since the impacts of omission are much smaller. Hopefully, many decisions do not need group input at all and we can let the team get on with the project.

However, it is often preferable to err on the side of inclusion with a brief statement about the decision you are considering. For example, you might mention to the team, *The team development licenses are up for renewal. I am going to suggest the same number of licenses for next year. Does that sound okay to everyone?* This informs the team about a decision you will be making. Likely, if people do not care much, they will just shrug or nod and the whole process will have taken 10 seconds. However, someone might explain that Team Beta bought some licenses they are no longer using or that the point has been reached where a site license is cheaper—these inputs could be valuable.

Define

The next step, assuming the decision warrants group participation beyond a mention of it, is to define the decision. It is important that we gain consensus on an accurate summary of the problem before moving on to generating solution ideas. People will only feel comfortable thinking of potential answers to an issue once they believe they understand it enough.

The key part here is believing we understand an issue enough to start generating ideas. Often, we do not fully understand the issue and partway through our solution implementation we discover new information. However, that is just the nature of emergent work: sometimes, the most efficient way to discover the full scope of an issue is to try something out to learn more information.

So, we need to explore, discuss, and agree on an accurate synopsis of the issue or problem. We must make sure everyone has time to provide their input and ensure everyone agrees that we have a mutual understanding of the problem before moving on.

Diverge

This is where we generate multiple potential solutions for the problem at hand. The goal of this step is to cast our net wide to include any solutions that might be missed through a conservative review of potential next steps. During the diverge stage we do not overly concern ourselves with implementation practicalities or costs. Instead, it is an open invitation to generate as many diverse potential solutions as possible.

Team diversity assists with generating a wide range of ideas. Teams comprising people who largely share the same gender, age group, social interests, and race will not generate as many unique or wide-ranging ideas as more diverse teams will. This is another great reason to have diverse teams: when everyone looks, acts, and speaks the same, we are exposed to the risk of being blindsided by groupthink.

This is probably an appropriate time to discuss the dangers of brainstorming and some better alternatives. Brainstorming, the free-flowing calling out of ideas by a group, is a popular technique that has several downsides. First is the Ringelmann effect, or social loafing. Studies have shown that when in a group, people generate fewer ideas than when working individually. Additionally, their ideas are less valuable and practical.

Ringelmann conducted experiments in 1913 on the force with which people pulled a rope both individually and as part of a group. He discovered that when people are part of a group, they do not try as hard as when they are working individually. This phenomenon has been replicated in a number of studies involving creative work and idea generation.

Case Study

I worked on a project to install portable tablets into semitrucks for hauling rocks, sand, and water. The system handled dispatching, tracking, and routing for drivers, telling them where to go next and what loads to pick up and drop off. We were concerned about making the tablets robust enough for a hostile work environment, so provided ruggedized protective cases and performed drop, heat, cold, and water tests.

One factor we initially overlooked is that tablet touch screens do not work with calloused fingers. During our first demo, we showed how the functionality worked for logging in and selecting the next dispatch order—using our soft office-job hands—then passed a tablet to the driver to let them have a try. They tried pressing the same icons and dragging orders, but nothing happened.

After a comical exchange (developers: "Give it here. Look, like this!"; drivers: "Yep, I'm doing that, and nothing is happening!"), a driver pointed out that he has the same problem with his phone. Our team's lack of workplace diversity (all indoor, office workers) resulted in our being unaware of the issue. People doing hard manual labor can have difficulties using capacitive touch-screen devices. We joked about providing manicures with the installs, but the fix was not that far off: drivers had to keep at least one finger soft and in good shape, through filing and moisturizing if necessary, to use the tablets.

A better way to generate ideas in a group is to ask people to think of them individually. For instance, have them write one idea per sticky note, then come together as a group, sticking the notes on a wall and removing duplicates and combining similar ideas. Generating ideas independently and then removing duplicates may sound wasteful, but the process of independently creating duplicates reveals broad agreement for that idea, which is useful information in itself.

So, when possible, generate ideas independently and use the collaborative power of teams for the next step of refining them.

Converge

This is where we move from many potential solutions to our preferred one. Engaging the team in generation and then selection of the chosen approach is critical. It is important that we bring a singular closure to the process and provide undisputable clarity regarding the decision selected. People are often uncomfortable with ambiguity; even the process of temporarily discussing multiple solutions makes them uncomfortable as they try to juggle the impacts of one candidate solution versus another.

So, make sure you do not leave anyone with doubt about which option was selected. Explain that the other options discussed, but not selected, will not be taken forward at this time. Let people park those thoughts, close any "mental brackets" opening in their minds, and now focus on the selected solution.

For people who are comfortable with ambiguity and evaluating many options, this step may feel redundant, obvious, and labored. However, it is vital and necessary for the many people who like clarity, plans, and predictability. On too many occasions, I have plowed forward after making group consensus only to be met with confused stakeholders afterward.

When you are facilitating a problem-solving exercise, you are totally engaged and keeping up with the conversation. Sadly, likely not all your participants are as attentive; it is always worth going around the room or through the participants list on a call to check in with them either with eye contact and a nod or by asking if they have any questions about this decision before moving on. A lack of clarity at this stage undermines the entire process and sets a team up for failure, not progress.

Cautions of Team Problem-Solving

People do not want to be treated as work drones. Ask them to think and they will amaze us with innovative, practical solutions that have strong backing from the people that need to implement them. Of course, this is no silver bullet or panacea. Here are some cautions we need to be aware of.

Real problems only: As mentioned in the introduction to problem-solving, we should use this only on significant issues, not on which brand of coffee to buy. Remember, we are modeling desired behavior: if people take it too far and consult their teammates when deciding what color dialog box to create, no work will get done. Team problem-solving is a tool for when you are stuck, and the problem is significant.

Poor team cohesion: If the team is currently fragmented and has opposing groups, then resentment for "fixing other people's problems" may undermine the process. We need to get the team aligned for team-based problem-solving to be effective.

Team and project changes: Over an extended period, if a significant portion of the team changes, we need to recanvass the team to ensure they are still on board with the approach. Exercising the bright ideas of others is nearly as bad as not being consulted; we need to ensure people still agree that this is a good policy. Likewise, if the project changes significantly, we need to recheck in light of these new facts and get the team to review the approach.

Follow-through: Once we ask for solutions, we must follow through by executing them. It is pretty demoralizing to be asked to work on a solution and then see it wither. It is fine to go back with implementation problems that need to be solved, but do not waste people's time by asking for input and then ignoring it.

Review

This step involves evaluating the effectiveness of the chosen solution. It is one thing to arrive at what we think of, today, as the best solution, but reality often proves that we were wrong or missed some other variable. So, it is necessary to review how things are working out after an appropriate amount of time and adjust or rethink our solution.

The appropriate amount of time has passed when the results (or problems) are uniformly acknowledged. Often, new approaches take some time to bed in and settle down. We should not abandon a potential solution just because of an initial stumble, but if it is just not working and people can see that, it is time to adjust.

If your team is working with one- or two-week iterations, then retrospectives are a good time to review decisions made and experiment with new processes. We can ask the team if it is time to make a decision on a new approach. Maybe they need another week or two or maybe problems are apparent already. Maybe it is working like a charm and can be adopted as a new standard. Be guided by team reaction to it; canvas the inputs from silent stakeholders too. Maybe what is great for a vocal development team is less than ideal for a quiet quality assurance (QA) squad or business group. Do not assume silence means consent.

Repeat

This is the last step in the review, adapt, and improve cycle. We need to continue improving and to reserve the right to be smarter tomorrow than we were yesterday and today. So, we need to circle back and see if the original problem still exists in any form. Also, we need to check if our solution introduced any new problems itself.

If we discover the original problem still exists in some form, or a new problem has come into being, then it is time to repeat the process and engage the team in the process again. This is not a failure. We tried something and likely learned more about the problem in the process. We are better equipped than before at solving the problem and at least know one more approach that does not solve it.

So, assemble the players again, summarize the issue, review why the last solution did not work, and repeat the process. Redoing it is okay; if your work were easy, likely it would have been automated by someone else by now and you would not have a job in the first place. Learning from setbacks is natural and healthy, provided we keep trying and keep improving.

Closing Thoughts on Problem-Solving

Your team has the best solutions to your project problems. When Toyota took over the old General

Motors (GM) assembly plant in Fremont, California, they proved they could engage the internal problem-solving skills of a workforce, previously written off by GM management as "hostile, uncooperative, and lazy,"[2] as an empowered group. So, it is ironic that many projects are populated by smart, well-educated people, yet organizations treat them like production-line robots.

Team Decision-Making

Once we have consensus on a single solution that was arrived at through team activity, we get the following benefits:

By asking the team for a solution, we inherit consensus for the proposal: The fact that the solution came from the team and not you as project leader, means you do not have to sell it—it already has support. It is easier to steward a suboptimal solution with good support to a successful outcome than it is to build support for an optimal solution and ensure its successful execution. If challenges arise and team members subconsciously ask, *Whose bright idea was this?* the answer is, *Oh yeah, it was ours,* and they are more likely to continue with the work.

Solutions are practical: Anyone who has worked hard to craft a solution only to be told *That will not work here because. . .* will know how frustrating and disheartening these words are. Team-suggested solutions have been vetted for practicality and, because created internally, solutions will be found for implementation issues.

When consulted, people work hard to generate good ideas: The simple act of asking for suggestions engages team members beyond the role of coder or tester. People appreciate having their inputs valued and generally work hard to create innovative and effective solutions. Treating workers as interchangeable resources is a poor model, inherited from the command-and-control methods of the Industrial Revolution. Leading companies such as Toyota and 3M recognize that their best ideas come from inside their companies and it is important to make use of this intellect. It is partly due to team problem-solving that these companies innovate better, and have higher-quality products, and better labor relations.

Asking for help shows confidence, not weakness: Asking for ideas and solutions to problems is not a sign of incompetence or an inability to manage. The fact that we ask for input does not mean we are dumb. Instead, it demonstrates valuing the opinions of others and being thoughtful. In essence, it demonstrates how all problems should be tackled, which is the next benefit.

Seeking ideas models desired behavior: Project leaders have the role of modeling desired behavior, i.e., behaving as we wish others to behave. If we stay silent, make decisions with incomplete awareness of the facts, and do not ask for help when we need it, what message is this sending to the team? Well, it is a clear message that we expect team members to behave the same way and work in isolation. Frequently, organizations waste time and money on team-building activities that are then eroded by management-in-a-vacuum. By demonstrating good problem-solving techniques, team members are encouraged to solve their problems this way too. Teams that can effectively problem-solve and build support for solutions are the real powerhouses of successful projects. As leaders, we need to make sure we are supporting and mirroring these best practices.

Design Thinking

Design thinking is popular these days—and for good reason. Design thinking is the modern application of the *diverge, converge* problem-solving process we just reviewed to the product-design world. Design thinking is increasingly being used in the service and business design fields too.

Design thinking is based on three pillars:

1. Empathy: Understanding the needs of those we are designing for
2. Ideation: Generating lots of ideas (the *diverge* component discussed earlier)
3. Experimentation: Testing those ideas with prototypes and trials

The empathy component captures the mindset and needs of the people we are creating for. It helps us understand their needs and frustrations. By using quick, low-fidelity prototypes and experiments, we learn about user needs quickly and without a large investment. Similar to the incremental approach from agile, we then conduct iterations of building features and getting feedback until the customer and/or business need is satisfied.

The five phases of design thinking are:

1. Empathize with the users
2. Define the users' needs, their problems, and our insights
3. Ideate by challenging assumptions and creating ideas for innovative solutions
4. Prototype, to start creating solutions
5. Test the solutions

Empathize   Define   Ideate   Prototype   Test

However, these phases are not necessarily linear and there are opportunities to loop back and repeat activities as new information emerges.

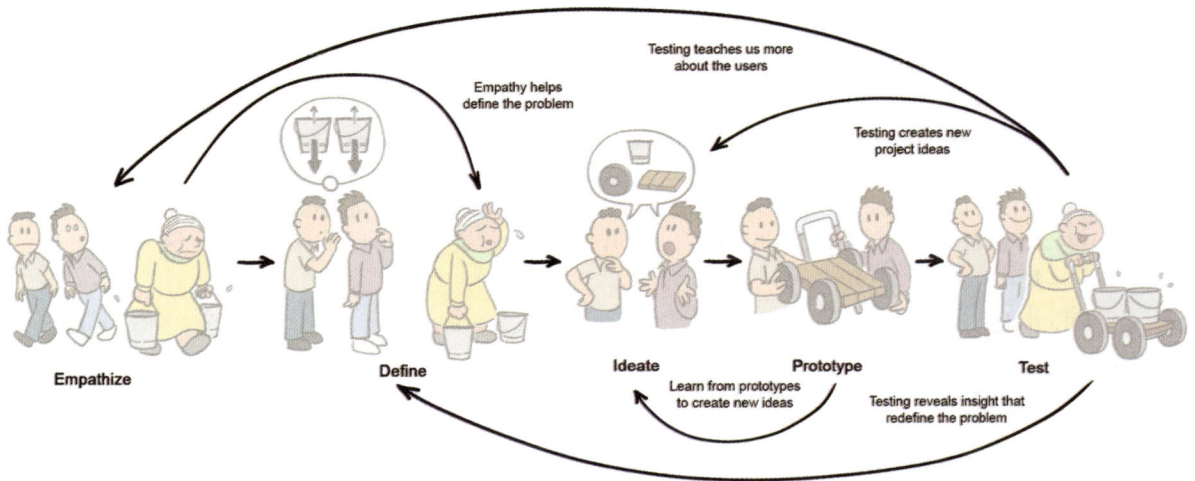

Empathize   Define   Ideate   Prototype   Test

Design thinking is a huge topic and an industry in its own right. For our discussion here, I just wanted to explain how it is another instance of engaging people collaboratively. Like agile approaches and lean startup, design thinking uses the power of divergent thinking and convergent agreement to find possible solutions. It then employs short experiments and develops prototypes to test ideas and adapt based on feedback.

In the software world, we may call this *agile* or *Kanban*. In the product development world, we may see these ideas called *design thinking* or *lean startup*. There are differences between the approaches but they share many core ideas. They all tap into the power of interpersonal relationships and EI.

Flexibility

Flexibility is our ability to adjust our thoughts, emotions, and behaviors to fit changing situations or conditions encountered. It includes being able to change our mind when it turns out we were wrong about something. It includes being open to different ideas and tolerant of alternative views. Being flexible allows us to better understand problems, create solutions, and deal with the inevitable issues and conflicts that arise with people on projects.

Chapter 8 Summary

In a way, it seems crazy to have taken this long to get to discussing how teams solve problems and make decisions. That is what they do all day long. That is what projects are: a long stream of problem-solving and decision-making with some collaboration and old-fashioned "doing" thrown in there too. Yet without understanding how to organize and execute work—without understanding and sorting ourselves out first—we would be no use to our teams. At best, we would be helpful observers, perhaps providing out-of-date technical suggestions.

Yet, when we understand and can apply empathy, we listen and we appreciate the feelings and thoughts of others—and people notice. When we demonstrate social responsibility, we show we are acting for others, not for personal benefit. When we test realities with others and facilitate problem-solving and decision-making through a structured *diverge*, *converge* process, we are beginning to serve the team and earn our keep.

Often, people cannot identify what defines a good leader or facilitator, but they recognize it when they experience it. It is not magic; it is the careful application of social awareness and relationship management, built on a foundation of strong interpersonal skills, all grounded in a healthy outlook and resilience. That is the secret sauce, and now you have the recipe. It took a while to explain because it needs to be built up block by block.

Key topics covered in this chapter:

» Empathy

» Team problem-solving

» Team decision-making

» Design thinkingas an empathy driven team approach

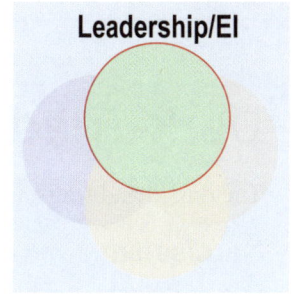

Chapter 9
EQ for Dealing with Difficult and Toxic People

Most of us will experience difficult and downright toxic people at some point in our careers. If you ever have then you can probably see, in retrospect, how much those people differed from socially acceptable norms. Yet at the time, their impacts are so upsetting and jarring that it is quite common to question whether we contributed in some way toward the situation.

So, having some strategies for dealing with these people can save your sanity and provide pathways through the issues, while also protecting others.

Fortunately, truly toxic people are few and far between. Most people we deal with are generally helpful or at least neutral. Some got into their careers because they had an interest in it or aptitude for it; others, because the job paid a wage and they needed the income. Whatever the reason, their skills and usefulness typically vary from zero to extremely valuable and highly value-adding.

Occasionally, we encounter people with difficult personalities: people who unknowingly or deliberately bully, undermine, manipulate, or sabotage work, relationships, and people's self-esteem. Being unaware of these personality types can derail projects and cause high levels of personal distress to ourselves and other team members.

While terms like *vindictive*, *argumentative*, and *manipulative* might begin to describe these people, a more scientific understanding is helpful. The term *dark triad* is used in psychology to describe three negative and harmful personality traits. Some people have one or two of the traits, while others have all three.

Dark-Triad Traits

The dark-triad traits are narcissism, Machiavellianism, and psychopathy.

Narcissism

Narcissism is vanity, self-love, and having an overly inflated view of yourself. It is manifested through characteristics such as perceived superiority, entitlement, dominance, and self-admiration. Narcissists are egotistic, often lacking in empathy, and overly sensitive to criticism, and have inflated views of themselves. Unfortunately, that self-love and inflated ego mean they generally dress well and interview well, and are happy to talk about their accomplishments, and so get hired into positions of power and influence.

Machiavellianism

Machiavellianism is manipulation to get what is wanted. It includes a disregard for morals and the ready use of deception. It is driven by self-interest and is marked by traits such as being self-serving, immoral, deceitful, and cunning. Machiavellian people are often emotionally detached, cynical, and lack principles. They can be domineering and, because they are so sneaky, often do well in office politics, rising to positions of power and influence.

Psychopathy

Psychopathy is having little or no empathy for others, combined with high levels of thrill-seeking, impulsive behavior. Psychopaths exhibit aggressive, antisocial behavior without guilt. They are remorseless but can appear extraverted and superficially charming. Unfortunately, this can lead to—you guessed it—promotions and positions of power and influence.

You probably recognize these personality traits in people you work with, even if you do not apply the same labels. Like all personality traits, they exist on a spectrum. In mild forms or infrequent bursts, they do much less harm than severe or prolonged exposure.

Knowing about these traits is extremely important because it allows us to adjust the "volume control" in terms of how these people impact us. Without an understanding of these traits, it is easy to be swayed and confused, and even question our own contributions toward the conflict and

problems these people create. Once we understand how to recognize these traits, we can adjust our behavior around and involvement with these people.

A safe default strategy is to disengage and avoid people with dark-triad traits. However, we sometimes find ourselves managing people with these characteristics, working alongside them, or reporting to them. In these cases, it is not possible to avoid them, so here are some strategies for minimizing their impact.

First, we need to make sure we are not the problem (i.e., that we do not have dark-triad personality traits ourselves). Dr. Peter Jonason and Gregory Webster developed the Dirty Dozen rating scale to roughly assess dark-triad traits.[1] It asks people to rate themselves on a scale from disagreeing to agreeing with these statements:

> » I tend to manipulate others to get my way.
>
> » I have used deceit or lied to get my way.
>
> » I have used flattery to get my way.
>
> » I tend to exploit others toward my own end.
>
> » I tend to lack remorse.
>
> » I tend to not be too concerned with morality or the morality of my actions.
>
> » I tend to be callous or insensitive.
>
> » I tend to be cynical.
>
> » I tend to want others to admire me.
>
> » I tend to want others to pay attention to me.
>
> » I tend to seek prestige or status.
>
> » I tend to expect special favors from others.

The higher the score, the higher the concern and the greater the need for some empathy training. Most people continue to develop their EI, including empathy, as they get older. I know early in my project-management career, I was liable to employ some Machiavellian approaches to increase the success rate of my projects. I did not do anything too sinister, but I would book meeting rooms far in advance, in case we needed them, and claim favorable go-live dates when the best support staff were available. Now I am much more willing to give up/trade rooms/dates for the greater good of the organization or just to help people out when I can. It was not a monster-to-saint transformation, but rather a more considerate mellowing with age. But let us talk about the real problem cases.

Anger, Aggression, and Bullying

These are usually linked to psychopathic traits. If you see people frequently getting angry, shouting, or acting aggressively, or their anger spills over into bullying, you need to act quickly but carefully. Also, be aware that some people suppress their anger and instead brood, sulk, or ignore people. These are passive-aggressive behaviors that also need dealing with.

First, stay safe: do not put yourself in a situation where there may be physical conflict. It is always better to just walk away and engage HR. However, assuming the anger levels are lower, such issues need to be dealt with. Resist the temptation to match the person's raised voice; instead, listen dispassionately and try to diagnose the cause of their issues. Techniques like questioning, active listening, and appreciative inquiry might help to reveal why they are behaving as they are. If not, then it may be time to recommend counseling, either directly to the person, if they acknowledge the issue, or to HR, if they will not acknowledge it.

When bullying is involved, be it verbal abuse, threatening behavior, or just unnecessary criticism, it is important to support the victim in addition to addressing the perpetrator. Leaders should listen for concerns both formally and informally. We are closer to team members than the senior level and can better spot shifts and pattern changes in behavior.

When someone does something that you feel is disrespectful, have a conversation with them about it (if you feel it is safe to do so). We cannot assume that someone is a bully if we have not told them that their behavior appeared disrespectful, because we have not given them the opportunity to understand our view and the opportunity to change.

We must also walk the talk, treating all stakeholders respectfully and encouraging respectful interactions at all times through all communication channels. We often set the overall tone for workplace behavior, and people are watching us for cues.

We should arrange, support, and attend training, then provide ongoing training on respectful workplace interactions. Having people acknowledge workplace policies during orientation is not enough. Everyone needs to know specific behaviors that are acceptable and unacceptable and be trained in how to handle aggression and bullying when it occurs.

Manipulation and Double-Dealing

These are Machiavellian traits. Manipulative people are skilled at hiding their behavior. They often present one face when it serves them well and then another, altogether different persona when that serves them better.

Look for people who will not take no for an answer, who always have reasons and excuses for their hurtful behavior, or who switch personas to suit their circumstances. Due to their chameleon-like nature, we need to be specific about pointing out what behaviors we have noticed and how they are negatively impacting the team.

Talk to them privately first. If you see behavior that looks manipulative in a meeting, hallway, or desk conversation, try calling out the manipulator in private first. It gives them an opportunity to explain (but be prepared to see a different persona) and change their ways.

If that does not work, call out the behavior publicly to show that it will not be tolerated. This reduces the opportunity for the manipulator to lie or play dumb about the situation. It also shows everyone what is going on and builds allies for additional intervention and support. Follow up with them in private again, clearly explaining how their behavior must change, and consider implementing conduct agreements or performance agreements to hold them accountable.

Manipulators are often driven by insecurity. They are trying to build power through knowledge and connections. They often start out acting friendly with people to learn about them and gain personal information they can potentially use later for their own purposes.

An effective strategy for disarming them of power and influence is to form closer relationships with other people in their network. If the manipulator is a network architect, have lunch with some of the other network architects and the manipulator's boss. Once they see their source of power dwindling, they feel threatened and switch from manipulating others to defending their own career that they believe is linked to their connections and knowledge.

Ultimately, we want offenders to see the greater good of the team members and the organization they work in. Information does not become less valuable as it is shared. Helping others is a more powerful strategy for self-promotion than undermining them—it just takes longer to germinate.

Entitlement and *How Does That Help Me?* Mentality

These are signs of narcissism. There is less to worry about here. Excessive use of *I* and *me* language, as opposed to *us* and *we* language, is a telltale sign that we are dealing with a narcissist, who can upset team harmony and performance.

With big egos often comes denial of fault and an expectation of not being challenged, so it is important to be direct and specific about how their actions are impacting team performance. Confront the perpetrators and explain the impact of their behavior. Come prepared with feedback and recent examples or evidence of their selfish actions. Provide suggestions about how to be more inclusive and supporting and better serve the team.

Follow up with team members to see if they are keeping these characteristics in check. It is unlikely they will transform into selfless servant leaders, so toning their behavior down to tolerable levels is often the best we can hope for.

Chapter 9 Summary

Unfortunately, manipulative, nasty people are part of life. Being aware of the dark-triad traits can help us spot them a little earlier, somewhat negate their impacts, and provide us with some strategies for dealing with them.

The traits include the following: narcissism, characterized by self-love, superiority, dominance, and an inflated view of oneself; Machiavellianism, characterized by a disregard for morals, the use of deception, and cynicism and cunning; and psychopathy, characterized by thrill-seeking, impulsive behavior, aggression, and a lack of empathy and remorse or guilt.

Review the Dirty Dozen categories to see if 'we are surrounded by gullible idiots' (i.e., you are the problem) and, assuming you are not, ask yourself if you see those characteristics exhibited by others. Bullying needs to be dealt with and HR should often get involved. Double-dealing often stems from insecurity, which can be used to rein people in and neutralize their impact.

To be forewarned is to be forearmed. In other words, knowing a little about toxic people can help us avoid them or reduce their impact.

Key topics covered in this chapter:

» Dark-triad traits – Narcissism, Machiavellianism, psychopathy

» Dirty Dozen quiz: Diagnosing your own traits

» Tips for dealing with people who exhibit dark-triad traits

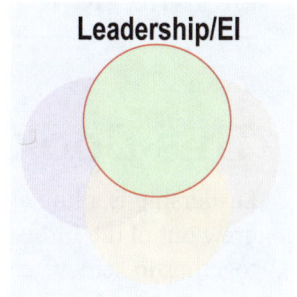

Chapter 10
Leadership

A s we saw at the start of the EQ section, leadership is built on top of EQ and uses it to deliver powerful results. A firm grasp of EQ, either gained intuitively or improved through study or training, brings us to the starting line with engaged, willing stakeholders. Leadership involves bringing this collective willpower to bear on a purpose, a vision, or a journey to our project or product milestone.

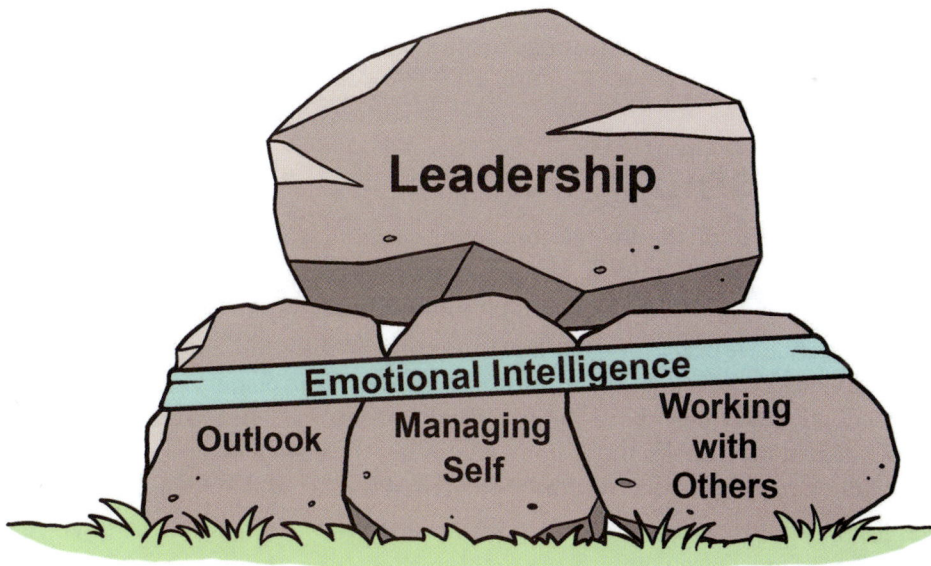

Leadership

Emotional Intelligence

Outlook   **Managing Self**   **Working with Others**

We can create backlogs and release plans all we like but until there is a motivated team with a shared vision of the end goal, it is like trying to push a rope—it is ineffective. Leadership is focused on creating the pull from the team and giving the team the goal and tools to overcome obstacles.

This Book's Focus on Leadership

Leadership is a huge topic. It has been around far longer than project management, which largely grew out of the Industrial Revolution. It goes back as far as people have lived together and worked together to achieve common goals, whether that meant invading a neighboring tribe, traveling to new lands, or building a large structure.

There are over 70,000 published English-language books on leadership. If you read one per day, it would take you 191 years to finish them (by which time there would likely be 70,000 new ones to read). With such a deep history and broad scope, we need a focus to best direct our guidance toward knowledge-worker team execution.

This book takes a product-focused view toward leadership. It concentrates on the leadership traits and steps necessary for building and leveraging high-performing teams in complex knowledge-work environments. Unlike many leadership books available, we will not cover leading companies or even leading organizational change; instead, we will focus on leading projects and programs to deliver business results.

This attention to project execution means the guidance provided is 100 percent applicable to project leads and PMs. However, if you are looking for leadership guidance beyond the project team, then consult some of the recommended reading sources in the Futher Reading section of this book.

So, this book will not teach you all there *is* to know about leadership, but it will teach you all you *need* to know about leadership.

What Leadership Is Not

Unfortunately, there are more myths and misconceptions around what leadership means than any other subject we will cover in this book. So, before we get into how to become a better leader, we should dispel some of these myths that are common barriers to understanding.

The best metaphor I have heard for dispelling leadership myths is the "cowboy leader" by Pinto et al.[1] When we think of a cowboy, we often picture the stock movie character of a lone-wolf type who acts independently and often above the law, thinks on his feet, and saves the day. He cuts through bureaucratic red tape, circles the wagons, and rallies the people to overcome the bad guys. Then our hero rides off into the sunset with the pretty schoolteacher and onto his next adventure.

Yet this is just a movie-star definition of a cowboy, portrayed by the likes of John Wayne, Roy Rogers, and Clint Eastwood. Do you know what a real cowboy does? They lead cows. They use their dogged determination to turn and drive bovine herds toward a desired goal. I am not trying to be derogatory here, comparing your company's staff to unintelligent cows; I am making the point that real cowboys do not typically do a lot of shooting of bad guys and rescuing of damsels in distress.

Also, John Wayne, Roy Rogers, and Clint Eastwood are Hollywood actors, not cowboys. They live in big, fancy houses and do not spend much time around farm animals. Would you really trust them to look after cows? Your cows?

The term *leadership* is often loaded with this romantic notion of a swashbuckling go-getter with a larger-than-life personality. Yet, in reality, some of the best leaders are quiet, introverted people who care deeply for their teams and stakeholders and who quietly grind away toward a common goal.

True leadership is based on sound theory. It can be learned and exercised on a small scale before being brought to bear on larger groups. True leadership is practiced on mundane things, yet when larger events occur, the skills and trust of others can be used to overcome major hurdles.

Additional leadership myths include the beliefs that leadership needs to reside in a single person and that all groups need leaders. Quite often, leadership roles are shared between team members. In fact, it is unlikely that any one person would be solely equipped to lead a team in all circumstances. Establishing environments where people can step up to lead when the need arises creates resilience and competitive advantage. Likewise, some small teams without the need for high-consequence decision-making can operate just fine without a leader.

What Leadership Is

So, having established that leadership is *not* swashbuckling behavior or an innate predisposition of character, let us look at what it *is*. We will first examine the components of leadership: This is the easy stuff of understanding what it is we are trying to achieve. We will then focus on the more difficult topic of how we achieve it, given all the challenges of project constraints, opposing demands, and people conflicts.

Leaders exhibit the following attributes:

» Vision

» Good communication skills

» Ability to inspire trust

» Ability to empower

» Energy and action orientation

» Emotional expressiveness and warmth

» Willingness to take personal risks

» Use of unconventional strategies

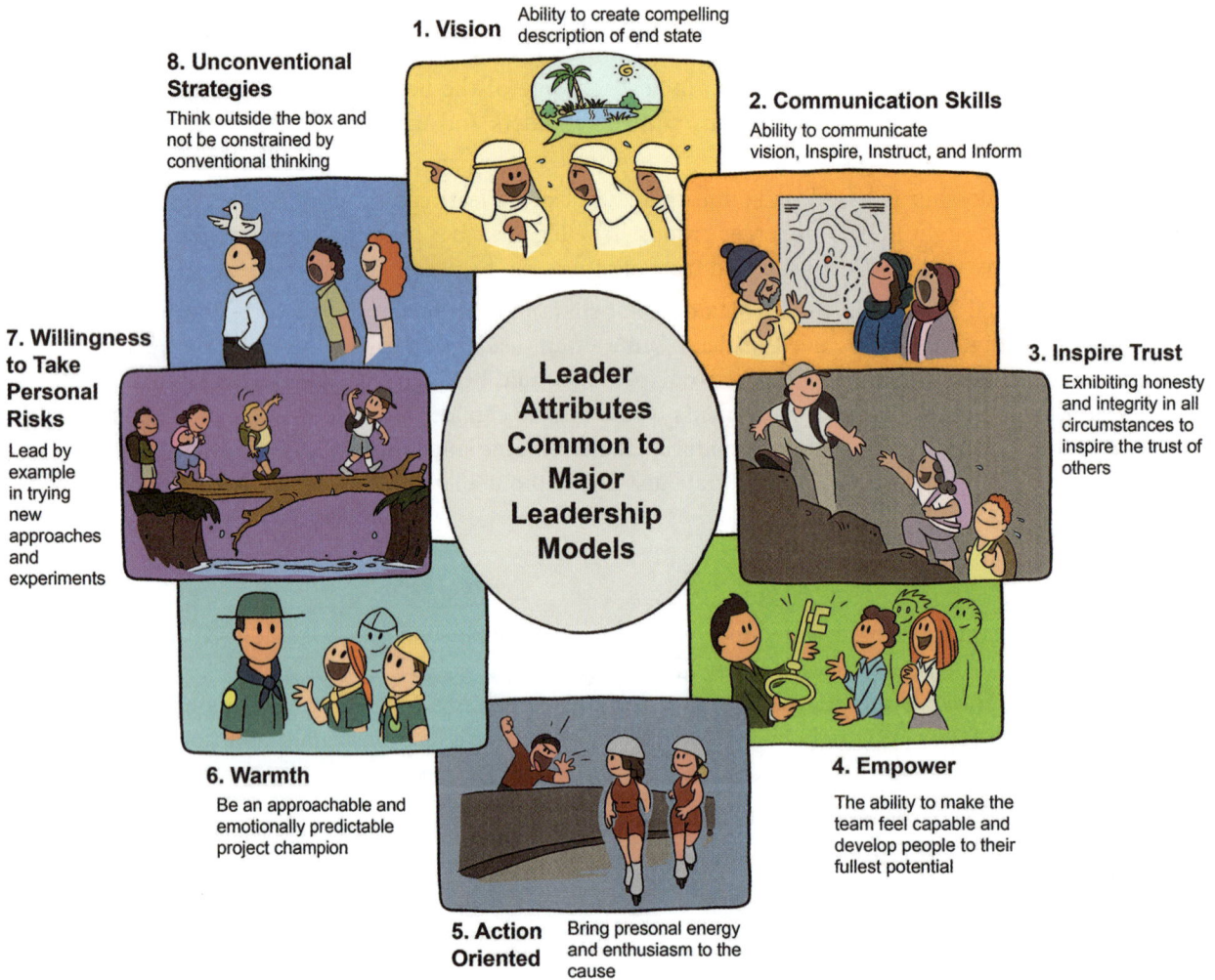

Figure 10.2 *Leadership Attributes Common to Major Leadership Models*

Let us look at each of these characteristics in turn.

Vision The ability to create and describe an exciting view of the future state. This includes what success looks like and the benefits it will bring to the sponsoring organization, the users of the end result, and the team members who created it. It provides a common goal to guide the team in times of questioning and decision-making. It is what we are aiming for.

Good communication skills A vision, support, and guidance are useless unless we have a way to communicate them to people. Communication skills are required to inspire, inform, and advise stakeholders. They are also important for receiving information and being able to quickly build rapport with a wide variety of groups and individuals.

Ability to inspire trust Studies show that the greatest attribute people look for in leaders is honesty and trustworthiness. Working for someone we do not trust undermines our feelings of self-worth and respect in the long run. To be an effective leader, we must act honestly and with integrity—otherwise, people will not work with us.

Ability to empower We should make use of people's knowledge and skills by trusting them to do a good job. We must also be able to make the team feel capable and develop team members to their fullest potential.

Energy and action orientation Effective leaders have elevated levels of energy and enthusiasm for work, which is contagious. We need to understand that it is impossible to inspire others if we are apathetic or lukewarm in our reaction to the challenges at hand.

Emotional expressiveness and warmth Leaders must be able to express their feelings openly, but without venting or alarming people. They should not keep others guessing about their emotional state, but instead be approachable and warm cheerleaders for the endeavor.

Willingness to take personal risks It is desirable to have some skin in the game, to be personally invested beyond just a role, and to have some reputation or repercussion invested in the outcome. Like successful entrepreneurs, leaders are not risk averse.

Use of unconventional strategies Leaders must think creatively and not be constrained by conventional approaches. They are happy to model the desired behavior of trying new approaches and experiments.

These characteristics are the goal; things get more difficult when it comes to the strategies and tactics to achieve these characteristics under challenging circumstances. To start, we need a primer on some leadership theory. As with anything human-nature related, these models are great if they help us improve or gain new insights into behavior. However, when dealing with people, there are always shades of gray and exceptions. So, view these leadership theories as maps to understanding the leadership landscape, but do not expect them to cover every aspect of human nature. When the landscape we are in diverges from the map we are carrying, we must trust the landscape—nobody should drown in a lake that is not supposed to be there!

Leadership Theories Primer

The following outlines of popular leadership theories provide a primer for the main models in use. They are helpful in determining which ideas resonate and for expanding upon our own mental models. They can also be useful when dealing with different stakeholders who do not think like we do. Maybe we can recognize their thought process in one of the models listed, and so better interact with them using concepts they align with.

In the following section, we examine several popular leadership theories. Reading through these descriptions may be a little confusing as we jump from one idea to another. However, understanding these different approaches gives us a tremendous advantage when reviewing leadership recommendations.

There is so much seemingly contradictory guidance on leadership behaviors that many people bounce from one leadership book to the next feeling overwhelmed by the variation. Looking at the theories that underpin leadership broadens our perspective. It allows us to view the recommendations from a higher level of abstraction where we can see how the parts fit together. It also enables us to see how we can combine approaches and improvise our own responses for unique situations that still encourage the best outcomes.

After understanding several agile practices first at a *shu* level, eventually we can rise to *ha* and *ri* levels to create our own rules. So, as you read through these popular theories, try to extract the central theme and key takeaways; we will be bringing these ideas together later to form a generalized leadership framework.

Traits: Nature or Nurture

Great leaders are born, not made. That is one side of the "nature versus nurture" argument. Aristocrats, kings, and noblemen were keen to propagate the idea since they had the most to gain and preserve. Machiavelli's 1532 book *The Prince* argued that "it is better to be feared than loved" and promoted positional power as the way to operate, even if most followers do not appreciate it.

However, the counterargument—that leadership skills can be learned and developed—dates back even further. Chinese general and strategist Sun Tzu suggested, around 500 BC, that leaders need to develop and balance the virtues of:

» Intelligence

» Trustworthiness

» Humaneness

» Courage

» Discipline

Tzu cautioned: "Reliance on intelligence alone results in rebelliousness. Exercise of humaneness alone results in weakness. Fixation on trust results in folly. Dependence on the strength of courage results in violence. Excessive discipline and sternness in command result in cruelty. When one has all five virtues together, each appropriate to its function, then one can be a leader."

Most would agree that some people are born with higher quotients of leadership attributes than others. They have a higher natural predisposition for leading. However, every attribute we have seen listed so far (except, perhaps, intelligence) can be developed and improved.

A related situational question often comes up: Do people create the situations, or do the situations create the people? Winston Churchill was a great wartime leader who united and motivated a country at a time of great stress, but after the war, he struggled to connect with the people and lost support for reelection. Did the leader rise to the occasion and then subsequently fade or did the situation (wartime) allow a suitable leader to emerge? Likely, it is a little of both, but history is littered with leaders who become inconsequential in a new context.

Key Takeaways

- As leaders, we need to exhibit a core set of traits to be trusted, respected, and followed.
- Some circumstances lead to the emergence of suitable leaders.

Trait Theory: Transactional and Transformational Leadership

A common differentiation made between leadership styles is that of transactional versus transformational. Trait theory describes people's view of culture, workers, and their role as a leader.

Transactional leaders believe their job is to get work done within the system. They are people managers who are aiming to get the most work out of employees, who recognize accomplishments, and who encourage contributions toward the end goal. They are not trying to change the world, rock the boat, or mess with the process. The mantra *do the work and manage the system* summarizes their philosophy.

Transformational leaders, on the other hand, focus on improving the whole even if it means shaking things up. In fact, challenging the process and developing people are their main objectives. In doing so, the work should also get done and the capabilities of workers and the organization are improved, allowing more work to get done.

The table below summarizes the differences between the two types of leaders:

Category	Transactional Leader	Transformational Leader
Leadership agenda	Planning and budgeting	Establishing direction
View of workers	McGregor Theory X: Workers are generally lazy and need monitoring	McGregor Theory Y: Workers are generally self-motivated and want to improve
Path-goal approach	Define goals, describe goals, follow procedures, supervise, monitor performance	Define problem, empower team, develop people, challenge the process
View of organizational culture	Work within the culture	Work to improve the culture
Motivation techniques	Carrot-and-stick: Reward achievements and take corrective action for failures	Treat people as if they have already delivered high performance, encourage and promote them
View of change	Responsive	Proactive
View of role	Task oriented	Relationship oriented

Theory X and Theory Y Summary

Douglas McGregor created his Theory X and Theory Y model in 1957, while working at the Massachusetts Institute of Technology (MIT), and further developed it during the 1960s. It describes two ways of thinking about workers and how to motivate them. The first, Theory X (imagine someone with their arms defiantly crossed in opposition), asserts that workers are inherently lazy and will do only the minimum of work required to get paid. They need close supervision and carrot-and-stick motivation to get work done. With an emphasis on controlling, Theory X thinking works best in strict environments such as component assembly, where consistency is important.

The second way of thinking, Theory Y (imagine someone with their arms raised in the air in jubilation, making a *Y* shape), asserts that workers generally enjoy their work and want to expand their skills and capabilities. The best way to motivate them is to support them, elevate them, and give them more responsibilities and freedom.

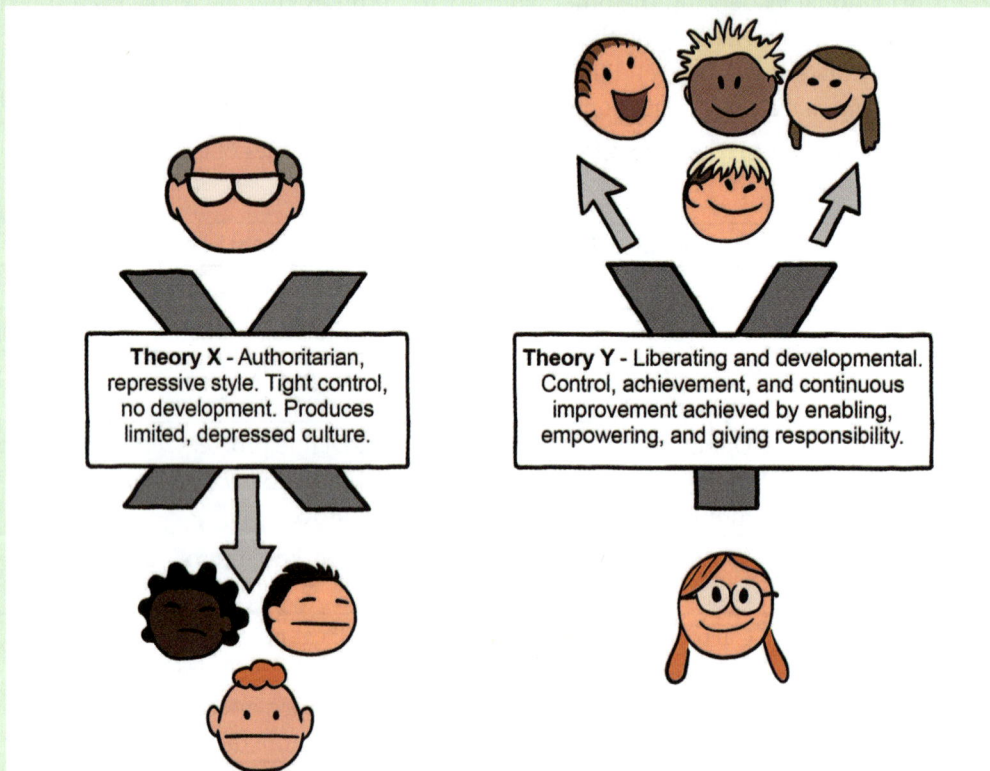

FIGURE 10.3 *Theory X and Y*

An aspect of the model that some people overlook is that rather than seeing the workforce as just two camps, McGregor used the groups to illustrate why contingent leadership is useful. To achieve the best results, a combination of both theories is usually necessary. First, the workforce is examined and then based on where on the Theory X and Theory Y spectrums the groups or individuals reside, management styles are adopted accordingly.

Agile promotes this transformational, servant leadership that can also be described as encompassing the following:

1. Individualized consideration (IC): The leader takes a genuine interest in the needs and feelings of team members. This personal interest is a big factor in bringing out the best efforts of team members.

2. Intellectual stimulation (IS): The leader challenges team members to solve problems, innovate, and improve. Humans are hardwired to receive dopamine rewards for problem-solving and it is a more satisfying way to work.

3. Idealized influence (II): The leader serves as an ideal role model for the team. The leader models the desired behavior and is admired for it.

4. Inspirational motivation (IM): The leader aims to inspire and motivate team members, not direct them.

The transactional versus transformational view of leaders is a useful model for contrasting the command-and-control, "plan the work and work the plan" nature of traditional managers with the more inspirational and empowering nature of servant leaders. However, it is rarely so black and white. People who are new to organizations or leadership roles often start out leaning more toward a transactional view, then move to a more transformational approach once they learn about their role and the organization and gain confidence.

Organizational Fit

In 1990, John Kotter was credited with articulating the overlap and differences between management and leadership. Management copes with complexity by seeking to establish order and consistency, while leadership involves producing organizational change and movement. He showed that it is possible to be a manager without being a leader and vice versa.

I once worked at a large utility company, leading a software-development program. We were successful in our execution, had happy business owners, were taking on new projects, and challenging the process. So, I could not understand why the chief information officer (CIO) was not happy with us. Every process improvement met with resistance and every business endorsement was downplayed or squashed. It turned out that the CIO had plans to outsource the IT department. Our maverick process changing and heightened business engagement were the opposite of the standardized, lower-cost future he was selling to the CEO.

Once the outsourcing was announced, the CIO's behavior made a lot more sense. Until then, it seemed he just had a problem with our program and business group. Our program was transferred, the contract staff (myself included) were let go, and the products we had built were handed over to the new outsourced vendor. Despite producing good transition and support documentation, the sustainment and expansion of the products we had built did not go well with the new vendor. Technically, they were competent, but the business had grown accustomed to working directly with the development team.

The product owner went from requesting a feature one week and seeing it in production the next to submitting change requests and waiting months for them to work their way through approval and development. The business unit created such a fuss that many of the original contractors were hired back to continue development in-house.

It is natural to want to get the lay of the land and understand what you are supposed to be doing before trying to improve things. So, we sometimes see a blending of transactional and transformational approaches, in which people are trusted, empowered, and promoted (transformational) but the processes are followed, at least to begin with (transactional).

Key Takeaways

- Leadership encompasses more than just getting work done within the status quo. It also entails moving the group and/or organization to a better position through challenging and changing the status quo.
- Transactional leaders are more akin to managers. They are task focused and care about the work more than the team members or improvements to process. They plan the work and work the plan by supervising team members. Transformational leaders are more focused on people and culture. They are more proactive about change and empower team members to solve problems.

Motivation Theory: Intrinsic and Extrinsic

In 1959, Frederick Herzberg developed the two-factor theory around job satisfaction and motivation. The two factors are intrinsic (internal) and extrinsic (external). Through experimentation and interviews, he found that people are motivated by intrinsic factors (such as growth, advancement, and achievement) and extrinsic factors (or more like basic hygiene)—people need enough to be satisfied, but they are not motivators by themselves. A failure to address these extrinsic hygiene factors results in demotivation.

If we were to picture these motivators and potential demotivators (when not provided to sufficient levels) as enablers and obstacles in an agile retrospective sailboat chart, they would look as they do in figure 10.4.

Hertzberg's Two-Factor Motivation Theory

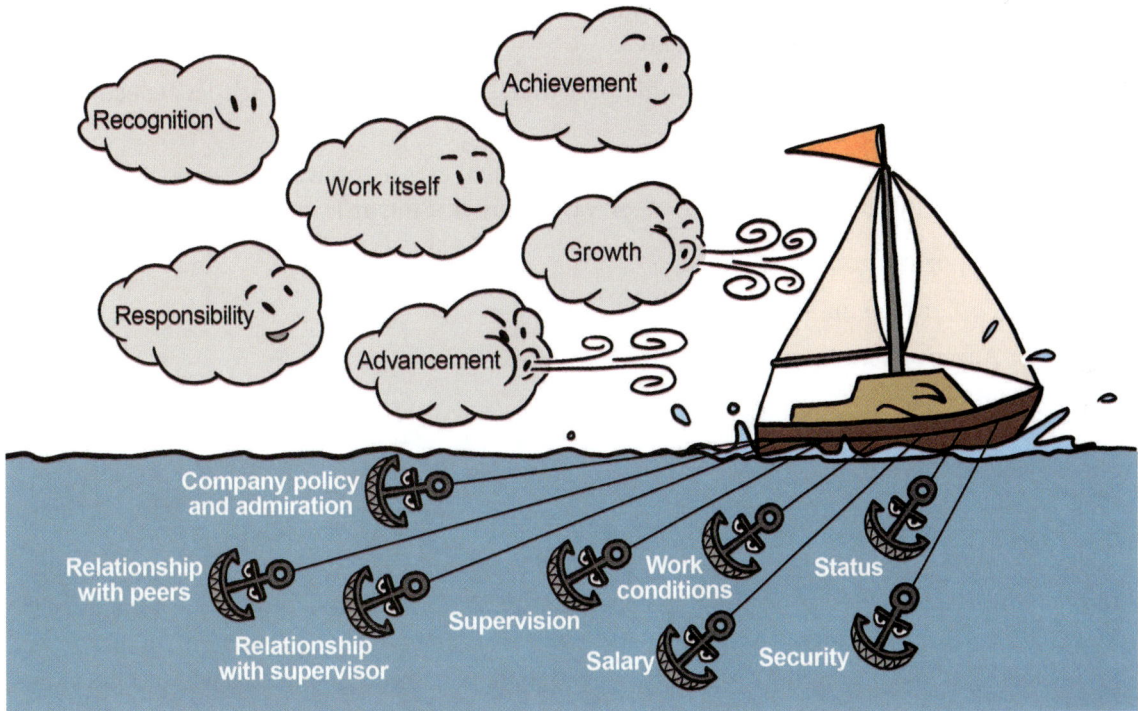

FIGURE 10.4 *Hertzberg's Two-factor Motivation Theory*

People are more strongly motivated by internal, intrinsic feelings of accomplishment, by interesting work, and by the ability to advance in their careers. These factors are depicted as gusts of wind blowing the sailboat forward. We can try to motivate people using external, extrinsic factors such as money and status, but they are not as motivating. At best, they have a net-zero drag on motivation when they are sufficient; more likely, they are potential demotivators when not adequately provided. These factors are depicted above as anchors.

This greater understanding of what motivates people to work to their fullest potential gave rise to different leadership behaviors. Switching from focusing solely on the work at hand to considering the people undertaking the work and their needs is an effective way to improve engagement and results.

Key Takeaways

- People are motivated to try hard and overcome obstacles by both internal (feelings-based) and external (rewards-based) factors.

- The external rewards do have some measurable benefits but are much less effective than internal, intrinsic rewards.

- When creating and working with teams, ensure that extrinsic rewards are met, but focus the most energy on providing a variety of ways to provide intrinsic motivation. These include:

  » Opportunities for growth

  » Recognition for work

  » Advancement in roles and skills

  » Responsibility

  » Interesting work

Behavioral-Styles Theory: Task Focus versus People Focus

As mentioned in the EI section, leaders must balance production and production capability (P versus PC balance). From a leadership perspective, this means having concern for both task performance and people's well-being. Leaders need to understand the project needs and the team-member needs, then act for the welfare of both the people and the project.

Leaders with a strong concern for the human aspect spend more energy helping team members meet their personal goals, improving their quality of life, and creating a safe, comfortable work environment. Leaders with a strong concern for production are output-oriented and tend to focus on increasing efficiency and meeting performance and quality goals.

Often, leaders emphasize one trait over another. When we are more skilled in one category and weaker in another, we are less likely to venture into our weaker domain. Some people will not crack the whip for fear of upsetting people. Others will be task focused and unable to summon much concern for the well-being of team members; through fear of intrusion or overstepping professional boundaries, they may appear indifferent to team-member feelings and aspirations. These traits are illustrated in figure 10.5.

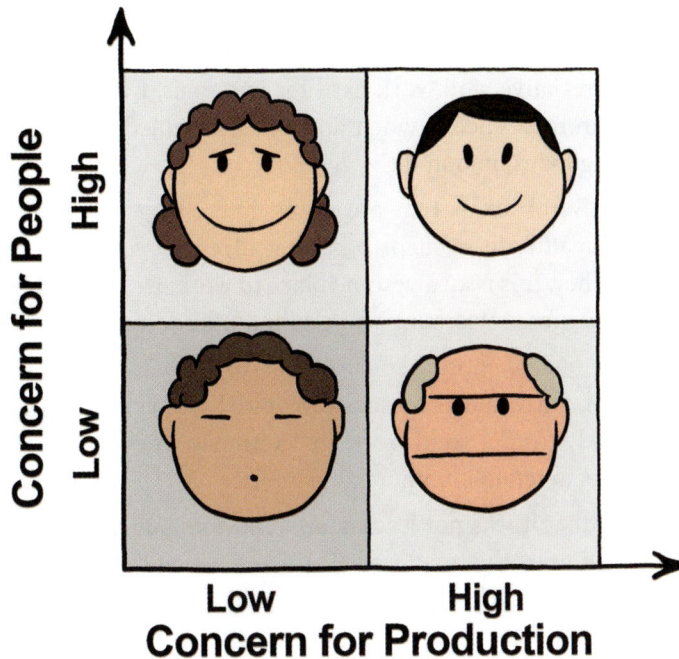

FIGURE 10.5 *Task Focus and People Focus*

Leaders with low concern for either tasks or people are apathetic and likely in the wrong career. A high concern for production but low concern for people describes a tyrant, who just wants to get the most out of teams and does not care about people's long-term development or well-being. This class of leader, once popular, is increasingly threatened by a more mobile workforce in which people are happier to change jobs. The other extreme shows high concern for people but low concern for production. This type of leader is all about personal development and happiness but does not care so much about output.

The optimal position is a balanced one, reflecting a high concern for both people and production; here, the needs of the project and workforce are respected and optimized. The trouble is that when we have a weakness in one area, it is often because we are blind to it or poor at assessing our abilities in it. Assessment surveys that incorporate 360-degree feedback from colleagues can help determine where people fit and then steer them toward addressing imbalances.

From our BAM perspective, it is important to understand the need for this balance. It not only addresses our goal of maximizing output and developing capabilities in people but also addresses the concept of focusing on the goal while optimizing the whole. When we examine agile-related frameworks, we can see elements of each approach.

Jurgen Appelo's "management for happiness" concept, outlined in his book *Management 3.0*, involves a high concern for people. He argues that if we make the work environment great, people will enjoy their role, be appreciative, and work hard for our goals. I think there is a lot of merit to this idea: people do perform much better when appreciated, valued, and supported. I also think there needs to be a balancing focus on output.

I have worked with several teams that are doing interesting technical work in a pleasant working environment. Their attitude seemed to be that if results got delivered that day, it was a bonus; if they did not, then, hey, this is an awesome place to work, we are learning lots and we get to come back tomorrow and do more interesting work with our buddies.

If I am honest, I was one of those people earlier in my career, working on cutting-edge technology projects for IBM, surrounded by smart people. I was excited to turn up for work and learn new skills. We definitely need a good work environment, but we also need strong direction and accountability for results to retain commercial viability.

Researchers suggested that it was not leadership behaviors but the ability of leaders to adapt their style to the needs of followers that mattered. This led to situational-leadership theory.

Key Takeaways

- When undertaking project work, we need to balance concern for the people involved with concern for the tasks at hand.
- While day-to-day focus may change based on circumstances, an ongoing deficiency in either area will be harmful.

Situational Theories:
Adaptive Leadership/Situational Leadership

Situational-leadership theory suggests that leaders should adopt a type of leadership that depends on the situation at hand. While this seems sensible, our ability to switch leadership styles depends on our understanding of and fluency in different situations and models. A common framework for situational leadership is Hersey and Blanchard's grid model that follows the forming, storming, norming, and performing phases of team development described by Bruce Tuckman. These stages are followed by a disengagement phase called *adjourning* or *mourning*, since people often miss being on a high-performing team after it has been disbanded.

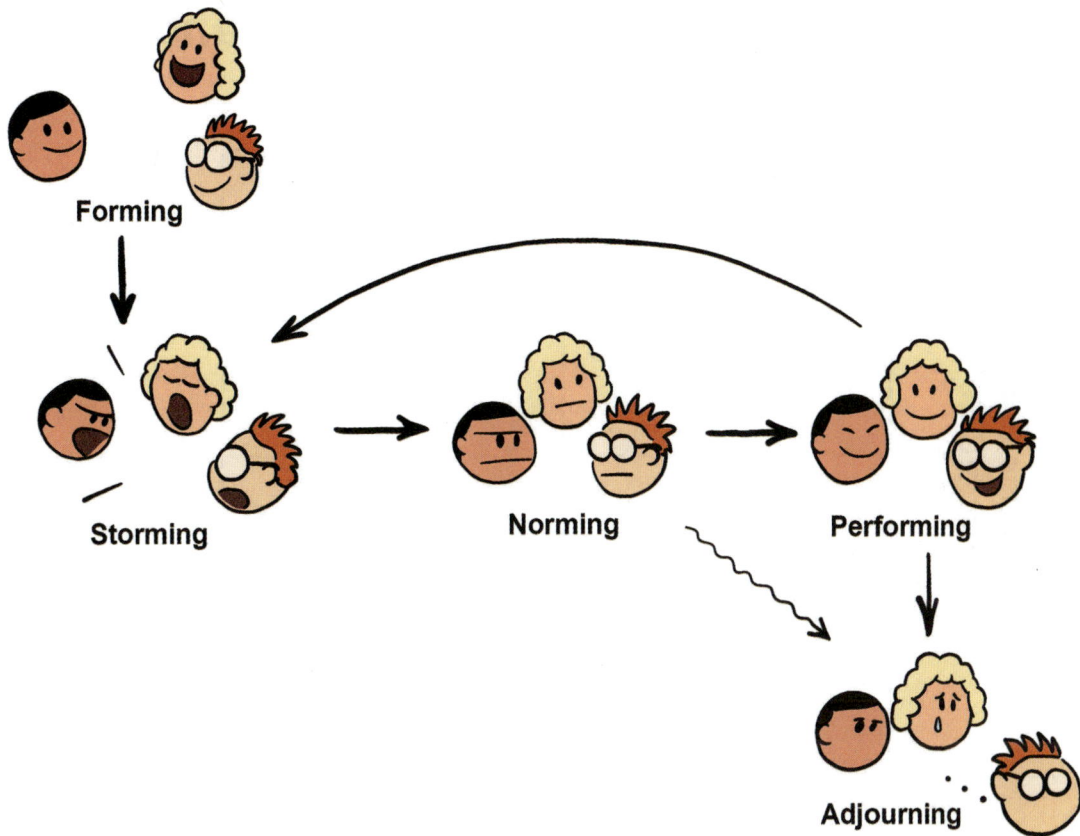

FIGURE 10.6 *Framework for Team Development*

In the forming stage, people come together as a team, then there is some turmoil, or storming, as people learn to work together. In the norming stage, the team normalizes, becoming comfortable in their roles and relationships. Eventually, they become a highly functional, or performing, team that works effectively together.

As depicted in figure 10.6, a team may cycle through storming, norming, and performing multiple times. This is likely to happen whenever there are changes to the project team, such as people leaving or joining the group. Each time, the team members have to reset and sort out their roles, relationships, and responsibilities within the new structure.

If we superimpose these phases onto a grid that shows a relationship focus and empowerment focus, we get what is depicted in figure 10.7.

Team Phases by Relationship and Empowerment Focus

Leader's Use of Relationship-Oriented Behavior

High

A **pseudo team** that is challenging each other and developing into a potential team

A **potential team** that is working with each other and developing into a real team

STORMING

NORMING

FORMING

PERFORMING

Low

Adjourning / Mourning

A **working group** that is learning about each other

A **real team** that is working as one and becoming a high-performing team

Low   **High**

Leader's Use of Empowerment

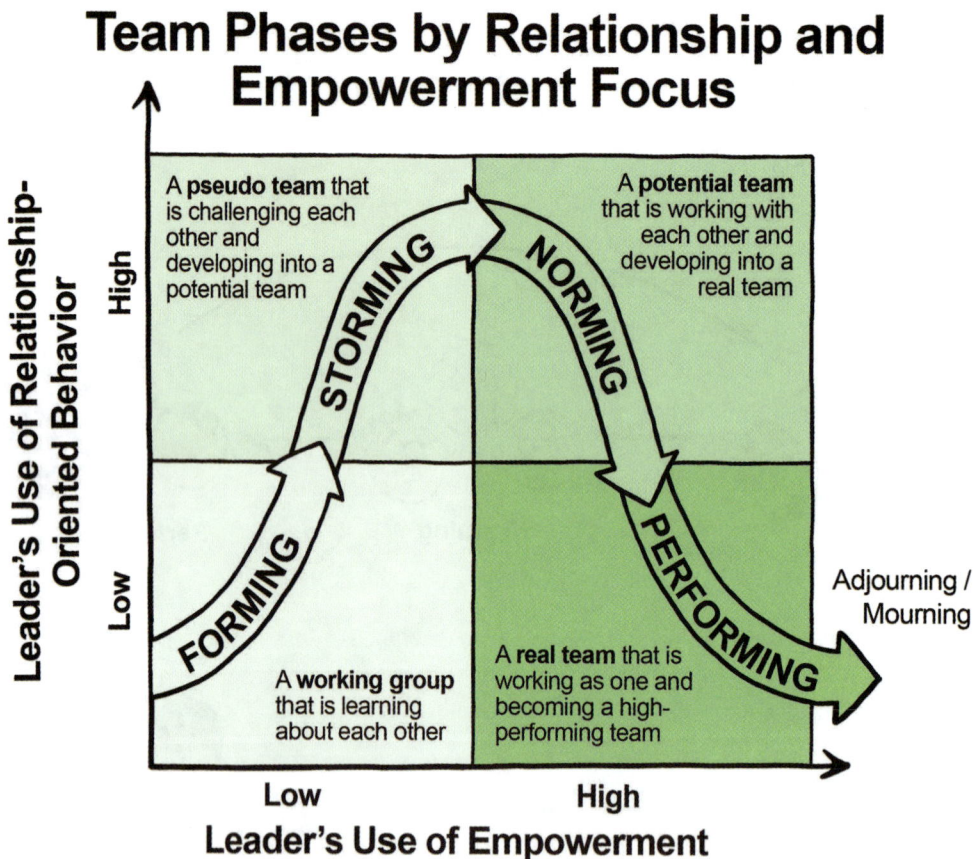

FIGURE 10.7 *Team Phases by Relationship and Empowerment Focus*

In this depiction of the model, a team starts in the lower-left quadrant (forming) as they learn about each other. Next, they move through storming, where they challenge each other, and norming, where they learn how to work together. Finally, they arrive at the performing stage, where they can start working as one to reach their full potential. In other words, we typically start a project with a collection of people who are a working group rather than a real team. During storming, we have a pseudo team, which transforms into a potential team during norming, and finally becomes a real team once they reach the performing stage.

It seems so neat and clean to define the stages of team formation like this. Does that mean all teams go through these phases in a predictable way? No—each team is different. The people who make up the team and factors such as whether any of the team members have previously worked together will affect the way in which a team moves through the stages.

This brings us to another question: Do teams progress as a whole unit through the stages? Not really. People and teams are complex and messy. As leaders, the best we can do is be aware of these models, look for signs that the team is in a particular phase, and then act accordingly. These general pointers can be useful, but we should never expect a team to proceed in an orderly fashion and follow the stereotypical stages.

Now that we have discussed Tuckman's model, we can turn to the concept of situational leadership. Blanchard and Hersey identified four leadership styles: directing, coaching, supporting, and delegating. Tuckman's stages of development can be mapped to Blanchard and Hersey's styles of leadership as shown in figure 10.8.

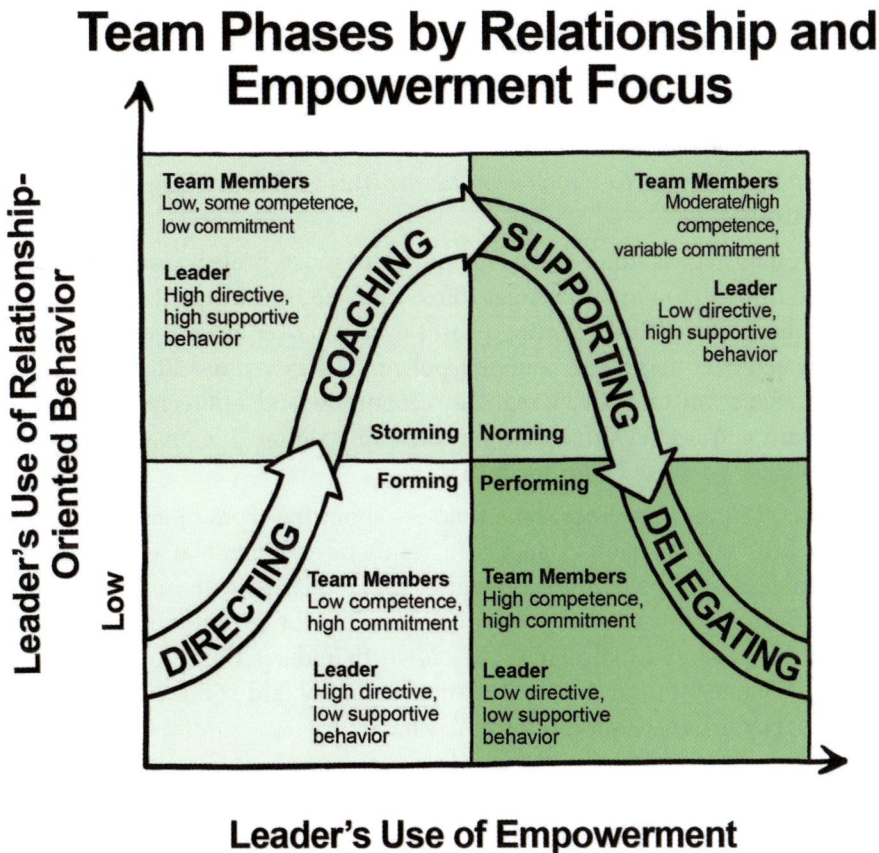

Team Phases by Relationship and Empowerment Focus

Leader's Use of Relationship-Oriented Behavior

COACHING

Team Members
Low, some competence,
low commitment

Leader
High directive,
high supportive
behavior

SUPPORTING

Team Members
Moderate/high
competence,
variable commitment

Leader
Low directive,
high supportive
behavior

Storming | Norming

Forming | Performing

DIRECTING

Team Members
Low competence,
high commitment

Leader
High directive,
low supportive
behavior

Team Members
High competence,
high commitment

Leader
Low directive,
low supportive
behavior

DELEGATING

Low

Leader's Use of Empowerment

FIGURE 10.8 *Team Phases by Relationship and Empowerment Focus*

Starting in the lower-left quadrant, we can see that Tuckman's forming stage corresponds to Blanchard and Hersey's directing style. Early in a team's formation, the role of the team leader is to directly help with project activities and present a clear, tactical picture of what needs to be done. The leader may also make a lot of requests, such as *Help me see it*, or ask questions, such as *Where is the problem?* to assist team members in identifying and articulating the issues.

As the team passes into the storming phase, there will generally be plenty of disagreement, open conflict, and harsh dialogue. During this stage, the leader needs to assume the coaching style to help team members resolve conflicts without damaging relationships. Keep in mind that some conflict is good, so we do not want to mollycoddle the team too much. Let the disputes occur, but act as a referee or safety valve to ensure the conflict does not go too far.

When the team reaches the norming phase, the members have successfully created rules (team norms) to help govern themselves. This does not mean the team leader can simply go into cruise-control mode, however. Instead, the leader needs to play a supporting role. The team will still need help with conflict resolution, as well as reminders to enforce the norms they have created. This is a good time for the leader to challenge the team with high-level goals such as *The team is responsible for tracking velocity on the project* or *Everyone owns testing*. This is also an appropriate time to tackle the issues raised at retrospectives.

The final performing stage is not a given—many, if not most, project teams never reach this phase because they go through too many changes (often initiated by the organization), which sends them back to repeat the storming and norming phases over and over again. Performing teams are autonomous, empowered, self-managing, and self-policing. They require little more than to be pointed in the right direction and given regular recognition and appreciation for their high performance. Blanchard and Hersey's delegating leadership style for this phase means the leader brings work and challenges to the team for them to solve.

The model is useful since it provides some pointers about the types of activities or emphasis that leaders should focus on at various stages of a team's development. It is also quite a blunt instrument. Often, the team may be in a storming or norming phase, yet an individual on the team may be in need of directive or delegating type help that is not in line with the broad-brush recommendation for that phase. So, like all models, it is worth understanding, but not basing all our judgments on. It is an input into our evaluation engine: It may add some credit to a particular choice, but should not be the only way we determine what to do.

Key Takeaway

» Situational leadership recognizes that people need different types of support and direction at various stages of a project

» By understanding the likely needs of a team during its formation and maturity, leaders can adapt the styles to be most useful and productive.

Functional Theories: Leadership Practices

There are a couple of popular theories based on what good leaders do. The most popular one relating to knowledge work is Kouzes and Posner's five practices of exemplary leadership, described in their best-selling book, *The Leadership Challenge*.[2]

After interviewing over 75,000 participants to determine what leaders do and what attributes describe the best leaders, they defined five leadership behaviors:

1. Model the way: Demonstrate the desired behavior in your actions and communications. Clarify your personal values and find your voice to express yourself. Set an example by aligning actions with values.

2. Inspire a shared vision: Describe a beckoning summit toward which others can chart their own course. Be forward-looking and envision the future as an exciting and worthy destination. Develop a shared sense of destiny. Enlist others in a common vision by appealing to shared aspirations.

3. Challenge the process: Improve, grow, and further the capabilities of the team and individuals. Innovate, create, and look outward for fresh ideas. Search for opportunities by seeking innovative ways to grow, change, and improve. Experiment and take risks by constantly generating small wins and learning from mistakes.

4. Enable others to act: Support and facilitate the growth of team members. Foster collaboration by promoting cooperative goals and building trust. Support face-to-face interactions. Strengthen others by sharing power and discretion. Promote competence, confidence, and self-leadership. Foster accountability and generate power all around.

5. Encourage the heart: Provide frequent recognition and thanks. Expect the best and pay attention to results. Recognize contributions by showing appreciation for hard work. Celebrate the values and victories by creating a spirit of community.

Kouzes and Posner's research has spanned over thirty years, six continents, and 1.3 million survey respondents. They ask what people look for and admire in leaders; given a choice of twenty attributes, the same four repeatedly emerge as the most significant. In order of significance, they are:

Honest

Forward-looking

Competent

Inspiring

1. Honest: The single most important ingredient for an admired and effective leader is honesty. No one wants to be lied to or misled. In fact, knowingly following a dishonest leader erodes our feelings of self-respect and self-regard. It makes us feel bad and we will not willingly do so for long,

2. Forward-looking: Leaders must know where they are going if they expect others to join them on that journey. This is not some magical vision, but a down-to-earth view of a desirable destination, revealing a beckoning summit toward which others can chart their own course.

3. Competent: Effective leaders are competent enough to guide us and have a track record of getting things done. They should have a good understanding of the technological and market sector, but not necessarily one superior to the technical expertise they call upon. They should also have experience leading groups in this field.

4. Inspiring: Admired leaders are enthusiastic, energetic, and positive about the future. Their emotions are contagious. After all, if the leader displays no passion for the cause, why should anyone else?

Grounded first in credibility and honesty, leaders use the behaviors of modeling the way, inspiring a shared vision, challenging the process, enabling others to act, and encouraging the heart to build high-performing teams and deliver results.

Key Takeaways

» The act of developing a uniting vision is powerful for gathering consensus and aligning efforts toward a common goal.

» By challenging the process and enabling and encouraging team members, leaders can leverage the stronger intrinsic motivators of opportunity for growth, recognition for work, advancement in skills, and responsibility.

» Certain personality traits are necessary in order for team members to trust and follow a leader. Understanding and modeling these desired behaviors will lead to better acceptance and improved likelihood of success.

Chapter 10 Summary

Leadership builds on EI. Without a strong EQ base, our leadership will be unstable. Leadership is often misrepresented; it is not acting like the charismatic hero portrayed in movies, but rather the ability to:

» Describe and convey a vision

» Apply good communication skills

» Inspire trust

» Empower others

» Provide energy and action orientation

» Be emotionally expressive and warm

» Exhibit a willingness to take personal risks

» Use unconventional strategies

Leadership can be a combination of nature and nurture. Often, effective leaders emerge during a crisis. All effective leaders understand how to motivate people, having knowledge of intrinsic and extrinsic motivators and recognizing that workers have task- and people-focus preferences.

Lastly, we examined situational-leadership styles that vary based on the project phase or team need, and functional theories of leadership that get to the heart of what leaders actually do.

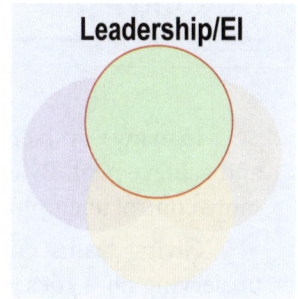

Chapter 11
Servant Leadership

Servant leadership is often referenced as a preferred approach on agile projects. ScrumMasters are encouraged to perform servant leadership roles for the team.

The concept of leaders serving followers is timeless and can be found in the teachings of the *Tao Te Ching* (550 BC) and in nearly every religion. The phrase *servant leadership* was coined by Robert Greenleaf in 1970 and used to describe a philosophy and set of leadership practices. It involves flipping the power pyramid, so instead of the team working to serve the leader, the leader works to support the team.

Team members serve team leader **Team leader serves team members**

Servant leadership is the opposite of autocratic (centralized) power, concerned instead with participative sharing of power. It encourages the development of people's abilities and potential, uses participative decision-making, and aims to satisfy employees. Servant leaders are focused on how to better serve others, not increase their own power.

In many ways, servant leadership makes use of the intrinsic motivators of growth, advancement, and achievement. By emphasizing these factors, employee engagement is greatly increased. Giving more control to employees is another powerful motivator.

Giving teams control over their work (autonomy), when coupled with encouraging and preserving flow, goes a long way to improving motivation and productivity. Daniel Pink, author of *Drive: The Surprising Truth About What Motivates Us*, popularized the work of motivation researchers Deci, Ryan, and Grant and explains why traditional if-then, carrot-and-stick-type rewards do not work in the long run.

Pink cites several MIT studies in which adults and children were rewarded for conducting work, hobbies, and play activities. Once the reward was removed, people stopped doing these activities, even if they had previously been happy to do them voluntarily. Once tainted by if-then rewards, the motivation evaporated.

Pink asserts that the common if-then, extrinsic motivation used by many corporations is flawed and needs an upgrade. Hence the need for and rise of a new form of motivation based on:

» Autonomy

» Mastery

» Purpose

Autonomy means giving people control over how they work. This includes the following aspects:

» Task: The work, and how they undertake it

» Time: When they choose to work in the day, week, or year

» Technique: How and where they perform tasks

» Team: How they organize, interact, and collaborate together

Mastery comes from:

» Flow: Having the time, space, and freedom to find and exercise your passion for a profession.

» Goldilocks tasks: Not too difficult and not too easy, but just right. We need enough Goldilocks tasks to stretch, engage, and indulge our desire for completion and satisfaction.

» Mindset of learning: People who believe intelligence and knowledge are not fixed capabilities we are endowed with, but rather a muscle or skill we can grow. People who are happy to face their limitations and who continually find new learning opportunities more easily achieve mastery.

Purpose describes tapping into people's belief that there should be more to work than just making money and being successful. It involves aligning company goals with people's aspirations for doing good and meeting a higher guiding principle.

This is why companies such as TOMS have been successful; for every pair of shoes sold, they give away a pair to those in developing countries. Buyers feel good because their purchase has a charitable impact and the workers at TOMS feel good because they are doing more than just generating shareholder value, by tapping into their motivation principle of a compelling purpose.

Motivation for Agile Teams

The good news is that agile teams are halfway toward providing autonomy. The stepping-stone to autonomy that empowered teams have provides a huge leg-up on those people caught in command-and-control hierarchies.

Agile teams already have good autonomy over task, technique, and some aspects of team. Time, the remaining component of autonomy, is seeing some progress too. Kanban approaches that are being adopted by agile teams have a more pragmatic view of iteration structures and scheduled meetings. If these time structures add value, then go ahead and use them; if they do not, then try using more of a pull model of task selection and work scheduling. This not only removes delays and eliminates waste, but also affords the team more autonomy over their time.

Some agile organizations go further and allow 20 (or 10) percent of time for pursuing new ideas and experiencing the joy of flow (being in the groove, doing work you love). These one-day-a-week (or half-day-a-week) opportunities for self-directed work provide more autonomy and an opportunity to experience work mastery and pursue a goal with a purpose (perhaps for a good cause).

A component from Adam Grant's original research on motivation that Pink does not address in his *Drive* book is relatedness. Relatedness refers to the desire to avoid letting down or disappointing other members of the team. Feeling that your work is connected to others' efforts and that you are part of something bigger than yourself creates a powerful sense of affiliation. Appreciation and a sense of support from colleagues is a powerful motivator. We do not want to let others down, so when we know others are looking out for us, we appreciate that and, in return, have a tendency to try harder.

Returning to the servant-leadership theme, Larry Spears, a former president of the Greenleaf Center for Servant Leadership, lists ten characteristics of a servant leader:

» Empathy

» Awareness

» Listening

» Foresight

» Conceptualization

» Persuasion

» Stewardship

» Commitment to the growth of others

» Healing

» Building community

Key Takeaways

- Servant-leadership principles reinforce the significance of empowering team members to do their work and providing intrinsic motivation.

- Daniel Pink and others are finding practical ways to reinforce Theory Y views of team members (smart, diligent) and the importance of focusing on intrinsic motivation.

Shared Leadership: Primary Colours® Model

The Primary Colours Model of leadership was one of the first to recognize that it is extremely difficult, if not impossible, for any individual to possess all the attributes needed to be a complete leader. Instead, it recommends leaders build leadership teams that comprise all the necessary skills.

The Primary Colours Model offers ideas similar to those found in "In Praise of the Incomplete Leader," a 2007 paper published in the *Harvard Business Review*. Its authors suggest that successful leadership comprises four capabilities:

1. Sensemaking: Understanding the context of the company and how people operate. Having a talent or knack for explaining these complexities to others.

2. Relating: Being able to build trusting relationships with others.

3. Visioning: Creating compelling images of the future by collaborating with others on what they want and then explaining it.

4. Inventing: Developing new ways to bring the vision to life.

The Primary Colours Model contains three intersecting domains of strategy, operations, and interpersonal skills. It also uses a human-anatomy metaphor to explain these functions and how they interact. The strategic domain is like the head, responsible for thinking; the operational domain is the hands and legs, responsible for getting things done and moving the organization or product forward; and the interpersonal domain is the heart and deals with forming relationships, motivation, and EI.

These domains and functions are shown in figure 11.2.

The Primary Colors of Leadership

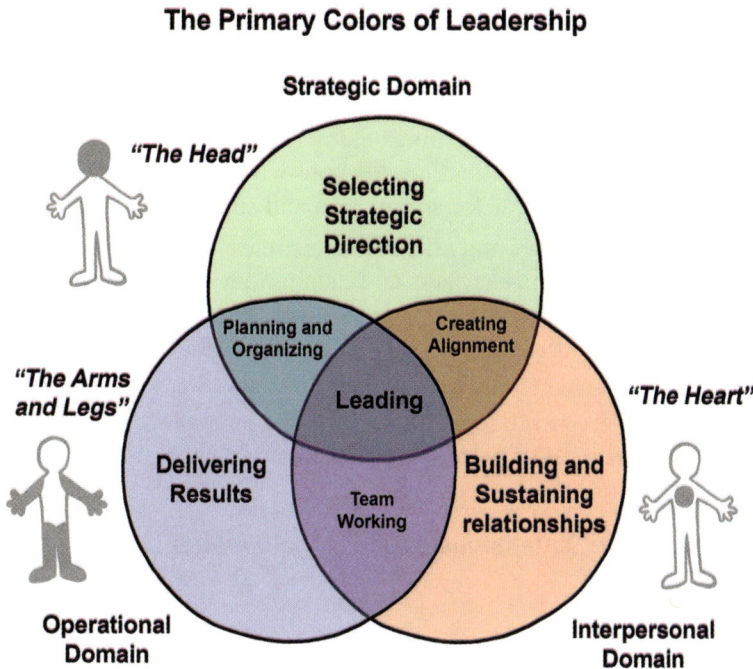

FIGURE 11.2 *The Primary Colours Model of Leadership*

In this human-anatomy analogy, the Primary Colours Model places *leading* at the center, like a central nervous system. It senses, balances, and coordinates all the other functions.

At the intersection of these overlapping functions are three key roles of a leader. Creating alignment is at the intersection of strategy (head) and interpersonal (heart) since it deals with creating a rational and emotional commitment. Team working, the skill of getting things done, is at the intersection of operational (arms and legs) and interpersonal (heart) since it deals with work and motivation. Finally, planning and organizing is at the intersection of strategic (head) and operational (arms and legs) since it deals with planning the work that needs to be done.

Now we know what functions need to happen and that it is unlikely that any single person has all the necessary skills. So, the next logical step is to assess our own skills, recognize our gaps, and go find people with the skills to fill those gaps. This is another instance where having diversity on the team is helpful. Diversity is Darwinian: The greater the diversity in the resource pool, the greater the range of external events that can be responded to successfully.

> Tom Peters, author of *In Search of Excellence*, once joked, "If you find anyone in your organization who agrees with everything you say, fire them! Why pay twice for the same opinions?"

So, diversity is good, but how do we measure it? A simple approach is to assess people's affinity for or attraction to work types. Vocation-planning tools used in schools try to determine likely "fit" by assessing people on two ranges. The first range is things or people, and asks if individuals are happier working with things (be they animal, vegetable, mineral, or machine) or happier working with people. People who are interested in things enjoy collecting, constructing, and categorizing them, and analyzing them and their functions. People who prefer people enjoy emotions and idiosyncrasies; they are drawn to people for stimulation and support.

The second range is data or ideas, and asks if people prefer working with data and facts or with ideas and possibilities. People who prefer facts and data tend to be practical, data-analytics types. They are persuaded by logical, here-and-now facts and data. People who are drawn to ideas, possibilities, and theories enjoy what-if scenarios and are divergent thinkers. They may be thought of as creatives or dreamers.

Assessing people on these two ranges helps us determine where we fit and where others on our teams fit. The ranges and categories of preferences are shown in figure 11.3.

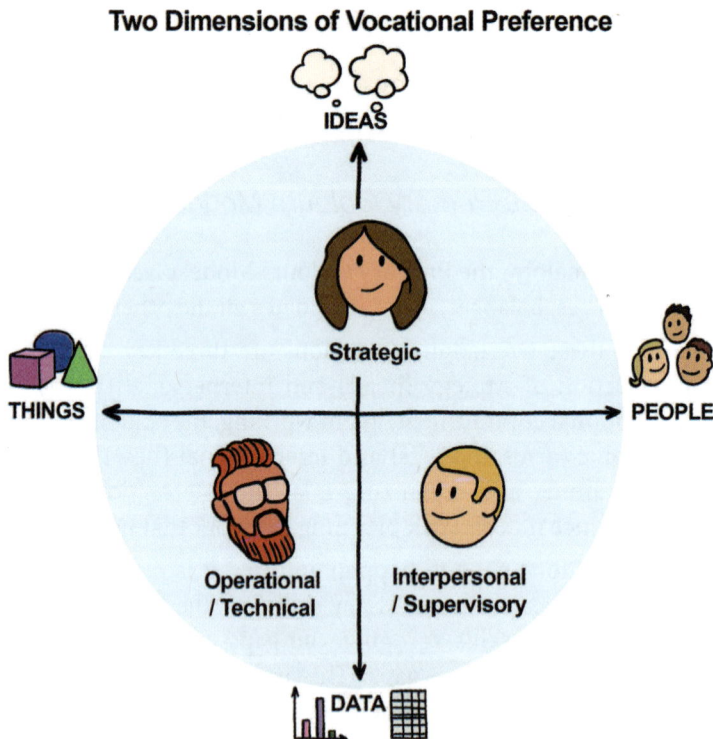

FIGURE 11.3 *Two Dimensions of Vocational Preference*

Here we see three roles and their positioning based on work preference. Position A, strategic, indicates someone who leans more toward the *ideas* end of the data-to-ideas spectrum and who is happy dealing with ambiguity. Position B, operational/technical, shows someone who leans more toward the *data* end of the data-to-ideas spectrum and toward the *things* end of the things-to-people range. Finally, position C, interpersonal/supervisory, shows someone who is more comfortable with people than things and who prefers data over ideas.

Incidentally, full personality assessments such as Myers-Briggs, Belbin, or the Big Five typically take about an hour or so to administer. But having team members indicate where on this chart they rate themselves is quick and makes a great retrospect or team-building exercise to illustrate and respect diversity.

In figure 11.3, it is difficult for people to move between these roles as it requires major shifts in focus and interests. The nearer people are toward the center, the easier it will be for them to move into each of these roles.

Combining the Primary Colours Model of leadership with these personality traits reveals additional useful ways to categorize the functions and roles of leadership. Figure 11.4 shows the two models superimposed.

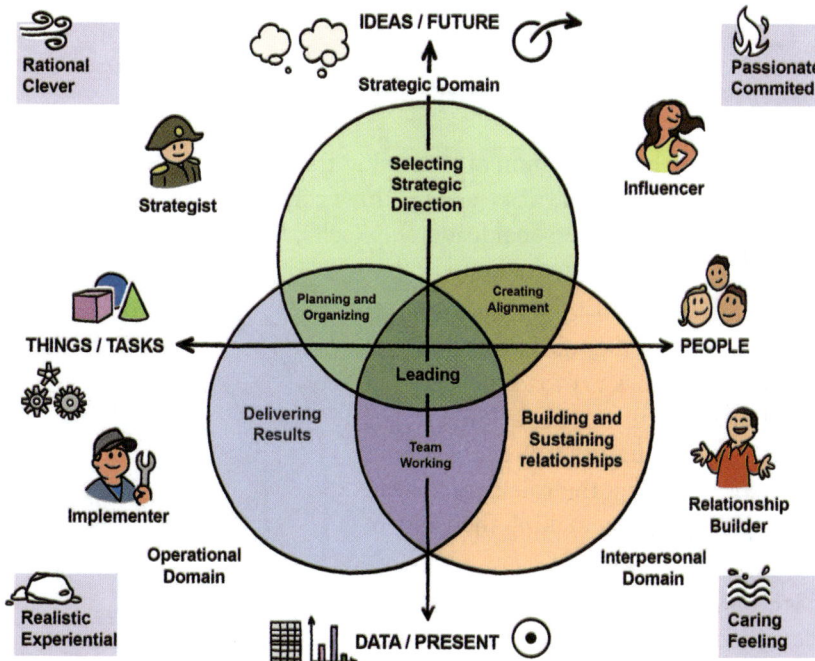

FIGURE 11.4 *Primary Colours Model Combined with Personality Traits*

Here we see the two job-preference dimensions of *things/tasks* to *people* on the x-axis and data/present to ideas/future on the y-axis. Also shown are ovals representing the personality traits of the people who operate well in that domain and boxes representing the classical elements of air, fire, earth, and water.

The Primary Colours Model is powerful for several reasons. First, it legitimizes the idea of shared leadership and the need for collecting a set of competencies from the team and distributing power. Second, the human-anatomy metaphor creates an easily understood structure for uniting the skills and functions necessary for leadership, which are often described as discrete, unconnected, or vaguely connected elements in other models. Finally, it aligns well with vocational preference models and work types.

Key Takeaways

- Leadership can be shared.
- People have distinct preferences for dealing with things or people, hard facts or ideas.
- Holistic leadership needs to address all these dimensions.

Shared Leadership: Three Levels of Leadership

The most recent and talked-about evolution of leadership theory is James Scouller's Three Levels of Leadership. This model defines the role of a leader as three concentric circles radiating outward like ripples on a pond. At the center is personal leadership (self), then private leadership (one-on-one with others), then public leadership (with groups).

At the center, the personal-leadership level is concerned with understanding the role of a leader and gaining the individual skills necessary to lead effectively. The Three Levels of Leadership model acknowledges that the leader does not have to perform every role in the leadership repertoire and that the role may instead be shared between several people, making the most of individual strengths.

The model is clear about the fact that a leader's role is to ensure leadership occurs. In other words, while no one person may have all the necessary skills to be a whole and rounded leader, somebody is required to

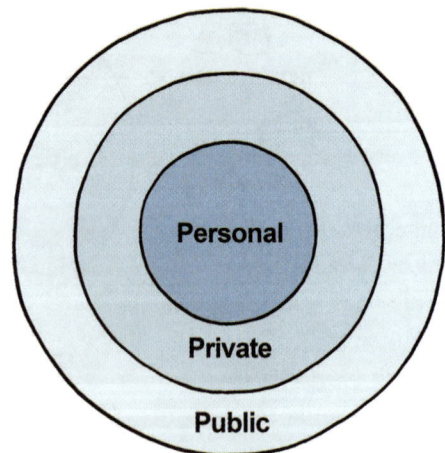

make sure whole and rounded leadership occurs, either through one or many people. As such, it separates the leader from the role of leadership. Leadership is all the activities that need to occur for a group to perform. The leader is someone tasked with ensuring that all these activities occur, even though it is unlikely that they will be performing all the tasks themselves.

Scouller defines leadership (all the stuff that needs to happen) with a four-quadrant diagram similar to the Primary Colours Model.

Leadership's Four Dimensions

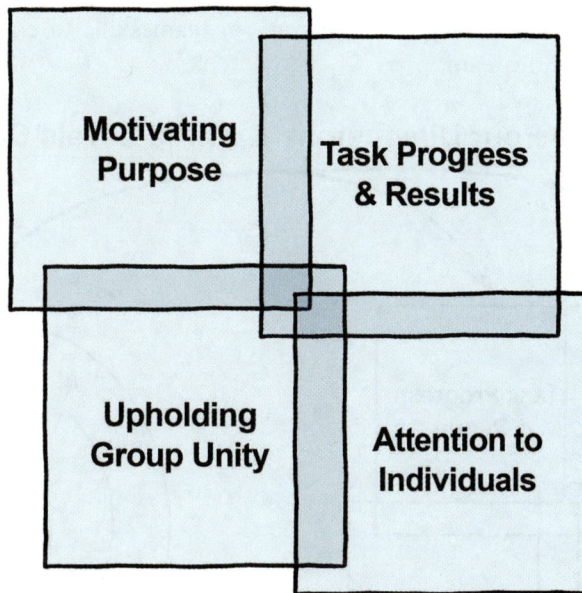

The four quadrants overlap because they are interrelated and support each other. The motivating purpose aligns with the vision component of other leadership models. When leaders focus too much on task progress and results, they are managing but not really leading. We do need the management function, so paying attention to task progress and results is important, but it is not enough on its own. Likewise, leaders will not be successful if they omit group unity or attention to individuals.

The main distinction between this model and the Primary Colours one is the addition of the *upholding group unity* function. It is different from the Primary Colours Model's *building and sustaining relationships* trait in that it speaks more about the sense of team and community than respect for individuals.

Scouller provides a nice example to illustrate that the role of the leader is to ensure leadership occurs. He asks us to imagine that a leader and their team are traveling in a small plane that crash-lands on a desert island. The leader asks the group if anyone has survival training; one person explains they were in the Army Reserve and have had survival training. The leader says, "You take charge of survival for the moment. What do we need to do first?" In this scenario, the leader does not pretend to be some all-knowing expert, but rather enlists the skills of those best fit to help. They ensure that leadership occurs in all four dimensions but leverage the unique skills within the team.

The realization that there is no one way to be a leader should bring us considerable relief. When we look at lists of leadership traits and behaviors, it is exhausting to think that we need to be and do all these things. In addition, assuming an individual focus underutilizes our colleagues' strengths. Instead, leaders should make the best use of team skills to ensure all dimensions of leadership are addressed for the team.

How the Four Dimensions & Three Levels Connect

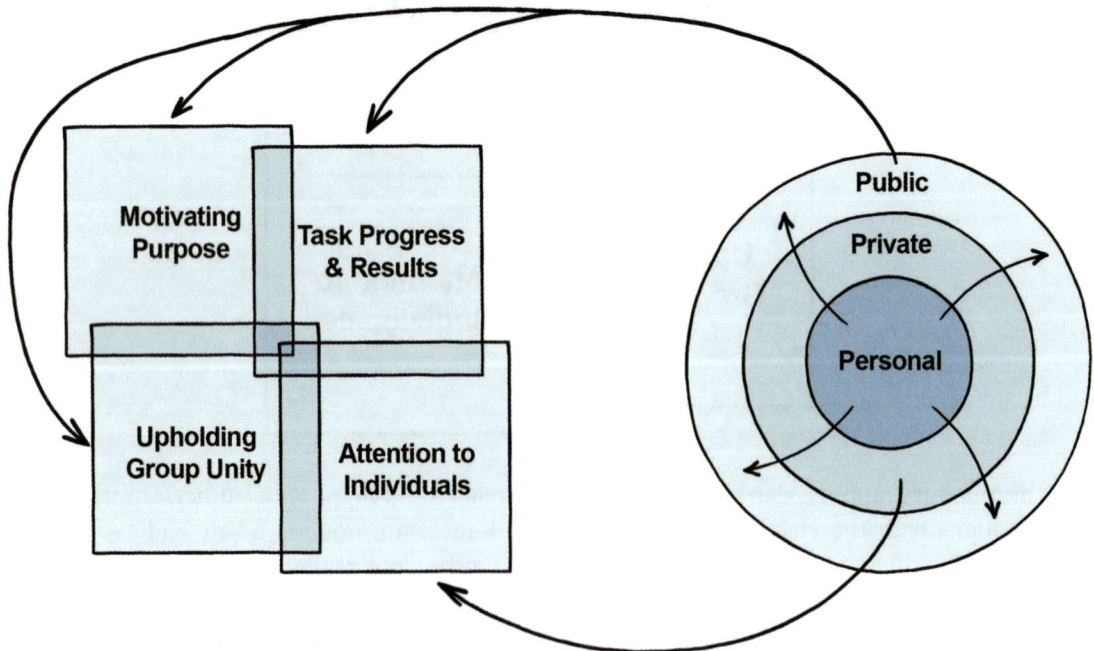

FIGURE 11.7 *How the Four Dimensions and Three Levels Connect*

After establishing the four roles of a leader and the link to the three levels of leadership, Scouller then expands on the three levels themselves.

As shown in figure 11.7, the innermost ring is personal leadership, which focuses on expanding your know-how to widen your range of behaviors and increase your skills. It includes working on your presence (Scouller's term for being the authentic you), attitude toward others, technical skills, and self-mastery. These are essentially the topics we covered in the section on EI. Presence is aligned with self-mastery, feeling comfortable on the horse, and being grounded.

Moving outward, the next ring is private leadership, which deals with one-on-one interactions with people and treating individuals as individuals. It includes recognizing the different levels of confidence, commitment, mental toughness, and experience that everyone brings to a team. It also addresses adjusting what you do to suit each individual, including goal setting, reviewing, attracting, consulting, developing, intervening, recognizing, and understanding.

A memorable and valuable quote about this layer of leadership relates to the importance of supporting team members. It comes from Vince Lombardi, a famous American football coach in the 1950s and 1960s who was an outstanding motivator: "I don't necessarily have to like my players and associates but as their leader I *must* love them. Love is loyalty, love is teamwork, love respects the dignity of the individual. This is the strength of any organization."

I like this quote for a couple of reasons. First, the "I don't necessarily have to like my associates, but I must love them" part is sticky (memorable) because it is paradoxical and unexpected. Loving someone without liking them seems odd. Second, it is a great summary for a couple of important leadership points: We may not necessarily get on with our coworkers, but that is understandable and okay. On high-diversity teams, we will likely have little in common with many of our peers. However, as effective leaders, we must respect them, support them, and back them up faithfully like we would for a loved one. Leaders need to demonstrate unwavering trust in and support of their teams if they are to be supported. So, you do not need to like your team, but you do need to love them.

The final ring in the Three Levels of Leadership model is public leadership. This involves group interactions and responsibilities, including creating unity of purpose, often around an inspiring vision; building and protecting a sense of togetherness based on trust, mutual respect, dedication to the goals, and the group-wide standards of performance; and getting the group's tasks done on time. The activities required to achieve these goals include:

- Setting the purpose and staying focused
- Organizing, giving power to others
- Ideation, problem-solving, decision-making
- Executing work
- Group building and maintenance
- Honoring, representing, setting an example, updating, encouraging, gatekeeping, compromising, harmonizing

Key Takeaways

- The role of the leader is to ensure leadership occurs, even if it is not done by the leader.
- Leadership is rarely one person's role. Thinking so will likely lead to an underutilization of your colleagues' skills and capabilities.

Leadership-Model Evolution

Through this discussion of leadership models, some general themes and trends emerge. Classical leadership theory, popular before the 1970s, is dominated by command-and-control thinking. Leaders saw a large part of their role as providing direction and answers. Then, in the 1970s to mid-1980s, transactional leadership emerged, creating more of a balanced rewards-and-expectations model for leaders and followers.

Visionary-based leadership started becoming popular in the mid-1980s. It inspires followers by capturing their hearts and minds via a uniting image of a better future that is typically created by or communicated by the leader. While visionary leadership remains popular to this day, new models for shared/organic leadership have emerged. These are based on mutual sensemaking and collective creation of a vision. These waves or eras of leadership are depicted in figure 11.8.

The Primary Colors of Leadership

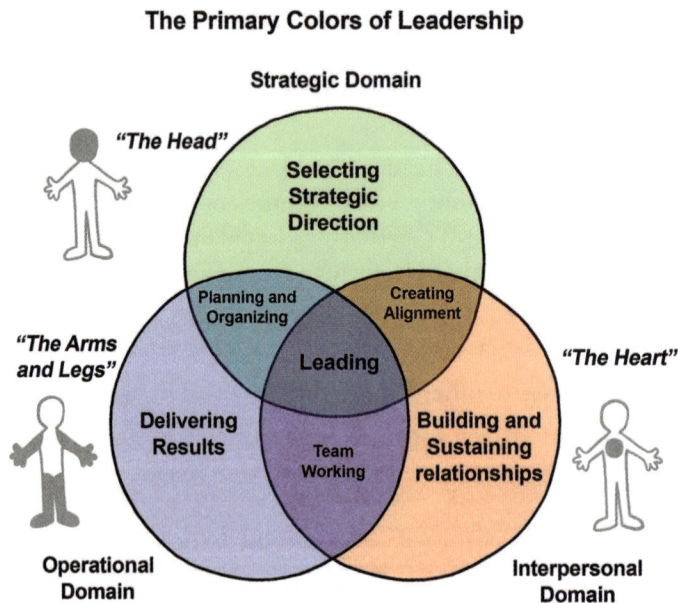

FIGURE 11.8 *Leadership Eras*

Here, we see the progression from domination through negotiation, inspiration, and cocreation.

These changes reflect the change in the types of work being undertaken as much as they reflect evolutions in leadership thinking. Prior to the 1970s, much of the work was industrial in nature. Knowledge work started with the widespread outsourcing of manufacturing work and the transition to more design and novel problem-solving work. So, it is only natural that new ways to lead these workers would be required from the 1970s onward.

Directing and telling people what to do is more appropriate for defined and repeatable processes. Adding rewards and incentives is a natural reaction when struggling to hire and retain the best workers when an industry is under threat from outsourcing. Visionary leadership helps build consensus and clarity when tackling unique initiatives that have not been done before. Finally, organic and plural models of leadership embody the shared leadership mindset of younger workers who grew up in the digital age and value inclusion.

This high-level summary makes some broad generalizations about sixty years of leadership theory but does correlate with the transition of work from the industrial era to the knowledge- and learning-worker era. If you find yourself leading an industrial-worker project—maybe a landscaping project or a Habitat for Humanity charity house build—you may want to revert to more of a command-and-control directing approach to provide clarity and clearly communicate the plan. Alternative, more modern approaches that employ inclusive visioning and joint decision-making might be overkill and inappropriate.

Crafting a Generalized and Practical Leadership Framework

Given the leadership approaches we have reviewed, and what we already know from agile approaches, it is possible to create a robust, practical leadership framework.

- Start with a strong foundation of EI: Before we can be useful leading teams, we need to be grounded and have our own headspace and confidence sorted out. We must possess the requisite soft skills for interacting with others, overcoming adversity, and managing our outlook.

- Learn the traits of leadership and be mindful of your behavior: People expect leaders to use their Intelligence and be trustworthy and approachable. They also expect leaders to be disciplined enough to follow through on commitments and courageous enough to chart a course into new territory. If we want people to admit to mistakes and ask for help, we must model this behavior ourselves. Tell the team that you missed some information on a status report and will be sending it again; admit that you forgot to include an activity in an estimate. As the saying goes, "Be the change you want to see in the world."

- Favor transformational leadership: By aiming to improve the capability of the team and organization, transformational leaders will build stronger followings that tap into challenging the status quo and Theory Y views of workers.

- Utilize intrinsic and extrinsic motivators: While extrinsic motivators are weaker than intrinsic ones, do not overlook them. Failure to meet these external needs can create unnecessary drag within the project team. Have a plan for addressing each of your team members' intrinsic motivators. Find out what makes them tick and what they want to achieve in the short and long run, then find ways to link those goals to the project journey. Check back with them frequently because perceptions of a situation vary from person to person and goals will change over time.

- Balance care for results with care for people: Act toward the simultaneous care for people and tasks. While it is fine to concentrate on one aspect (people or tasks) for short periods, we need to ensure that both critical team aspects are attended to at a global level. Use the vocational-preference tool outlined in the discussion of the Primary Colours Model to determine your natural preference and periodically check if you are giving enough attention and energy to your weaker trait. Where possible, engage other team members to assist you in your weaker areas, whether as progress and task champion, or as team leader, monitoring morale and team development.

- Apply situational leadership support where appropriate: Be mindful of the different types of support and direction that team members need at various stages of a project. Understand that people move through Tuckman stages at different speeds and new members and team changes can reset the process. Offer both directional and supporting assistance through open-ended questions and listen to what is requested. For instance, saying to the team, *I know you are all busy planning the new release. Can I help with organizing some business reviews or assist with getting those software tools you were asking for?* allows the whole team, or individual people, to approach you with requests for direction (business involvement) or support (tool and environment) help.

- Apply functional leadership: Practice the functions we know that followers look for in their leaders. Deliberately engage the project stakeholders to build a uniting vision. Use retrospectives and business demos as opportunities to challenge the process. Apply servant leadership and team empowerment to enable and encourage team members. Encourage the heart by finding the motivating purpose behind the work and making it relevant and meaningful.

- Practice servant leadership: One of my favorite paradoxical quotes about leadership is "You lead people by standing behind them." It reminds me that servant leadership means supporting people, looking out for them, and protecting them. It is typically the team members who add value, so the best thing a leader can do is clear a path for them to do that, shield them from interruptions, and provide the things they need and sincere thanks. Servant leaders should also tap into the motivating power of providing more autonomy to the team so the team can control as much of their time, tasks, tools, and team-member selection as possible.

- Shared leadership: Leadership is rarely one single person's role; it can and should be shared. We all have distinct preferences for dealing with things or people and data or ideas. Use shared leadership to address all these dimensions. The role of the leader is to ensure leadership occurs, even if it is not done by that leader. Utilize the team's capabilities to the fullest.

The US Marine Corps' 11 Principles of Leadership

Many of the principles of leadership described in this chapter are reflected in Tom Deierlein's article "11 Timeless Principles of Leadership (US Army 1948)":

1. Know yourself and seek self-improvement:

    a) Honestly evaluate yourself.
    b) Learn by studying the causes of success and failure.
    c) Develop a genuine interest in people.
    d) Master the art of writing and speech.
    e) Have goals and a plan to obtain those goals.

2. Be technically and tactically proficient:

    a) Seek out education.
    b) Practice being a leader.

3. Know your team and look out for their welfare:

    a) Know the people on the team.
    b) Support the team.
    c) Correct grievances.

4. Keep your team informed:

    a) Explain the work to be accomplished.
    b) Ensure information is passed on to the entire team.
    c) Publicize successes.
    d) Spread truth, not rumors.

5. Set the example:

    a) Show the team you are willing to work at the same level you are asking them to.
    b) Maintain an optimistic outlook.
    c) Avoid favoritism.
    d) Leadership is taught by example.

6. Ensure the task is understood, supervised, and accomplished:

    a) Encourage feedback.
    b) Make sure the team has the resources they need.
    c) Check progress
    d)

7. Train your team:
   a) Project success will be because of teamwork.
   b) Develop mutual trust among team.

8. Make sound and timely decisions:
   a) Plan for every event possibility (risk awareness).
   b) Announce decisions as soon as possible.
   c) The team must know the plans.

9. Develop a sense of responsibility among your team:
   a) Provide clear, well-thought-out directions.
   b) Tell the team what to do, not how to do it (develop responsibility).
   c) Recognize accomplishments.
   d) Accept honest mistakes.
   e) Resist the urge to micromanage; it can destroy initiative.

10. Employ your command in accordance with its capabilities:
    a) Make sure the team you developed is up to the task required.
    b) Make sure tasks assigned are reasonable.

11. Seek responsibility and take responsibility for your actions:
    a) Accept responsibility for your own actions
    b) Evaluate failure by subordinates; it could be a leadership mistake.
    c) Build up team members but replace them when it must be done.

The list is old now and, due to its military context, uses terms such as *command* that seem off in today's knowledge-worker domains. However, the concepts are timeless and universal. We lead teams by supporting their members. We build trust by demonstrating honesty and integrity. Once people see that we care about them, they will likely care about us and the goal at hand.

Chapter 11 Summary

We covered a lot of ground in this chapter. Servant leadership is central to agile approaches and lean thinking. It makes use of the more potent intrinsic motivators of autonomy, mastery, and purpose, as opposed to the carrot-and-stick strategies employed by command-and-control authoritarian rule.

Shared leadership teaches us that the role does not have to be occupied by one person. Perhaps the best person for the job is not one person at all, but a collection of people performing a variety of roles. The Primary Colours Model describes these critical roles as sensemaking, relating (building trust), visioning, and inventing.

Scouller's Three Levels and Four Dimensions of Leadership models describe how leaders work through personal, private, and public methods and address creating a motivating purpose, task progress and results, upholding group unity, and attention to individuals.

Finally, we looked at the evolution of leadership models, seeing the trend and progression from classical, central authority, through transactional negotiating rewards. Then on to visionary and inspirational leadership and ultimately organic and plural leadership that involves mutual sensemaking and a vision owned by all.

Key topics covered in this chapter:

» Servant leadership

» Shared leadership

» Leadership evolution

» Creating your generalized practical leadership framework

Chapter 12
Plan-Driven

This section focuses on smart integration—integrating plan-driven tools and techniques with agile approaches in ways that do not invalidate either the plan-driven elements or the agile values or principles.

Why Plan-Driven Again?

At this point, after learning about the intrinsic motivational benefits of empowered teams, it may seem odd to suggest that we learn more about and adopt traditional, plan-driven project-management approaches. However, the truth is that many organizations and many people have not converted to or fully embraced the new era of knowledge-worker approaches. We could try to convert them or just ignore them, but, depending on their role, they likely have the ability to make our lives and project success difficult.

Also, plan-driven approaches still have their place in many environments. Not all portions of our whizzbang new technology project will be learning based. Ordering equipment, building facilities, then training people is still primarily a defined, repeatable process. These activities can benefit from simple to understand plan-driven approaches.

This is an example of being smart over being inflexible and dogmatic. Yes, we favor empowering the workforce, but not when it takes more energy or costs more than using a defined, predictable way while delivering no benefit. We use lean and agile approaches to be successful, not to make a point; our end goal is success at minimum expenditure.

Finally, understanding plan-driven approaches, knowing how to undertake them, and being able to talk the talk is essential for converting plan-driven stakeholders to more modern, post-industrial methods. Without knowledge, appreciation, and experience of plan-driven techniques, we are not going to be compelling advocates for change. To be credible and convincing, we must be capable in both camps. Only then can we make persuasive arguments for trial and change.

I never allow myself to hold an opinion on anything
that I don't know the other side's argument better than they do.

—Charlie Munger

Working with Traditional PMOs

It is quite common for project teams to be further along in their agile-adoption journey than the PMO in an organization. As leader of that team, you might be asked to provide metrics that are better suited for predictive project execution than a more lean or agile approach.

When faced with this request, you have a couple of options. Likely the easiest will be to just create a one-off version of what they have asked for, be it a green, yellow, or red status; percent-complete figure; or even a development-phase update. All these metrics can be determined and defended based on features-delivered versus features-remaining metrics from an agile-backlog perspective.

The bigger issue is whether we should try to convert the requesting group (in this example the PMO) to more suitable post-industrial metrics. My views on this question have varied over the years as I transitioned from youthful optimism, through goal-focused ruthlessness, to (hopefully) a more balanced value-based view.

Initially, I wanted to try to educate everyone about the benefits of the lean and systems-thinking ideas that underpin agile and modern project approaches. If I received a misaligned PMO request, I would try to explain why the agile alternative was preferable. However, I soon learned to pick my battles; converting people takes a lot of time and effort that should really be dedicated to the project you have been hired to execute.

So, I then applied a harsher filter. If this is a group that we will frequently deal with, then perhaps it is worth the conversion effort. This typically requires producing what they asked for, along with what they should have asked for, and explaining why the new approach or deliverable one is preferable to their old one. People do not typically take things at face value, so it is normal to have to produce both sets of artifacts for a trial period before getting permission to convert to the new approach. This all takes a lot of time and effort, hence the *will-we-be-doing-this-lots?* filter.

Now, I leave the option open for conversion if the group expresses an interest. The process is described in figure 12.1.

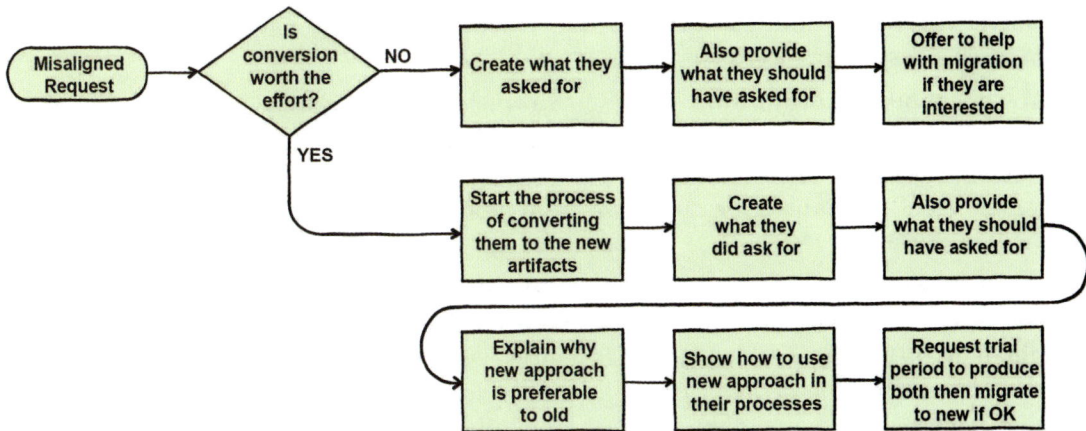

FIGURE 12.1: *Determining if Conversion to an Agile-based Method is Worth the Effort*

It starts with a misaligned request (1), perhaps for a sequential phase status report on an iterative, incremental project. We then determine if the education and conversion of this person or group is worth the likely investment of effort, which will probably require parallel running of both sets of artifacts and education sessions. If this is a one-off request—let us say for a project-status poster requested by a marketing group we infrequently interact with—then conversion might not be worth the effort. We answer *No* and produce what they asked for (3).

It may be tempting to leave it there but adding the steps of also providing what they should have asked for (4), such as a burnup graph or release road map, and offering to help with migration if they are interested (5) is worthwhile. Helping someone requesting information is much easier than converting someone more skeptical, and we can often point them to reading on the subject and provide them with artifacts we already have on the project to illustrate the ideas in a local setting.

If we answer *Yes* to the effort question (2), we start the process of converting them to the new approach (6). This will likely involve producing what they initially asked for anyway (7) because refusal will be met with opposition rather than the partnership mindset we are hoping to establish. By providing what they asked for and what we believe they should have asked for, we are now complying and showing an interest in their domain—for many compliance groups, that is a welcome change.

By meeting their request with something akin to *Here is that nail fastener you asked for, and I would like to show you this screw fastener we use*, we create a space for collaboration. We can then explain why we think this new approach is preferable to the old (9) and how it could be used in their own follow-on processes (10). We should not expect permission to transition straight away, but if we request a trial period during which both sets of metrics or artifacts will be provided (11), this is often a successful strategy.

You might be thinking that this sounds like a whole bunch of work you would rather avoid. I agree, but when you consider the alternatives, it makes sense. We could refuse to comply and just produce the new alternative. However, now we have created issues and strife in an internal group that we may want to approach for exceptions from process or to advocate for us with some other group in the future.

Alternatively, we could just produce their outdated artifact and move along. Taking the path of least resistance is tempting, but it does not best serve our organization. We have an obligation to do the right thing, up to the point of uneconomic returns (when the right thing no longer makes sense). This not only models the desired behavior we hope for from our team members (who will be watching and listening to us and the feedback from others), but also gets noticed by others in the organization.

This mindset comes back to the leadership traits of integrity, honesty, transparency, and following through on doing what you said you would do. The other point it illustrates is the power of forming relationships with people before attempting to convert them. Arguing with logic alone is rarely effective, especially with people we do not know well. We need to make an emotional connection with people first and sell them a vision before they will even begin to listen to our logic.

Mapping Traditional to Agile Artifacts

Many of the traditional project-management artifacts have agile equivalents. The trick to finding them is to apply the lean Five Whys principle to discover the reason we are being asked for something. So, when asked for the project WBS, we can ask ourselves *Why do they want a WBS?* Likely because they want to see the breakdown of work. Why do they want to see the breakdown of work? So they can get some reassurance that we have performed due diligence in analyzing the expected work, and so they can better understand what the project will entail.

Following this line of questioning, we will then see that a prioritized backlog may answer many of these questions. While probably not in the format the requester expected, we can use our answers to the Five Whys to explain how the elements of a WBS are shown in a prioritized backlog. Here are some common traditional-to-agile mappings:

Business-requirements document (BRD) -> Export of user stories: Sometimes, PMOs, QA groups, or architecture groups ask to see the approved, signed-off list of requirements. This presents a challenge in iterative environments where the project teams know the requirements will continue to evolve and be discovered as the evaluation of candidate functionality built to date uncovers remaining requirements and prompts ideas for new ones. The discovery and development is iterative and will likely continue throughout the product life cycle, bounded by schedule and budget.

In these circumstances, it is usually preferable to supply the available requirements and explain they are continuing to evolve through progressive elaboration than to say it is not possible to provide a full list right now. These groups typically care less about the project's requirements-elicitation methods than their own review process they are waiting to undertake. The concept of progressive elaboration is a traditional project management term, outlined in the *PMBOK® Guide* and other predictive project management documents. It describes the process by which designs, requirements, and understanding continue to evolve as further project work is undertaken. While lean and agile projects often take the extent and speed of progressive elaboration to the limits of what can be expected in more traditional project environments, it is still the same process.

So, it is accurate and defendable to export the current epics, features, and user stories from an agile backlog and provide them as a BRD proxy. Make sure to include non-functional requirements and explain that this is today's best view and is subject to update and expansion through progressive elaboration. Should significant change to these backlog elements occur during project development, we should reach out to these groups and let them know. They should take notice and update their analysis but may not.

Earned Value (EV) Reporting -> Velocity and feature-based reporting: Traditional EV reporting shows progress against a plan at a given moment in time. It can show how far ahead or behind we are in terms of progress and spend. It can also be used to estimate completion timeframes and final costs. However, it is tied to the accuracy and quality of the plan we are tracking against.

The phrase *the map is not the territory* speaks to the fact that if reality diverges from our map or plan, then we have to accept reality and draw a new map. Unfortunately, the uncertainties of new technology projects often show us that our initial "map" was flawed. Plan the work and work the plan is a fine approach when your plan is solid, but a recipe for failure when change rates are high.

All the same estimate to complete, cost, and schedule performance indices can be calculated by tracking velocity (number of features/points completed per iteration) and checking these delivery rates against the total number of features.

Work Breakdown Structure (WBS) -> Prioritized backlog: As mentioned previously, when asked to show the WBS, sponsors and PMO are likely looking for a breakdown of the project deliverables. Traditional project-management approaches recommend creating a WBS early in a project life cycle after gathering requirements and defining scope.

Agile projects acknowledge that this up-front design is likely to change and so deliberately go a little lighter on these definition activities, preferring to invest the time in building portions of application and arriving at agreement of functionality through feedback.

Detailed Gantt Chart –> Release plan: Detailed Gantt charts are another example of a detailed up-front design deliverable that is likely to be brittle and change too frequently to warrant the update effort in project environments that have high levels of requirements uncertainty or technology uncertainty. It is not that we cannot create Gantt charts for agile projects—we can for some stakeholders who really need one—but rather that the time and effort required to update them is probably best used elsewhere in gaining agreement of the true business requirements.

So, instead of producing detailed Gantt charts that list tasks but do not survive contact with the reality of technology projects, use release plans that layout iterations and release timeframes that are a more robust and quicker-to-update planning instrument.

Alignment with the PMI Model

BAM, with its four domains of agile, leadership/EI, plan-driven, and domain-specific, aligns well with the PMI Talent Triangle®, as depicted in figure 12.2.

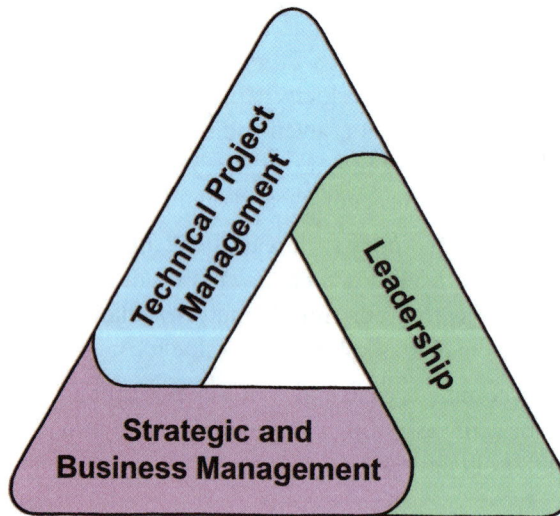

FIGURE 12.2 *PMI's Talent Triangle®*

In the PMI Talent Triangle®, the portion labeled *technical project management* is similar to the plan-driven domain in the BAM. PMI has a strong legacy of plan-driven guidance and is the source of many standards, guides, credentials, and other offerings in this field.

More recently, PMI has added agile-related offerings including the PMI-ACP credential, the

Software Extension to the PMBOK® Guide, the *Agile Practice Guide*, Disciplined Agile, and an appendix to the *PMBOK® Guide, Sixth Edition*. It is promising to see PMI moving in this direction, addressing the needs of project practitioners in the knowledge-worker domain. This was why I volunteered my time to coauthor each of these PMI offerings; it is what the project-management industry needs to move toward.

However, there is a limit to how much agile material PMI will incorporate into their standards and guidance. A portion of their membership base still operates in industrial-worker domains. When work is defined and repeatable, it is appropriate, and recommended, to plan the work in detail up front and then execute that plan. There is less benefit in continuously operating short-build feedback loops for scope verification.

So, while lean and agile methods fall under the technical project management domain, their coverage is lighter than typically required by today's high-uncertainty/high-change knowledge-worker projects. Also, PMI as an organization has a culture born from predictive, plan-driven approaches. Having worked extensively with PMI on getting more agile techniques adopted into their standards over the last fifteen years, I know firsthand that they have many progressive thinkers in their leadership team who are eager to adopt more agile approaches, but it will take time and only go so far. That is just a feature of their culture and it will be slow to change—but it is moving in the right direction.

The *leadership* portion of the triangle is well aligned to the BAM's leadership/EI domain; it speaks directly to the need for the same set of skills, tools, and techniques. However, it does not provide much tangible guidance, instead pointing to leadership textbooks and related self-study options.

This is understandable: Leadership is a huge domain and getting a team of SMEs from PMI to collate and agree on a single set of leadership topics would be a difficult project. For every SME present, there would likely be a unique set of recommendations. The ones listed in this book were selected because I have seen them work on real projects and they are compatible with the other recommendations provided. The net has not been cast so wide, but everything caught is proven.

The *strategic and business management* portion of the PMI Talent Triangle® is similar to BAM's industry-specific domain. *Strategic and business management* refers to the boundary between the project and the business unit. It refers to the zone immediately surrounding the project being managed. This is shown in figure 12.3.

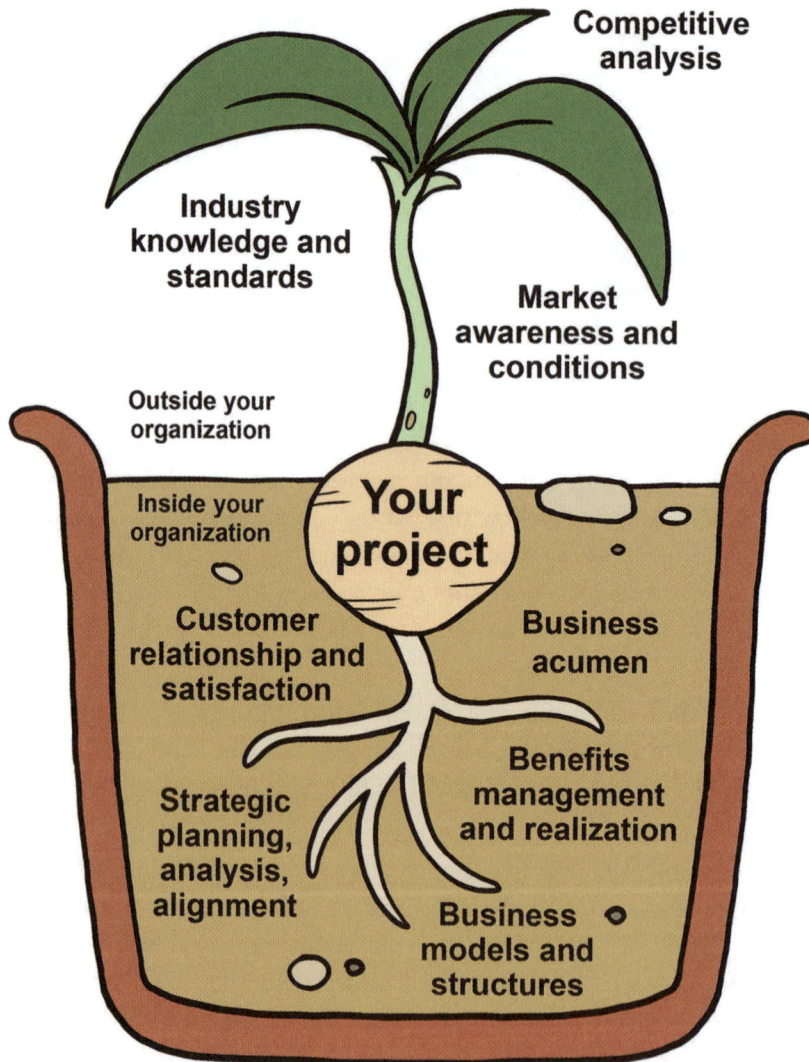

FIGURE 12.3 *Strategic and Business Management Concepts*

Strategic and business management covers any preproject interactions with the business to determine project opportunities, feasibility, ROI, and also competitive analysis. Then, as the project progresses, track performance against these models (financial analysis, benefits analysis, competitor-product tracking). It is more concerned with interacting with the business than getting into the business itself.

PMI publishes a list of categories of work embodied by this portion of the Talent Triangle®. They include:

» Benefits management and realization

» Business acumen

» Business models and structures

» Competitive analysis

» Customer relationship and satisfaction

» Operational functions (finance, marketing)

» Strategic planning, analysis, and alignment

» Market awareness and conditions

These are all important topics. We need to understand them to be effective in and useful to our organization. Yet we also need to go deeper and address not only how to interact with these functions from a project perspective but getting in there and learning the business too. We need to be credible business participants to be listened to and trusted when making recommendations.

In summary, the PMI Talent Triangle® is well aligned with the BAM. Organizations that use it for their training or professional development will have no problems finding a home for topics from either model. Where the Talent Triangle® differs is in its lighter coverage of agile/lean approaches and in the fact that it does not recommend getting as immersed in industry knowledge. This is understandable: The Talent Triangle® comes from PMI, whose domain and remit are project based. BAM's is success based, regardless of whether the approach recommended is a project technique, an empathy technique, or industry knowledge.

Another key difference is BAM's emphasis on the direction of energy. It is one thing to develop knowledge and awareness of these different talents or domains, but we must always focus on delivery over doing work in these domains. The focus means understanding these topics but then deliberately doing the minimum necessary to retain focus on delivery.

Alignment with PRINCE2 and PRINCE2 Agile

PRINCE2 (Projects in Controlled Environments) is a popular project-management approach. It is an alternative to PMI-inspired project management, and there is much debate about which approach is more widely used. While PMI typically reports on "active members," PRINCE2 counts the total trained or certified practitioners that may no longer be actively practicing, so the numbers are not an apples-to-apples comparison. Both approaches boast over one million users and between them probably constitute 80 percent of the market.

PRINCE2 is a structured project-management method comprising seven principles that describe the mindset and are consistently applied, including *tailor to suit the environment*, *learn from experience*, and *use defined roles and responsibilities*. It has seven themes that are functional categories or knowledge areas, including *quality*, *risk*, and *change*. It also has seven processes that describe executing the work, including *starting up a project*, *directing a project*, and *managing product delivery*. These principles, themes, and processes describe the *why*, *what*, and *how* of executing projects with an emphasis on strategy and governance.

PRINCE2 Agile is the deliberate combination of PRINCE2 and agile concepts. Since many teams were using agile approaches for execution, PRINCE2 Agile was created to combine the strategy and project-management elements from PRINCE2 with the delivery focus of agile.

PRINCE2 Agile is agnostic and open to using any agile approach. It works with iteration-based approaches such as Scrum, and flow-based approaches such as Kanban. It also uses elements from Cynefin, lean startup, and design thinking to increase compatibility and relevancy with these emerging techniques.

At the sponsor level, it establishes a common vocabulary for project stakeholders and retains a focus on strategy, budgets, and deadlines. At the team level, it empowers the team members to deliver value while encouraging exploration through frequent, iterative collaboration with the business and customers.

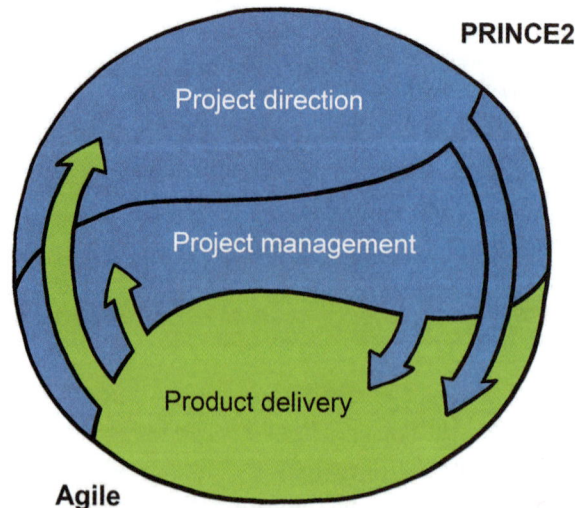

FIGURE 12.4 *The Interaction between PRINCE2 and Agile*

I contributed to the forerunner of PRINCE2 Agile when I helped create a PRINCE2 and DSDM white paper and mapping framework. Since then, PRINCE2 Agile has matured tremendously and been fleshed out with a lot more detail and practical guidance on how to combine the structure of project management with the adaptability and delivery focus of agile.

PRINCE2 Agile has an accompanying Agilometer with project-suitability sliders. These look and operate similarly to the project characteristics sliders in the BAM. They were both inspired by the DSDM-suitability filter I helped define in the 1990s and draw on Alistair Cockburn's ideas about varying approach formality based on characteristics such as team size and project criticality. However, unlike the BAM, the Agilometer is not user-data driven and so does not allow teams to add their own dimensions.

Like every framework, it has its downsides and critics. Some people claim the PRINCE2 components stifle the agility and limits the freedom of the team. I suspect that is only when it is being applied too zealously, beyond the original intent.

The BAM fits perfectly well within a PRINCE2 Agile environment. The inclusion of the plan-driven component of Beyond Agile aligns with the PRINCE2 strategy and project-management components. The agile/lean domain meshes well with the PRINEC2 Agile's agile product-delivery portion.

Where there is some disconnect is at the leadership/EI level. PRINCE2 Agile takes a process-mechanics focus without paying much attention to how we leverage soft skills such as intrinsic motivators within the team. It does not offer much guidance on leadership approaches, nor does it recognize or emphasize the need for industry-specific knowledge or development. As such, it is compatible with BAM because there are no apparent conflicts. At the same time, practitioners would benefit from adding concepts from BAM to the PRINCE2 Agile framework to be more productive and successful.

Alignment with Disciplined Agile (DA)

DA was mentioned earlier in the section about agile scaling frameworks. There, we reviewed how these agile scaling frameworks suffer from agile myopia, which is the belief that everything can be solved by agile techniques when a distinctly non-agile approach is sometimes the best way to go. They also often exhibit buffet syndrome by suggesting many tools and methods that tempt teams to take on too much process, reducing their capacity to work on the project goal as a result.

These risks aside, of all the scaling frameworks available, DA shares the closest conceptual fit with BAM. DA is approach agnostic, acting as an umbrella over all agile approaches and some plan-driven approaches too. It uses a tool kit metaphor and provides tools to help users choose their most appropriate way of working. All seven principles of DA align to some degree with the values and concepts of the Beyond Agile approach.

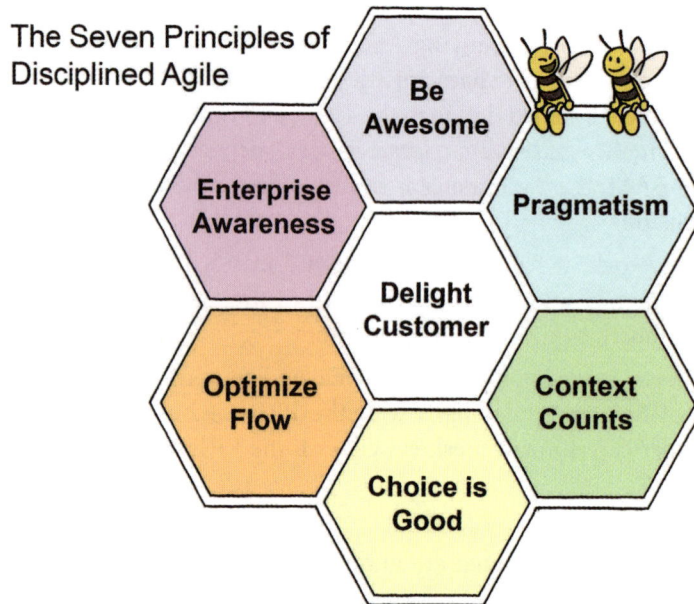

FIGURE 12.5 *The Seven Principles of DA*

The first principle, shown in gray in figure 12.5, *be awesome* comes from Modern Agile and relates to empowering and growing the team members and aspiring to create a better environment for all stakeholders. DA is light on soft-skills development, but this is covered extensively in the BAM sections on team motivation via intrinsic motivators and EI.

The next principle, *pragmatism* promotes being practical and useful rather than being a purist. Beyond Agile is also pragmatic and goes a step further to actively promote raiding frameworks such as DA, SAFe, and LeSS for anything that can work in your environment. Knowledge is weightless—gain all you can.

The *context counts* and *choice is good* principles speak to tailoring your approach and deliverables for the environment at hand from a broad tool kit of techniques and deliverables. These are great concepts and are at the heart of BAM that expands and contracts based on our context and choice.

Like DSDM, PRINCE2 Agile, and BAM, DA also promotes project characteristics sliders to help choose our way of working. The slider choices are fixed and also inspired by the Crystal family of methods.

The *optimize flow* principle borrows from lean and Kanban approaches to visualize our WIP and identify and remove bottlenecks, all to help maximize throughput. BAM also draws from lean and Kanban approaches.

The *enterprise awareness* principle is about recognizing and using the ecosystem of our organization. It includes integration, coordination, and leveraging other assets and groups, along with building capabilities. This is related to growing our industry-specific knowledge and strategic focus from the plan-driven area.

At the center, *delight customers* extends the Agile Manifesto principle "Our highest priority is to satisfy the customer through early and continuous delivery of valuable software" to not only satisfy them but also strive to delight them—or, in modern language, adopt a customer-centric philosophy. The BAM achieves this by ruthlessly stripping away process that does not add value or directly contribute toward building the best product we can for our customer. We also encourage frequently engaging the customer to gain feedback, learn insights, and check their mood.

So, there are lots of great ideas in DA that fit exceptionally well with the BAM concepts. This book can help anyone working in a DA environment.

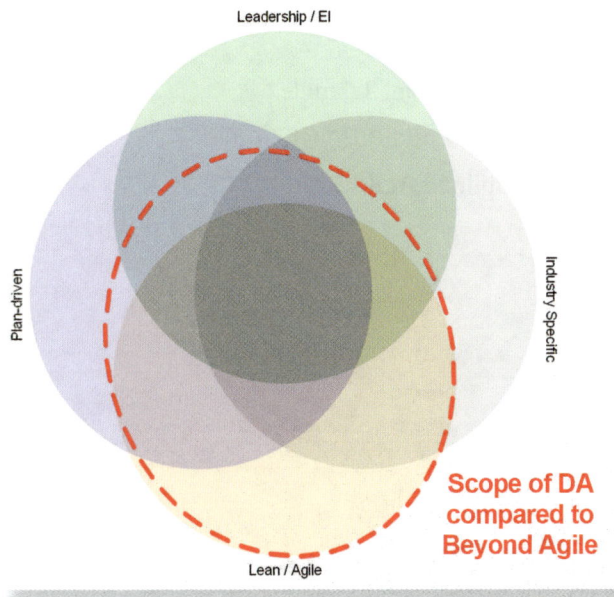

FIGURE 12.6 *Scope of DA as Compared to BAM*

As shown in figure 12.6, BAM provides more coverage and tools that go deeper into plan-driven, leadership/EI domains.

Chapter 12 Summary

This chapter brought us back to what many of us were rebelling against in the first place: plan-driven project management. However, I suspect what we were rebelling against was the misapplication of plan-driven thinking in the knowledge-worker environment. There is nothing wrong with a plan-driven approach where it makes sense, and we often need a combination of both types of thinking.

We often encounter plan-driven thinking when working with traditional PMOs. Here we have an opportunity to help transition them to more of a value-delivery office by giving them what they asked for but also supplying what the organization would be better served by.

We also looked at the alignment of the BAM with the PMI Talent Triangle®, PRINCE2 Agile, and DA. These are not plan-driven approaches, but it made sense to keep the model-alignment discussions grouped for comparison. Many of these other frameworks contain compatible and similar concepts but without the completeness of scope or explanations of how to gain more information.

Key topics covered in this chapter:

» Plan-driven project management

» Working with PMOs

» Alignment with the PMI Talent Triangle

» Alignment with PRINCE2 and PRINCE2 Agile

» Alignment with Disciplined Agile

Chapter 13
Industry Specific

Why Is Industry Knowledge Important?

This section deals with increasing our understanding of the business domain within which we are operating. All significant product development or project execution efforts run into problems during their execution. There will be times when we need to talk to the business sponsors, senior executives, or product owners about an issue, the options available, and what to do next. To be treated as trusted advisors by these people, we need a good understanding of the basics of our industry. We also need an in-depth appreciation of the value proposition and main competitors to the product or service we are engaged in.

There is a point of view that PMs can manage any kind of project without industry knowledge. They are simply conduits for passing information, coordinating work tasks, and managing communications. While all true, if this is all they are doing, then it sounds to me as if their job could be replaced by some decent project-portal software! Where is the value-add? Where is the application of urgency to critical matters and filtering out of trivia? That extra something we bring to the table is what separates us from being merely competent to truly valuable.

In addition to being valued and respected by the business, industry-specific knowledge is necessary to be credible when interacting with the user community, vendors, and, of course, the project team. One of the attributes of an admired leader identified in the Kouzes and Posner survey is competence.[1] This includes competence in our role as leader and in the domain in which we operate. Nobody wants to work for someone who could embarrass them.

Likewise, an important motivation for any worker is having a supervisor whom they respect take an interest in them. So, being respected and at least competent is central for creating effective teams and retaining good people.

This section provides guidance on how to obtain this industry knowledge so you will be respected when discussing critical product or project issues.

Starting in a New Domain

Starting with a new client or with a new domain can be daunting. Perhaps you have been hired to solve problems and so do not want to appear too "green" or naive. Yet, the perfect time to ask lots of questions is when you are new in a role. People do not expect you to know all the nuances of their business. There is a golden period in the first few weeks of an engagement when you can ask all kinds of questions.

I am upfront about my level of knowledge on a subject and do not mind admitting when I do not know anything about, say, credit insurance, missile guidance, or aircraft financing. When working in each of those fields, I met many people who were happy to explain the basics to me. Expressing a genuine interest taps into people's tendency to want to explain their work; usually, people are willing to share knowledge.

If you are concerned about admitting to not knowing the basics, one strategy is to ask, *How does process X work at MegaCorp? Can you walk me through the process?* This should get people explaining the process. You can make a note of terms you do not understand and then go off and research them. Do this with a couple of people and you should get some basics established so you can start asking better questions.

I like to start by asking how the person I am talking to got into the business and what roles they have had. This not only demonstrates an interest in the person but often uncovers useful background information that you may not be aware of. Maybe the area lead you are talking to previously worked for ten years in another role that is also important to your product or service. It is as useful to learn who knows what as it is to gain information yourself.

Nonprofit Organizations

For nonprofit organizations, it is essential to understand where the group gets its funding, who it reports to, and who sets its budgets and strategic direction. Then learn about its goal, mission, and strategies. These are then typically exercised through programs, initiatives, or projects. Learn the organization's history: Who founded it, and when? How do the goals and programs offered today differ (if at all) from the original vision? Learn about performance, funding, and achievements year over year. Often, much of this is on the organization's website or intranet sites, but create your own summary to make sure you know it.

Annual reports are dull to read but usually start with an excellent review of the year, significant achievements, and breakdown of spending by function. Ask how they differ from other nonprofits in the same field. Ask about the plans for the next year, three years, or five years. Ask people what motivated them to get involved and where they see the organization going.

For-Profit Organizations

There is some basic information you need to know. The more you can find out before starting your role, the better, but those golden first couple of weeks when you are still the new person are a great time to get the basics covered.

- How do we generate revenue?
- How much revenue is it?
- What is the composition of the revenue?

  » By product

  » By season

  » By region

  » By customer

- Who are our competitors?

  » Direct

  » Biggest in industry

  » Our percentage of market

  » By revenue

  » Our differentiators—our unique value-add

These are all basic things we should know about a company.

How to Gain Industry Knowledge

The following suggestions are other ways you can gain knowledge about an industry. You do not have to use all of them but you do need to use enough of them to get up to speed and then stay current with the industry you are working in. You may think your industry is IT or mechanical engineering, but if your customer is in the shipping or pharmaceutical supply business, then you are in that businesses too.

Ask for Onboarding Training

Even though you may be a consultant rather than a full-time employee, there might be some onboarding training available that would be helpful. I took over from a PM at a trucking company and worked with a team that was building a new dispatching system. They had training videos for new drivers demonstrating the old system we were replacing. Watching those videos on my lunchtime, I learned lots about the basic functionality of the system and trucking in general. Sure, most of the content was on driver safety and materials handling, which was of little systems-and-process use to me, but I learned lots of trucking terms and acronyms that came in handy.

Business 101 Sessions

If you can find an SME to provide some basic business training, they are worth their weight in gold. Take them to lunch, do whatever it takes, to learn about the business objectives and challenges. Whenever I have had the opportunity to have someone walk me through the business, it has been tremendously valuable.

Seek Mentors

Finding a mentor can both increase our knowledge and highlight areas where we need further learning. Often, we do not know what we do not know, in other words we are blind to our omissions. Having a mentor can not only fill in some of our gaps but also recommend what we need to study next.

Request Site Visits

Going on-site for a team visit is a great learning and motivational experience.

Host Lunch-and-Learns

If you lead a team, a great way to increase everyone's understanding of the business is to arrange for the business to provide a speaker for a lunch-and-learn. You should of course gauge the team's interest first, to make sure they want and are ready for one, then get suggestions for topics and speakers. Then work with the business to request someone who can deliver a thirty-minute presentation on any of the requested topics.

An approach I have found effective is making the ask after a product demo. We have the business there and have just completed a show-and-tell from the product development side. It is perfectly logical to request a reciprocal presentation from the business to learn about the process in question for the next or some upcoming portion of the business that will be tackled or impacted by the project.

Requesting a lunch-and-learn is also a useful litmus test for team and business relations. I have noticed that the projects I have worked on that went really well had an equitable, sharing, and cooperative relationship between the project team and the business representatives. Projects where the business unit was consistently reluctant to provide speakers for lunch-and-learns had more adversarial relationships between the project team or, more commonly, within the department they came from. As the old saying goes, sharing is caring; groups unwilling to share likely care less about their results (or are understaffed or bound by confidentiality).

For example, a business unit sees the IT group as incompetent and would rather engage them at arm's length just to build the product and service they asked for and then get out of their space, as opposed to viewing the project as a joint discovery and learning exercise for both groups and trying to raise the knowledge and cooperation levels on both sides.

Sign Up for Trade Newsletters

Some industries still produce newsletters and magazines. These are great sources for learning about emerging trends, who the major vendors are, and maybe even new job opportunities in your industry. These days, most physical newsletters have migrated online.

By using inbox filters, you can safely sign up for many newsletters and mailing lists and have them funnel into dedicated folders rather than clogging up your regular email. Once a week, or more frequently when you are learning a new domain, spend some time reviewing them for useful content.

Add the Industry to Your News Feeds

News aggregators such as BuzzFeed, Feedly, Google News, and Flipboard will allow you to collect and read current articles and posts in a single news feed. Most of these tools have categories you can subscribe to such as *wearable technology*, *senior advocacy*, or *coal mining*. Others allow the entry of keywords that can include technologies and product and company names.

Keeping up-to-date on industry news makes you more useful to project sponsors because you are plugged into current issues, products, and regulatory changes. It also makes you more approachable and engaging for typical business representatives since they can at least talk to you about work issues without having to apply a layman's filter first.

Visit or Speak to Vendors

Product and service vendors usually have a vested interest in supporting the customer. If you explain that you are new to ABC Corp and would like to chat to someone at the company about their product offerings in that space, a salesperson will often be happy to talk to you.

To be in sales, vendors need to understand the industry of their clients and be decent at talking to people about the industry and their products. These qualities make them good people to connect with.

There are obviously a couple of potential downsides: you will get a sales spiel about their products and you will be added to their contacts database and sent emails about their products and services—but these might be useful too.

Just make sure you clearly explain that your goal is to understand how their products fit in this new domain. Do not oversell your interest, pretend to be buying anything, or represent your role as anything it is not. After reaching out, let them come to you, meet, and explain your position. If they are happy to talk to you, ask about their products, how they fit in the industry, and what ABC CORP is doing with them.

Go to School

Community colleges and universities provide a wide array of courses that can help increase your industry knowledge. When moving from defense and finance roles in the United Kingdom to the oil- and gas-dominated economy of Calgary, Canada, I found I was in need of an education. I read what I could online but attending an Oil and Gas 101 evening course at the University of Calgary pulled it all together for me. Approaching the topics from the broader scope of geology and macroeconomics helped me understand more about the *whys* and *hows* of the industry.

The six-week course was only two hours a week, plus an extra couple of hours of reading, but it was probably one of the most useful studies I have undertaken. Another advantage of attending courses outside of work is that nobody is judging you. There is no *Oh, I thought you already knew that* stigma for those signing up for a beginner's class and no expectations or performance anxiety, unlike when dealing with colleagues. You are just another member of the public attending an evening class and meeting some new people.

Learn Online

With so much content available online, it can sometimes be a problem to find the most relevant and high-quality content. In addition to YouTube, learning sites like Udemy, Lynda, and Coursera provide a variety of free or low-cost courses.

Exercising Your Business Knowledge

We must remember what we can learn about a business from a few weeks or months of part-time study is unlikely to be significant compared to what anyone in the business knows. Like a relative who is not technologically savvy and asks someone with a computer science degree for IT support, or someone who has diagnosed their health condition via a search engine and is now speaking to a doctor, our analysis is probably, at best, rudimentary.

So, we must approach with humility and position our thoughts carefully. Even if you have a firm conviction of being correct, nobody likes a know-it-all consultant. For example, saying, *Jane was telling me a little about the new generation of widget-x's that have XYZ functionality. Could we use something like that to help in this situation?* is preferable to saying, *Why do we not just use a new widget-x? They do this for you by default now!*

As with arguments between spouses, there is a huge difference between being right and being happy—or, in the project space, being successful. Projects are long-term endeavors where acts of support and collaboration pay dividends throughout the project life cycle. If you are a consultant, especially a well-paid contract hire, some people may dislike you because of your role. There is no need to add *pretentious know-it-all* to the list of prejudices against you.

So, downplay your knowledge. Consider suggesting your ideas in private. Work to make the business look good. Position your thoughts from a novice, outsider perspective, at least with stakeholders you rarely interact with. Contributing freely within your team is usually safer.

I recall a steering-committee meeting where I had outlined an issue with a vendor and summarized our resolution steps to date and alternative options going forward. The chief financial officer (CFO) asked me how much I had paid to be educated by their best managers, the best in their industry. It was an awkward moment because he knew full well I had been billing them for the entire education.

Exercising your business knowledge is a tricky balancing act. People do not like know-it-alls, especially if they have paid for the education of a temporary person who will be moving on after the project is complete. That effort could and should have been invested in training juniors within the company. So never assume you know enough and be humble and appreciative of what you have learned. That way, your ideas are more likely to be accepted and appreciated. We are not out to get appreciation or accolades, but instead to quietly and stealthily orchestrate the smooth flow of successes toward the project goal.

Chapter 13 Summary

We need to build and then keep developing our industry knowledge. This allows us to be treated as trusted advisors on the project by the sponsors and executives. Knowledge of the business domain helps us solve issues and determine what to do next. Industry knowledge allows us to identify urgency, filter out the trivial, and focus on the critical.

We also need industry knowledge to take a relevant interest in our team members' professional development. We cannot help them along their career paths if we have no idea what their next steps or options might be. We can build industry knowledge by asking lots of questions when we are new to a role and exploring the business case for a project with our sponsors. We should learn the economics of the business within our organizations and from competitors. If working for nonprofits, we need to research the motivating cause and reason for being.

These days, it is easier than ever to learn about any topic. We can ask for onboarding, mentors, and site visits. We can also study up via news feeds, vendors, online courses, and conferences. Be humble and never stop learning.

Key topics covered in this chapter:

- » The importance of industry knowledge
- » Strategies for how to gain industry knowledge
- » Learning through site visits
- » Applying your knowledge

Chapter 14
Collaborating with Stakeholders (Key Topics)

Projects and products are commissioned by people, developed by people, and consumed by people. In complex engineering environments, it is easy to get caught up in the technical details, but we should never lose sight of the people involved. Collaborating with stakeholders deals with some of the common interactions in the BAM.

Stakeholder Analysis

Products and projects involve and impact a wide array of people. Some of the common groups and their typical interests are listed in the table below:

Stakeholder Group	Typical Interests
Owner/investor	Profit, share price, reputation, competence, consumer loyalty
Sponsor/business champion	Business benefits, time, price, competitive advantage, ROI, relationships, reputation
Consumer/user	Time, price, features, future development
Project team	Time, cost, performance, learning, camaraderie, retention, well-being, new technology, skills, reputation, relationships, job security, future projects
Operations/support group	Time, cost, performance, reliability, ease of operation, ease of maintenance, technology
Public	Environmental impact, social costs, social benefits, cost-benefit ratio

When analyzing the people in these groups, it is worth asking the following:

» Do they support the initiative?

» Can they influence the outcome?

» Are they knowledgeable about the product/project?

Often, some people may oppose rather than support a project. People who believe the project will damage the environment, take away revenue (competitors), or make their lives worse (consumers/users) are likely to resist and oppose a project.

Knowing the degree to which these people are aware of and involved in the project helps us determine the most appropriate course of action to take with them. The Knowledge-Attitude Strategy grid shown in figure 14.1 provides some useful insights.

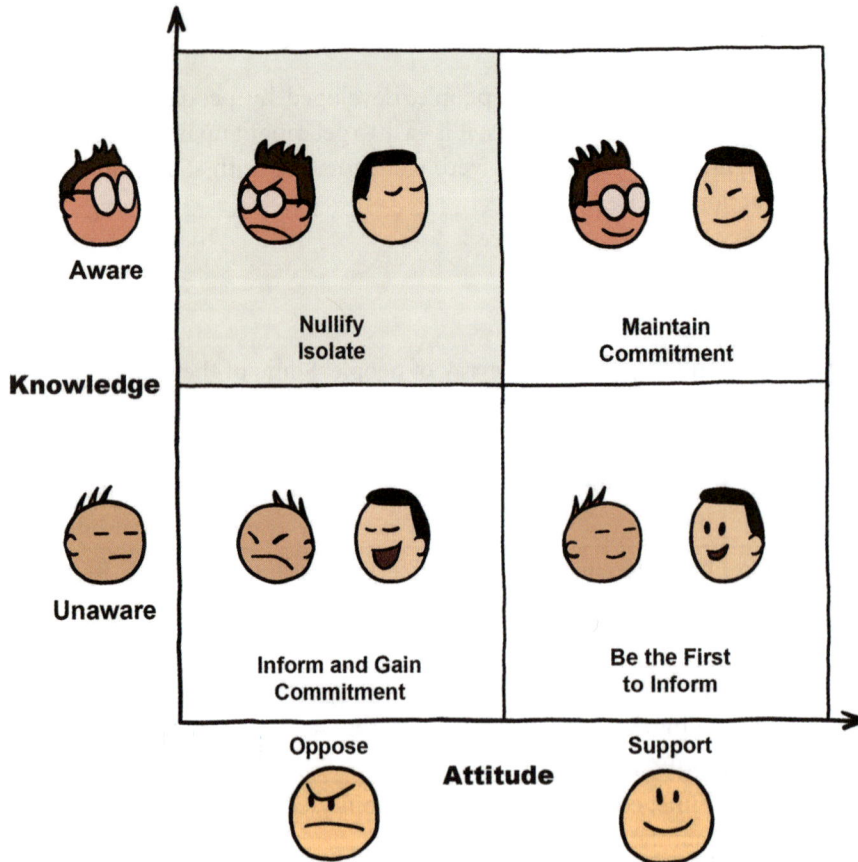

FIGURE 14.1 *Knowledge-Attitude Strategy grid*

The top-left quadrant represents people who are knowledgeable about the project but oppose it. They can create problems for us. Educating them is not going to help, so we need to use empathy, sensitivity, and influence to try to win them over. If that does not work, we may need to nullify and downplay their objections while trying to isolate them. This may sound sinister, but it does not have to be.

For whatever reason, people sometimes decide to object. If we cannot convince them to be supportive by providing them with more information (building their knowledge), it is best to reduce their impact and the airtime we give them.

Below this quadrant is the unaware, opposed group. Hopefully, they are just misinformed about the project. Providing education may be enough to turn them around and gain their support and commitment. Here, we use the EQ skills of empathy, sensitivity, effective communication, and influence.

In the bottom-right quadrant is the supportive but unaware group. These are potential allies and cohorts; we need to tell them what we are working on and get them on board as soon as possible. This should involve restating the project vision and employing other engaging communication techniques.

Finally, the top-right quadrant comprises supportive and aware people who are our friends and allies. However, we must not take them for granted because they could slip into another quadrant if neglected. Instead, we keep them informed and use empathy and effective communication.

A slightly different but equally important measure to consider is the stakeholder's degree of power and influence. On a web design project, your graphic artist may have a big impact on the project, but not a lot of power to influence the project execution. Someone in the PMO may have hierarchical power, but a limited role in and impact on the project overall. A project sponsor or business champion likely has both a high level of power and a high impact.

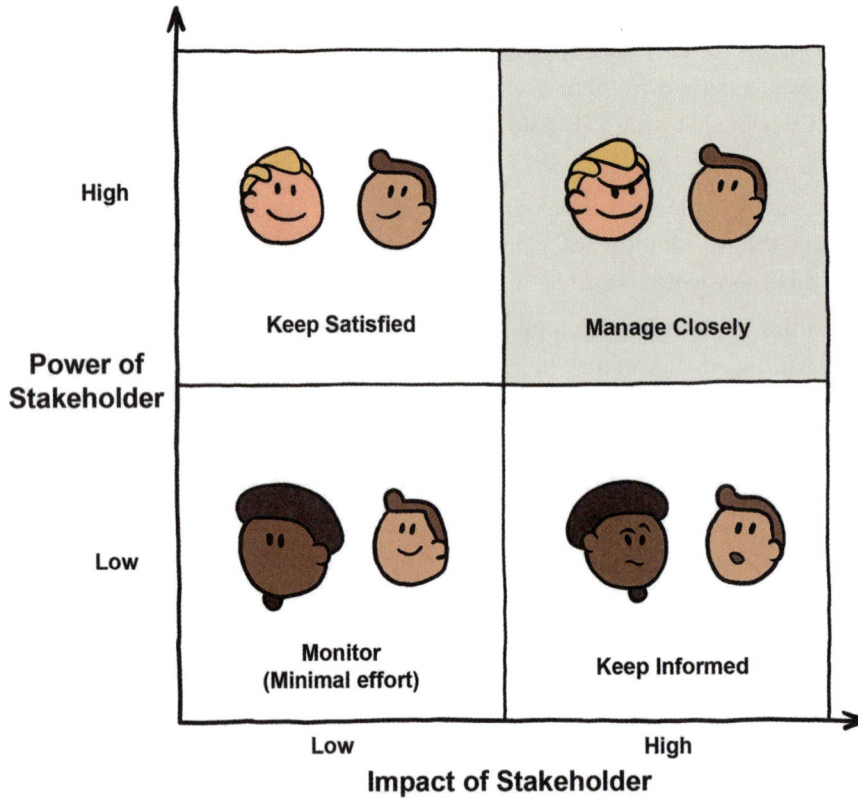

We should not dedicate a great deal of time to engaging with people in the low-power, low-impact quadrant of the grid. Our time is better spent elsewhere, so we should just monitor these people to make sure there are no major issues or power/impact changes.

People in the high-power, low-impact quadrant need to be kept satisfied because they are in positions of power and could make life difficult for those working on the project. Likewise, people in the high-impact, low-power quadrant need to be kept informed.

Finally, it is those in the high-impact, high-power quadrant who require most of our attention. This group is managed carefully and given the bulk of our timely attention.

Categorizing people and changing our behavior based on their power and influence may seem callous and manipulative. However, we are just taking an economic, risk-based view of interactions. Agile teams already prioritize work based on business value and threat reduction—it is the most responsible thing to do. We do not get upset about low-priority tasks that fall to the bottom of the backlog. The same is happening with stakeholders and communications—they are being prioritized to maximize positive outcomes.

Project Communications

A big part of successful project execution is effective communications management. People accept news about issues and setbacks better than nasty surprises about issues and setbacks. Also, it is easier to under-communicate than it is to overcommunicate. The fact that something was said once, somewhere, does not mean that everyone who needs to know about it is aware of it.

The suggestion that we should repeat things five or seven times so they will be remembered may not be underpinned by exact science, but the sentiment rings true: we must repeat communications, many times and in many different mediums, to stand any chance of reaching the majority of our target audience.

The cost of under-communicating is high, resulting in misaligned effort, errors, and surprised stakeholders. The cost of over-communicating, however, is low because people quickly move on when presented with the information they already know, so we should err on the side of over-communication.

It comes back to the difference between being right and being successful. We can communicate all the pertinent information clearly and accurately once and be correct, then still fail, or we can continuously communicate our messages in different ways and check for understanding, then be successful. Yes, it is redundant and takes much more time and effort, but less than recovering from a project that failed due to misunderstandings or alienated customers.

By now, you will realize that I have said the same thing in a few different ways so as to illustrate the *communicate, then communicate it again* message. So, how do we do this best? First, we need to understand our stakeholders, then we work out a plan for how best to build relationships with them, and then, finally, communicate and interact with them.

Communication Channels Increase Exponentially

As we add team members to a project, the number of communication channels we need to manage to keep everyone informed rises in a nearly exponential fashion. With just two people on a project, there is only one communication channel between them; three people have three communication channels; and four people have six.

The number of communication channels on a project follows the formula $n(n-1)/2$ and rises quickly.

Channels: 1   Channels: 3   Channels: 6

$$\text{Channels} = n(n-1)/2$$

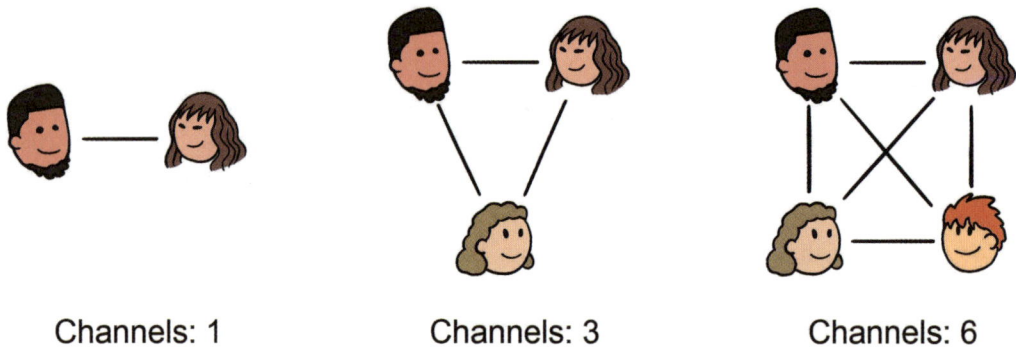

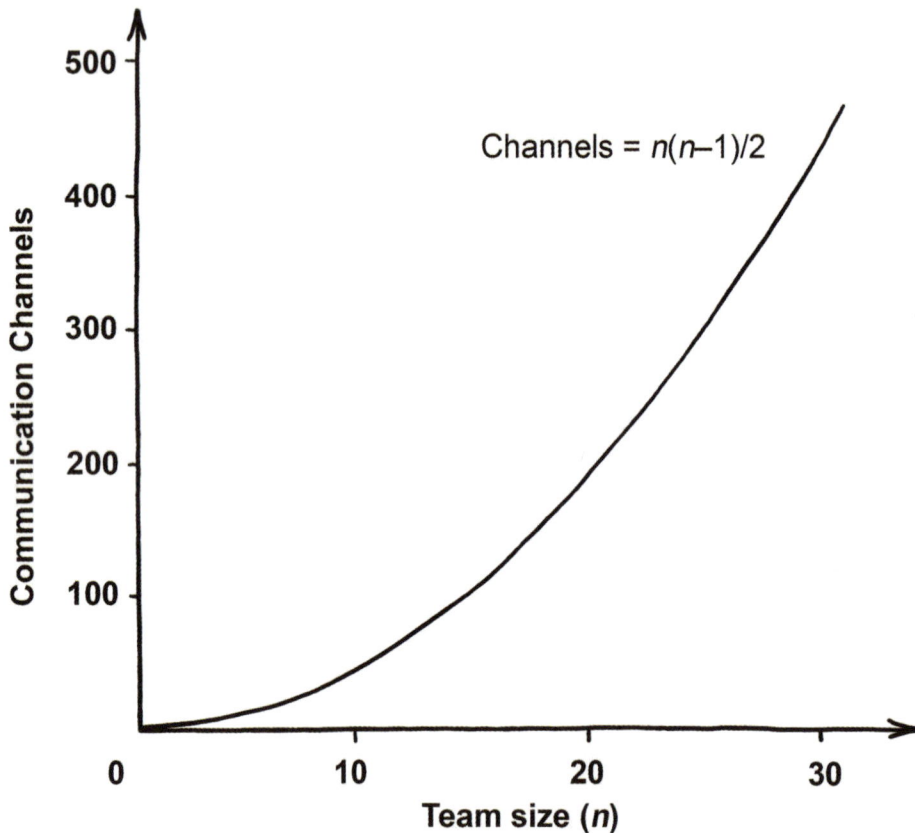

FIGURE 14.3 *Communication channels and team size*

As we can see in figure 14.3 above, on small teams of 8 people, the communication channels are small (28), but as team size reaches, say, 15 people, the communication channels rise to 105; with 30 people, the number of communication channels reaches 435. This is why small teams can do more face-to-face meetings and need to commit less to documentation. When team size exceeds 10 people, face-to-face communication tends to break down and more needs to be written down, which takes longer and conveys less information. The larger the project, the higher the probability that communication gaps will occur.

> *Poor communication is probably the*
> *single most significant contributor to project failure.*
>
> —Lois Zells, *Managing Software Projects*

What to Communicate

Communication needs to occur throughout the project via multiple mediums. There should be a combination of push, pull, and interactive communications. Push-based communications involve sending the information with little expectation of receiving feedback. Push-based communications include:

- » Status reports
- » Project updates
- » Meeting or workshop minutes

Pull-based communications are resources that people pull from a central repository to consume themselves. This repository could be a project website, SharePoint site, or wiki. Examples of artifacts they may contain include:

- » Video recordings of demonstrations or workshops
- » For software projects, links to product downloads
- » Project documents

Pull-based information does not have to be electronic. Information can also be displayed where people will see it. Big visible charts (information radiators) are large graphs showing project data (velocity, burnup, burndown, cumulative flow diagrams, quality statistics, etc.) displayed in prominent places so people cannot help but notice them.

Interactive communications include:

» Workshops

» Meetings

» Conference calls

» Video conferences

These interactive forms of communication allow immediate questions and answers. Because we can test people's level of understanding, these communications do not have to be geared to a lowest common denominator of understanding. They allow the high-bandwidth flow of face-to-face communications while also allowing us to interpret body language and gauge people's emotions and reactions to ideas and discussions.

Now let us talk about how to craft and deliver those communications.

Sharing the Project Vision

All project approaches need to unite people around the vision for the project. To get a feeling for the importance of establishing a clear vision for a product or project, consider what it is like when we do not have good vision. Think about driving in fog. What do you do?

Without a clear vision, we slow down, uncertain of what to head toward and what obstacles there may be. Vision, by contrast, brings clarity and direction that allows for focused effort and speed. It unites and concentrates our efforts and helps replace personal agendas with a common project agenda. To be effective, a vision should be both worthwhile (taking us to some better state) and a stretch (but still possible).

In his book *Managing the Design Factory*, Donald Reinertsen describes an exercise called *design the brochure description*; Jim Highsmith, in his book *Agile Project Management*, outlines a *design the product box* exercise. Both are excellent vision-building exercises that engage the team, customers, and sponsors in imagining what a product box would look like for the completed project outcome.

Kick-Off Meeting Vision Exercise

Design the Product Box - Alignment Exercise
- **Mixed Teams**
- **20 minutes**
- **Rules**
  - **Name**
  - **Top 3 features**
  - **10-15 subfeatures**
  - **Logo**
- **Team present**
- **Timeboxed discussion of options**

Facilitates: Early collaboration, prioritization of features, timeboxes, flexing of requirements

FIGURE 14.5 *Product box vision-building exercise*

To conduct this exercise, we split the kickoff meeting participants into two or three mixed teams (some sponsors, developers, and customers) and ask each group to imagine we were to sell the completed, successful project outcome. Their job for the next 20 minutes is to design the box the product will ship in following some simple rules. On the front of the box, they must have the product name, a logo (optional), and the top three features (not four or five—just the three most important features) for the project/product to deliver. On the back, they can list the next 10 to 15 most important features.

After the 20 minutes are up, each team presents their product box and explains why they thought their three items were the most important. The ensuing dialogue is incredibly valuable as sponsors and customers who were split between teams debate the merits of their top-three list.

Kickoff meetings can otherwise be limp, introduction-focused sessions, but by using the product box exercise, we quickly home in on the key project issues. Then, as a group, the final product box is created (sometimes with executive tiebreaking) and a strong sense of purpose and vision is established.

This exercise is useful because it embodies the five principles of a good project vision:

1. Ideal: It represents some future preferred state.

2. Unique: It is not generic (like statements such as *happy stakeholders* and *conforms to requirements*), but the product of a specific team addressing a definite problem.

3. Visual/image: Images are important because they connect the right and left sides of the brain, enabling us to better understand the preferred end state.

4. Future oriented: Providing a target to aim for in the future.

5. Common purpose: Provides a common goal that stakeholders who have differing skills can all work toward.

By creating a clear image of the completed product or service goals, stakeholders can check and align their decisions and work toward this common objective. James Kouzes and Barry Posner, authors of the best-selling book *The Leadership Challenge*, describe it like this: "Leaders need to reveal a beckoning summit toward which others can chart their own course." Put simply, a common vision helps keep people pulling in the same direction.

While this may sound obvious, it is common for divergent views to develop between well-intentioned team members. Developers' desire for simplicity or new technology can diverge from user requirements. Analyst or QA desires for completeness and conformance can diverge from PM and sponsor requirements for progress and completion.

Having created a vision for a project, we are not done with it. We must also frequently re-communicate this project vision. Found in Jim Collins's book *Good to Great*, a survey of the most effective executives reveals that the best leaders spend over 50 percent of their time communicating the project/corporate vision. It is almost impossible to overcommunicate vision. Employing a variety of analogies and metaphors is an effective means to help communicate vision.

So, do not just have one vision exercise at project kickoff, develop your iteration goals, and then assume you are done. Continually look for opportunities to communicate the project vision and new ways to illustrate and reinforce that vision. You may sound like a broken record to yourself, but the *aha* and *Okay, now I get it* connections made by internal and external project stakeholders will pay dividends.

Vision should be reiterated frequently, preferably using new analogies and metaphors. Sports analogies are overused and poorly understood and therefore should be used with caution. Having created a compelling vision during a kickoff meeting, work with the team to generate elevator pitches, overviews for the steering committee, and quick starts for new stakeholders. By engaging the team this way, leaders can get a true measure of team understanding and generate a variety of valuable new ways of describing the project.

Recently, a development team at a product development company generated the following elevator pitch to describe their view of the project: "To create a flexible reporting engine that links both sales and production data, the 'AceReports Project' is replacing the existing static reports with a new user-defined report system, that allows custom reports to pull data from across the company." While not the snappiest of pitches, it is reassuring as a leader to confirm that the team has a similar view of the goals of the project.

Defining What *Done* Looks Like

Project vision is an important snapshot of what the end result of the project should look like. However, it is just one view, akin to a 30-second movie trailer: it tells an abbreviated story but should leave people asking for more.

We also need to provide more information about what we are doing, why, and when. This is the realm of the project charter. Not necessarily a bloated description of project management basics, but instead a focused account of the W5+ (why, what, when, who, where, and how) we will use to get there.

Project Charters

Predictive, agile, or hybrid, we typically still need to describe the project vision and goals at some level and acknowledge approval to start.

The project charter is our formal agreement about what *done* should look like for the project and how we will get there. Every charter should cover the five *W* questions (why, what, when, who, where) and explain the extra (+) question of *how*. A lightweight, to-the-point description of each of the following points is all that is required:

> » What the project is for: A brief scope outline
> » Why the project is being undertaken: An explanation of the business benefits
> » Who will be undertaking the project and who will be impacted: Identify the stakeholders
> » When the project will occur: Provide an outline of the schedule
> » Where will the project be done: Provide a logistics outline and resources required
> » How the project will be undertaken: Outline the approach being used along with what is expected of people

How much detail and depth we need to provide around these subjects should depend upon the size and criticality of the project. Project size can be measured by the number of people or amount of money involved—whatever best describes the magnitude of the undertaking for your organization.

For project criticality, I like to use a variation of Alistair Cockburn's "Failure results in loss of <X>" scale, which he uses in his Crystal family of methodologies.

This scale assesses what a failure in the product or service would result in. Failure of a video game means we waste some of our leisure time. Failure of a word processor means we may lose some work time or discretionary funds. Failure of a commercial service may result in a major loss of funds. Failure of an aircraft system or medical device may result in the loss of life.

As projects get larger in size or criticality, we typically apply more process, documentation, and communication rigor to help ensure success and the correct level of due diligence. Figure 14.6 shows this relationship.

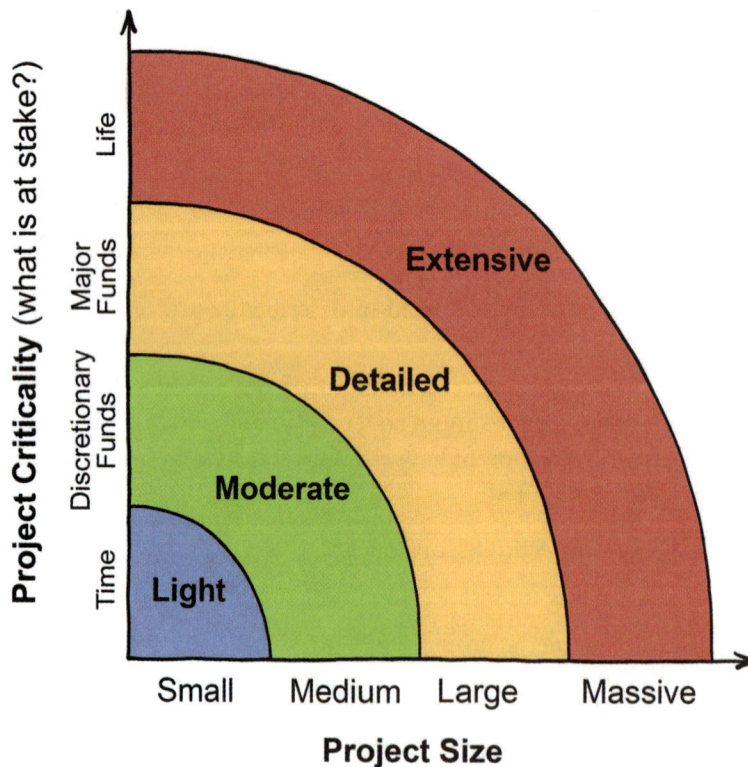

FIGURE 14.6 *Relationship between project criticality and project size*

We use project size and project criticality with an "OR" function to indicate the level of rigor required. So, if you have a large project or if major funds are at stake, then "detailed" documentation would be typical.

Defining What *Broken* Looks Like

Vision statements and project charters help us define what *done* should look like. However, it is also important to discuss and agree on what *broken* or *challenged* looks like. When we agree up fronton what constitutes *delayed* or *substandard*, it is far easier to quickly execute escalation procedures if these circumstances occur.

Also, at the beginning of a project, vendors are much more amenable to agreeing on these things because they often have a rose-colored view of flawless execution and contented customers. Getting vendors to agree on the escalation process for missed deadlines while these events are theoretical is much easier before they have actually fallen behind. However, we can later hold them (and ourselves) accountable to the project tolerances, exceptions, and escalation procedures we develop.

Ongoing Communications

Throughout project execution, we have an obligation to communicate—to try to overcommunicate—project status, issues, and progress. This leads us to the discussion of what metrics we should be tracking and reporting.

Good metrics are simple and relevant to the goal; they should fall out of the process, not be onerous to produce. Value-based metrics, such as stories developed (and tested) compared to stories remaining, meet the criteria of simple and relevant.

The evolving product is the primary measure of progress. Look at what has been built and tested! The product shows where we are in the project; missing functionality is what we still need to complete, directed by the business prioritization of features in the backlog. Agile reporting tools such as cumulative flow diagrams, burnup and burndown graphs, parking lot diagrams, QA stats, etc. also play a role in explaining important project information.

All these topics that are critical to our project success and perceived success (which should matter less but matter more than we think) are embodied in the BAM and discussed in the next chapter on performance analysis.

Chapter 14 Summary

Projects are people-based. We need to study, analyze, and come to understand how best to work with people and communicate with them. This includes asking them what they want, then communicating with them in that way.

Some of the communications that are universal to all projects include a vision, a charter, status reports, what *done* looks like, and what *broken* looks like. If we can agree on those core elements, many of the communication and collaboration problems with stakeholders will be solved.

Key topics covered in this chapter:

» Stakeholder analysis

» Communication complexities

» Defining done and broken

» Ongoing communications

Chapter 15
Organizational Change

Leading teams and implementing new solutions requires us to become change agents. Projects are only successful when they achieve the benefits they were commissioned to deliver. Nobody wants to build a product or service that does not get used. So, to be effective, we need to understand how organizational change works. We need to know how to identify and minimize resistance and facilitate positive change.

Being a change agent requires us to understand the common change frameworks and models. They each offer some useful tools for our organizational change toolbox.

The Kübler-Ross Model

Elisabeth Kübler-Ross introduced the "five stages of grief" model after her work with the terminally ill in 1969. The model became known simply as the Kübler-Ross model in 1969; it describes how change progresses through stages in a similar way to grieving. By understanding the steps and progressions associated with a significant loss, such as a death, we can recognize and help people who are dealing with less severe changes.

- Denial: Initial shock and disbelief about the event or change: *This must be a mistake…*

- Anger: When denial cannot continue, people become frustrated: *It is not fair!*

- Bargaining: *If I do this, can we make it somehow better?*

- Depression: *It is useless. Why bother with anything?*

- Acceptance: *It is going to be okay; I can move on.*

These stages can occur at different times for different people experiencing the same event. The sequence and morale level is shown in figure 15.1.

The Kübler-Ross Change Curve

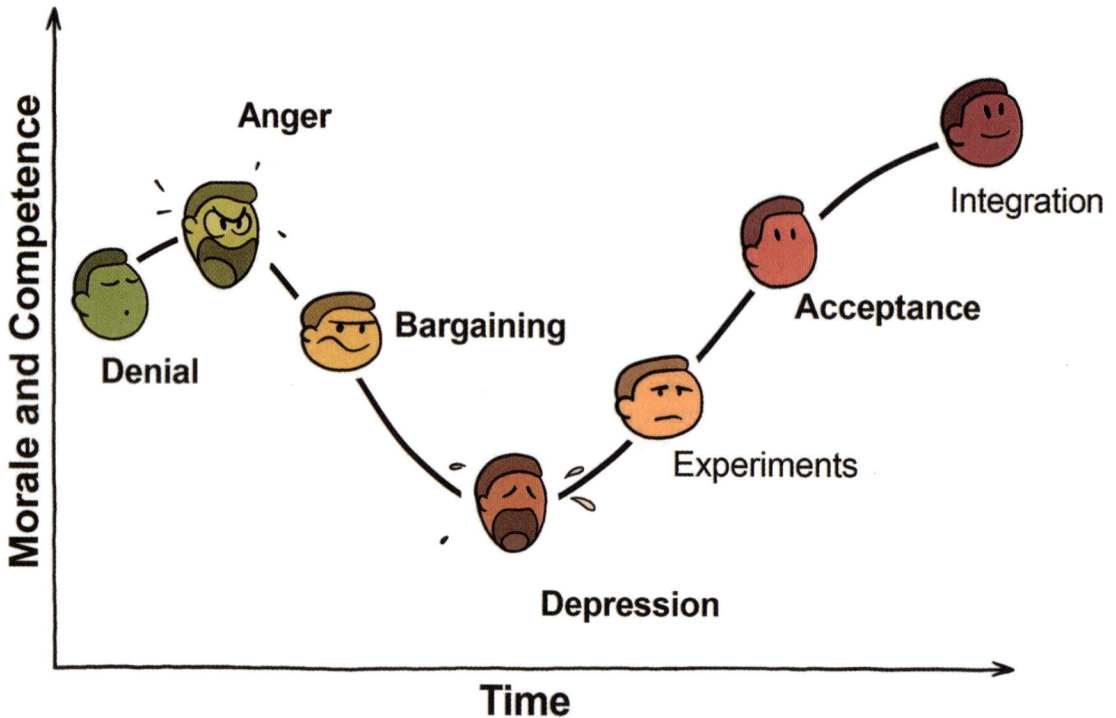

FIGURE 15.1 *The Kübler-Ross Change Curve*

Sometimes, we see the additional stages of *experiments* and *integration* added to the model. Experiments are small-scale attempts at the new environment that lead to eventual acceptance. Integration is encoding the "new normal" into our personal and organizational lives.

When introducing change in an organization, we often see these stages of grief. Knowing where people are in this cycle helps us in helping them move forward through the process. Below are some observations we might recognize from people being exposed to agile concepts for the first time.

1. Denial: *Nice ideas, but they do not apply to my project or how I work.*
2. Anger: *No, I will not change. You cannot make me use these stupid user stories.*
3. Bargaining: *Okay, how about if I have six-month iterations?*
4. Depression: *This is not working, nothing makes sense.*
5. Acceptance: *It was difficult, but I can now see how it helps.*

Satir Change Model

The Satir Change Model, introduced by Virginia Satir, helps us predict how people are likely to react and how to support people emotionally through the change process. It focuses on our comfort levels and confidence as we try something new.

Think about learning to drive, playing a musical instrument, or speaking a foreign language. First, our confidence is high as we consider the prospect of gaining independence, becoming a rock star, or traveling with ease. This is illustrated by the initial high score of confidence/comfort at point 1 in figure 15.2.

FIGURE 15.2 *Satir Change Model*

Then we start our learning and quickly realize that driving, playing the guitar, or learning Spanish is difficult and we are not as good at it as we are at all the familiar things we do every day. This is the confusion/loss period of the Satir Change Model shown at point 2. Many adults who have not had to learn significant new skills for many years find this uncomfortable.

Next, comes the "groan zone" of turmoil and despair, where some days go well, some days go poorly, and we seem to be moving backward (point 3). Understanding that this is perfectly normal is a great relief for many learners. It is helpful to point to the graph and explain that it is okay to feel bad because there is turmoil/despair in learning a new skill, but it will be followed by growth and confidence if they persevere.

Finally, with perseverance and practice, we acquire the new knowledge or skill, and our confidence and comfort rise above our original level (point 4), along with our usefulness.

There are parallels with the Kübler-Ross model, which focuses on the roller-coaster ride that change brings to our lives. Anyone who has been doing the same thing for a long time will experience these rollercoaster curves and emotions when we ask or force them to change.

ADKAR® Model

The ADKAR Model from Prosci is a goal-oriented model for individuals and organizations. ADKAR is an acronym that stands for awareness, desire, knowledge, ability, and reinforcement—the five outcomes that people need to achieve for lasting change.

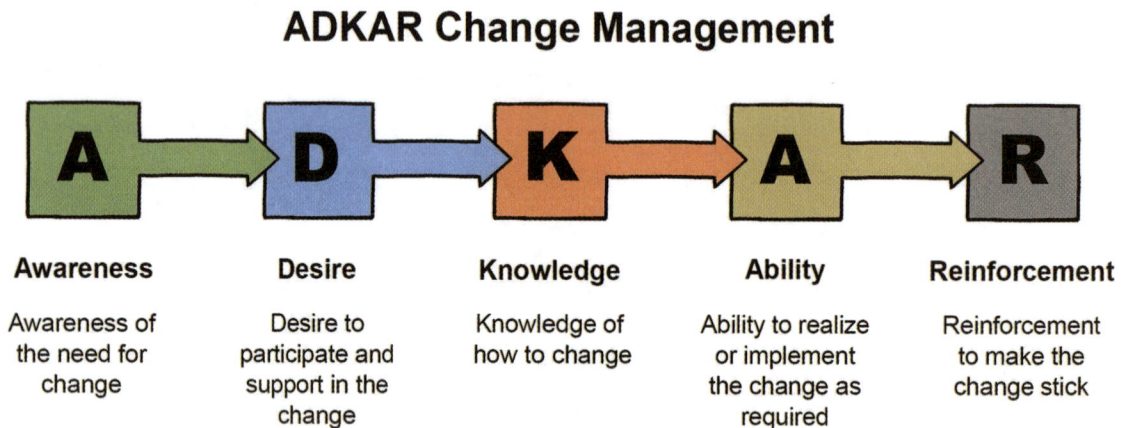

ADKAR Change Management

Awareness	Desire	Knowledge	Ability	Reinforcement
Awareness of the need for change	Desire to participate and support in the change	Knowledge of how to change	Ability to realize or implement the change as required	Reinforcement to make the change stick

FIGURE 15.3 *ADKAR Model*

By outlining the goals and outcomes of successful change, the ADKAR Model is a useful tool for planning change-management activities. It is often used as a basis for communications and training programs associated with organizational change.

Some organizations also use it as a checklist of activities to help ensure they have prepared groups for upcoming changes. For example, they would ask, *What did we do to spread awareness? Did everyone who wanted to get an opportunity to participate in the change? Were resources and training made available for people to increase their knowledge and practice their abilities in the new situation?*

Kotter's 8-Step Change Model

John Kotter is a change-management and leadership professor at Harvard Business School. He introduced his 8-Step Change Model in his 1995 book *Leading Change*. The model sets out the eight critical steps in the changes process and argues that neglecting any of the steps can be enough to cause the whole initiative to fail. The steps are:

1. **Create urgency** Describe the *need* for change, not just the *want* for change

2. **Form a powerful coalition** Recruit people to do the work and spread the message

3. **Create a vision for change** Encapsulate and promote the goal and benefits

4. **Communicate the vision** Utilize the coalition to continuously spread the word

5. **Remove obstacles** Enlist people to clear the way early and keep it clear

6. **Create short-term wins** Justify continued investment by promoting benefits

7. **Build on the change** Cement the change and avoid complacency

8. **Anchor the changes in corporate culture** Make the changes core and lasting

FIGURE 15.4 *Kotter's 8-Step Change Process*

I have had success using a change model roughly based on Kotter's 8-Step Change Model in several organizations. I call it a *change road map*; it considers both strategic and human-related steps of change.

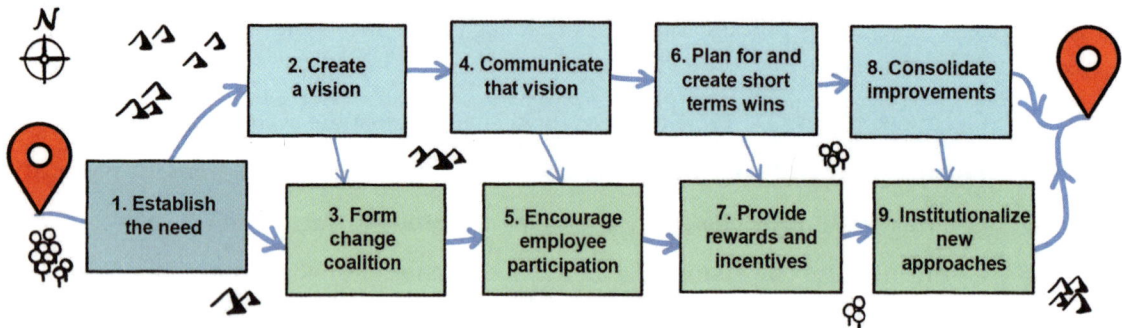

FIGURE 15.5 *Organizational Change Road Map*

The change road map shown in figure 15.5 uses parallel strategic and human threads to achieve successful change.

1. **Establish the need** Gain consensus as to why a change is needed. Qualify and assess the organization; analyze and document current problems and shortcomings. Capture previous stakeholder complaints, and issue log and postmortems problems. Keep it real, but if there is a burning platform from which we have to move forward, document it fairly. Determine the business benefits and describe where you are now.

2. **Create a vision** Describe a better state. Outline the goals and objectives you are aiming to create. Unite everyone with a common end goal of what success would look like. Describe where you want to be.

3. **Form a change coalition** Identify key stakeholders. Get people involved, not only on the initial project but also on advisory and review boards. Provide mechanisms for general input and information exchange. Use websites, lunch-and-learns, etc. Be civil, be humble, and be nice. Do not assume or give the impression the change team has all the answers. Ask people, *How should we get there?*

4. **Communicate the vision** Provide a clear outline of what is going to happen. People generally need to hear things five times in five different ways to ensure it sticks. Use different formats, analogies, and styles. It is usually impossible to overcommunicate a change-initiative vision. Plan and promote the organizational changes.

5. **Encourage employee participation** After inviting people to be involved, make sure they are. Schedule follow-up sessions and speak to people about their concerns. Ask for volunteer reviewers and give praise and thanks for their reviews, especially the negative ones. This is the opportunity to turn people around while the resistance is only at levels one and two. Work on forming good relationships, and select and train the team.

6. **Plan for and create short-term wins** Identify the initial project. Schedule some early small victories to build momentum, demonstrate progress, and reassure sponsors. People only trust for so long—give them something to justify their continued support.

7. **Provide rewards and incentives** Change on top of a regular job is a lot of extra work. Reward contributions as well as organizational norms will allow. If you cannot give bonuses, plan for some decent food for the lunch-and-learns. Give good mementos and freebies. Arrange for time off if teams work hard on initial projects. People have to see benefits in taking part, otherwise they will not bother. Goodwill, loyalty, and corporate benefits do not cut it with everyone.

8. **Consolidate improvements** Make sure the successful changes get repeated. Document the successes and spread the word. Monitor and perform mid-project retrospectives.

9. **Institutionalize new approaches** Complete and review the initial project. Measure and promote business benefits; get the sponsors and users to promote the benefits. Identify the next project and broader rollout plan. Make the changes stick by institutionalizing them—make them part of the standards and culture. Support other groups who are trying to repeat the process.

SCARF Model

The SCARF model is a neuroscience-based model for collaborating with and influencing others. It gets its name from the five social domains that influence our behaviors. These are:

1. **Status** Our relative importance to others

2. **Certainty** Our ability to predict the future

3. **Autonomy** Our sense of control over events

4. **Relatedness** How safe we feel with others

5. **Fairness** How fair we perceive the exchanges between people to be

FIGURE 15.6 *Domains of Social Behavior (SCARF Model)*

These five social domains trigger the same threat and reward circuits in our brain that we use for physical survival. We will consciously and subconsciously try to avoid these threats and move toward these rewards. So, when planning organizational change, we need to make sure we do not inadvertently introduce threats by, say, omitting a group from the change discussions and creating an exclusion threat to their feelings of relatedness. Instead, we want to provide all the reward feelings we can to attract people to the other side of the change.

These ideas are further supported by books, such as Donald Kirkpatrick's *How to Manage Change Effectively: Approaches, Methods, and Case Examples*, that list many circumstances in which people will resist or accept change. Anyone who is trying to roll out agile methods would do well to be aware of them.

People will resist change under any of the following circumstances:

- When there is a sense of loss, be it of security, pride or satisfaction, freedom, responsibility, authority, good working conditions, and/or status

- When the change initiative and its implications are misunderstood

- Where it is believed that the change does not make sense for the organization:

  » The change is misdirected; the current state or alternatives are better

  » It may create more problems than it is worth

  » Our extra efforts are not being rewarded

- When there is a low tolerance for change in their lives, perhaps because there are already many changes at home
- When change violates a principle or commitment that the organization must stand by, such as customer service or quality
- When there is a lack of respect for those initiating the change
- When people are excluded from the change initiative; this is a great way to generate resistance
- When changes are viewed as criticism of how things were done in the past: *You are so bad at development that we are going to have to adopt agile methods!*
- When the change effort occurs at a bad time, such as when other issues or problems are also being handled (for example, just before a company takeover)

Fortunately, people will accept change under the following circumstances:

- When the change is seen as a personal gain, be it in security, money, authority, status or prestige, responsibility, working conditions, or achievement
- When it provides a new challenge and reduces boredom; when we create more interesting work
- When they are given the opportunity to influence the change initiative; when we involve people in the changes
- When the time is right for organizational change
- When the source of the change initiative is liked and respected
- When the approach of the change and how it is implemented appeals to them; when they buy into the approach being taken

These characteristics remind me of one of my first opportunities to roll out agile before it was widely known. I was working for IBM, and our client was a government department. Having struggled to get dedicated business input on previous projects, I commandeered a large boardroom to collocate the development team and business SMEs. It seemed like a good setup: everyone was together in one room and we had direct access to the business representatives for requirements elicitation, clarification, and demo feedback. We were getting lots of features built, but the business representatives were not happy.

Luckily, I had access to many people at IBM more experienced than I was. I was given the Donald Kirkpatrick book mentioned previously, which outlined when people resist change because they see it as a threat and when they support change as an opportunity for reward or improvement.

Within government, the most junior hires work in open-plan cubical offices. As they are promoted, they are given bigger cubicles with higher walls that are more like mini offices. Next comes a real office, then an office with a window, and, eventually, a corner office. In short, their work space defines their status, responsibility, and authority.

By bringing these business representatives into a shared boardroom to work on the project, I had unwittingly triggered threats about the loss of status, certainty, and autonomy. Making them sit and work together like the most junior recruits had caused a loss of good working conditions, status, freedom, pride, satisfaction, and perceived authority—a bad idea when hoping to develop a productive working relationship with someone.

After reading the Kirkpatrick book, I changed the approach. Instead of the business SMEs being colocated with the team all the time, they returned to their fancy corner offices, long lunch breaks, and afternoons spent reading the newspaper—which they could not do when everyone sat together. Instead, I reserved their mornings for questions, review sessions, and demonstrations. This was better received because their morning calendars were blocked with important-looking project meetings, but I rarely called on all of them at once unless it was for a business demo.

Now they had their offices back, enjoyed a little more free time, and were engaged more respectfully. The team was skeptical at first. However, it is much better to have one hour with someone who is cheerful, engaged, and helpful than to have eight hours with someone who is bitter, obstinate, and causing issues. The project went much smoother after these changes, and it taught me a valuable lesson: never try to introduce a process or practice without considering the human element first.

We completed the project early, primarily due to the input and hard work of the business SMEs during acceptance testing, and IBM got their successful case study. I learned to temper my enthusiasm and consider other stakeholders, who will undoubtedly have a view of the project that is different from mine. Individuals and interactions are indeed more important than processes and tools, even if they are your pet agile processes and tools.

Chapter 15 Summary

There is a plethora of recognized change-management frameworks and models, including many others that we did not cover here, such as the OODA (observe, orient, decide, act) loop and drama triangles. They all have something to offer and provide insights that can help us get our projects accepted and their benefits realized.

Leaders should be aware of the change models and tools for a couple of reasons. First, they can help us be successful. Delivering a project output is not enough; when the operation is successful, but the patient died, there is no success. We need to look at the outcomes, not outputs, of our work.

A big part of getting to success is organizational change—greasing the tracks ahead of the project, to ease its introduction.

The second reason is that, much like understanding the basics of finance or your industry's vocabulary, you will likely hear the terms ADKAR, Kübler-Ross, and Satir as you take on more senior roles or work with executives. While transparency and the willingness to ask for help are good traits, it is preferable to be the person explaining the concepts rather than the person asking, *What the heck does* X *mean?* should someone else mention a model.

So, get acquainted with the models and test your own experiences against them. See if you can find some examples where actions led to resistance and think about what a better strategy may have been in those circumstances. These are useful tools; we do not need to use them all the time, but it is better to know about them and have them stashed away than to try to invent something in the heat of the moment.

Key topics covered in this chapter:

» Understanding organizational change

» The emotional rollercoaster of change

» Models for navigating change (ADKAR, Kotter, SCARF)

Chapter 16
Performance Analysis (Key Topics)

Is what we are doing working? Are we getting closer to our goal of building our new wonder product or service? Are the people happy or at least engaged and in agreement? These are all critical questions to ask and answer to ensure we are doing the right things and doing things right.

The BAM encourages honest review and reflection, not only within our teams but also within the broader stakeholder community.

Status Reporting

Ah, the good old project status report, loved and hated by PMs, PMOs, and sponsors alike. It seems like a litmus test or amplifier to show organizational execution competence. Productive organizations use good versions of the status report while struggling groups often have awkward, irrelevant templates that seem to reflect their organization's likely future. So, how do we create great ones? Do we even need them if our evolving product speaks for itself?

Even if our project is agile with a preference for "working product over documentation" and for "face-to-face meetings over written documentation," I believe there is merit in a written status report. It describes a snapshot of progress and standing to stakeholders who cannot be present. It also forces the regular assessment of basic project attributes.

Effective status reports typically combine some or all the elements of a four-way review and the project constraints.

Four-Way View

As its name implies, a four-way view describes four assessments of the project.

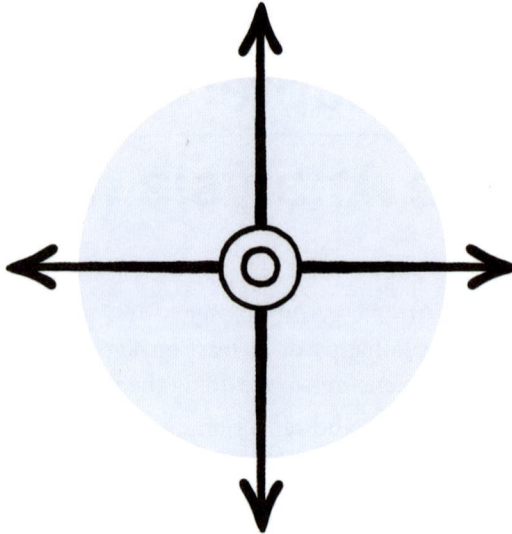

FIGURE 16.1 *Four-way View*

These four views are:

← A look back at what has been achieved since the last report,

→ A look forward at what is planned and scheduled next,

↓ A look downward into the team to surface any personnel or project execution issues or risks,

↑ A look upward to review any competitor analysis, ROI, and sponsorship direction changes or inputs that may have occurred.

Addressing these four views of a project ensures good coverage of the project accomplishments and issues. It provides a logical framework for discussions at a high level and assures stakeholders that the context of the project is being considered. It does not, however, go into the specifics of a project, such as performance against the plan or budget reporting, so it is normal to accompany a four-way view with a review of the project constraints.

Measuring Project Objectives and Constraints

Organizations are transitioning from assessing project success as meeting time, schedule, and cost targets and focusing instead on delivering value and delighting the customer. With this transition has come the adoption of measuring attributes such as:

- Customer satisfaction: Are customers satisfied with the benefits, outcomes, and experience when using your product or service?

- Market responsiveness: The ability of the organization to change direction and pivot quickly to respond to changing market needs and external factors.

- Innovation: The ability to adopt technology or new ideas that are often sourced or suggested internally.

- Continuous improvement: The ability of the project team to contribute to the organization's ongoing pursuit of optimizations and improvements in all its functions.

- Productivity: Teams maintain a predictable cadence of value delivery, enabling the business to make informed business predictions and decisions.

- Employee engagement: Are team members satisfied in their work? Are they willing to go the extra mile? Do they demonstrate a passion for their jobs and for the direction of the organization?

- Concept speed: The time it takes to develop an idea and deliver it to the market.

- Quality: The product or service meets the market's expectations of usability and reliability.

- Predictability: Increasing the business value is realized while maintaining or reducing costs.

Organizations that have not made this transition typically still use project constraints as a way of evaluating project performance. In an agnostic or hybrid environment, we can anticipate being expected to report on some or all the project constraints shown in figure 16.2.

The project-constraints view provides a deep dive into the major attributes of the project. This includes the basic measures of scope, schedule, and budget, along with the secondary measures of risks, resources, quality, and customer satisfaction. Many people do not like the term *resources* when applied to people, but in this context, it means both physical resources, such as the availability of tools and materials, and the availability and suitability of people and roles.

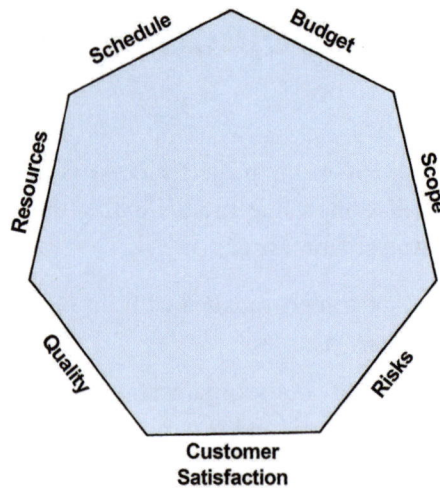

FIGURE 16.2 *Project Constraints*

Depending on the size and criticality of the project, the status report would describe performance against each of these categories. A small and noncritical project might just provide a summary statement for each constraint. The status report for a large or high-criticality project would have more detail and a discussion of performance compared to expected ranges. Deviations from forecast tolerances for each constraint would trigger an escalation.

Spend, Progress, and Earned Value Management (EVM)

Project leaders need to understand the basics and application of EVM. At its simplest level, EVM combines the tracking of spend and progress against a baselined plan. Before we examine EVM, let us look at how we usually track the components of spend and progress separately.

S curves are great for tracking project spend. They are simple to interpret and quickly let us see if we are over or under budget.

Project Expenditure

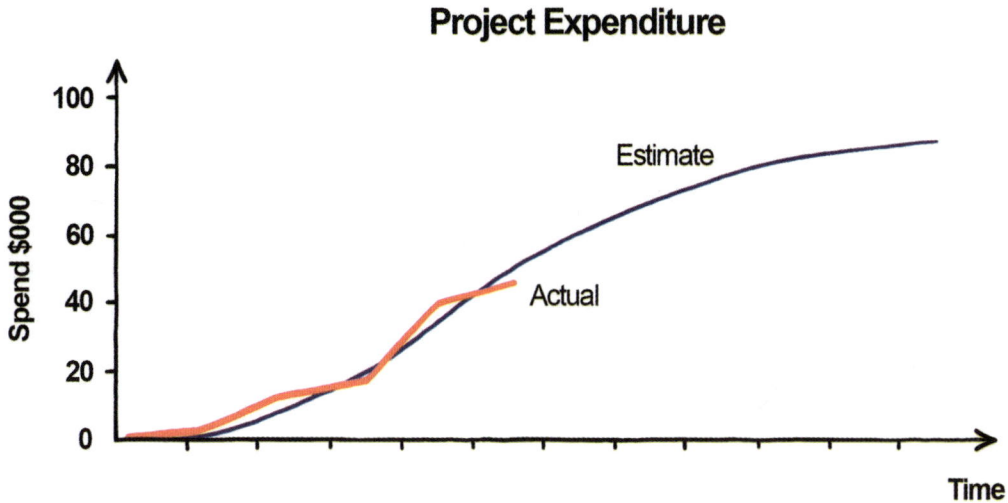

FIGURE 16.3 *S Curve*

However, we could be doing fine spendwise, but behind from a schedule perspective. This is where tracking Gantt charts are helpful in showing the project schedule.

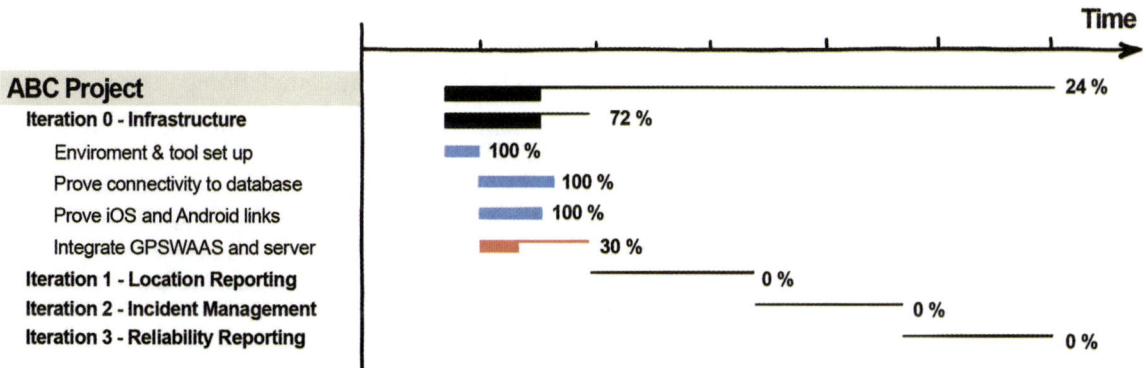

FIGURE 16.4 *Gantt Chart*

Yet, Gantt charts lack the spend component. Pretty soon, most projects get ahead or behind in spend and time, so trying to gauge overall project health becomes difficult.

EVM was created for this reason; it combines both spend and progress variables to produce a comprehensive set of project measures and metrics.

Benefits of EVM

- It is a leading indicator: Hindsight is not of much use to people. At least EVM tries to predict completion dates and final costs. *Imperfect leading metrics are always more valuable than perfect trailing metrics because they give us options to replan and change our approach.*

- It is visual: It is easy to forget the EVM graphs and focus on the numbers, but at the heart of the process are some useful graphs. Visual is good because it engages the right side of the brain and helps us draw on more mental power to understand, interpret, and plan appropriate responses. Visual things are also better to discuss and collaborate on because we can point, annotate, and extrapolate easier than with words or numbers alone.

Issues with EVM

- Accuracy of the baseline plan: EVM compares actual project performance to planned performance at a point in time. So, if our initial plan is wrong, we could effectively be trying to do the equivalent of tracking our progress on a road trip from Paris to Rome using a map of South America. The quality of the baseline plan is a critical success factor of EVM. In agile projects, we acknowledge that initial plans will likely need to change and so the basis for effective EVM is quickly eroded with evolving plans.

- Assumes linear progression: The idea that a linear extrapolation of past performance to predict future performance is suspect and works better for defined, repeatable, low-risk tasks. However, most knowledge-work projects have nonlinear completion patterns.

Figure 16.5 shows the differences between linear and nonlinear completion patterns.

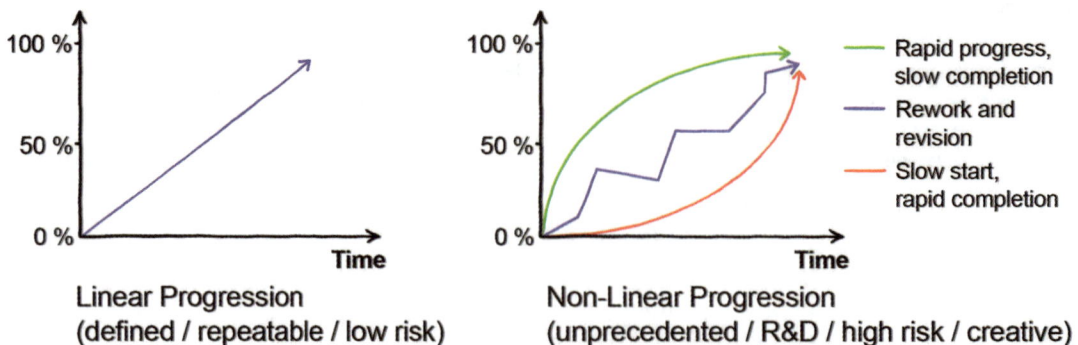

FIGURE 16.5 *Linear and Nonlinear Progression*

The first graph shows a linear progression of work progress. We get linear progressions for defined, repeatable work, such as painting a fence or digging a ditch, where work is stable and low risk. If it takes us two and a half days to do the first 50 percent, then it will likely take us another two days to do the remaining 50 percent. Linear extrapolation of progress is relatively accurate.

However, if we are doing anything unprecedented, based on research and development, or high-risk or creative, we generally do not experience linear progression. Instead, we get curves or stepped progression as depicted in the second graph.

The top green line shows a rapid start and slow completion. We get this profile when the easy work goes well, but the last, difficult elements take longer to solve—common in engineering problems. The opposite curve (shown by the red line) shows a slow start and rapid completion. We see this shape when creating a class or pattern in software that takes a long time to create initially, but then we can reuse it in many places to quickly solve a large number of problems. Finally, the stepped middle progression depicts trial and error—some things go well, some things do not. Progress is sporadic, with lulls and breakthroughs that are difficult to predict.

Knowledge-work projects have more of the nonlinear progression tasks than industrial-work projects do. It makes the application of techniques like EVM more problematic. They can still be used, but they may be less accurate at predicting final project costs.

- Where is the quality? We could be on time and on budget but building a horrible product that the business does not like or is low in quality. We should be aware that cost and schedule are not the whole picture. EVM and agile alternatives are just part of the picture.

Agile EVM

Traditional EVM metrics like schedule-performance index (SPI) and cost-performance index (CPI) can be translated into agile terms. For example, if we planned to complete 30 stories this iteration, but only completed 25, then our SPI is 25/30 or 0.83 (we are working at only 83 percent of the rate planned). Likewise, CPI is the EV (completed features value) to date divided by the actual costs to date, in the example above, $2,200,000/$2,800,000 = 0.79. This means we are only getting 79 cents on the dollar compared to what we had predicted (but, of course, who is to say that what we predicted is correct?).

For a full description of how EVM can be used on hybrid and agile projects, see my book *PMI-ACP Exam Prep* (available at rmcls.com).

Some Issues with Metrics

Whether our metrics are goal based (customer satisfaction, innovation, etc.) or constraint based (scope, schedule, etc.), there are some issues about metrics we should be aware of. Metrics are like fire. When controlled properly and used appropriately, they are useful, but if they are not used correctly or allowed to get out of control, they cause a lot of damage.

The BAM provides a well-rounded view of projects that considers both human engagement and performance data. By focusing on the needs of the stakeholders we are reporting to and acknowledging the uncertainty and variability in making future projections, we can try to produce the most useful reports possible.

Unfortunately, not all the things we can measure or observe are that helpful to us. In fact, many observations can, without proper understanding, lead us to the wrong conclusions. Such as:

» The sun rises up in the sky in the morning and then falls down again at night.

» Planets revolve around Earth.

» Stars come out at night.

» Heavier objects fall faster than lighter objects.

While these observations seem valid, they are all based on flawed understandings of the underlying systems. So, we need to be careful that we understand what we are measuring and how the systems work. We also need to be careful to measure and collect the right attributes because there are so many things we could measure, most of which are less valuable than the smart metrics we should be focusing on. With not enough metrics, we are flying blind; with too many, we are flying blinded.

> *There are so many possible measures in a software process that some random selection of metrics will not likely turn up something of value.*
>
> —Watts Humphrey

Often, the things we really want to measure are kind of hard to discern or objectively measure. Such as:

» Spouse's mood

» Sponsor confidence

» Team commitment

This leads us to recognize that many of the most useful metrics are subjective and intangible, and challenge us to try to measure them.

Not everything that counts can be counted,
and not everything that can be counted counts.

—William Bruce Cameron

Use Design-Factory Metrics

One of my favorite project-management books has nothing to do with software development or even project management, really. It is *Managing the Design Factory* by Donald Reinertsen and it is packed full of valuable project truths from the world of product design and development that apply equally well in the design-heavy world of software.

Reinertsen has many valuable lessons for planning and estimation, but what I want to draw on right now are his guidelines for valuable metrics. First, they should be simple; the ideal metrics are self-generating in the sense that they are created without extra effort in the normal course of business; second, they should be relevant to the end goal of the project; and third, they should be focused on leading indicators that are future focused.

So, given these characteristics of good project metrics, let us see how many of today's traditional project metrics measure up.

Desirable characteristics:

- » The Hawthorne effect is positive
- » Simple, self-generating
- » Relevant to the end goal
- » Leading, future focused

Beware the Hawthorne Effect

The Hawthorne effect describes the phenomenon of influencing what you measure. It gets its name from the Hawthorne Western Electric plant in Illinois, where Elton Mayo and others conducted experiments on work productivity in the 1920s and 1930s.

They selected a group of workers and put them in a controlled environment where they could measure their productivity. They made the working environment brighter and remeasured worker productivity to find it had increased. Upon installing more lights and making the workplace even brighter, they found worker productivity increased yet again. I am sure Western Electric could see the marketing potential for installing more electric lights in factories. However, Mayo was a good scientist and, as a control, reset the lighting to the original levels and measured productivity. Once again, it went up, seemingly unrelated to lighting levels. The simple act of measuring a group of people against something influences their behavior.

In the years following, there has been lots of speculation about exactly what caused these increases. Was it the special treatment of separating out a group, the public way the measurements are taken, or where the data was displayed? However, it is widely accepted that you will influence what you measure. So, the takeaway is to be careful what you measure, because the side effect may have adverse consequences for your project.

Traditional Metrics

- Lines of code written: Poor, does not reward simplification, leads to code bloat
- Function-points delivered: Poor, effort to generate, not relevant to the end goal of project
- Hours worked: Poor, leads to long hours, burnout, defects, consumed budgets

The list goes on (budget consumed, conformance to plan, etc.). Many of the project metrics that companies collect and publish violate these basic goals of design-factory metrics and acknowledgment of the Hawthorne effect. I am not saying that we do not measure things like budget consumed; obviously, we have a responsibility to do so, but not overtly—not with big graphs on the wall and in-your-face collection. Instead, be more aware of the nuances of metrics collection and focus on smarter project metrics.

Smarter Project Metrics

Okay, so if the previous metrics are not optimal, what constitutes a better set? Well, metrics that recognize that you will influence what you measure and that focus on simple factors related to project success in the future. Such as:

- » Features accepted
- » Sponsor confidence
- » User satisfaction
- » Defect cycle times

Here are some examples:

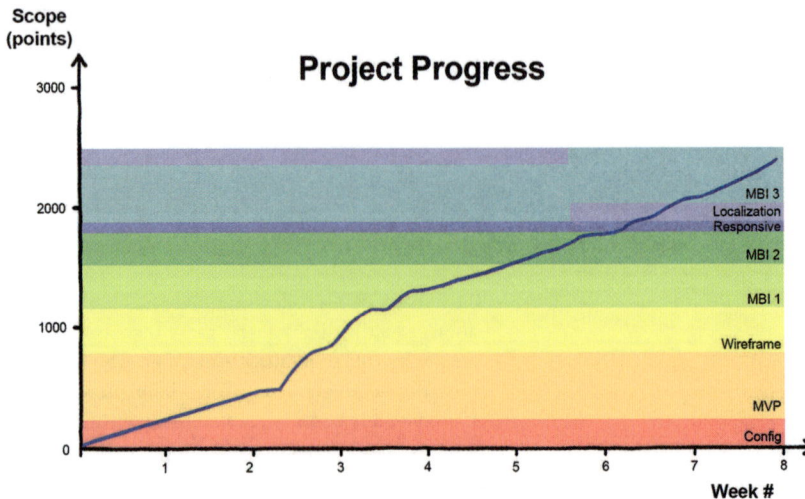

FIGURE 16.6 *Cumulative Graph of Accepted Features*

Figure 16.6 shows a cumulative graph of features accepted by the business. The colored bands in the background show different functional areas and the blue line shows progress against these areas. Note that we are tracking features accepted, not features developed or features tested. The end goal of the project is to have the system accepted by the business, so this is what we need to track.

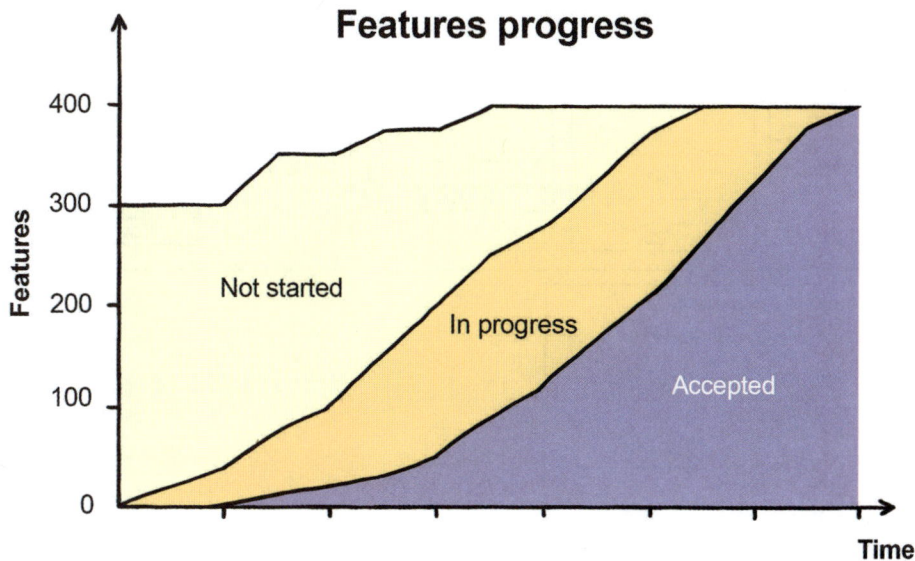

FIGURE 16.7 *Smarter Metrics*

Figure 16.7 is a cumulative flow diagram that not only shows features accepted, but also WIP. Queue size is a useful leading metric that can help us determine likely completion times.

Feature Based Reporting

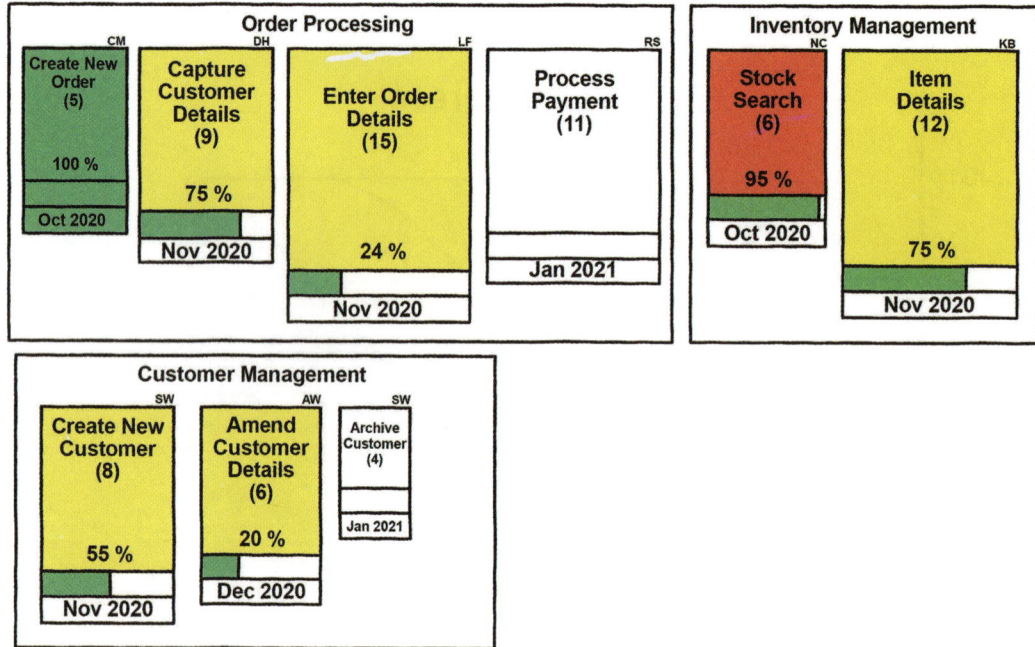

FIGURE 16.8 Parking Lot Diagram

Parking lot diagrams (figure 16.8) are a nice way of summarizing progress against a variety of goals in a single-page executive summary. Color-coding helps highlight areas behind (red), done (green), in progress (yellow), and not yet started (white).

Net Promoter Score is another tool we can use for sponsors and customers. It measures how likely people are to recommend the product or service to others. It is an index that ranges from −10 to 10. (Some organizations use a range of −100 to 100, but the concepts are the same.)

Net Promoter Score is calculated by asking stakeholders if they would promote the product, advise against using it, or take no action. Stakeholders are classified as promoters (with a score of 9 or 10), passives (score of 7 or 8), or detractors (score below 6).

A final Net Promoter Score is calculated as the percentage of promoters minus the percentage of detractors, creating a strong predictor of business success and customer satisfaction. A positive Net Promoter Score is a reliable indicator of success, while a net negative score indicates that there is probably something wrong that needs improvement.

Measuring Up

Measuring up means raising the level of measurement one level higher than you might initially expect.

Robert Austin, in his book *Measuring and Managing Performance in Organizations*, makes three key observations[1]:

1. "You get what you measure."

2. "You get only what you measure, nothing else."

3. "You tend to lose the things that you can't measure: insight, collaboration, creativity."

The first observation correlates with the Hawthorne effect. The second says that if you do not measure things, they may not get done. The third observation is that we need to be careful that our measures do not promote local optimization and suppress desirable behaviors like collaboration.

A company that understands this is Nucor Steel. Growing quickly since they were listed on the stock market in 1971 into a $4 billion leader with a great record for employee retention, collaboration, and labor relations, they attribute a lot of their success to their incentive pay based on productivity.

The interesting thing is that plant managers are not paid based on how well their plan performs, but on how well their plant and other plants perform. This may sound unfair: How can they influence how other plants perform? Well, through collaboration, sharing ideas, and cooperation. Likewise, departments are measured across multiple departments (to avoid silos), teams across teams, and individuals by team results. This rewards collaboration and cooperation that would otherwise be difficult to measure and encourage.

In the software world, defects could be traced back to individual developers, but they may well be the result of environmental challenges. So rolling defects up to an entire team and getting the testers involved earlier to provide more timely and valuable feedback to developers may be a better way to go.

> *Instead of making sure that people are measured within their span of control, it is more effective to measure people one level above their span of control. This is the best way to encourage teamwork, collaboration, and global, rather than local, optimization.*
>
> —Mary Poppendieck

Favor Leading over Lagging Metrics

We touched on this briefly earlier. Design-factory metrics should be leading versus lagging, focusing on the future so that they can help us change direction and make better project choices. For an accountant, a perfect view of the past might be useful, but for a PM, a perfect, or even imperfect, view of the future is far more useful.

So, we should pay less attention to lagging metrics that have already past, including actual values. Instead, we should pay more attention to leading metrics, such as trends and the likely impacts of their projections.

Trends

Observations	Mar 3	Mar 10	Mar 17	Mar 24	Mar 31
Defects Opened	5	25	30	20	10
Defects Closed	1	16	35	22	15
Defects Remaining	4	13	8	6	1
CR Opened	0	18	20	23	12
CR Closed	0	11	21	16	9
CR Remaning	0	7	6	13	16
Clarif. Opened	9	12	14	8	2
Clarif. Closed	6	14	11	9	5
Clarif. Remaining	3	1	4	3	0
Total Observations	7	21	18	22	17

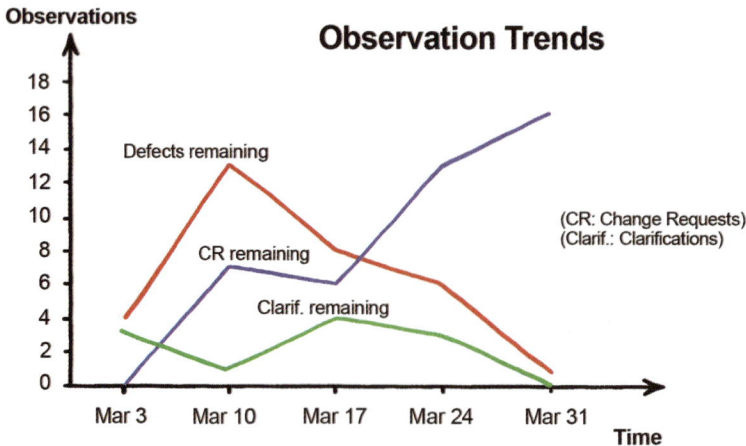

FIGURE 16.9 *Trends*

In figure 16.9, we can see the trend for unresolved change requests is increasing month over month. Perhaps we do not allow enough time to fully understand user expectations and are pushing too hard to build features.

Risk Short Name	Jan Imp	Jan Prob	Jan Sav	Feb Imp	Feb Prob	Feb Sav	Mar Imp	Mar Prob	Mar Sav	Apr Imp	Apr Prob	Apr Sav
JD BC driver performance	3	2	6	3	0	0	3	0	0	3	0	0
Calling Oracle stored via web service	2	2	4	2	0	0	2	0	0	2	0	0
Remote app distribution to PDAs	3	2	6	3	1	3	3	0	0	3	0	0
Oracle Warehouse Builder stability	2	2	4	2	3	6	2	2	4	2	0	0
Source system availability	2	1	2	2	1	2	2	0	0	2	0	0
Access to user community	2	1	2	2	2	4	2	2	4	2	1	2
Availability of architect	2	2	4	2	3	6	2	2	4	2	0	0
Server upgrade necessary	1	2	2	1	1	1	1	0	0	1	0	0
Oracle handheld Warehouse Browser Launch	3	1	3	3	1	3	3	3	9	3	1	3
PST changes for BC	0	0	0	0	0	0	2	2	4	2	1	2
			33			**25**			**25**			**7**

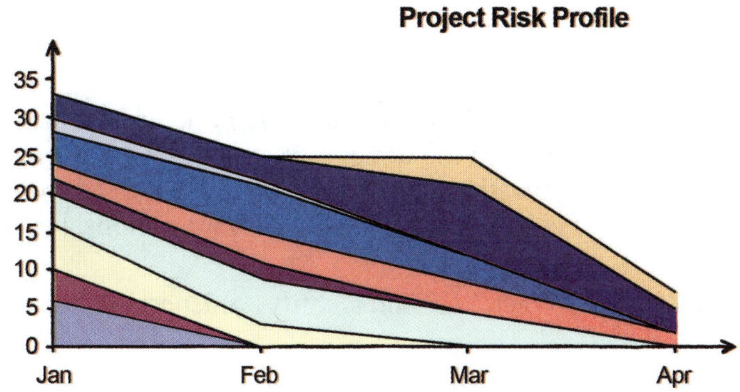

FIGURE 16.10 *Trends: Risks Reduced*

In figure 16.10, we are trending project risks and can see that the overall trend is down, toward risk reduction and avoidance. Risk-profile graphs like this can be useful to explain project progress in the early phases of a project when we are doing technology trials (via development spikes) and risk mitigation is a strong focus and there may not be a lot to demo to the business.

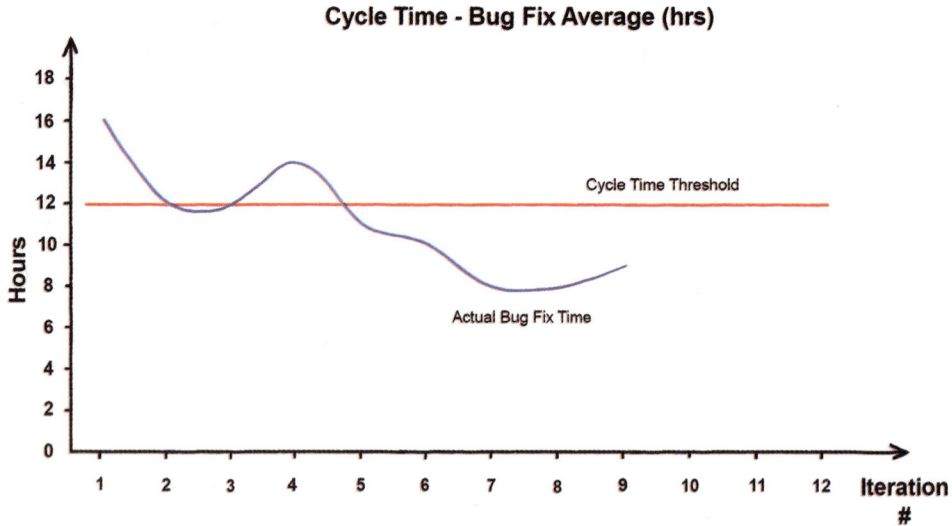

FIGURE 16.11 *Cycle Times*

Cycle times are also a great leading metric for identifying bottlenecks in a process. In the example depicted in figure 16.11, the user interface (UI) designer is the bottleneck in the process, handling 30 stories an iteration, a lower number than anyone else on the team. Micromanaging people and measuring individual productivity is not effective, so how do we gain insight into these bottlenecks?

Cumulative flow diagrams can be used to track WIP and identify bottlenecks without the need for micromanagement.

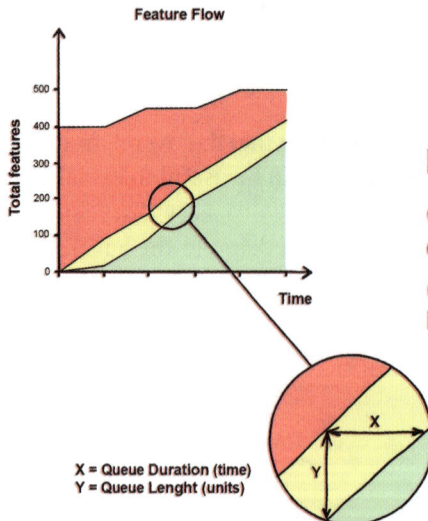

Little's Law

Cycle times are proportional to queue lengths

(We can predict completion times based on queue size)

X = Queue Duration (time)
Y = Queue Lenght (units)

FIGURE 16.12 *Little's Law*

Little's law tells us that queue size is proportional to queue length. So, by measuring WIP we can gain insights into completion times. However, we need to be careful how we measure and report queue size because we do not want to influence it to make it larger, but rather aim to reduce WIP.

Task Boards and Kanban

Tolerances, Exceptions, and Escalation Processes

When caught in a fire or other urgent situation, it is useful to have an escape plan already developed, and to have emergency equipment on hand and know how to use it. The same goes for project exception processes: If something untoward happens, it is not the best time to be creating new processes to deal with the event and explaining how to use them; emotions are high and people respond to bad news in different ways. It is better to practice an agreed-upon procedure than to figure out new rules.

Project tolerances and exception plans provide an agreed-upon emergency plan for when bad stuff happens to our projects. They act as guardrails, helping us avoid going off track and providing a mutually understood and agreed-upon resolution process. So, just as an emergency situation is not the best time to collaborate on improvising a rope ladder, a major project-scope change is not the best time to define a resolution process between project stakeholders.

We will look at the two elements (**tolerances** and **exception plans**) individually and then examine how they work together. Project tolerances are the guardrails, the upper and lower boundaries the project stakeholders are willing to tolerate for a given project metric. Another way to think of them is the amount of slack rope we have as a project team to do our own thing (or hang ourselves with). Tolerances can be set on a variety of metrics and the degree of variation will depend upon the individual risk tolerances of the collective stakeholders. Some projects might be time-critical, while others are more concerned with budget or user satisfaction.

Budget Tolerance

Figure 16.14 shows a budget tolerance set at +10 percent (red) and −20 percent (green) of the predicted spend rate.

Projected and Actual Project Spend with Tolerances

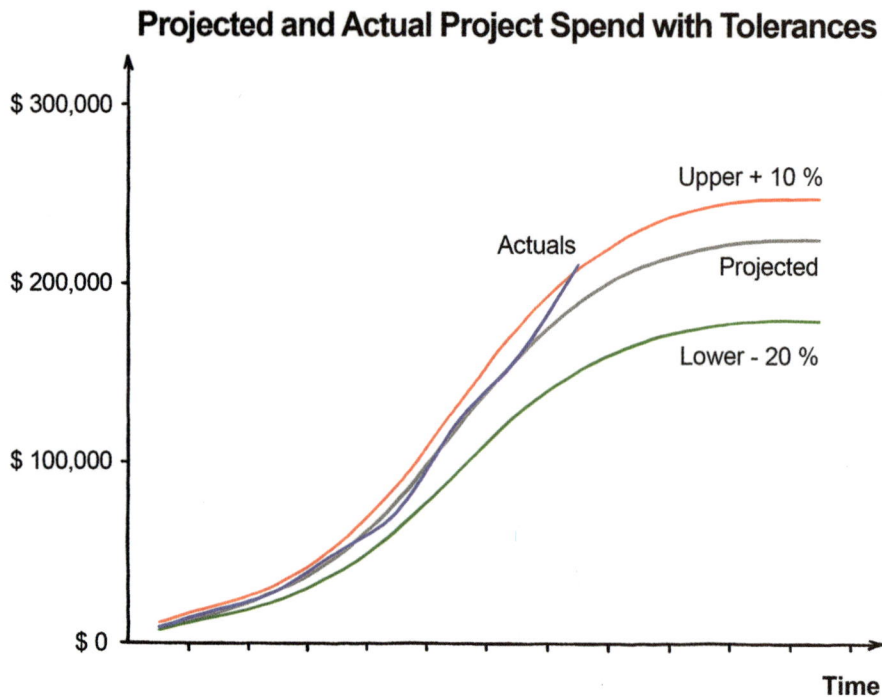

FIGURE 16.14 *Projected and Actual Project Spend with Tolerance*

The blue line is tracking the actual spend; in August, it has exceeded the +10 percent upper tolerance that would trigger the exception plan.

Significant project underspending can be a problem too, hence the lower green threshold.

Returning a large portion of unspent funds at the end of a project represents lost opportunity; this money could have been used to fund other profitable projects during this project's lifetime had it been returned. As a junior PM, I once thought that finishing under budget was a good thing, until it was pointed out to me that this represented poor reporting and a failure to fully utilize available capital for ROI!

Iteration Velocity

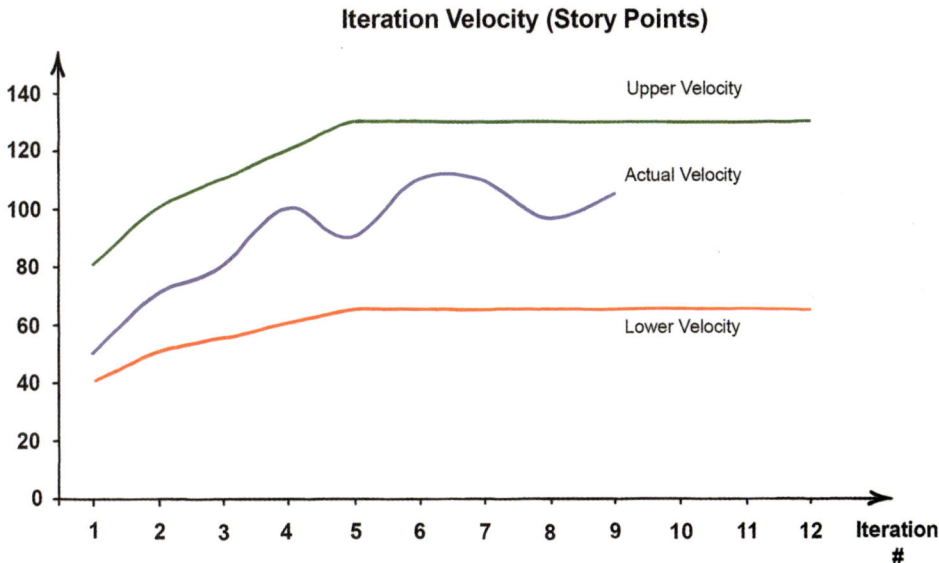

FIGURE 16.15 *Iteration Velocity (Story Points)*

Figure 16.15 shows iteration velocity that tracks story point completion per iteration. It is a good indicator of productivity throughput, and tolerances can be used to trigger further investigation if it drops below a certain level. In our example, the lower tolerance is set to 65 story points per iteration for iteration 5 onward (the red line). While you might think high velocity is good, I would like to investigate whether velocity appears to skyrocket, because this could be a sign of gaming (fudging) the metrics. (When things appear to be too good to be true, they usually are.)

Sponsor Confidence

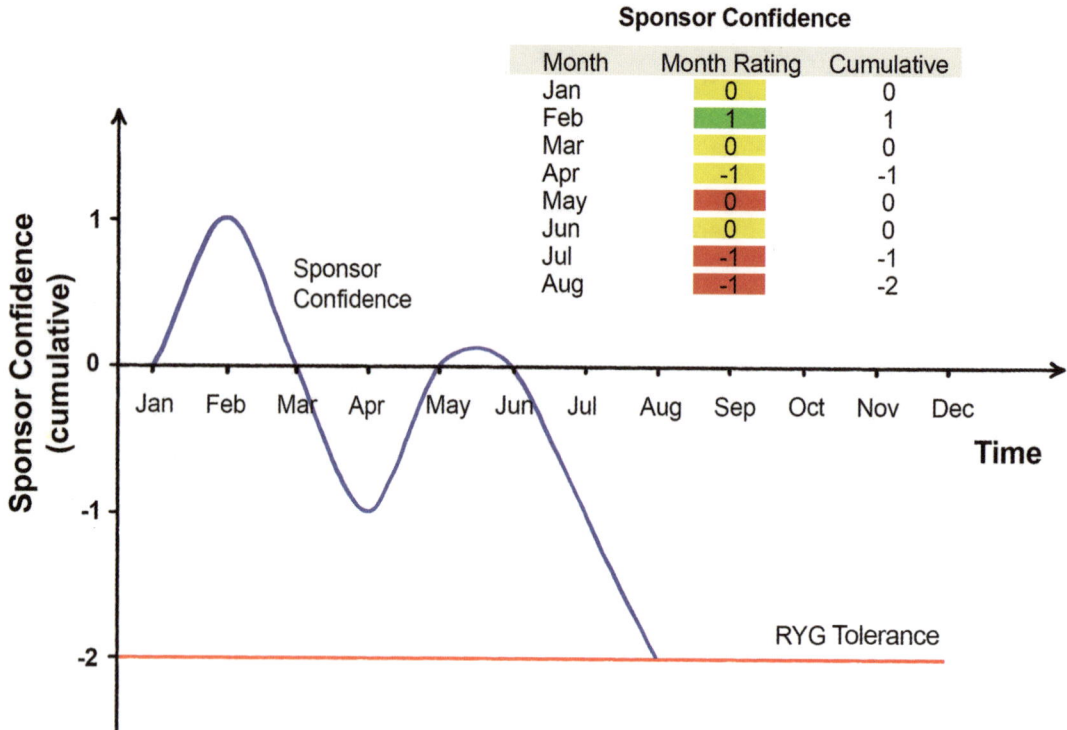

Sponsor Confidence

Month	Month Rating	Cumulative
Jan	0	0
Feb	1	1
Mar	0	0
Apr	-1	-1
May	0	0
Jun	0	0
Jul	-1	-1
Aug	-1	-2

FIGURE 16.16 *Sponsor Confidence*

Sponsor confidence is another metric we could set tolerances for. It is quite common to canvass sponsors for a simple green, yellow, or red flag for each iteration. While the odd yellow, or even a single red, might not be cause for notifying the steering committee (or whatever group of stakeholders we wish to engage), a persistent trend of yellows or reds indicates that something is clearly wrong and we need to intervene. The model used in figure 16.17 keeps a running score of greens, yellows, and reds. A green earns +1, a yellow 0, and a red −1. If the total drops below −2, we need to investigate.

User Satisfaction

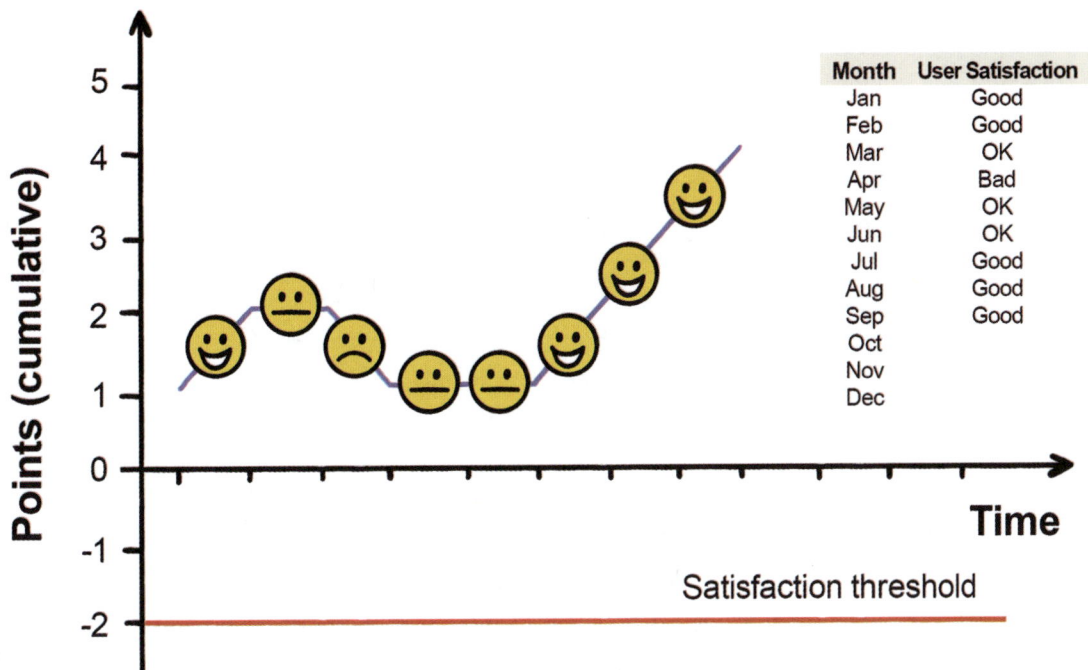

FIGURE 16.17 *User Satisfaction*

A similar approach can be used for user satisfaction. Tracking application satisfaction via simple smiley faces (happy, neutral, sad) and keeping a cumulative score can be useful for tracking mood and identifying trends and issues.

Cycle Time

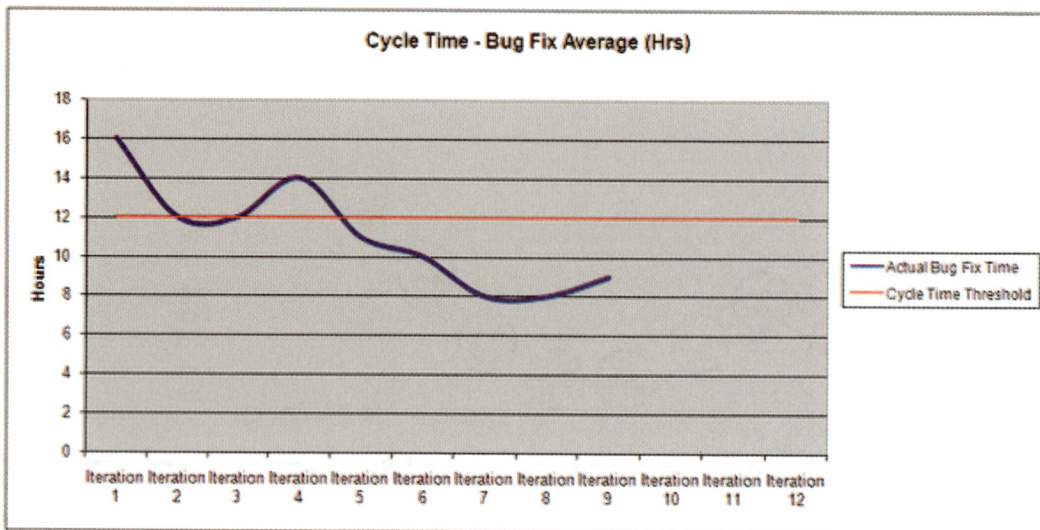

Figure 16.18 *Cycle Time: Bug Fix Average (Hours)*

Cycle time (the time it takes for something to move through the system) is an important metric for agile projects. Reducing cycle time (for developing new features or defect correction) is a main objective for creating efficient processes. In figure 16.18, we are plotting average bug-fix time, from detection through to confirmed resolution. The tolerance threshold was set as an average of 12 hours, and we can see that in iterations 1 and 4 this was breached, but since then, cycle time has generally been reducing (which is a good thing).

Why Bother with Tolerances? Why Not Just Adapt?

Why track metrics and have a process for sorting things out if they go off track? It might seem easier to just ask everyone to try their best and let the project run its course. Unfortunately, subgroups rarely evolve into totally symbiotic ecosystems.

Developers tend to want to work on cool technology, users want every bell and whistle, QA folks want to get things right, and PMs just want to get the thing done. While ants may self-organize into productive colonies, people tend to gravitate toward what is easiest for them or suits their personal goals the most.

While these opposing forces are at play, tolerances and exception reports provide a high-visibility, high-transparency way of keeping us all honest and pulling in the same direction within the guardrails of project tolerances.

Also, the act of exploring tolerances with project stakeholders is extremely valuable. Learning where their issues and sensitive areas are helps with project decision-making. So, even if metrics and tolerances are not outwardly graphed, understanding their thresholds is important.

Tolerances can be applied to any measurable project characteristic. These include the traditional measures:

- » Cost
- » Schedule
- » Scope

- » Risks
- » Resources
- » Quality

They can also be used for more creative measures like:

- » Team retention
- » Adoption rates
- » Pairing diversity

- » Amazon scores
- » Team celebrations held

Basically, whatever metric you care about and should have an agreed-upon plan to execute in the event of a deviation from healthy levels.

Forecasting Breached Tolerances

Ideally, we do not wait until a tolerance has been breached before taking action. If a breach can be forecasted via a trend or new information, then we can be proactive about dealing with it. Just as we should use the guardrails to help guide our car down the road when driving, we can go faster and be more effective by steering before tolerances are encountered.

Exception Plans

An exception plan is an agreed-upon set of actions to be taken if a tolerance is breached, or, more usefully, if a breach of tolerance is forecast. It does not have to be formal; it can just say something along the lines of *we will call a stakeholder meeting*, but typically an exception report with the following information is generated:

- **What has happened** A brief description of what occurred.
- **Why it happened** Some explanation of the events that led to the situation.

- **Options available to us now** Options to sort out the issue.
- **Recommended action** Stakeholders want to hear about solutions, not just problems, so we should include the team's recommended solution.
- **A request for the stakeholder to decide on the course of action.**
- **A review of the tolerance values to see if they need updating.**

The main point is to discuss the issue and do something about it. Plan what needs to be done and then follow through to ensure it occurs. Continue tracking the metrics and determine if the actions are working. If similar problems occur again, consider trying something else; evolve, adapt, and overcome.

Failure

While this book is focused on improving our likelihood of success, it is important to talk about setbacks and failures. Expanding our skill set requires trying new things and stretching our capabilities. Sometimes we will come up short, and sometimes we will fail. That is okay if we can learn from it. The saying *failure is intelligence gained* is apt. It defines *intelligence* as new information, in the sense of intelligence gathering, not in the sense of being better at math, for example. Failure is a sign that we are still learning and gives us the opportunity to learn. So, while outwardly, we might be a little ashamed and embarrassed, we should try to find the learning opportunity.

Failure should be our teacher, not our undertaker. Failure is delay, not defeat. It is a temporary detour, not a dead end. Failure is something we can avoid only by saying nothing, doing nothing, and being nothing.

—Denis Waitley

We must keep trying new approaches if we are to continue learning. John Augustus Shedd said, "A ship in harbor is safe, but that is not what ships are built for." In other words, we must get out of our comfort zones if we are to achieve anything and improve.

While today there is much talk about organizational learning and learning organizations, all learning is personal. As Peter Senge said, "The organization does not learn, it is the people in the organization who learn, since the organization is made up of individuals." So, learn, try, perhaps fail, learn from that, and try some more. This is how we advance.

Objectives and Key Results (OKR)

Objectives and Key Results (OKR) have been made famous by their use at Google and other high-profile companies such as Twitter, Spotify, ING Bank, and Walmart. They were popularized by venture capitalist John Doerr who introduced them to many start-up companies and pioneered them at Google in 1999.

Unlike traditional metrics, OKRs are frequently set, tracked, and reworked, usually every quarter. They are simple but fast-paced metrics that engage teams in their creation and measurement. Setting direction and ensuring teams are aligned with organizational goals are some of the core benefits of OKRs.

As the name implies, OKRs have two components, the Objective and the Key Results:

I will [Objective] as measured by [this set of Key Results].

Here is an example:

Objective: Become the market leader in our industry.

Key Result #1: Acquire 80 new customers.

Key Result #2: Increase marketing leads by 40 percent.

Key Result #3: Increase customer retention to 90 percent.

It sounds simple, but there are some guidelines to follow.

» OKRs describe both *What will be achieved* and *How it will be measured.*

» Objectives should be short, memorable qualitative descriptions of what we want to achieve. They should be engaging and inspirational; teams can get creative and build compelling goals.

» Key Results are a set of quantitative metrics that can be measured to track progress toward the Objective. Each Objective should have two to five Key Results that are numeric. As Marissa Mayer, Google's Vice President said: "If it does not have a number, it is not a Key Result."

Another example could be:

Objective: Create the best customer experience

Key Results:

Improve Net Promoter Score from 25 to 50.

Increase renewal rates 75 percent to 85 percent.

Increase referrals to over 50 percent.

Reduce cancellations from 20 percent to 10 percent.

OKRs work well with agile teams since they are lightweight, transparent, and frequently updated. The regular cadence of setting, tracking, then retiring keeps them exciting for teams while maintaining alignment with organizational goals. Changing the objectives often reduces the likelihood of abuse or gamification that might be counterproductive.

Goal-Question-Metric (GQM)

The Goal-Question-Metric (GQM) is an approach to metrics that has gained popularity recently. It is designed to drive measurement and assessment toward desired goals. It does this by acknowledging the Hawthorn effect (you influence what you measure) and working backward to create a set of questions and metrics related to something we genuinely care about and want to assess.

Here is an example. Let's say the goal was to determine if our development team is on track to deliver on time. Delivery on time is the goal. Then we determine a set of questions that relate to that goal and a set of metrics that answer the questions. For our example team, this may be:

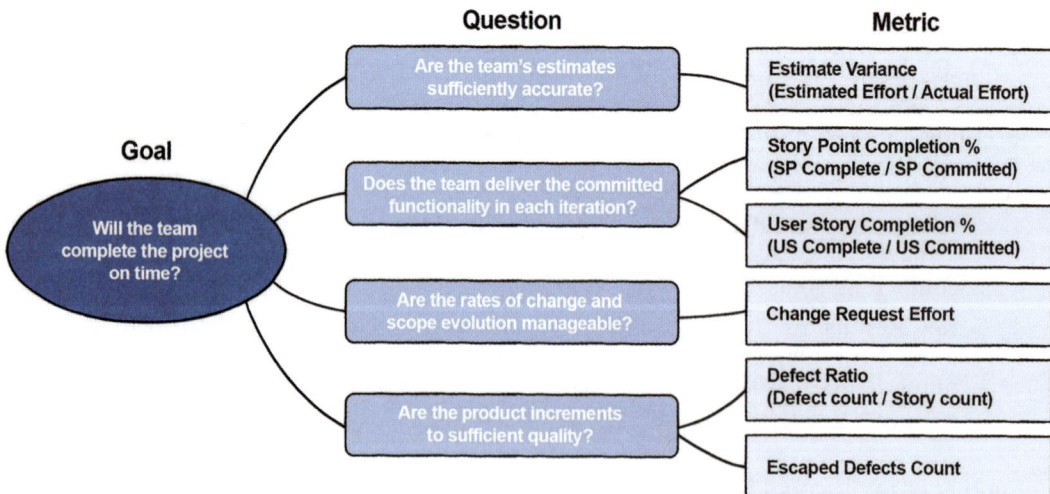

The process for developing GQM has six steps. The first three define business goals to identify the right metrics, and the last three steps gather measurement data to drive decision making and improvements.

1. Develop a set of corporate, department, and project goals and associated measurement goals for productivity and quality.

2. Generate questions (based on models) that define those goals as completely as possible in a quantifiable way.

3. Specify the measures needed to be collected to answer those questions and track process and product conformance to the goals.

4. Develop mechanisms for data collection.

5. Collect, validate, and analyze the data in real time to provide feedback to projects for corrective action.

6. Analyze the data in a post-mortem fashion to assess conformance to the goals and make recommendations for future improvements.

GQM helps address the high cost of maintaining useless metrics. Instead of measuring and analyzing all manner of metrics, it allows organizations to target those they care about; similar to putting your metrics in a prioritized backlog and only working on the highest priority ones. GQM are unique to each group, driven by meaningful questions, and based on agreed-upon metrics. It is usual for a group or team to develop a Goal-Question-Metrics collection to analyze their performance and target corrective action.

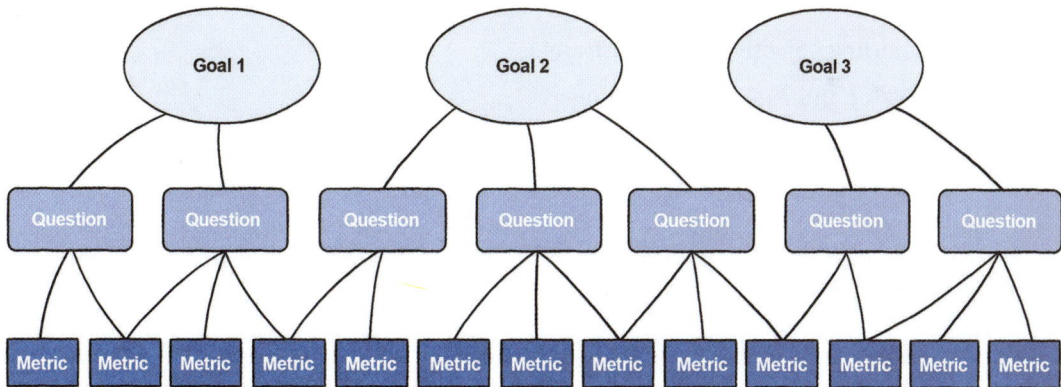

FIGURE 16.21 *Shared Metrics*

As seen in figure 16.21, metrics can be shared between multiple questions.

Chapter 16 Summary

Questions such as *Are we there yet? Can we afford it?* and *Is it worth it?* are common in any endeavor. So are the secondary questions of *Are we going the best way?* and *Is everyone okay?* This is the world of performance analysis—the process of trying to ensure we are doing the right things and doing them right.

We examined EVM in all its genius and inherent flaws for knowledge-work environments. We saw how it could be applied in an agile environment and why other measures might be more appropriate. We examined the Hawthorne effect, which describes the tendency to influence what we measure. We looked at design-factory metrics that are simple, self-generating, and relevant to the end goal, and that favor leading, not lagging, indicators.

We looked at ways to measure the critical but intangible, such as cooperation and knowledge sharing. We saw how Nucor Steel uses measuring up to achieve some of these goals. We also reviewed measuring other subjective factors, such as engagement, satisfaction, and the use of tolerances, exceptions, and escalation. Finally, we examined the new kids to the metrics party, Objectives and Key Results along with Goal Question Metrics. We may still fail in the end, but that can also improve our performance, if not for this attempt, then in the next thing we try.

Key topics covered in this chapter:

- Understanding objectives and constraints
- Earned Value and Agile Earned Value
- Common metric issues and dumb metrics
- Smarter metric alternatives
- Tolerances, exceptions, and escalations
- OKRs and GQMs

© 2021 RMC Publications, Inc.™ • 952.846.4484 • info@rmcls.com • www.rmcls.com

Chapter 17
Estimating Time and Cost (Key Topics)

Regardless of whether we follow a predictive, hybrid, or agile approach, sponsors and other stakeholders want and deserve to know our best estimates of how long something will take and its likely final cost. Depending on the project characteristics, this could be as definitive and predictable as summing up known costs and times, then adding margins for variation, or something much more elastic. Novel, creative, and complex projects will likely have higher levels of uncertainty.

The Need for Accountability on Hybrid Projects

While some agile teams seem to shy away from time and cost estimation, that is not a recommendation I have ever seen outlined in an agile approach. Nowhere in the *Scrum Guide*, the XP outline, or DSDM overview does it say that we do not have to produce estimates of completion date or final costs. Instead, this view that agile teams do not estimate is an extrapolation of some observations about the difficulty of estimation in the presence of uncertainty and complexity.

Yes, estimation on projects is difficult. Yes, we will likely have larger ranges of probable values and higher margins of uncertainty. Sometimes, even when providing our estimates as ranges with probabilities, we will still be wrong, but that does not mean we should not estimate. In my opinion, we have more of an obligation to estimate the final costs and schedule on an agile-type project because we are asking for acceptance of faith and permission to proceed in the face of uncertainty from the sponsors.

This acceptance of uncertainty and permission to proceed anyway, given to us by our sponsors, deserves our best and ongoing communication. People are going to ask about and speculate on when the work will be done and how much it will cost. I prefer to put that on the team, since they have the best insights and control over the situation—even though the process is difficult.

Think about the leap of faith required to sponsor something you are not an expert in, to create something that you cannot precisely define, but you will know only when you see the results. If you have spent your career embedded in technology, it is sometimes difficult to think like sponsors, but this is what sponsors often have to do. Put yourself in their shoes and imagine commissioning work, with money you are accountable for, in a domain you are by no means an expert in.

Imagine you commissioned an artist to paint an abstract picture or a poet to write you a poem for a new sweetheart. You know you want to delight your customer (your new sweetheart) but their tastes and talents are still an enigma. What exactly would they love? This uncertainty around the end goal is often shared in knowledge-work projects too. In addition, the process the artist uses is an unknown to most people, as much knowledge work is to many sponsors. As a sponsor, you accept that this process is difficult to predict, but surely you would prefer regular checks and communications on progress from the artist rather than nothing, instead receiving insights from outsiders who speculate that artists are notoriously hard to work with and unreliable.

These circumstances exist on knowledge-work projects. If the team does not produce estimates, other people will fill the void with speculation, which can be more damaging than explaining the challenges and uncertainty being faced. Rather than remaining silent, it is better to meet regularly with the sponsor, explain the work done to date and what is planned next, and share today's best estimates of completion-date ranges and costs.

In our sweetheart analogy, this would be like a weekly update from the artist, saying they have followed our new love around to study what they do and like and asked them about their preferences to gain a better understanding of what a successful product would look like—slightly creepy, but much like what product and project teams do!

Many forms of knowledge work are not a purely creative process. They are often systematic, but still difficult to interpret, follow, or appreciate for external stakeholders. So, we need to share the work done, reiterate our understanding of the sponsor's time and cost goals, and update them on our current estimates.

I recall a steering committee meeting that took place shortly after I took over the leadership of a delayed software program for a trucking company. The sponsors had become frustrated by the program's multiyear delays and lack of estimates for completion or final spend. I had been asked to review the projects and make suggestions for trying to make them successful or shut them down. Having worked with the business sponsor and project teams for a month, I had decided they were close to delivering some useful functionality, but we needed CFO support to continue.

In the steering committee meeting, I explained the uncertainty regarding the work required to complete the next release. The CFO replied, "It sounds like you don't know what you are doing!" (He used a stronger word; it being a trucking company, cursing seemed obligatory.) Not sure of the best course of action, I decided to share some of the uncertainty we faced and replied, "It's more that we don't know what the hell you want. We still need more drivers for the pilot and a decision is required on if satellite modems are required." I was not thanked but being candid about the uncertainty made it difficult to press the point further. In the absence of some key business commitments and decisions, the uncertainty was justifiable.

Conversations are often difficult, but it was the absence of such discussions that had gotten the previous program manager fired. Maybe I would have been next to go, but I did not want to continue working on a program where information was not shared. As it turned out, I continued and the program struggled on and delivered its benefits a couple of months later. By then, it was already years late and over budget, so there was no celebration party or congratulating of the team from the executive. We pushed through the final months with frequent communications and honest reporting of estimates and issues. No one liked the news, but I think they appreciated the honesty.

When estimating knowledge-work projects, we have a couple of factors in our favor. First, knowledge-work projects aim to establish stable teams, so the project burn rate is usually relatively stable. We should always know how much we have spent and the burn rate of our teams on a daily, weekly, and monthly basis. This allows us to estimate likely completion costs (minus closure costs) at any given time.

Dividing our burn rate into our remaining budget provides a valid indicator of how much time remains before we use all the project funds. For example, if our budget remaining is $600,000 and we know the team costs, on average, $120,000 per month for labor costs and other charges, this allows us to calculate that we have five months left until we consume all the budget ($600,000/$120,000 = 5$).

Next, we can use team velocity as a measure of their capacity to do work, and an input metric for estimating the remaining work schedule. If the team had been averaging 20 points of work completed and accepted per month, then the remaining 5 months at 20 points per month indicates that another 100 points of functionality could be completed. Then we can share what this looks like from a backlog perspective.

Applying Velocity Expectations to the Backlog

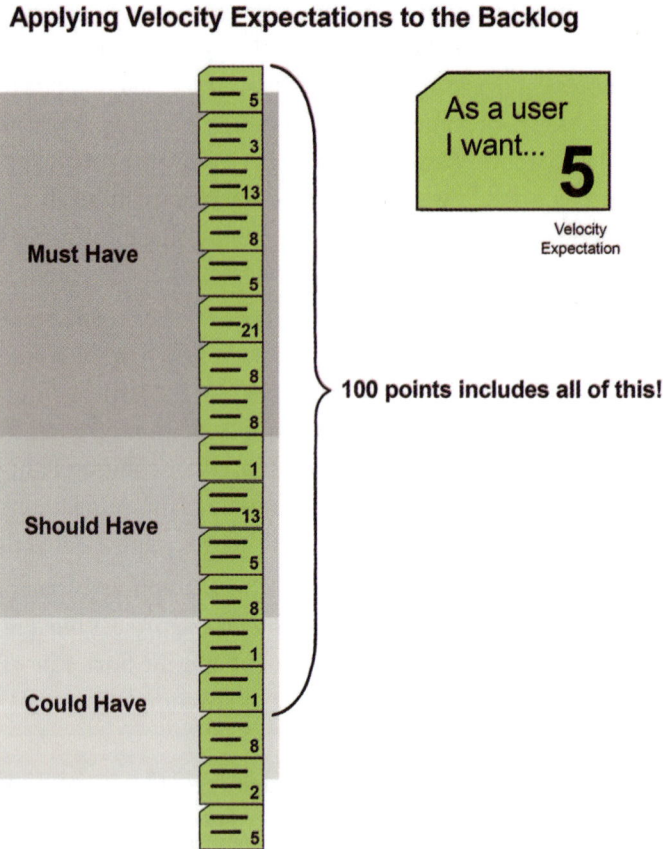

FIGURE 17.1 *Applying Velocity Expectations to the Backlog*

The results may not be what the sponsor wants to hear, but at least they are based upon defendable assumptions. For figure 17.1, I kept the math simple, but we should be clear about the fact that there is variability and uncertainty. Perhaps the team velocity varies between 19 and 25 points per month. An average of 19 points would only allow us to deliver so much, while an average of 23 would allow this much (a 24- or 25-point average is probably not likely enough to merit discussion).

Other factors, such as requirements growth, should also be addressed. If as features are worked on their points estimates tend to increase, then we should apply that average increase to the remaining stories in the backlog. Now the 100 points capacity remaining may not take us as far.

These are all inputs and concerns we need to be clear about. Yes, they introduce uncertainty, and yes, the sponsor often just wants to know when we will really be done and how much this thing will really cost. So, show the process, keep the communication channels open, and be open to new insights and issues. This is the only way to remain credible and trusted through the estimation and reporting process.

#NoEstimates

There is a movement, a trend, or line of thinking called #NoEstimates that asserts that estimation is a form of waste. Like most trends, it is based on some valid observations we can make use of, but I feel it goes a little too far at the macro level. The #NoEstimates line of thinking parallels lean thinking that invites us to review all the steps in our work stream and eliminate any steps that do not add value.

In software and many other knowledge-work domains, estimation of the everyday tasks team members undertake is fraught with uncertainty. Work is often exploratory, involving trying new approaches to solve a problem. This type of research and development is hard to predict: We might get lucky and our first try might work, or it might be the fourth or fifth try that is successful. Trying to estimate this type of work generally yields large degrees of variation because some team members assume the happy path of success on the first try; others try to average the number of tries it generally takes to get things working; and still others, tired of never meeting their estimates, just default to the worst-case scenario so they can comfortably get on with their work, not bothered about impending, self-imposed deadlines.

The combination of high variability, poor accuracy, and the tendency to game estimates understandably gave rise to people questioning their usefulness. Teams were spending a lot of effort estimating the points value of tasks, only to be wrong as often as they were correct. So, an alternative to estimation based on flow was suggested.

Instead of estimating all the work and tracking how many points' worth of work was completed per iteration, we simply count how many stories are complete and assign an average points value for those stories. Many teams that tried this found that due to the difficulty of accurately estimating the points value of stories, assigning an average points value to each story was just as valid. In other words, they could get similar (but not great, due to all the uncertainty) levels of accuracy without all the estimation effort.

So, by tracking the count (flow) of stories completed per iteration (say, 10 done per iteration), they achieved the same goals of tracking without any of the problematic story-point estimation process. In fact, flow increased slightly, compared to historical counts of story totals, because they were now spending more time doing work and less time estimating work.

Start of Iteration

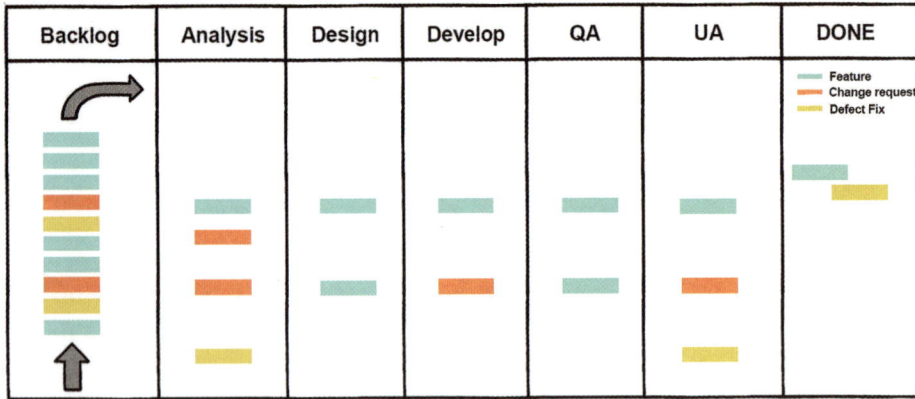

End of Iteration

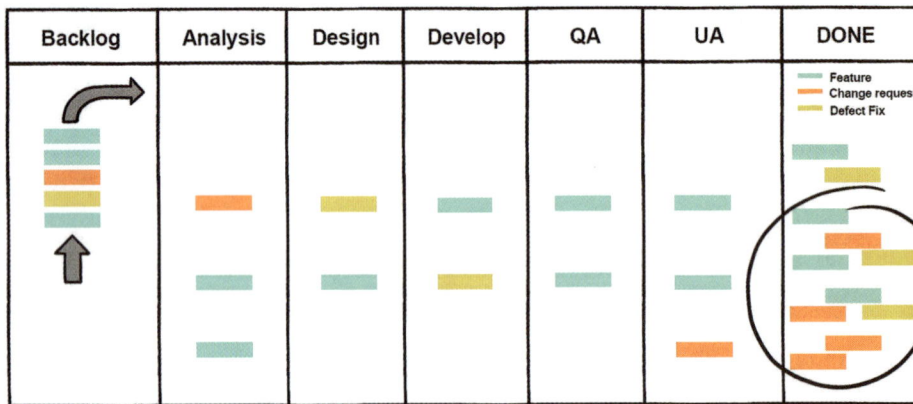

These items have been completed

FIGURE 17.2 *Tracking the Count of Stories Completed per Iteration*

There are variations on flow-based, #NoEstimates project tracking. On one project I worked on, featured later in the case studies chapter, we stopped using points-based estimation and switched to a flow-based approach with great results. Rather than totally abandoning estimation of stories, we did some analysis of past stories and characterized them with the T-shirt sizes of small, medium, large, and extra large. Looking back at work we had done over the last six months, 90 percent of the stories we had tackled could be put into one of these categories.

We then did some research in our story-tracking tool to see how long it had taken us, on average, to move these stories from *ready for dev* through to *accepted*. Armed with these averages, we assigned the following points values to our stories:

» Small: 2 points

» Medium: 4 points

» Large: 10 points

» Extra large: 25 points

When we switched to flow-based tracking, our development lead quickly assigned a T-shirt size to each upcoming story. It was not a group activity; we trusted the story to be assessed and assigned a probable size, knowing it was not an exact science. Freed from estimation in points, people just got on with doing the work. Every week, we tracked how many small, medium, large, and extra-large stories we completed and calculated the appropriate points velocity value.

Using this approach allowed me, as team lead, to continue tracking progress and divide the remaining backlog, whose stories had also been assessed in T-shirt-size points, by the team's average velocity. The process seemed about as stable and predictable but freed up the team for more development work.

So, while I am a fan of the #NoEstimates philosophy, which asserts that many forms of estimation in new fields of development are likely fraught with issues and can be replaced by flow-based analysis, I have some cautions. #NoEstimates carries a stigma that estimates are not necessary, and this too easily could include estimates of completion, both for schedule and cost. Now I know that nowhere in responsible #NoEstimates arguments is it suggested that we abandon macro-level predictions of completion. However, in a field already tarnished with an attitude that we cannot estimate knowledge work, it is further fuel for that fire.

On one project I worked on, we simply called our approach *flow-based estimation*, not #NoEstimates. We were working in an amber organization with a traditional PMO and did not need further scrutiny or to invite suspicion of avoiding process.

Along the same vein of removing processes that no longer added value, we reevaluated stand-up meetings, iterations, and scheduled retrospectives. The team had been working together for several years at this point and communicated constantly, even with remote members who used voice-over-internet-protocol (VoIP) headsets to contribute to conversations. Daily stand-ups lacked value; people were aware of what everyone was working on through our tracking tool and conversations. We switched them to every other day, then twice a week, then weekly, before finally dropping them. Nothing fell apart and rates of progress continued to rise.

Likewise, iterations were dropped for a continuous flow of work pulled from the backlog. We still maintained a biweekly cadence for business demos but detached the retrospective process. The team now met to review issues and improvements immediately. Waiting for a retrospective to make an improvement seemed wasteful and irresponsible. I would not recommend teams start here, but for this one established team, these changes were all positive.

When You Do Need to Estimate

Some teams do need to estimate, either because they are required to for compliance reasons or want to improve their ability to analyze work. The following steps still hold true for knowledge work:

1. Determining the size of the project in story points or ideal days
2. Calculating the effort for the work in hours or person-months by determining the availability and capacity of the team
3. Converting the effort into a schedule by factoring in the team size, required resources, and dependencies
4. Calculating the cost by applying labor rates and adding in other project cost elements

Let us go through each in turn.

Step 1, determining the size of the project in story points or ideal days can be achieved using techniques such as Wideband Delphi or planning poker.

Step 2, calculating the effort for the work in hours or person-months, is achieved by determining the availability and capacity of the team. This means that if, for the sake of simplicity and speed, we estimated the work in ideal days, we now have to determine what the blended team availability is likely to be. This can be calculated by summing everyone's estimated average availability.

Let us use a small team of three people—Bob, Bill, and Mary—as an example. If Bob was available 80 percent of the time, Bill 70 percent, and Mary 75 percent, then the team's average availability is $(80 + 70 + 75)/3 = 75$ percent. If the estimates in ideal days totaled 500 days, the likely effort would be $500/75\% = 667$ days.

As the project progresses, we need to check the teams' availability and capacity to determine if the original approximations were correct. If the same team of three people repeatedly completes a combined total of 100 hours' worth of work per 40-hour workweek, then their actual capacity is $100/(40 \times 3) = 83$ percent (or they actually work a little faster than they estimate).

As work progresses, we increasingly rely on the actual velocity of the team to gauge their future progress. Using the availability rate of 83 percent, the 500 person-day project will likely take $500/83\% = 603$ days to complete.

Step 3 is converting the effort into a schedule by factoring in the team size, required resources, and dependencies. Now, we have to determine if our 603-day project will be completed by our team of three people in 201 days (603/3=201) or some other period.

Questions will arise; for example, is all the work truly independent in that it can be worked on by any developer at any given time, or are there dependencies or skill constraints that will require a longer duration? The *I* in INVEST, a mnemonic for remembering the characteristics of good user stories, stands for *independent*. Good user stories should not be tightly coupled to other stories. Reality has a way of messing up these goals.

Anyone interested in understanding the relationship between effort and schedule more deeply or anyone asked to complete the same project in 101.5 days with 6 people, need to understand the Putnam-Norden-Rayleigh (PNR) curve.

Research by Putnam Norden found that for projects that require communication and learning (such as software projects), the effort-to-time curve follows a Rayleigh distribution. Putnam confirmed that this curve applied to software projects in his article "A General Empirical Solution to the Macro Software Sizing and Estimation Problem" and the curve became known as the Putnam-Norden-Rayleigh curve or PNR Staffing curve, as shown in figure 17.3.

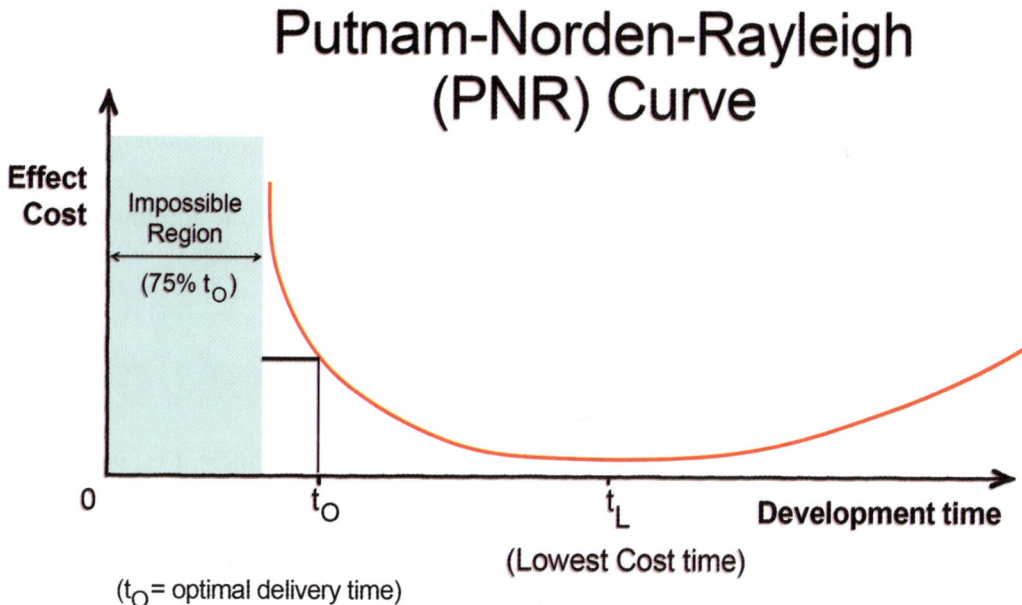

FIGURE 17.3 *Putnam-Norden-Rayleigh (PNR) Curve*

The PNR curve shows time (x-axis) against cost (y-axis). As we add more resources to a project, the reduction in effort is not linear, but instead follows an ever-steepening curve. As we move to the left (shortening the project timeline), the *adjusted staff months* curve (red curve) gets steeper and steeper, indicating increasing costs, but not much of a shortening in timeline.

There are some important points on the curve to understand. The lowest-cost delivery time (shown as t_L: the lowest point on the curve) indicates the lowest cost that the project could be delivered for. However, it does not factor in delayed ROI, inflation, or work-in-progress costs. Most companies are looking for the best compromise between low cost and short timelines, as indicated by the optimal delivery time.

Barry Boehm did an interesting study on attempts to shorten project schedules; he examined over 750 projects that attempted to deliver code in less than the optimal delivery point T_o. None of the projects were successful in reducing the schedule below 75 percent of optimal delivery point T_o, and he christened the area the *impossible region* to indicate that you cannot compress schedules beyond this point.

Intuitively, we know this; as Fred Brooks stated in *The Mythical Man-Month*, "Adding resources to a project that is already late will make it later."

As you approach the impossible region, the gradient of the line becomes vertical. Adding resources increases the project spend but does not shorten the timeframe. Following Fred Brooks's observation, the line starts to curve back, so adding more people not only adds costs, but makes delivery longer. I can see how this would be the case as decisions and communications become more complex and extra people actually slow things down.

So, how do you determine the best compromise between short timeline and low cost? Barry Boehm provides the following formula in the constructive cost model (COCOMO) estimation engine:

To = F x Effort ^ 0.33

(The effort in person-months cube rooted multiplied by a scaling factor.)

Where *F* is a factor that varies on project type:

COCOMO II default F factor is 3.67, but other environments have different values, including Web Development 3.10 and Embedded Dev. 4.00.

So, for example, 603 person-days divided by 21 working days per month is 29 person-months for the project (603/21 = 29). Putting 29 into the formula and assuming we are making a web application that has a scaling factor of 3.1, this would be:

Tn = 3.1 * 29 ^ 0.33

   = 9.5 months

This indicates that a 29 person-month web-development project would be optimally implemented in 9.5 months by a team of 3 people (29/9.5 = 3). So, thankfully, 3 people is a good size for a 29 person-month project, but could we get it done in 9.5/2 = 4.75 months with 6 people? No, that would be in the impossible region. Knowledge of the PNR curve is useful to validate that we are not being asked to undertake unrealistic plans and to better understand the true cost of adding more and more resources to projects.

Finally, step 4, calculating the cost by applying labor rates and adding in other project cost elements. Once we have a duration for our project, it is relatively easy to calculate the costs in monetary terms, as shown in figure 17.4.

- Cost = (Time x Rate) + Other Project Costs
  - Hardware and Software
  - Training Courses
  - Expenses

FIGURE 17.4 *Calculating Costs in Monetary Terms*

So, we would take our project time estimate (9.5 months), multiply it by everyone's rates to calculate the project costs, then add in any other project costs.

Rates are as follows: Bob, $50 per hour; Bill, $80 per hour; and Mary, $95 per hour. Labor rate = 9.5 × 160 hours per month = 1,520 project hours. Labor cost = (1,520 x $50) + (1,520 x $80) + (1,520 x $95) = $76,000 + $121,600 + $144,400 = $342,000.

Now we need to add other project costs, such as other part-time resources, hardware, software, travel, backfill for business representatives, warranty period after go-live, plus whatever else the project needs to fund.

Chapter 17 Summary

Like the children's question, *"Are we there yet?"* anyone paying for a service or job done wants to know how long it will take and how much it will cost. Put yourself in the sponsor's shoes: if you were having work done on your house or car, these would be reasonable questions. The idea that agile projects do not have schedules or budgets did not originate from the Agile Manifesto. Instead, it is an undefendable notion spread by people who are uncomfortable explaining variability and uncertainty.

Throughput (the rate of completing work) can be used for estimating durations. Estimates can be determined by multiplying burn rates by estimated durations, then adding in fixed costs and contingency. We need to be aware of the lack of accuracy in our estimates and be careful to explain the variation and likely ranges.

Attempting to apply too much precision is a waste of time. Given the variance in estimate ranges, it is often also wasteful to spend too much time making estimates if there is a lot of uncertainty. This is where the #NoEstimates movement took root, in deeming estimation as a waste, but that is flawed logic. Too much effort expended on estimation when there is much uncertainty is a waste. However, most projects will never get off the ground without a preliminary estimate. How else could you determine value? Since value = benefits − costs, we nearly always need some form of cost estimate. It might be rough and it might change, but we need one.

Finally, we examined the PNR curve and learned how project schedules cannot be shortened simply by adding more people to the project. Collaboration, communication, and problem-solving often go slower as team sizes increase. Be wary of requests to ramp up team sizes to get things done faster.

Key topics covered in this chapter:

» The need for accountability: Accountability when entrusted to spend other people's money

» The #NoEstimates movement: Where it originated and what we can learn from it

» When we do need to estimate: How to avoid being pressured into the "Impossible Region"

Chapter 18
Risk Management (Key Topics)

Risk management is critical for project success. All too often, we focus on avoiding the negatives, but we should also be looking to capitalize on and exploit opportunities and favorable characteristics too. The BAM encourages a more collaborative approach to risk management.

Unfortunately, there are lots of problems with how risk management is commonly undertaken on projects. Too often, risk management is conducted as an "alongside" activity by a project manager, as opposed to a "driving and defining" activity undertaken by the entire team. Other examples of correct but insufficient behavior include:

Poor engagement: Dry, boring, academic; done by PM; does not drive enough change

Done once: Typically near the start when we know least about the project

Not revisited enough: Often "parked" off to one side and not reviewed again

Not integrated into project life cycle: Poor tools for task integration

Not engaging, poor visibility: Few stakeholders regularly review the project risks

Techniques such as planning poker and iteration planning make estimation and scheduling a team activity. This gains the technical insights of engaging people who are closer to the work. These ideas are repeated in using collaborative activities for risk management. After all, why leave risk management to the PM, who is furthest from the technical work?

Most knowledge-worker projects resemble problem-solving exercises more than plan-execution exercises. It is difficult to separate out the experimentation and threat mitigation from the pure execution. Team members are actively engaged in risk management every day. We can benefit from their input in the risk management process. When they are more aware of the project risks (by being engaged in determining them), then how they approach their work will be more risk-aware and successful.

The Benefits of a Collaborative Approach to Risk Management

The benefits of collaboration are widely acknowledged. A study by Steven L. Yaffee from the University of Michigan cites the following benefits:

1. Generates wiser decisions through the understanding of complex, cross-boundary problems via shared information
2. Promotes problem-solving rather than procedural decision-making
3. Fosters action by mobilizing shared resources to get work done
4. Builds social capital by building relationships and understanding
5. Fosters ownership of collective problems by valuing participation and shifting power downward

These are some powerful concepts that deserve a second look and application to risk management. It is pretty obvious that engaging a larger group of stakeholders will produce a better list of possible risks, and then yield more creative ways of avoiding or reducing those risks. However, the real benefits of engaging the team come from the changes that happen in the team.

By engaging the team, not only do we get better input data and ideas, but we also encourage problem-solving, foster action, build social capital, and foster collective ownership of ideas. No longer do we have a single PM worried about the risks; instead, we now have a motivated, energized, and empowered team proactively managing the risks.

Far too often, projects do a great job of identifying possible threats and a lousy job of doing anything about them. The result is that projects get derailed when a known threat becomes an issue. When the team is fully plugged into the project risks, small changes in their behavior eliminate many threats at the source, long before they get large enough to severely impact the project.

Finally, the last point in Yaffee's benefits-of-collaboration list is noteworthy too. Valuing participation and shifting power downward fits extremely well with the empowered teams and servant-leadership model promoted by agile methods. We already encourage these ideas in reporting progress via daily stand-ups, estimating via planning poker, and decision-making via fist-of-five techniques, so why not in risk management?

Of course, collaboration is no silver bullet. Brainstorming, for example, can actually stifle innovation and lead to groupthink. *New Yorker* magazine describes studies that show that brainstorming groups think of fewer ideas, of lower quality, than the same number of people working alone who later pool their ideas. So, let us be clear: collaboration does not only mean brainstorming; it also includes pooling individuals' ideas and group validation.

Before getting too far into risk management, we should clarify that the word *risk* refers to both risks that are good for us (opportunities) and risks that are bad for us (threats). To provide clarity, risk management professionals use the term *threats* to describe those risks that are bad for us, while the term *risks* is reserved for any event (good or bad) that may occur.

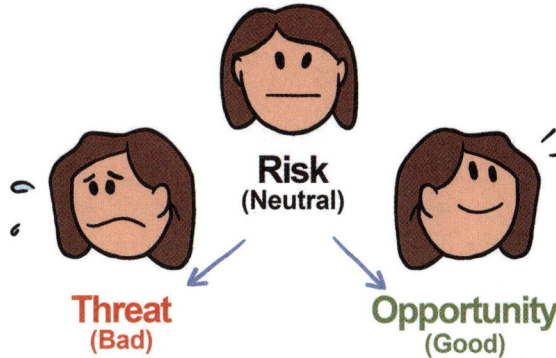

Risk
(Neutral)

Threat
(Bad)

Opportunity
(Good)

Agile and Hybrid Risk Management

There is a myth that agile approaches somehow magically have risk management processes built into them. This is, of course, false, but the section below outlines a couple of practical tools that we can borrow from agile to start improving risk management approaches on agile- and hybrid-centered projects.

Agile Is Not a Risk Management Approach

Some people believe agile approaches, with their short cycles and regular feedback, have a risk management approach naturally built into the process. It is easy to see why: the building blocks and attachment points for plugging in an effective risk management process are certainly present, but unfortunately, just building something iteratively or incrementally does not ensure risks are managed.

It is all too easy to develop iteratively and miss opportunities to actively address threats or exploit opportunities. Many agile teams also fail to actively look for risks, discuss and decide on appropriate actions, undertake those actions, reassess the risks, and evaluate if the risk management process is working.

It is a shame because, in many ways, agile methods provide an ideal framework for introducing effective risk management practices. They have short timeframes, active reprioritization of work, frequent review points, high team member and business engagement in planning, etc. However, similar to having a group of people to help you find something, "a beach party is not the same as a search party" — they need to be focused. We need a conscious effort of coordination and cooperation to make it effective.

Consciously Adding Risk Management to Agile and Hybrid Approaches

The good news is that when organizations and their participating teams decide to layer risk management onto agile and hybrid approaches, there are many self-reinforcing cycles and mechanisms to make use of. For instance, the frequent consideration of change requests and reprioritization of work in the backlog makes the insertion of threat-avoidance or threat-mitigation tasks an easier process to handle.

Likewise, the regular retrospectives that review progress and process are great points to examine the effectiveness of risk management strategies and take corrective actions. Daily stand-up meetings that surface issues and blockers can also act as early warnings for potential new threats.

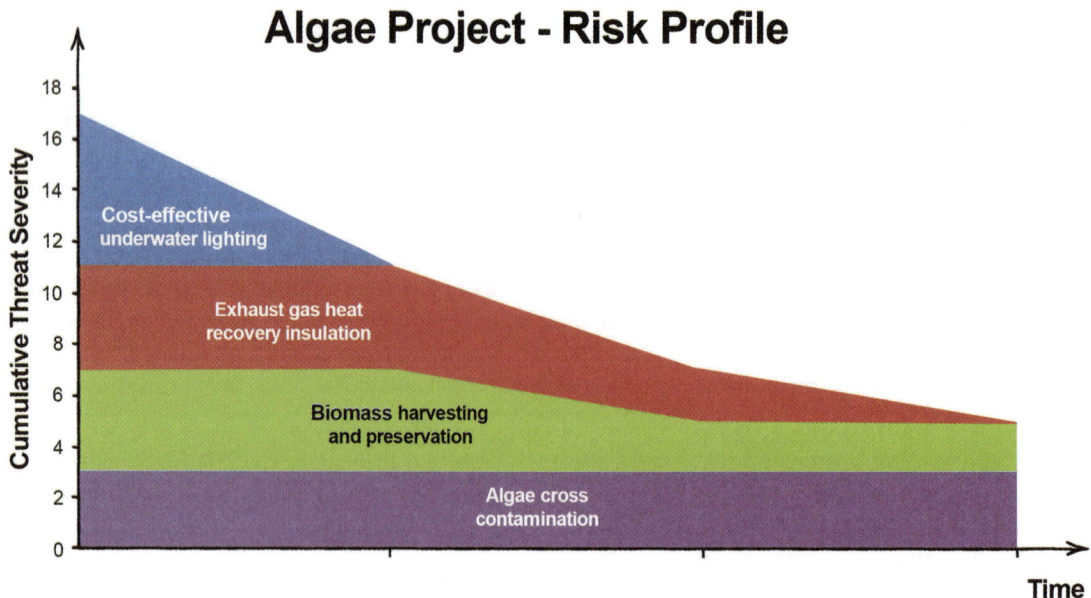

FIGURE 18.1 *Example of a Risk Profile*

Risk Management Tailoring

Listed in this section are some example tools, although not the recommended set to use on every single project. Your approach should vary based on your project and organizational factors. The risk management approach for a large military project would most likely be inappropriate for a commercial, in-house project and vice versa.

The key to adding an effective risk management approach is generating consensus on the importance and approach. Leaders of teams should communicate the links between threats, opportunities, and features, then get people engaged in building a shared framework for decision-making that is appropriate for the project type and domain. Empowered teams that frequently meet to review progress and process already have many of the techniques in place for effective risk management. However, they also need to be educated and equipped with the tools, time, and permission to execute them to start the journey to better risk management.

Risk Management Reminders

Risk management, like estimation, should not be just a project-management activity. We can greatly raise a project team's ability to manage risk—and therefore avoid project failures through socialization, collaboration, and practice. If nothing else, these team activities make the basics of risk management more accessible to a larger pool of project stakeholders, and in doing so provide more eyes to find and avoid risks before they can impact the project—which, at the end of the day, is the heart of effective risk management.

A Risk Management Framework

The *PMBOK® Guide, Sixth Edition* describes a seven-step process for risk management:

1. Plan risk management
2. Identify risks
3. Perform qualitative risk analysis
4. Perform quantitative risk analysis
5. Plan risk responses
6. Implement risk responses
7. Monitor risks

Through collaborative team-based activities (serious games) each of these seven risk management steps can be recreated as highly visual, team-based activities that create risk avoidance and risk mitigation stories for the product backlog. The same ideas can also be used to plan activities to exploit and maximize the impacts of opportunities.

We want visual collaborative games because visual representation helps engage the left and right hemispheres of the brain. They allow us to tap into our spatial awareness and memory to avoid forgetting about risks. This is why today's military still uses visual tokens on boards to represent enemy forces, despite having access to the world's most sophisticated tools. The impacts of forgetting about them can be fatal. The same goes for project risks.

The collaborative games that cover these steps are:

- Plan Your Trip (Plan Risk Management)

  a. 4Risk Cs: Consider the costs, consequences, context, and choices
  b. Are we buying a coffee, couch, car, or condo? How much rigor is appropriate?
  c. Deposits and bank fees: Understanding features and risks

- Find Friends and Foes (Risk and Opportunity Identification)

  a. Doomsday Clock
  b. Karma Day
  c. Other risk-identification forms (risk profiles, project-risk lists, retrospectives, user-story analysis)

- Post Your Ad (Qualitative Risk Analysis)

  a. Investors and help wanted: Classification and visualization of opportunities and risks
  b. Tug-of-war: Project categorization

- Today's Forecast (Quantitative Risk Analysis)

  a. *Shark Tank*: Next best dollar spent

- Decision Time (Plan Risk Responses)

  a. Junction function: Choose the risk response path
  b. Dollar balance: Risk/opportunity EVM to ROI comparison

- Backlog Injector (Implement Risk Responses)

  a. Report card: Customer/product-owner engagement
  b. Inoculator: Inject risk avoidance/mitigation and opportunity stories into backlog

- Risk Radar (Monitoring Risks)

  a. Risk burndown graphs: Tracking and monitoring
  b. Risk retrospectives: Evaluating the effectiveness of the risk management plan
  c. Rinse and repeat: Updating risk management artifacts, revisiting process

Plan Your Trip (Plan Risk Management)

This phase is about deciding and defining how to conduct risk management activities for the project. We want to tailor the process to ensure that the degree, type, and visibility of risk management is commensurate with both the risks and importance of the project to the organization. The other goal we have for this phase is to teach some risk management basics to the team because they may not be familiar with the concepts or terminology.

The name of the first exercise, Plan Your Trip, speaks to the goal of determining the appropriate level of rigor. Planning for a walk or hike is an activity most people can relate to, so this is the analogy we will use for the activity called the *4Risk Cs*. Early in any collaborative workshop, I like to get people working. If you let them spectate for too long, some will retreat into observer, rather than participant, mode.

Working individually (to encourage active engagement and avoid groupthink) ask the team to consider what they would pack for a two-mile hike in the country on a warm day. Give them a couple of minutes to create lists on sticky notes and review their responses as a group. Some will suggest taking nothing, or just a bottle of water; others, rain jackets, bear spray (I live near the Rocky Mountains in Canada), and all sorts of other things. Then review the pros and cons of these items; they are useful if you need them, but a burden to carry. We then repeat the exercise, changing some parameters, such as making it a ten-mile hike or multiday trip, in the mountains or in wintertime. Now the lists get longer as people prepare for more eventualities.

For each situation, we review the 4Risk Cs: the costs, consequences, context, and choices. What we bring (and how we prepare for risk management) varies based on the cost of bringing/using it and the consequence of not having it (for example, getting wet without a raincoat or suffering cold/hypothermia without a warm jacket). We also examine the context we are talking about: Are we making preparations for elite ultramarathoners who are hardy, capable, and resourceful, or for a kids' group that needs more protection? Finally, the choices we make should be an informed balance of cost versus consequence in the frame of the context.

Another tool to relate the need to tailor the process appropriately is to ask the team to consider the decision rigor they put into their purchases. The way we consider buying a coffee ($3), couch ($3,000), car ($30,000), or condo ($300,000) varies as the figures involved escalate.

For a coffee, we probably just find something close, maybe at our favorite coffee chain. For a couch, we will shop around and likely buy the one we like best without much further research. When it comes to a car, safety, economy, and resale factors are routinely examined and we may take along a car-savvy friend for the test ride. For a condo purchase, the stakes are so high that most people engage professional help from home inspectors and condo-document reviewers. We need to do the same for our projects and ask what level of caution and support is appropriate for the endeavor.

Finally, if the team is new to risk management, then a discussion or trade-off between business value and threats might be necessary. We usually undertake projects for the potential upside (or, for compliance projects, to avoid the downside). Getting business value out of a project is like receiving deposits into our bank account: we want them as often as possible and as large as possible. Given the uncertainty in the world, we want the biggest gains as soon as possible, before anything changes that may threaten future deposits.

In this bank analogy, threats are like withdrawals or bank fees: should they occur, they set the project back, take resources away from delivering business value, and threaten the delivery of future value. So, to get the most out of a project, we need to maximize business value while avoiding or reducing threats.

These exercises and discussions aim to get the team thinking about the appropriate level of risk management for the project and gain consensus and support for the strategy that is agreed upon. Without this shared understanding of *why?* we will not get people invested in the process.

Find Friends and Foes (Threat and Opportunity Identification)

The next step in the process is to identify potential risks and opportunities. Opportunities are the "good" risks or fortuitous events that have a positive impact. We want to avoid threats and exploit opportunities.

Referring to a clockface drawn on a whiteboard or flip chart, we ask team members to think of project risks associated with each of the topics, which are represented by the hour markers—12 in total.

This is the doomsday part: We encourage the team members to think of and record as many threats as they can about that topic. We work topic by topic, but if thinking of threats triggers ideas in other areas as we progress, it is not unusual for risks to be added to previously discussed risk topics. Again, I prefer that people work individually to come up with ideas, then put them all up and consolidate and remove duplicates as a group—a process that sometimes identifies new threats.

Discourage people's tendencies to want to score, rank, and solve the threats. This is threat identification; we will have plenty of time to process the threats later.

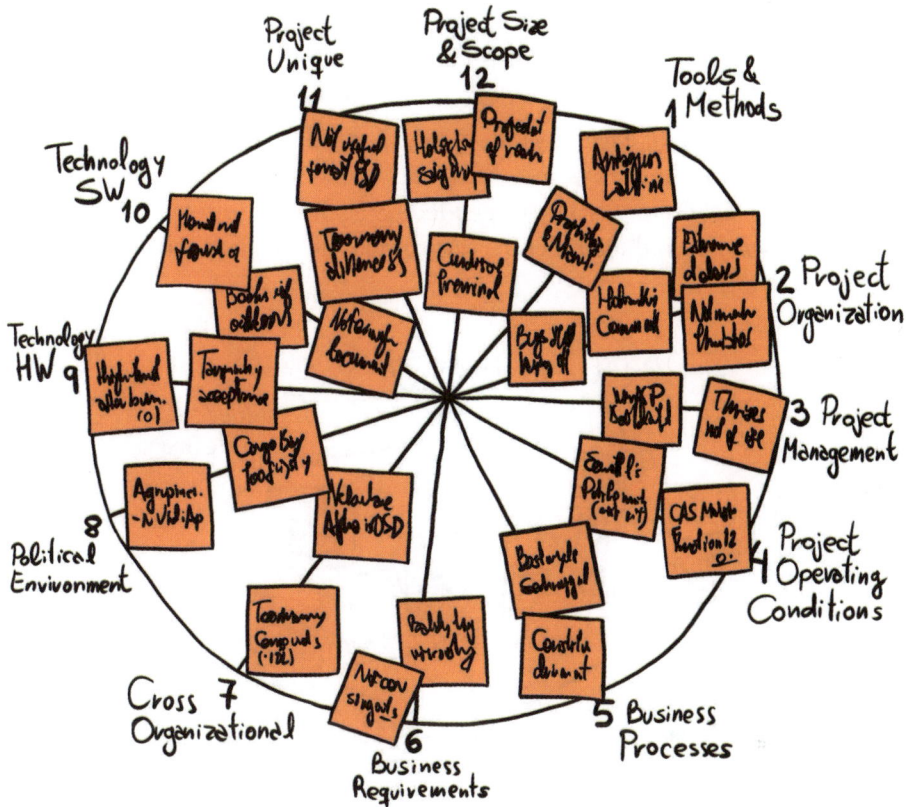

FIGURE 18.2 *Doomsday Clock Threats*

A wall filled with threat stickies around every aspect of the project can seem like a discouraging prospect for some, but it is also a useful eye-opener as to why risk management is so important. This project is not magically going to work out all by itself. We have some real obstacles in front of us and we need to work as a team to overcome them.

Always within the same session, I like to run the flip-side exercise, Karma Day. In this exercise, we generate opportunities for events and outcomes that would assist the project. Using a clockface drawing again, we come up with lists of all the good things that could occur to help the project go well.

Cynical team members may continue to gripe, suggesting opportunities as "inverted issues" such as *actually getting a one- or two-day turnaround on our database requests, for a change* or *support, not resistance, from the PMO,* but these can be really useful. Just as we later ask in risk management, *How do we avoid or reduce these risks?* in opportunity management, we ask, *How do we ensure or maximize these opportunities?* If spending a couple of hours explaining the project goals and approach to supporting groups, or proactively asking them how we might best engage with them, makes a difference, then this work could have a huge return on the time invested.

Without asking the team for a list of all the good things that can happen, team leads and PMs will likely be unaware of all the ways in which they could serve and support the team. The ScrumMaster as an obstacle remover is a one-sided, glass-half-empty view. Why not explicitly add *opportunity implementer* to the job description and let us see if we can arrange some mutual wins by being proactive?

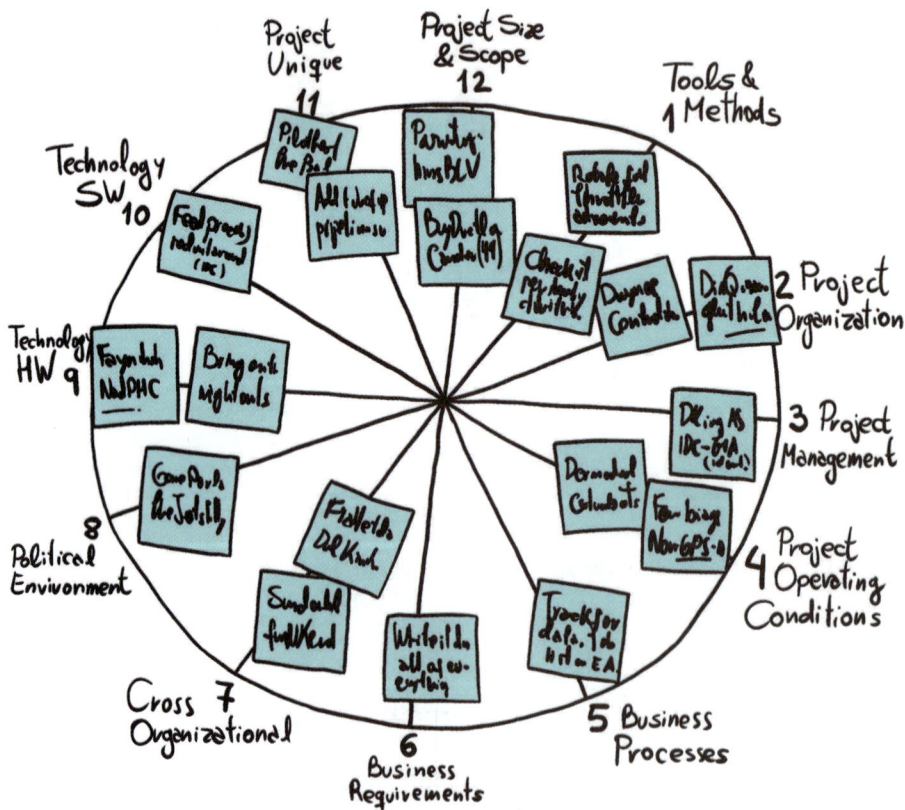

FIGURE 18.3 *Karma Day Opportunities*

These facilitated workshops are techniques for identifying threats and opportunities, but they do not stop us from also applying more conventional approaches, such as risk profiles; project-risk lists; SWOT (strengths, weaknesses, opportunities, and threats) analysis; retrospective findings;

user-story analysis; etc. Let us not throw out the baby with the bathwater: Use traditional approaches, but augment them with team-based approaches for better insights and buy-in.

Post Your Ad (Qualitative Risk Analysis)

Having found threats and opportunities, we now need to classify and rank them. The duplicates found in Doomsday Clock and Karma Day can be removed, and related threat and opportunity ideas might be better consolidated under new headings (provided they truly are the same risks). Then we need to categorize and prioritize them.

The traditional way of doing this is to assign numeric probability and impact scores using something like the matrix shown in figure 18.4. While mathematically valid, it seems counterintuitive to many people that the highest-ranked threats are grouped right next to the highest-ranked opportunities because they represent opposite extremes of bad and good outcomes for the project.

Probability and Impact Matrix

Probability	Threats					Opportunities				
0.9	0.05	0.09	0.18	0.36	0.72	0.72	0.36	0.18	0.09	0.05
0.7	0.04	0.07	0.14	0.28	0.56	0.56	0.28	0.14	0.07	0.04
0.5	0.03	0.00	0.10	0.20	0.40	0.40	0.20	0.10	0.00	0.03
0.3	0.02	0.03	0.06	0.12	0.24	0.24	0.12	0.06	0.03	0.02
0.1	0.01	0.01	0.02	0.04	0.08	0.08	0.04	0.02	0.01	0.01
	0.05	0.10	0.20	0.40	0.80	0.80	0.40	0.20	0.10	0.05
	Very Low	Low	Moderate	High	Very High	Very High	High	Moderate	Low	Very Low

FIGURE 18.4 *Traditional Threat and Opportunity Matrix*

Another issue with assigning estimated probability and impact values is that people are much better at relative estimation than absolute estimation. We get hung up on whether something has a 0.7 or 0.9 chance of happening but could tell you that it is more likely that the lack of C# experience will bite us before a lack of MSBuild experience will. This is one reason why many agile teams use effort estimation based on points rather than ideal days. People are better at relative estimation than absolute estimation, which is why we give directions in reference to landmarks rather than distances.

So, recognizing these human traits, I prefer to get teams to gauge impacts and probabilities in a more intuitive and relative way. For this we use *Investors* and *Help Wanted* board concepts. Threats are things we need help with; opportunities are things we need investors and supporters for. Using scales of impact to the project in terms of costs for risks and benefits for opportunities on the x-axis and probability of occurrence on the y-axis, the threats and opportunities can be visualized by the team as shown in figure 18.5.

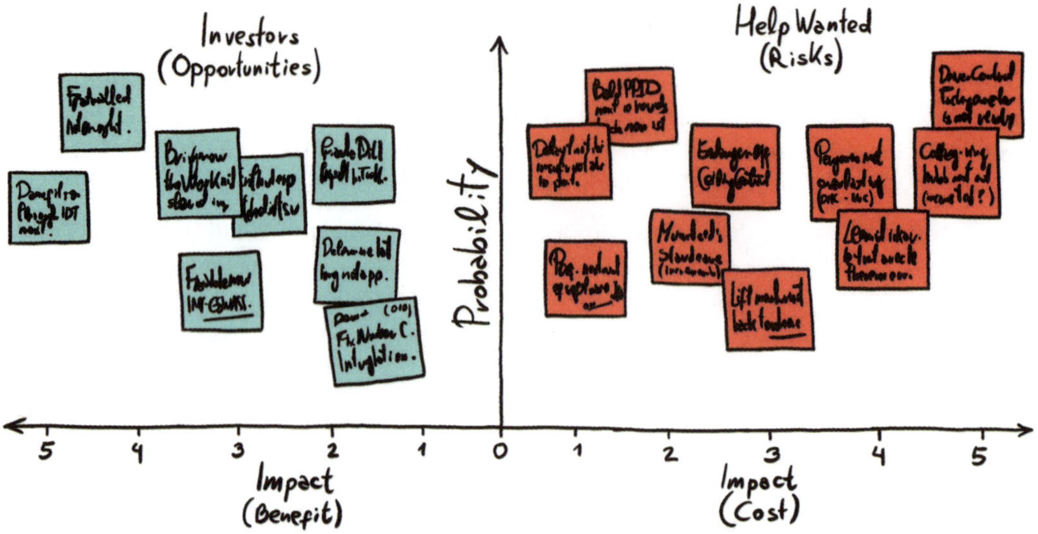

FIGURE 18.5 *Investors and Help Wanted Boards*

In this layout, the x-axis of impact to the project in terms of benefits and costs creates a spread where the greatest opportunities are furthest removed from the greatest threats. We do not worry too much about numeric analysis of probabilities, but instead use relative ranking to determine the vertical positions. The benefits at this stage really come from the conversations amongst team members about analyzing the threats and opportunities, and gaining consensus as to where they belong relative to each other on the charts.

Visualizing and agreeing on a spatial reference for the threats and opportunities also engages the right hemisphere of the brain and makes us less likely to forget them. (Assigning a location to the things we want to remember is a common memory-improvement technique. We can better recall things that are assigned a physical location, which is probably due to our hunter-gatherer days when our survival relied upon remembering where to find food and water.) This is useful for us as the project progresses, because if we better remember the threats and opportunities at play, we are more likely to appropriately tailor our behavior and everyday decisions for them.

Finding and categorizing risks is a start but is not sufficient. The real value comes from converting them into actionable stories for the prioritized backlog, then tracking and adapting based on review and reflection of the system's effectiveness.

Today's Forecast (Quantitative Risk Analysis)

The quantitative risk analysis process attempts to quantify (assign some numbers to) the threats and opportunities under consideration. It helps us understand the magnitude of individual threats and, viewed together, the overall project-risk profile. Before quantifying threats, let us talk about the dangers of applying math to estimates and speculations.

Remember this quote from William Bruce Cameron? *Not everything that counts can be counted, and not everything that can be counted counts.* In other words, some of the things we can quantify are not that useful, and some of the things we would like to quantify cannot easily be measured. Also, some research claims that quantitative risk approaches divert attention from precautionary or preventative measures.

However, as long as we are aware that trying to quantify risks may be problematic, we can still gain some valuable insights into their likely importance that can help us with prioritization. The usual way of quantifying risks is to express the impact of the risk in monetary terms and the probability of it occurring as a percentage. We can then calculate the expected monetary value of our risks, be they threats or opportunities.

For example, in a software project we may have a threat that our in-house reporting engine may not be up to the performance needs of the project. If the cost of swapping it out was $80,000 and we thought the likelihood of needing a replacement reporting engine was 50 percent, then we could calculate the expected monetary value of the threat as:

Expected monetary value = impact ($80,000) × probability (50%) = $40,000

Calculating the expected monetary values of our threats allows us to prioritize them. The general idea is that, much like an agile project's prioritized backlog of features, we want to tackle them (find ways to avoid the threat or make it smaller) in order of priority to minimize threats to the project as soon as possible.

The exercises we use here are more about showing the team risk management concepts to better illustrate why backlog items may shift, and less about taking action. Action comes in the next step, risk response planning, which is all about deciding what to do about the risks and putting work in our project backlog of things to do. For now, we are just concerned with quantifying the risks.

Dragons' Den

Agile addresses the concept of the "next best dollar spent," which reminds us to always be looking for where we can next add the most value. This may be in developing a new feature from the backlog that will generate an increment of ROI once it is released to the business, or it may be in investing some time in avoiding or reducing a threat that could negatively impact the project through expensive rework, delays, or additional costs.

The popular TV shows Dragon's Den and Shark Tank, in which entrepreneurs pitch investment proposals to investors, can be a useful metaphor for modeling the next best dollar spent. By comparing features from the backlog with threats to mitigate, we can get the team more comfortable with the seemingly shifting priorities that may come from the product owner or business representative when they consider the next best dollar spent and prioritize the backlog accordingly.

Decision Time (Plan Risk Responses)

After analyzing the options and possible responses to the risks, we then need to act on this information and decide what to do. This is the Plan Risk Responses step in the traditional PMI risk management process. It is the step for deciding and acting on the risks.

Junction Function

The Plan Risk Responses step is where we decide what to do about the risks we have identified, ranked, and measured. The options generally available to us are:

Avoidance: Eliminate the cause of the risk

Mitigation: Reduce the probability of the occurrence

Transference: Insurance, outsource, etc.

Acceptance: Accept and communicate to stakeholders

A fifth option, denial, is a widely practiced threat-response approach, but is not a valid option. Generally, it is best to avoid threats by finding ways to eliminate the root cause of the risk. Failing that, make them smaller or pass them to a party who is better able to handle them (for instance, outsource that work to a specialist in that field). Finally, the least preferable option is to accept the risk. For example, perhaps we just need to wait for service pack 2 from the vendor to fix the issue and, until then, we accept the risk of performance slowdowns.

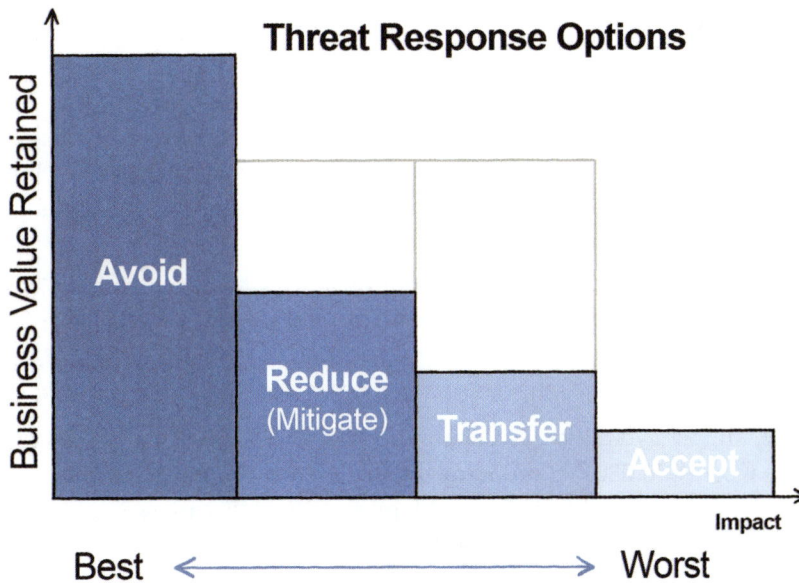

FIGURE 18.6 *Threat-response Options*

We need to explain these options to the team and make sure they understand the order of preference and how the threat-response options impact the residual risk to the project.

Residual risk is the remaining risk to the project even after we have taken the best threat-response option we were able to. Perhaps in our reporting performance example, we chose to run the reporting engine on a high-performance server. This helps somewhat, but we still have the residual risk that the higher-spec machine is not sufficient.

Secondary risks are new risks occurring as a result of our risk response strategy. Maybe we decided to do the report processing on the company's new scalable cloud platform. This may sound like a good idea, but if the company cloud platform is new and untested, then maybe this secondary risk is more significant than the original one we were trying to avoid or reduce. So, we need to quantify secondary risks to ensure they are indeed smaller than the risk we are responding to.

Once the team is familiar with the concepts of risk response options, residual risks, and secondary risks, we can engage them in the initial step of putting action items in the backlog. Backlog prioritization is a business/product owner role, but they will need help determining the priority of risk response actions. This is where steps to normalize the risks and feature values are required.

Dollar Balance

Not all threats can be avoided or reduced; we just reviewed how some threats might have to be accepted. When accepting a threat, there is no backlog action to create or balance against new functionality. However, if we can avoid a $50,000 expected monetary value (EMV) threat, then this threat avoidance is worth $50,000 to the project and should be inserted in the backlog above features worth $49,000 to the business.

We need to compare the value of risk response actions to the value of prioritized features and insert them in the appropriate place. When doing so, we also have to be aware of residual and secondary risks. So, the value of a risk response action is net monetary value (EMV) = EMV of residual threat + EMV of secondary threat.

For example, simply avoiding a risk with an EMV of $40,000 that has no residual risks or secondary risks is worth $40,000. Yet reducing the impact of a $60,000 risk by trying an alternative approach that only addresses half of the problem and in itself carries a $10,000 EMV is only worth $60,000/2 = $30,000 + $10,000 = $40,000.

So, we need to normalize all the risk responses to values to take into account residual and secondary risks before asking product owners to prioritize these actions in the backlog.

Backlog Injector (Implement Risk Responses)

The Backlog Injector step is where we take action on the risks, in other words, it is where we implement the risk responses. The name comes from the activity of creating and inserting new activities in our product backlog.

Of course, the product backlog is controlled by a product owner, so we need to determine, based on "where is the next best dollar spent" thinking, where in the backlog our risk response activities belong, then have a conversation with the product owner about inserting the risk response activities.

Report Card

The report card is a list of recommended risk responses, normalized by net EMV, for consideration by the business representative/product owner. It is prioritized by net EMV.

Threat	Initial EMV	Residual EMV	Secondary EMV	Net EMV
Reporting engine performance	$60,000	$30,000	$10,000	$40,000
iOS integration	$30,000	-	-	$30,000
Facebook compatibility	$50,000	$30,000	-	$30,000
Third-party components	$40,000	-	$20,000	$20,000
QA continuity	$15,000	-	-	$15,000

FIGURE 18.7 *Normalized threat values*

With this information, the product owner can now discuss adding these risk response actions into the backlog.

Inoculator

Inoculator is the name given to the process of injecting threat-avoidance/mitigation and opportunity stories into the backlog. It is done by the product owner, but with the consultation and guidance of the development team. It is this ability and frequent opportunity (every iteration planning meeting) to reduce remaining threats and capitalize on opportunities that sets agile methods apart from other, slower review cadence approaches that inspect and adapt less frequently.

By avoiding and reducing threats closer to their identification, this shortens the project horizon of risk. By making changes earlier in the life cycle, the cost of changes is reduced. On the flip side, capitalizing on opportunities is like making investments early; they have longer to accumulate. These are the compounding benefits of early and rapid threat and opportunity management.

Getting the risk response actions into the backlog is how these tasks are scheduled and undertaken. We want to make sure that all our risk management work is not supplemental to the project plan but baked right in. All too often, risk management is an activity done up front or alongside the project, but never really integrated into the day-to-day activities of the project. By inserting these new stories into the backlog, we drive risk management actions from analysis to action.

Prioritized Risk List	Prioritized Mitigation Actions	Prioritized Feature List	Prioritized Feature/Risk List
High x High		MUST	MUST
High x High	Action	MUST	Action
High x High		MUST	MUST
High x High	Action	SHOULD	MUST
High x High	Action	SHOULD	SHOULD
High x High		SHOULD	Action
High x High	Action	COULD	Action
			SHOULD
			SHOULD
			Action
			COULD

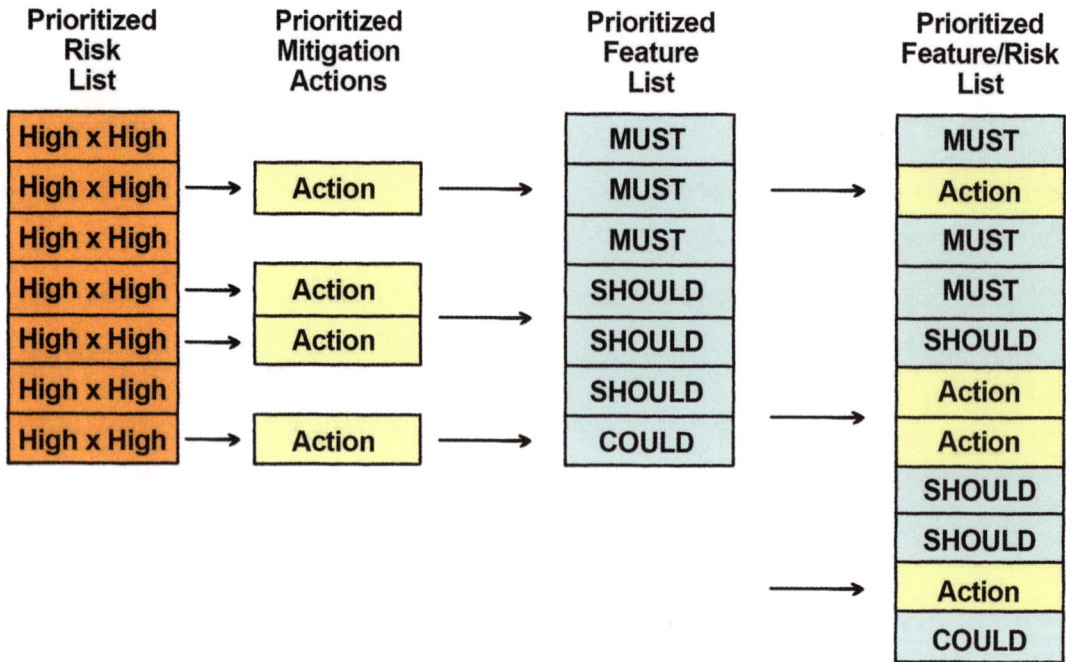

FIGURE 18.8 *Inserting Risk Responses into the Backlog*

Risk Radar (Monitoring Risks)

The last step in the process is monitoring and controlling the risk management process by making sure our strategies are effective, continually looking for new or escalating risks and ways to improve.

Risk Burndown Graphs

Risk burndown graphs are a great way of showing the project's cumulative threat position and trends over time. They are stacked area graphs of threat severity that allow trends, along with new and escalating threats, to be easily identified.

Algae Project - Risk Profile

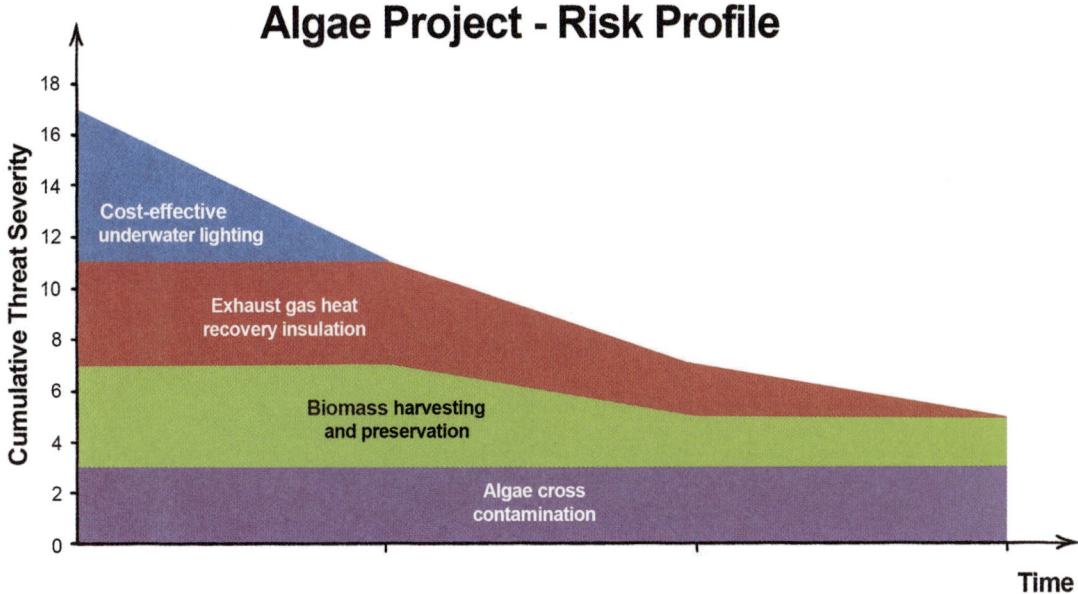

FIGURE 18.9 *Threat-profile Graph*

Risk Retrospectives

Risk retrospectives are periodic reviews of the risk and opportunity log and risk management processes being used on the project. Just as we review the evolving product and team processes throughout the project, so should we be evaluating the effectiveness of the risk management plan and processes being used by the team.

There are questions we could/should be asking when we regularly review our risk management approach. These questions ask about the current threats and opportunities:

- Do we have any new or escalating threats?
- Are we eliminating or reducing our threats?
- What are the root causes of our threats, and can we eliminate any of them?
- Which threat avoidance or elimination strategies are working, and which are not?
- For threats we choose to transfer, how are the third parties managing them? What can we learn from them, or would we be better off bringing them back in-house?
- How is our remaining threat EMV burning down?

- What is our threat EMV-reduction velocity per iteration?
- What opportunities have we been able to exploit this iteration?
- What new opportunities have been identified this iteration?

Questions that probe into whether the process is working:

- Are there any trends in our opportunities we can mine/develop for additional benefits?
- What is our rate of opportunity value delivery?
- Looking at our work done, where was our money best spent? Was it on feature delivery, threat reduction, or opportunity exploitation? What can we learn from this?
- How are the team's risk management capabilities developing?
- Where do we still need mentoring and support?

Rinse and Repeat

Finally, reviewing is not enough; we need to update our risk management artifacts, update our risk lists and EMV scores, and groom the backlog with new features and new risk responses. Always be rebalancing the priorities. Update the risk information radiator graphs (such as our threat burndown graphs) and make sure people are not only looking at the impacts of new work in terms of estimates, but potential risks too.

Chapter 18 Summary

Risk management is all too often a mostly passive analysis-and-reporting process focused mainly at the start of the project (when we know least about it) and fixated on threats. However, with the support and involvement of the business and project team, it can reach further and be active and more productive.

Risk management is traditionally the realm of PMs who might not have a good understanding of many of the technical risks. The team likely has a better handle on these, and we should engage them in the process.

Engaging the team generates wiser decisions. It promotes problem-solving as a sought-after skill, rewards being proactive, builds social capital, and creates ownership of collective solutions by shifting power downward.

Agile approaches can help risk management but do not magically manage risk for us. Risk management still needs to be an active, deliberate process engaging the team and business in the form of a product owner, if you have one, or, if not, a sponsor. We reviewed a comprehensive and collaborative risk management framework that mirrors the PMI-endorsed process but focuses on team interaction and revisiting the process often.

We can make management a valuable source of new revenue and loss prevention when we bake it into the ongoing planning and prioritization processes. With regular insights and updates from the team, and an equal focus on opportunities, it becomes a potent source of suggestions and valuable safety net.

Key topics covered in this chapter:

- » The benefits of collaborative risk management
- » Agile and hybrid risk management
- » Collaborative games for risk management
- » Tools to visualize threats and opportunities

Chapter 19
Bringing It All Together

First, a Warning about Models

These last four sections on agile, leadership, industry-specific knowledge, and plan-driven approaches have covered a lot of ground. We have examined a host of models and extracted elements from them to create new models. This is a useful and necessary part of how we learn.

David Kolb, an educational theorist, describes a four-step learning process, step 3 of which is based on mental models:

1. Concrete experiences: What we already know

2. Observation and reflection: What our retrospectives help us identify

3. Abstract conceptualization: Thinking about the problems and designing potential solutions

4. Active experimentation: Trying something new

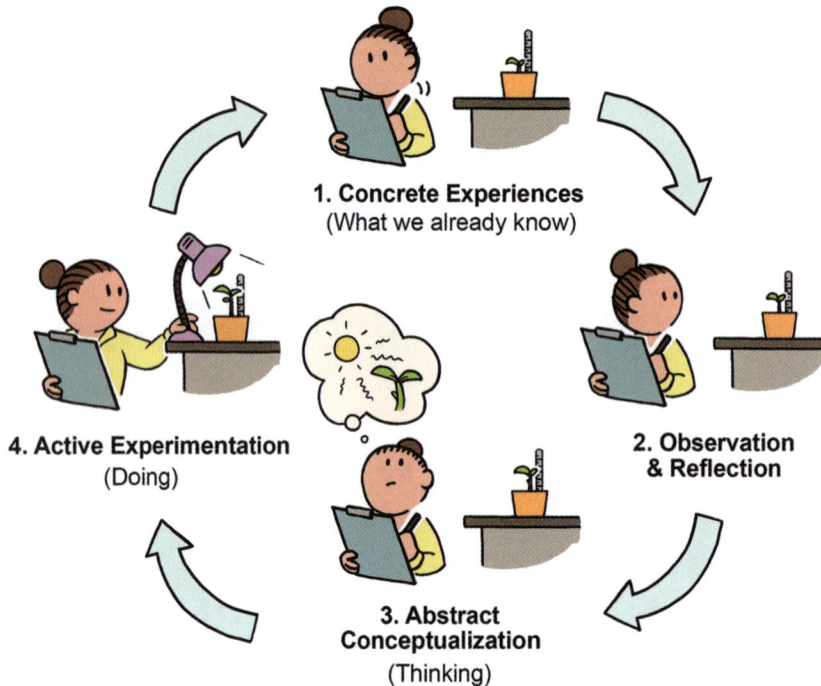

FIGURE 19.1 *Four-step Learning Process*

These stages act as part of an experimental learning cycle. The third step, abstract conceptualization (thinking), describes our use of models before we start using our knowledge in the last step, active experimentation.

However, we must understand that models, no matter how useful, are just simplified views of a more complex reality. They can help us frame and develop our thinking but cannot describe every situation or how best to behave. In our organizations, we will encounter complex situations where models can only take us so far. We will need to combine approaches, improvise, and experiment to be successful.

This warning should also bring some relief. If knowledge work were easy, it would be automated soon. If our work, as leaders of SMEs, could reliably be reduced to a set of best practices, then AI software (such as that used by the IBM Watson service) could begin to remove these roles.

We are in an era when we still laugh about being replaced by robots or AI. However, I believe it will be in our lifetime that this transition occurs. Tasks, such as some forms of diagnostic imaging, that were once in the realm of highly skilled specialists are now being performed by AI. The fact that people's behaviors are complex and messy means that leadership will be one of the last roles to be replaced.

I expect we will see AI-driven helpers reminding us of things like time allocation on tasks such as "Determining Task Progress and Results" is out of balance compared to tasks like "Upholding Group Unity." These tools should not replace people as leaders but make them better at their roles.

Focus on People

There are no silver bullets, shortcuts, or process frameworks that will solve all our problems. We must do the nitty-gritty work to overcome the challenges we face. Having said that, we do not need to go on this journey without a road map, that is what BAM provides. Nor do we need to do it alone—there is a community of people using and improving it.

Success is gained through the smart and respectful engagement of people. We cannot push people through doors; we can only open doors in front of them and describe the scene on the other side of the threshold. Managers try to influence with logic, but good leaders know they must build an emotional connection before appealing to arguments.

Program and Portfolio Management

Products and Programs

Projects are temporary endeavors. They are undertaken to create a result or service, then they end. Projects are often measured on delivering a defined scope within schedule, cost, and quality constraints. This works well for defined, repeatable, physical endeavors such as building a bridge or planning and executing an office move.

The temporary project framework does not work so well for developing digital products that have long life spans. Amazon's websites and apps will only be "done" when they go out of business and are no longer competing in the industry, evolving their products or services, or keeping up with technology change. The same goes for banks, music streaming services, and utility companies. Their digital products (websites, apps, integrations, back-end systems) will only ever finish development when they are obsolete. Until then, ongoing support, maintenance, and evolution is the norm.

This is different from the level of support and maintenance a bridge may need after it is turned over to operations. Physical assets still need maintenance, repair, periodic retrofits, and upgrades, yet the knowledge, skills, and team roles needed are typically not the same as those required for the initial plan, design, and build.

In the digital space, given the complexity and typical degree of uniqueness, it is advantageous to keep the original team together to do ongoing development. Handing over a software product to a different maintenance team will nearly always result in a degradation of development speed and capability due to a loss of knowledge.

So, digital-first organizations are built around stable product teams, a trend that is now spreading to traditional organizations. Movements and books like #NoProjects and Continuous Digital explain how the economics of software development differ from those of the physical world.

We have diseconomies of scale where digital elements are cheaper to build in small batches due to the improved ability to respond to change and the fact that communication and learning costs are higher than development costs. This is why, when digging ditches or picking apples, adding more people gets the job done sooner, but when building something complex and unique it results in much more time and budget being consumed.

This all poses quite the challenge for PMs in charge of digital projects. The experienced ones know we want small, stable, cohesive teams. Then, ideally, we should keep these teams together and let them maintain and extend the project once it goes live.

Yet many project management processes suggest creating plans and estimates for time and costs up front based on today's requirements, then dividing up the work and farming it out to specialized workers economically, all the while measuring progress compared to these initial plans and estimates, before going live, handing over to operations, and disbanding the team.

In short, many of the traditional project constructs and processes do not map well to digital projects. Luckily, there is another construct we can use that is much better aligned: programs.

Programs as a Partial Solution

Programs are not just a collection of projects. Programs take a different view toward change and managing for benefits and outcomes, as opposed to deliverables and outputs. They are also typically run for much longer.

Here is an excerpt from PMI's *Standard for Program Management, Fourth Edition*: "The primary difference between projects and programs is based on the recognition within programs that the strategies for delivering benefits may need to be optimized adaptively as the outcomes of components are individually realized. The best mechanisms for delivering a program's benefits may initially be ambiguous or uncertain."

This acceptance of up-front uncertainty, need for adaptation, focus on benefits, and longer timeframes makes programs much better vehicles than projects for digital product delivery.

It would be logical to argue that digital products are different animals than physical projects and so we should manage them accordingly. I am all for that but would like to offer programs as a stepping-stone for getting from projects to products.

Programs already exist within traditional organizations; there are guides, constructs, and frameworks we can use, and they do not require educating everyone in a new way of thinking.

The table below summarizes the contrast between projects and programs shown in PMI's *Standard for Program Management*, with additional information for product characteristics.

	Project	**Program**	**Product**
Duration	Short-term, temporary.	Longer-term.	Long-term.
Scope	Projects have defined objectives. Scope should be progressively elaborated throughout the life cycle.	Programs produce benefits to the organization.	Products are benefits driven.
Change	Project managers expect change and implement processes to keep change managed and controlled.	Program managers expect change and manage and adapt to optimize the delivery of benefits.	Product managers expect change and manage and adapt to optimize the delivery of benefits.
Monitoring	Project managers monitor and control the work of producing the products, services, or results that the project was undertaken to produce.	Program managers monitor progress to ensure the overall goals, schedules, budget, and benefits will be met.	Product managers monitor progress to ensure the overall goals, outcomes, and benefits will be met.
Success	Success is measured by product and project quality, timelines, budget, and degree of customer satisfaction.	Success is measured by the ability to deliver its intended benefits to an organization and the efficiency and effectiveness of delivering those benefits.	Success is measured by the ability to deliver its intended benefits to an organization and ongoing viability for continued funding.

	Project	Program	Product
Funding	Largely determined up front based on ROI projections and initial estimates, then updated with actuals and change requests.	Up frontand ongoing. Updated with results showing how benefits are being delivered.	Continuous via funding development tranches and reviewing value delivery.

Organizations making the switch to product development can benefit from examining program management frameworks as a stepping-stone. Programs are much better aligned with product thinking through their acceptance of up-front uncertainty, need for adaptation, focus on benefits, and longer timeframes.

Adopting a program focus to long-running digital products and services can reduce the typical friction points generated by questions such as *When will this project ever be done?* They provide better management strategies, monitoring approaches, and funding models to improve fit.

Do Not Give Up on Other Approaches

In our search for new and better ways to do things, we sometimes neglect moderation. We get caught up in whatever the new fad is—be it upsizing, downsizing, lean, or agile—and we go all in and lose the benefits of the old ways. Typically, new ways of thinking offer incremental improvements, but have their own omissions and blind spots.

Instead of abandoning existing models, think of them as Russian dolls. We can use some of the self-managing concepts of teal organizations, but retain some elements the agile green organizational concepts, and maybe some of the orange goal-centered ideas too.

In this way, we do not need to continuously throw out the old to use the new, but instead embrace the

ambiguity—and power—of using multiple approaches. This really is the *ri* mindset and is also valuing pragmatism over purism.

This uncertainty and ambiguity is difficult to process at first. We have moved you from *not knowing* what you do not know to *knowing* what you do not know. It may feel uncomfortable, but this is progress.

Chapter 19 Summary

Models are thinking tools: They help us frame problems and choose solutions. They are also typically visual, so they help us share our ideas with other people.

While they are useful, they also have limitations. Models are, at best, just simplified simulations that reflect how things work in the real world. At worst, they are time-wasting distractions that are wrong and divert our attention from working with people. So, we need to use them where they add value, then, like everything else, abandon them the moment they no longer deserve the expense of their upkeep.

Many of today's digital projects, such as websites and services, will not be "done" until the organization goes out of business or migrates to something else. As such, they do not meet the classic *temporary* criteria of projects. Product management approaches that resemble program governance structures are often a better fit for these long-lived initiatives. They also better support long-lasting, stable teams, and ongoing funding.

Finally, we need to recognize that the evolution of the models, methods, and tools we have examined is ongoing. We need to keep learning and keep asking if they are worth the cost. By all means, try new approaches, but have the kill switch primed too. We do not want process bloat; we need to focus on the goal of delivering value and overcoming done drift.

Key topics covered in this chapter:

» A warning about models

» How products and programs interact

» Do not give up on other approaches

Chapter 20
Case Studies

Case Study 1: Techno Trucking

A trucking company asked for help with a long-running IT initiative. The project involved installing a custom truck-routing, tracking, and support system in a fleet of one thousand trucks across the United States and Canada.

The hardware installation involved connections to the trucks' onboard computer to monitor driving time and used to track vehicle wear items, along with driver behavior (heavy braking, hard acceleration, etc.). Other components included mounting an in-cab tablet, a tablet holder/charger, a Global Positioning System (GPS) antenna, and cellular and satellite two-way communications systems.

Most of the trucks were owned by the sponsoring organization, but about a third belonged to independent owner-operators working on contract who did not take kindly to having their trucks cut open and holes drilled through them to install equipment.

The software involved a commercial package for truck routing and safety monitoring, plus a custom software suite of additional driver tools that ran on the in-cab tablet and integrated with the organization's scheduling, maintenance, and driver-management solutions running at the corporate office.

The three-year project had been running for five years by the time I was brought in. It was over budget and only a small number of trucks had equipment running just a subset of intended functionality. The internal software team claimed that problems with the vendor package were hampering their development. The vendor claimed their software was fine, and it was the new custom software that was creating the problems.

The hardware and software teams were mainly independent contractors who worked colocated with the truck-dispatching business unit. Due to the size and budget of the project, the steering committee included the CEO and CFO, CIO, PM, and business sponsor.

The business sponsor and CFO were at odds. To the CFO, it looked like a runaway project showing no signs of finishing and throwing good money after bad. The business sponsor acknowledged the delay but thought the team was close and had been delayed by a string of technology setbacks that they had now overcome. However, since these conversations had played out for two years, the CEO told the CIO to sort it out.

I was brought in to determine whether the project should continue to completion or be canceled and handed over to a different vendor who had provided a fixed-price estimate for a replacement solution. The CIO had little trust in the current PM and no visibility into the project team performance, who were working outside the IT group in a different business unit.

My time spent talking to the CIO and business sponsor was an emotional roller coaster. The CIO explained the overruns, problems, and sunk costs. I would come away from our talks thinking it was time to cancel the current project and start again. Yet, the business sponsor was deeply committed to the project and believed they were ever so close to having something for broader deployment. After my talks with him, I could see all the hard work done and how a custom solution would provide a competitive advantage. I felt a little gullible being swayed so much by each of their arguments.

My talks with the PM initially did not go so well. They were guarded and unable or unwilling to provide even basic information about the project performance, issues, plans, or budgets. It became apparent that they, like the business sponsor, had deep expertise in trucking-logistics software, satellite communications, and trucking hardware, but less affinity for schedules, budgets, or release road maps. I was grateful for their help, and they taught me a lot about trucking before the CIO transitioned them off the project.

From discussions with the software development team, it became clear their time was being stretched too thin. Not only were they responsible for developing the new modules, but also for helping the package vendor debug their problems and migrate an aging truck maintenance system to a new version on a new system. There was simply too much work competing for their time to make meaningful progress on any initiative.

After working with the team and vendors, I recommended we continue the project and push for a release to get driver feedback. This is what the team and business sponsor had been advocating all along, but I think the CEO just needed to hear it from a more independent source. Completing the project was not without its challenges, and we certainly got to exercise all the aspects of the BAM.

Beyond Agile Implementation

Plan-Driven and Agile Domains

We created detailed plans for the hardware installs. Some of the parts had long lead times, and others were too expensive to stockpile in large numbers, so we needed an overall deployment plan to drive ordering the parts and scheduling the install teams.

Minimizing the distance traveled and downtime for expensive equipment and drivers is a complex mathematical problem to solve. Fortunately, the dispatching software we were deploying handled lowest-cost scenario modeling, and we were able to use it to calculate the optimal install locations.

Every time an install team did a batch of installs, we debriefed the process afterward. How long did trucks wait on average before their install? How many truck drivers were no-shows and how many were late? How often did the install or training team sit idle waiting for trucks? Using the answers, we adjusted the truck counts, timings, and schedules for future install sessions.

We learned owner-operator truck drivers do not want to be trained while equipment is installed in their trucks. Instead, they want to supervise and provide input on where modules are installed, holes are drilled, etc. So, we had to update our training plans accordingly.

The software development team planned using agile approaches. Once we showed the steering committee how much of the development team's time was spent on sustainment, vendor assistance, and data migration, we gained their permission to focus on completing planned functionality. This reduced task switching and finally allowed good progress on feature completion.

Lean Visualization

Lean emphasizes making policies and work visible. We used graphical representations of the team's workload to convince the steering committee that having the team multitask between so many initiatives was not in the best interests of the organization; actually, the process took longer. The steering committee did not care too much to begin with. They said everyone was busy, and they would love to work on just one thing, but that was not going to happen. We only convinced them by pausing the migration work for a week and showing the improved completion rate of features. Then they approved the reprioritization.

When I first joined the project, I struggled to understand the mixed in-house developed software and cloud-based services. I went through all the documentation but still could not picture how the elements worked together. To get up to speed, I knew I had to draw it all out to understand it.

I met with stakeholders, asked how their part worked, and drew it out with them. They provided lots of corrections and additions. I then showed the whole thing to the team, and they found even more omissions, which I filled in. I felt like they were humoring me, helping me get my little project manager brain around the complex system they had spent years developing. However, they then announced they had never seen it all mapped out in a single (huge) image before.

Going forward, we ended up using the diagram repeatedly within the team to discuss issues and to bring new members on board. I also used simplified versions and zoomed-in portions for explaining elements of the project to the steering committee. Taking the time to create a visual helped many stakeholders.

EI

As always, the toughest problems to solve were the people problems. Fundamentally, the truck drivers did not like being monitored. One of the reasons people take a job like being a truck driver is because they want to be independent, be their own boss, and sometimes just get away from everyone else. The project involved installing driver monitoring systems that tracked their working times, driving speeds, and even driving behavior.

It should not have been surprising that some of the systems "broke," wires became loose, and an unexpectedly high number of "coffee spills" rendered equipment inoperable. The project was changing the drivers' operating environment.

Thinking about the Kübler-Ross change model, or the five stages of grief, it should have been obvious that drivers were experiencing denial and anger about the new situation. Using ideas from John Kotter's 8-Step Change Model, we created a plan that got the drivers more engaged in the design and rollout of the project.

The pilot group was expanded to include members from all regions, and we invited anyone else interested in piloting the technology to get in touch as we built out a vocal community of early testers. They provided valuable feedback about installs, software feature priorities, and usability issues before less supportive drivers experienced them.

We incentivized this group to also answer questions from newly trained drivers. Ultimately, they played a big part in institutionalizing the solution and fielding adoption issues.

Industry Knowledge

Working within the truck scheduling department enabled the team to learn about the trucking business. The product owner was a former dispatcher and driver who brought in-depth knowledge and over thirty years of experience in the business domain.

The expanded test group provided additional industry knowledge about real-world usage. They helped explain how edge cases, such as trucks moving out of cell range and switching to satellite communications, impacted our over-the-air software updates.

No Parade

The project delivered a working solution and was deployed to the fleet of trucks. However, because the project was years late and over budget by then, the CFO and CEO did not see the result as a success. They were relieved that project spending had stopped and they did not have to listen to me explain how many trucks had been installed and how many features we had deployed since we last met, but there was no celebration or corporate thanks to the team or drivers.

This was a shame because, if nothing else, it was an excellent example of collaboration between departments, creative problem-solving, and a lot of hard work. Small follow-up projects popped up to make enhancements, but the original project name was deliberately avoided because its mere mention seemed to cause an involuntary facial-tick reaction in the CFO.

Instead, stealthy, ninja-like teams delivered an enhancement and quietly disbanded. Yet the business unit got their features, the dispatch system worked well, and the old maintenance system got migrated. Using a combination of plan-driven, agile, lean, and industry knowledge, a struggling program of projects was pushed across the finish line by a hardworking team.

Case Study 2: Pipeline Volumetric Solution (PVS)

Background

The PVS was a large custom software development project for a major energy company. It was undertaken to create a pipeline scheduling, balancing, and invoicing system after a review of commercial packages revealed a significant gap in features.

Industry Domain

It is logical to think that managing a pipeline is simple. You put oil in at one end, and (if there are no leaks) the same amount should flow out the other end. While correct in principle, there are some crucial factors that complicate things. First, the pipeline-gathering system looks like a tree with several boughs (mainlines), many branches (gathering lines), and hundreds of twigs (feeder lines) and leaves that represent the truck pits and tanks that put hydrocarbon products into the pipeline.

The pipeline transmits products from many supplier organizations and charges these suppliers based on the quantity transported, the quality of the product, and how much diluent is necessary to convert the thick, sticky raw material into something that will flow through the pipeline. Low-quality products that contain lots of sand or water are corrosive to the pipeline, and thus carry a transmission penalty fee, as do acidic products. The diluent is not available at each input location, so the pipeline operator adds diluent upstream of the incoming product and charges the customer for how much they added for that amount of product at that viscosity.

The pipeline mixes and transmits many products at a time. Interestingly, adding 10 units of product A to 10 units of product B does not produce 20 units of the combined product. Instead, the small molecules of one product mix into the spaces between the larger molecules of the other product in a process called *volumetric blending*. Like adding sand to a bucket of ping-pong balls, it means the total volume of the pipeline at any given time is not the sum of its inputs and diluents. Instead, it is calculated via complex cubic formulae that have to be calculated in real time as new product is constantly entering the pipeline and blended product is exiting.

The real complications come from the suppliers and operator contracts. This pipeline was transmitting a quarter of Canada's oil output, worth billions of dollars annually. With such values at stake, the suppliers and operators wanted the best deals available and so employed people with advanced mathematics degrees to draft the operator contract agreements. Their solutions were varied and complex. Companies can transmit at the daily (spot) rate with variable-rate discounts for more volume, or buy bundles of transmission-capacity units that expire like cell phone credits if you do not use them, or even bid on options for upcoming capacity in a futures-like trading market.

The producers want to optimize the prices they receive at market, transmitting more volume when prices are high and less when prices are low. The pipeline operators want to be running at near-maximum capacity to maximize throughput and revenue. This means estimating likely volumes, based on fluctuating oil prices and aiming to avoid penalties if they underpredict demand and fail to transmit contracted volumes.

Agile and Lean

The client wanted a flexible system that could perform the forecasting, scheduling, and balancing calculations practically in real time. They also wanted a custom calculation engine that would allow them to model new contracts, what-if scenarios, and billing formulas without having to change the software and roll out new versions for every change.

A scope outline of the system was sent out to vendors via a request for proposal (RFP) process and a vendor with relevant experience was selected. The initial estimate was around $3 million and had a +/− 20 percent range with a proposal to tighten that to a +/− 10 percent range after initial scoping was complete. Of course, scoping revealed more complexity, such as the need to interface with over ten other systems and high-end computing demands to run the blending calculations in a timely fashion. Finally, after a year of scoping/analysis and $1 million of the budget consumed, the vendor came back with an updated estimate that was ranged to +/− 10 percent as agreed, but had doubled to $6 million. The vendor was asked to wrap up their work and leave; the business unit wanted to complete development of the system within the original $3 million budget that they had agreed on with senior management and that now had only $2 million remaining.

The vendor's exit and internal discussions about what to do next and what could be salvaged took some time. A new PM was assigned but resigned shortly after. I was asked to come in and manage the project restart and determine what could be built toward the original scope statement for the remaining $2 million. Although the vendor team left, the business representatives and contractors who had been working on the project for the last year were still available.

Working with this core group who were familiar with the problem domain, we reviewed the processes being used and the now-vacant roles required to continue the project. A benefit of taking on a rescue/recovery project is that there is often leeway to change process and try new things. It was obvious to everyone that the original attempt did not meet objectives, so there was some freedom to make substantial changes.

Leadership and EI

We were fortunate to have a skilled architect who knew the business domain well, having worked on the previous incarnation of the pipeline volumetric balancing system that was still being used until the replacement was developed. We also had a strong and committed business lead who patiently shared their vision for the completed solution and made a team of pipeline schedulers available to the project team.

Working with this core team, we reviewed the current situation, which involved hundreds of pages of specifications but no running code in production. We reviewed which processes were working well, such as physical colocation with the business and daily stand-ups, and what was problematic, such as the time taken to document and validate requirements. Allowing the team to decide what processes to keep and which to stop doing was empowering for them.

Compared to the more controlling PMs that had come before me, I was seen as progressive. In reality, letting people create their own process is quite simple; the challenges only come if they want to adopt or abandon something you do not. Here, however, the contractors and client's permanent staff were all experienced and their suggestions made good sense; soon, we had useful prototype code running in test environments.

With the departure of the previous vendor, there were many project roles to fill. Engaging the team in the hiring process led to some great new hires. The existing team screened resumes, selected candidates for interview, and created the interview questions. For programming roles, they also created coding exercises and code-review workshops.

Creating the interview process was a valuable team-chartering exercise for the remaining project participants. It allowed them to discuss and gain consensus on what their values were and how they wanted to work going forward. The attributes and skills they identified as characteristics for good candidates reflected their own ideals. Since we were in "rescue" mode, with pressures to deliver something, we had not been given the freedom to formally reset and recharter the project. However, this team-based recruiting process provided many of the same benefits.

The effort and thoroughness put into the recruiting process impressed the candidates and we were able to add some great new people to the team. However, it was not all smooth sailing: the hiring rigor exposed the fact that some team members did not operate at the same standards or aspire to the same goals. That was no one's fault; we all have different aspirations and talents in life.

Some full-time staff were transferred to other parts of the organization and some contractors were let go.

This is when the motivation and productivity of the team really took off. There was probably no single factor responsible, but instead a combination of multiple factors that included a streamlined process and a newly expanded, cohesive, capable team. Freed from prescriptive, command-and-control management and given autonomy to "do anything morally acceptable to be successful," they made many tool and process improvements.

A substantial portion of the success was attributable to the business involvement. It is tiring to work hard and overcome problems to deliver a quality product in a complex environment. If no one is present to evaluate, understand, and discuss it, why would you bother going through all that trouble again? However, on this project, the business turned up in full for every demo. The team was led by the department manager, who played the sponsor role and product owner role, in combination with the architect who had built the previous system. The department manager encouraged participation and articulated the business need and benefits convincingly.

I learned a great deal from working with this sponsor/product owner, along with a staff member of hers who was our business math expert for the blending calculations and linear programming (LP) forecasting models. They had worked together for over twenty years and exhibited exceptional EI. They took the long-term view of investing in business training for the team members, caring for and nurturing people professionally, and sometimes personally. When people take an interest and care more than, say, direct line managers, people do their best not to disappoint them.

When reviewing prototypes and iteration demos, these business representatives were always appreciative of what had been accomplished and understanding of challenges and setbacks. Giving feedback is a skill. During feedback sessions, whether they are personal career reviews or demo reviews, people can be given five compliments and one opportunity for improvement and often come away disheartened, focusing only on that single shortcoming.

Analyzing how they gave such effective feedback and fostered such cooperation and sustained effort from the team uncovered a genuine care for the cause and the people involved. This is good news and bad news. The good news is that anyone can do it: just take the time, get involved, and take an interest in the people, not just the outcomes. The bad news is that it cannot be shortcut, replaced with a process, delegated to others, or made easier. It takes commitment, energy, and true involvement. If your heart is not in it or you are pursuing some other agenda or focus in life, it is not going to happen. It requires a singular, honest commitment.

Another feature of the business SME's involvement and effective demo feedback was an emphasis on the positive without ignoring deficiencies. It reminded me of the pattern from improv comedy called the "*Yes, and . . .*" rule. In improv comedy, to keep the story moving along, there is a rule of thumb that suggests participants avoid contradicting others' input by saying *no*, or even variations of *no*, such as *but* or *however*. Instead, participants should approve others' input with a *yes* and build on their contribution with an *and* . . .

I am pretty sure our business SMEs were not into improv comedy training, nor had they heard about *Yes, and* . . . in the period from 2005 to 2010, before it became popular in business literature. However, when the team presented an increment of functionality, the feedback was always along the lines of *Yes*, X *is great*, Y *works now*, and *and if we can get Z working next, we will be well on our way*.

This focus on what was working and framing of deficiencies as *and*, not *however*, was subtle and was achieved with many variations beyond just *Yes, and* . . . wording. Yet when I look back to determine why these experienced stakeholders were such a pleasure to work with and so effective at motivating the team members, it illustrates many EI skills. They had good control of their emotions (which may initially include frustration, if the team had underachieved that week) and an awareness of other people's feelings. They knew how to provide feedback that was more inspirational than critical and they cared deeply about the people and product involved.

Best Project Awards and Grants

Ultimately, the project was successful and delivered all the anticipated benefits. Other energy companies have inquired about buying or licensing a version of the system but have been declined because it delivers a considerable competitive advantage to the sponsoring organization. I wrote an account of the project turnaround and the delivery approach we used for the local PMI chapter's annual award ceremony and was thrilled when it won first place. Bringing the award back to the team was a great endorsement for their efforts.

Due to the research that went into developing the calculation engine, the project was also able to submit for and successfully claim research and development tax credits from the government. This, a first for the energy company, was another endorsement of the approach used and helpful in securing funding for further development.

Case Study 3: Programs, Project Problems, and Products

A Canadian telecommunications company that offers mobile phone, internet, and cable TV services was experiencing project delivery issues. The bulk of their new services were digital, but they also had significant investments in physical infrastructure (hardware boxes, cabling, networks) to integrate, manage, and maintain. They were experiencing problems scaling their agile practices, and diagnosing the issues led to the transition from using projects to using longer-lived product streams.

They had a challenging mandate, with over one hundred in-flight projects, many competing to link to the same websites and legacy systems. It appeared to be far too much WIP. Also, the staffing structures in place created many handoffs between groups. Opportunities were identified and defined by one business group, then assigned to in-house development teams that often worked with external vendor teams more experienced in the domain or technology involved.

Most applications and services being developed needed to integrate with existing systems that were managed by a legacy-systems management group. Infrastructure (creating technical environments) was supported by a separate department located in the United States. Finally, the support and sustainment of applications, once developed, were handled by a different support group.

This collection of separate teams and groups created many handoffs, dependencies, and delays as teams tried to get their work done. When we mapped the flow and transfer of work between groups, there seemed to be many opportunities for optimization. Reorganizing around products with long-running product teams should eliminate many of the handoffs.

Lean and Agile

First, we needed to illustrate the extent and impact of the interproject team dependencies. This allowed us to build support for remediation activities. We made the dependencies, blocked items, and queues visible by flagging these items on the project Kanban boards. A simplified model is shown in figure 20.1.

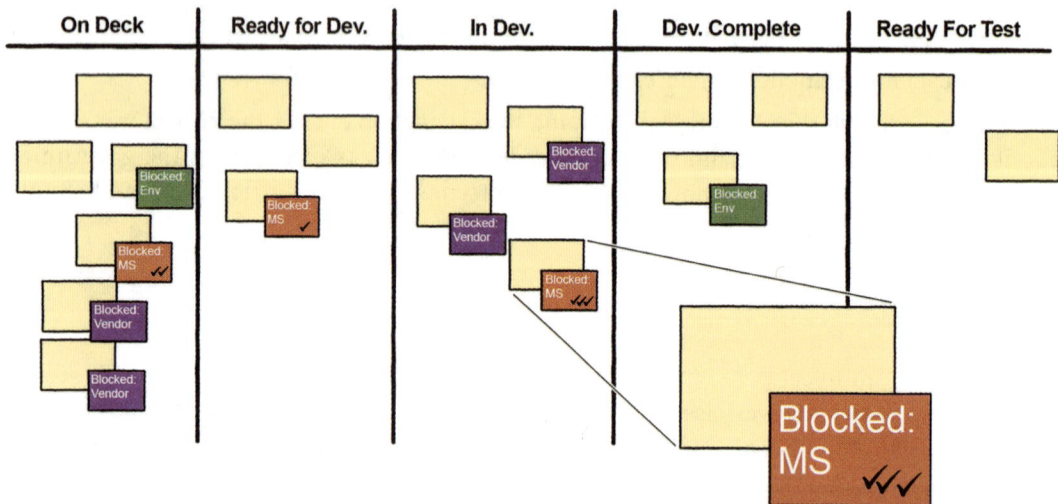

FIGURE 20.1 *Kanban Board*

Team members added blocked sticky notes to items waiting for other groups. The sticky note showed the initials of which group the task was waiting for. In the example above, *MS* stands for the microservices group. Each day at stand-up, team members added a tick to the sticky if the item was still blocked. This way, we quickly generated an easy-to-interpret score of the most impacted work items and the source of delays.

ScrumMasters and program managers worked to remove the blocked items and follow up with the groups creating the delays. Working with these groups, we discovered they too had many dependencies and delays that were preventing them from doing their work (or our requests) as quickly as they would have liked.

Creating dependency maps for the impacted team illustrated what we suspected. The web of project teams, vendors, and departments meant everyone was waiting on everyone else in an ensnarled mess. A simplified dependency map for one small project is shown in figure 20.2.

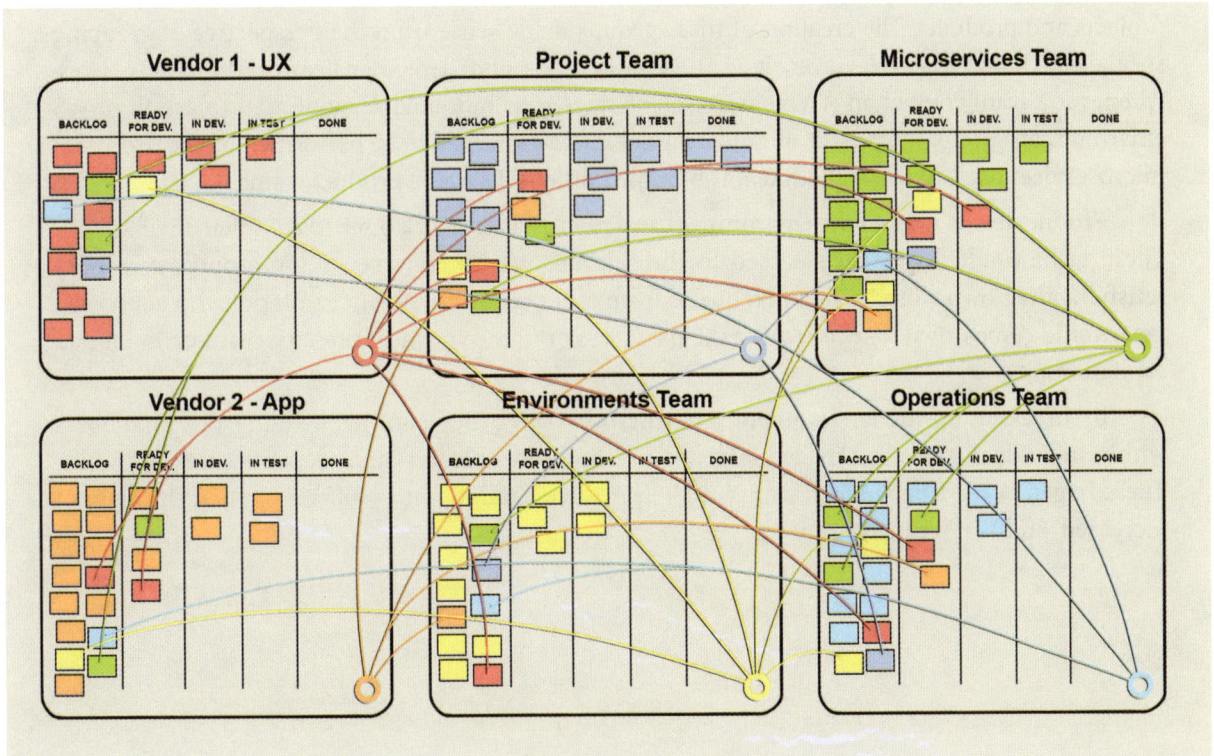

FIGURE 20.2 *A Simplified Dependency Map*

The lines on the dependency map indicate a task on one team's task board that is dependent and waiting on a task in another team. Analysis of how people spent their day revealed that many people spent as much time, if not more, following up on work and trying to get things expedited as they did undertaking development.

It was an example of global versus local optimization. Yes, small teams can operate the most efficiently internally, but if they are spending a large proportion of their time waiting for or escalating work within other teams, then they are no longer efficient.

Before making the switch to product-based development, the client had also recently adopted a microservices architecture and Amazon Web Services (AWS) cloud-based development. The two largest product development streams were using microservices and AWS for the first time.

The AWS environments were provisioned and managed by a separate team located at an office in the United States. A dedicated team was formed to create and manage microservices across all projects and products. The creation of these groups made sense from the perspective of grouping specialized knowledge. However, it created more silos and dependencies for the teams. Now, whenever a team wanted an AWS environment created or modified, they needed to ask the AWS environments group. Worse still, all microservice changes needed to be performed by the dedicated microservices team. Quickly, both teams became bottlenecks to the product teams.

Product teams needed the environment and microservice work done to complete their stories. These tasks would have to be passed to the relevant group. However, these groups were busy satisfying their own work items and requests from other teams. Often, the matter of who got served next would come down to who created the most fuss or found the most pressing justification for an escalation.

By breaking up the environment and microservices groups and embedding their members within individual teams, we created larger teams, but were able to reduce dependencies and waits. These larger, but less dependent, teams did help reduce handoffs and wait times. Their throughput increased, and WIP reduced.

Before Team Consolidation: Many Small Teams   **After Team Consolidation: Fewer, Slightly Larger Teams**

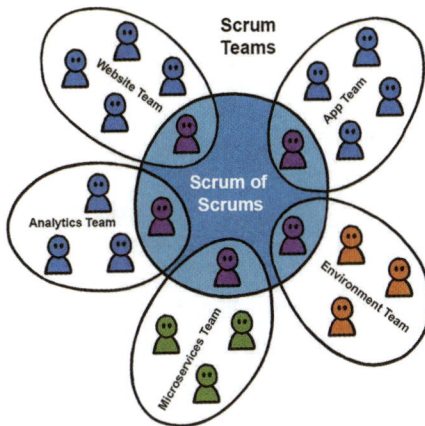

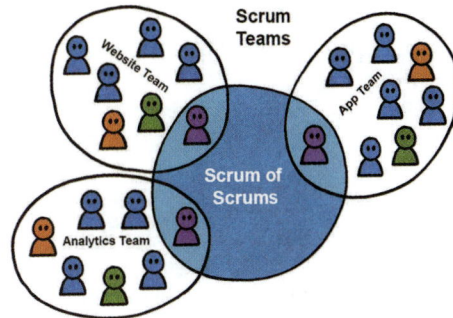

FIGURE 20.3 *Team Members Embedded into other Teams*

Along a similar vein, we asked the product owners who had previously worked out of a head office downtown to come out to the industrial park to work embedded within the development teams. Previously, they frequently reviewed and commented on the emerging product remotely, but always shared more information and provided deeper insights when on-site for weekly meetings. Of course, the downtown office location was more convenient for most people and had better lunch options, so the move was not universally welcomed or embraced. Luckily, the product director saw the benefits and encouraged the product owners to comply.

Forming dedicated, colocated, long-lived teams was the primary organization strategy for reducing handoffs. Embedding the support staff within the development team avoided a handover to another group at go-live time. So long-lasting development and sustainment teams were formed around the main websites and major applications. These websites and applications became the new product streams we organized around. These product teams would not be created just for delivery and then disbanded; instead, they would remain intact and undertake all subsequent updates and integrations.

The final team structurechange would be vendor staffing models. The client used a variety of outsourced vendors to undertake development work. This was either because the vendor possessed expertise in a software package or technology or because there were no people available internally to work on the initiative. Unfortunately, analysis of project throughput and delays showed that back-end integrations to legacy systems were often a bottleneck.

So, while initial development for vendor teams might go well, getting the system integrated and operational was difficult and competed for the same people and physical resources as in-house projects. The result was that, despite vendor promises, outsourcing a project did not result in it being completed when desired. Also, all these additional projects and integrations further hampered the in-house project-delivery plans since the in-house projects were also competing for these integration services.

A simplified schematic of the plan to transition from projects to products is shown in figure 20.4.

The general plan was to create a three-step transition, each step taking two team sprints or four weeks in total. The primary goals of the three steps are outlined below:

1. **Foundation:** Get everyone to a common starting point. Form the dedicated product teams and colocate them in the same workspace. Define the products and make sure each team has a definition of *done* and some basic metrics based on checking if the necessary roles are in place and people are functioning as a single team. Make sure teams have the tools and training they need. Also, provide support in the form of coaching and mentoring.

2. **Adoption:** Try to ensure the desired behaviors are being instilled. During the adoption step, we wanted to promote self-organizing teams. Most teams were operating this way, but some vendor teams were used to having tasks distributed to them. We also wanted to make sure the vendors were transitioning staff to be on-site. We started to measure throughput and team engagement metrics. In addition, we developed integrated product road maps that showed dependencies to other product teams at integration points.

3. **Development:** Encourage ongoing product-based development. By the third four-week productization step, we wanted to make sure vendor staff were on-site full-time. We also wanted to ensure that the product owners were now embedded with the teams permanently, and the teams were familiar with throughput-based reporting and running more experiments as a result of their retrospectives. We hoped to see mature product road maps, burn-rate-based budgeting and ongoing coaching and mentoring in place.

Sample Plan: An iterative and Incremental Approach to Transitioning to Agile Product Development

	Step 1- Foundation	Step 2 - Adoption	Step 3 - Development
People	• Organize teams around products • Co-locate Calgary staff	• Support teams toward self-organizing and self-managing • Vendor staff onsite as much as possible	• Teams self-organizing and self-managing • Vendor staff onsite only
Process	• Define products • Establish foundational metrics (roles, behaviors) • Robust DoD	• Create product ownership and architecture roles • Metrics based on number of deliveries, experiments & engagement levels	• Teams running frequent experiments and adapting process • Product road maps in place
Tools	• Set up Jira and Confluence • Create product and team boards • Agree reporting structures and process	• Integrated product road maps • Report manually	• Implement product and portfolio road mapping tools • Automate reporting
Support	• Assign agile coach • Provide team training	• More SM and PO training • Support and development	• Ongoing coaching and mentoring
O X Acceptance Criteria	• FTE, colocated roles • Tools ready • Products defined • Coaching	• Teams self-organizing • Supporting roles • Metrics in place	• Teams self-organizing & managing • Productive retrospectives occurring
	← 4 weeks →	← 4 weeks →	← 4 weeks →

Time

FIGURE 20.4 *Sample Pan: An iterative and incremental approach to transitioning to agile product development*

The idea was to take a single product team through this process and review how it went before rolling it out to the other product teams. The executive wanted to accelerate the move to product teams and so we were asked to overlap the transition for subsequent product teams.

The overall plan, for all product teams, was a nesting of the three-step process just described and is depicted in figure 20.5.

Following this approach, we would start with forming and executing one product team, then transition two more, then, finally, all the remaining product teams. It would have been nice to have started products 2 and 3 after product 1 had completed all three steps, so that lessons learned could be applied. However, the entangled, interdependent teams were struggling to deliver any systems to production, so the decision was made to overlap the product transitions by one step.

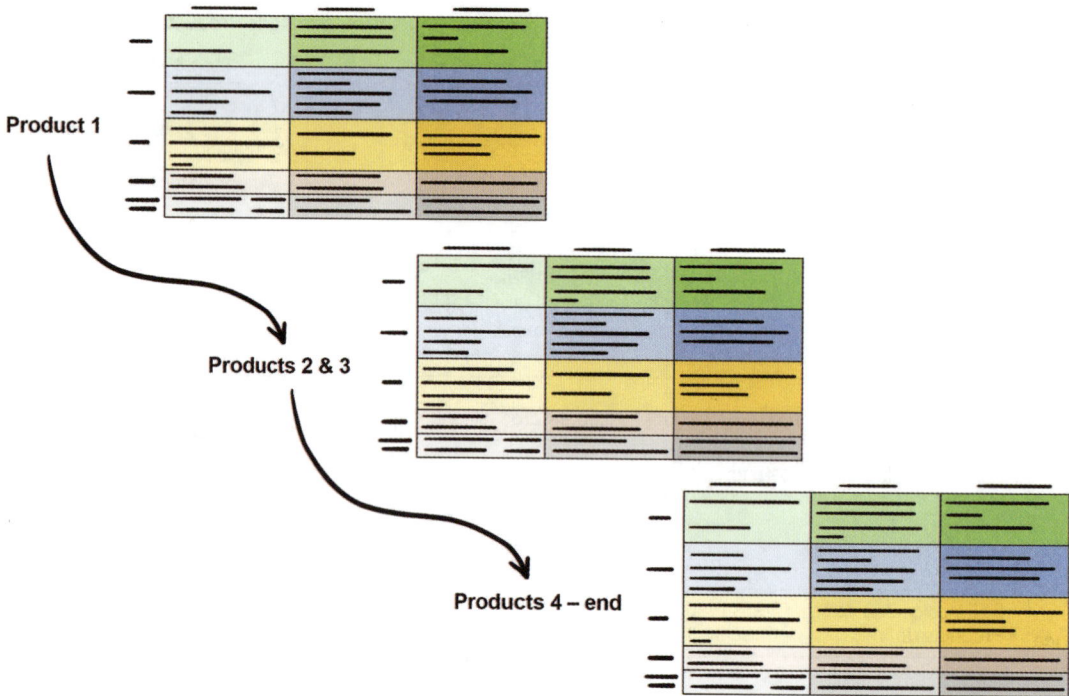

FIGURE 20.5 *Sample Incremental Rollout:*
One product first, then a couple more, then the remainder

Funding Problems

Previously, projects were funded based on their business case. If a sufficient ROI could be presented to senior management, then funds were allocated for the project. Project and program managers then tracked burn rates and reported on overall spend, along with requests for additional funds if necessary. It was an inexact process that lacked effective follow-through on delivered benefits, but everyone understood it.

Switching to a continuous product development stream presented some challenges. Predicting the expenditure was quite easy: we just totaled the anticipated run rates for the stable teams, and added vendor costs, software licenses, and some contingency funds for additional items. The problem was estimating the anticipated financial benefits for the investment. Without the standard ROI analysis for the backlog of planned features, there was less justification for authorizing the expenditure.

The issue was partially solved by requesting quarterly tranches of budget to fund the product teams for three months at a time. Each quarterly budget request was also accompanied by a list of planned features and enhancements provided by the product owner. The product owners also included business justification and ROI predictions. It was mainly a process similar to getting large projects approved. However, because the periods were shorter—and the dollar amounts smaller—it attracted less scrutiny.

The organization underwent structural changes that led to high rates of turnover and a change of technical leadership. These changes reset some of the advantages gained, yet many of the dependency problems were solved by forming larger, longer-running teams that had fewer handoffs and technical links.

Chapter 21
Final Guidance

This book has covered a lot of ground because today's knowledge-worker professional needs a wide repertoire of skills and strategies to be successful. We cannot predict the unique technologies or market segments that will emerge and require our skills. Before the COVID-19 pandemic, suggesting creating colocated teams seemed a safe bet. However, we can draw on traditional/linear life cycle approaches along with nonlinear/adaptive life cycles to handle complexity and ambiguity.

Likewise, whenever we deal with people, we can draw on leadership and EI to act with integrity, transparency, and respect toward others. As people become more mobile in where they choose to work, attracting and keeping the best talent will become critical for success. Admitting to our own mistakes and creating a psychologically safe environment demonstrates the desired behavior. By showing some vulnerability and allowing for experimentation and learning, we create work environments that people are attracted to and want to stay at.

We need to remember that knowledge is weightless: there is no downside to learning more about our domains, the needs of the customer, the business of the sponsor, or the preferences of the team members. It is only when we suggest or ask for approaches, tasks, and deliverables that we turn ideas into process that generates an execution burden. This is fine if the benefits exceed the costs. However, organizations often continue the process long after the costs exceed the benefits and they become inefficient and loaded with waste.

So, we need to take an economic view of our processes and always be asking what we can improve. What process can be paired back to provide the benefits with less burden to the team? If we operate in a safety-critical space, maybe there is little that can or should be tailored for efficiency. If we are generating ideas to validate new product or service ideas, maybe many things can be optimized. The idea to remember is that we should always be challenging the process by asking if there is a better way. Make this a team activity—teams should have more diversity than any one individual. Harness team members' ideas and let them run with them.

Even when we try to do everything right and have the best intentions, we still experience failure and awkward people. Try not to take these setbacks personally; if projects went well all the time, organizations would not need people like us. When setbacks happen, try to zoom out your perspective: look at the themes and repeating patterns you see. Once you have a plan for global improvement, the tribulations of daily work will seem more manageable and you will have a plan for reducing their occurrence in future.

If you always seem to have conflicts with the architecture group or marketing is making unrealistic promises to customers, then schedule some time with these groups. Listen to their frustrations with the project teams, who (to them) may seem to be cutting corners, diverging from agreed-upon standards, or dragging their heels and letting competitors launch features first. Only after hearing their side of the story will they be willing to listen to you. Take the time to find some common ground that might help both groups. Start there and keep the dialogue open and ongoing. Often, when in their eyes, our project starts to understand they will be more accommodating and focus their attentions and frustrations on someone else.

Finally, understand that it is okay (even desirable) to be vulnerable with your team. Daily meltdowns and displays of despair will not motivate any team, but the occasional sharing of your concerns with your team and superiors shows integrity, humility, and honesty. People will react well to it, see you as more human, and try to help, particularly if you have been a good listener and supportive of them.

Eric Shinseki, a retired United States Army general, has a great quote: "If you dislike change, you are going to dislike irrelevance even more." The skills discussed in this book will equip you for success in a world that is changing faster than ever. I wish you well in all your future endeavors and thank you for sharing your time and attention exploring the ideas described in this book.

Endnotes

Chapter 1

1. David Hyerle, "Visual Maps: Visual Tools for Activiating Habits of Mind," from *Learning And Leading with Habits of Mind: 16 Essential Characteristics for Success,* (Alexandria, VA: ASCD, 2008), 149-174, accessed 4/9/2021, http://www.mcoe.edu.my/Uploads/WMSTC2013_habits_of_mind.pdf.

Chapter 3

1. Stephen Covey, *The 7 Habits of Highly Effective People: Powerful Lessons in Personal Change,* (New York, NY: Simon & Schuster, November 9, 2004).

Chapter 4

1. Frederic Laloux, *Reinventing Organizations: A Guide to Creating Organizations Inspired by the Next Stage in Human Consciousness.* First Edition (Millis, MA: Nelson Parker, February 10, 2014).

2. Dr. David Rock and Dr. Al H. Ringleb. *Handbook of NeuroLeadership,* First Edition, (Charleston, SC: CreateSpace Independent Publishing Platform, October 30, 2013).

3. Daniel H. Pink, *Drive: The Surprising Truth About What Motivates Us,* (New York: Riverhead Books, April 5, 2011).

4. Ken Schwaber and Jeff Sutherland, Scrum Guide, accessed 4/9/2021, https://www.scrum.org/resources/scrum-guide.

5. Robert J. Anderson, William A. Adams, et al. *Scaling Leadership: Building Organizational Capability and Capacity to Create Outcomes that Matter Most,* First Edition, (Hoboken, NJ: Wiley, January 30, 2019).

Chapter 5

1. Ram Charan and Geoffrey Colvin, "Why CEOs Fail," *Fortune Magazine,* June 21, 1999, accessed February 17, 2021, https://archive.fortune.com/magazines/fortune/fortune_archive/1999/06/21/261696/index.htm.

2. Martyn Newman, PhD, *Emotional Capitalists: The Ultimate Guide to Developing Emotional Intelligence for Leaders,* (London: RocheMartin, March 31, 2014).

Chapter 6

1. Timothy J. Legg, PhD, "What Is the ABC Model in Cognitive Behavioral Therapy?," healthline.com, April 17, 2020, accessed 4/9/2021, https://www.healthline.com/health/abc-model.

2. Karen Reivich and Andrew Shatte, PhD, *The Resilience Factor: 7 Keys to Finding Inner Strength and Overcoming Life's Hurdles,* (New York, NY: Harmony, October 14, 2003).

3. Rick Hanson, *Hardwiring Happiness: The New Brain Science of Contentment, Calm, and Confidence,* (New York, NY: Harmony, December 27, 2016).

4. Angela Duckworth, *Grit: The Power of Passion and Perseverance,* (New York, NY: Scribner Book Company, May 1, 2016).

5. *European Journal of Psychotraumatology.* "Resilience definitions, theory, and challenges: interdisciplinary perspectives," October 1, 2014. Accessed February 16, 2021. https://www.ncbi.nlm.nih.gov/pmc/articles/PMC4185134/.

6. Duckworth, *Grit.*

Chapter 7

1. Jim Collins, *Good to Great: Why Some Companies Make the Leap and Others Don't,* (New York, NY: HarperBusiness, October 16, 2001).

2. Jaruwan Sakulku, "The Impostor Phenomenon," *International Journal of Behavioral Science.* 6 (1): 73–92, retrieved April 25, 2017.

3. M. Clark, K. Vardeman, S. Barba, (2014). "Perceived inadequacy: A study of the impostor phenomenon among college and research librarians," 2014, College & Research Libraries. 75 (3): 255–271, https://doi.org:10.5860/crl12-423.

4. Sakulku, "The Impostor Phenomenon," 75–97.

5. Mihály Csíkszentmihályi, *Flow: The Psychology of Optimal Experience,* (New York, NY: Harper Perennial Modern Classics, July 1, 2008).

Chapter 8

1. Augusto Vidaurreta, Gus Vidaurreta, and Tom Richardson, *Business is a Contact Sport.* (Minneapolis, MN: Alpha, August 1, 2001).

2. Susan Helper and Rebecca Henderson, "Management Practices, Relational Contracts and the Decline of General Motors," Harvard Business School Working Paper, No. 14-062, January 2014.

Chapter 9

1. Dr. Peter K. Jonason and Gregory Webster. "The Dirty Dozen: A Concise Measure of the Dark Triad," *Psychological Assessment,* 22(2), 420–432, accessed 3/10/2021, https://www.researchgate.net/publication/44653925_The_Dirty_Dozen_A_Concise_Measure_of_the_Dark_Triad.

Chapter 10

1. Jeffrey K. Pinto, Peg Thomas, Jeffrey Trailer, Todd Palmer, and Michele Govekar, *Project Leadership: From Theory to Practice,* (Philadelphia, PA: Project Management Institute, November 1, 1998).

2. James M. Kouzes and Barry Z. Posner. *The Leadership Challenge: How to Make Extraordinary Things Happen in Organizations*, 6th Edition, (San Francisco, CA: Jossey-Bass, April 17, 2017).

Chapter 11

1. Pink, *Drive.*

2. Larry C. Spears, "Character and Servant Leadership: 10 Characteristics of Effective, Caring Leaders," *The Journal of Virtues and Leadership,* 1 (1).

3. Deborah Ancona, Thomas W. Malone, Wanda J. Orlikowski, and Peter M. Senge, "In Praise of the Incomplete Leader," *Harvard Business Review*, February 2007. Accessed February 22, 2021. https://hbr.org/2007/02/in-praise-of-the-incomplete-leader.

4. James Scouller, *The Three Levels of Leadership: How to Develop Your Leadership Presence, Knowhow and Skill*, Second Edition, (Oxford, United Kingdom: Management Books 2000, August 2016).

5. Tom Deierlein, "11 Timeless Principles of Leadership (US Army 1948)," Academy Leadership, June 2014. Accessed February 23, 2021. https://academyleadership.com/news/201406.asp.

Chapter 13

1. Kouzes and Posner. *The Leadership Challenge.*

Chapter 14

1. Donald G. Reinertsen, *Managing the Design Factory,* Illustrated edition. (New York, NY: Free Press, October 1, 1997).

2. Jim Highsmith, *Agile Project Management: Creating Innovative Products,* Second Edition (Boston, MA: Addison-Wesley Professional, July 10, 2009).

3. Kouzes and Posner. *The Leadership Challenge.*

4. Collins. *Good to Great.*

Chapter 16

1. Robert Austin, *Measuring and Managing Performance in Organizations.* (New York, NY: Dorset House, June 1, 1996.)

Chapter 17

1. LH Putnam, "A General Empirical Solution to the Macro Software Sizing and Estimation problem," *IEEE Transactions of Software Engineering*, SE4 (4): 345-361.

2. Barry Boehm, *Software Engineering Economics,* (Hoboken, NJ: Prentice-Hall, 1981).

3. Frederick Brooks, *Mythical Man-Month, The: Essays on Software Engineering,* Anniversary Edition (Boston, MA: Addison-Wesley Professional, August 2, 1995).

4. Boehm. *Software Engineering Economics.*

Chapter 18

1. Steven Yaffee and Julia Wondolleck, "Making Collaboration Work: Lessons from a comprehensive assessment of over 200 wideranging cases of collaboration in environmental management," *Conservation in Practice,* 1(1): 17-24, March 8, 2006. Accessed 4/12/2021. https://doi.org/10.1111/j.1526-4629.2000.tb00156.x.

2. J. Lehrer, "Annals of Ideas: Groupthink: the Brainstorming Myth," NewYorker.com, January 30, 2012. Accessed August 1, 2012. http://www.newyorker.com/reporting/2012/01/30/120130fa_fact_lehrer.

3. B. Commoner, "Comparing apples to oranges: Risk of cost/benefit analysis," *Contemporary moral controversies in technology,* (Cary, NC: Oxford University Press, February 19, 1987). pp. 64–65.

Chapter 19

1. David Kolb, *Experiential Learning: Experience as the Source of Learning and Development,* Second Edition, (Hoboken, NJ: Pearson FT Press, December 12, 2014).

2. Project Management Institute, *Standard for Program Management,* Fourth Edition. (Philadelphia, PA: Project Management Institute, 2017).

References

Albert Ellis ABCDE model https://en.wikipedia.org/wiki/Albert_Ellis.

Anderson, Robert J., and William A. Adams, et.al. *Scaling Leadership: Building Organizational Capability and Capacity to Create Outcomes that Matter Most.* Wiley, January 30, 2019.

Clark, M.; Vardeman, K.; Barba, S. "Perceived inadequacy: A study of the impostor phenomenon among college and research librarians." *College & Research Libraries.* 75 (3): 255–271. https://doi.org:10.5860/crl12-423.

Commoner, B. *Contemporary moral controversies in technology.* "Comparing apples to oranges: Risk of cost/benefit analysis," pp. 64–65. Oxford University Press, USA, February 19, 1987.

Gangwar, Timothy. *Visual Thinking - Visual Impact, Visual Teaching: Using Images to Strengthen Learning*, Chapter 1. Skyhorse, November 3, 2015.

Hyerle, David. "Thinking Maps: Visual Tools for Activating Habits of Mind," *Learning and Leading with Habits of Mind.* http://www.mcoe.edu.my/Uploads/WMSTC2013_habits_of_mind.pdf. Accessed March 17, 2021.

Iacoviello, Brian M. and Dennis S. Charney. "Psychosocial facets of resilience: implications for preventing posttrauma psychopathology, treating trauma survivors, and enhancing community resilience." *Eur J Psychotraumatol.* 2014; 5: 10.3402/ejpt.v5.23970. Published online 2014 Oct 1. doi: 10.3402/ejpt.v5.23970.

Lehrer, J. "Annals of Ideas: Groupthink: the Brainstorming Myth." NewYorker.com, January 30, 2012. http://www.newyorker.com/reporting/2012/01/30/120130fa_fact_lehrer. Accessed August 1, 2012.

Perkins-Gough, Deborah. "The Significance of Grit: A Conversation with Angela Lee Duckworth." *Educational Leadership*, September 2013. 71(1): 14–20. http://www.ascd.org/publications/educational-leadership/sept13/vol71/num01/The-Significance-of-Grit@-A-Conversation-with-Angela-Lee-Duckworth.aspx.

Pinto, Jeffrey K., Peg Thomas, Jeffrey Trailer, Todd Palmer, and Michele Govekar. *Project Leadership: From Theory to Practice.* Project Management Institute, November 1, 1998.

Reivich, Karen and Andrew Shatte Ph.D. *The Resilience Factor: 7 Keys to Finding Inner Strength and Overcoming Life's Hurdles.* Harmony, October 14, 2003.

Rock, D. "SCARF: A brain-based model for collaborating with and influencing others." *NeuroLeadership Journal* 1(1), 44–52, 2008.

Sakulku, Jaruwan. "The Impostor Phenomenon." *International Journal of Behavioral Science.* 6 (1): 73–92.

Index

Further EI Reading

If you would like to read more about EI, the following books have been selected for both their approachability and relevance to the project-delivery space:

» *The Emotionally Intelligent Manager* – David Caruso and Peter Salovey

» *The Core Protocols: A Guide to Greatness* – Richard Kasperowski

» *Emotional Intelligence for Project Managers* – Anthony Mersino

» *The Emotionally Agile Leader* – Kevin Bowser

» *Emotional Intelligence: Why It Can Matter More Than IQ* – Daniel Goleman

» *Emotional Intelligence 2.0* – Travis Bradberry and Jean Greaves

» *Emotional Capitalists: The New Leaders* – Martyn Newman

» *The EQ Edge: Emotional Intelligence and Your Success* – Steven Stein and Howard Book

» *Primal Leadership: Unleashing the Power of Emotional Intelligence* – Daniel Goleman, Richard Boyatzis, and Annie McKee

» *Hardwiring Happiness: The New Brain Science of Contentment, Calm, and Confidence* – Rick Hanson

» *One Second Ahead: Enhance Your Performance at Work with Mindfulness* – Rasmus Hougaard, Jacqueline Carter, and Gillian Coutts

» *Flow: The Psychology of Optimal Experience* – Mihály Csíkszentmihályi

» *Thinking, Fast and Slow* – Daniel Kahneman